Religion and Culture in Early Modern Europe, 1500–1800

Religion and Culture in Early Modern Europe, 1500–1800

KASPAR VON GREYERZ

TRANSLATED BY THOMAS DUNLAP

OXFORD
UNIVERSITY PRESS

2008

OXFORD
UNIVERSITY PRESS

Oxford University Press, Inc., publishes works that further
Oxford University's objective of excellence
in research, scholarship, and education.

Oxford   New York
Auckland   Cape Town   Dar es Salaam   Hong Kong   Karachi
Kuala Lumpur   Madrid   Melbourne   Mexico City   Nairobi
New Delhi   Shanghai   Taipei   Toronto

With offices in
Argentina   Austria   Brazil   Chile   Czech Republic   France   Greece
Guatemala   Hungary   Italy   Japan   Poland   Portugal   Singapore
South Korea   Switzerland   Thailand   Turkey   Ukraine   Vietnam

Published by Oxford University Press, Inc.
198 Madison Avenue, New York, New York 10016

www.oup.com

Oxford is a registered trademark of Oxford University Press

Library of Congress Cataloging-in-Publication Data
Greyerz, Kaspar von.
[Religion und Kultur. English]
Religion and culture in early modern Europe, 1500–1800 / Kaspar von
Greyerz ; Translated by Thomas Dunlap.
p.   cm.
Includes bibliographical references and index.
ISBN: 978-0-19-532765-6 (cloth); 978-0-19-532766-3 (pbk.)
1. Religion and culture—Europe—History.   2. Europe—Religious life
and customs.   I. Title.
BL65.C8G7413 2007
274'.06—dc22   2007001259

Printed in the United States of America
on acid-free paper

To
Maya Widmer

Preface

When I wrote the foreword to the original German edition of this book in March 2000, I took the secularized social and cultural climate in which Europeans live today as a reason for reminding the reader of the special effort he or she had to make in order to grasp the central role of religion in the cultures and societies of early modern Europe. There is no need to repeat this caveat in a preface to the American edition of *Religion and Culture in Early Modern Europe*. To this day, North American society has not undergone the same thorough process of secularization. What will appear naturally more removed to American readers, however, is the specifically European context of what follows.

The attempt to familiarize a largely secularized public with the dynamics of religion in early modern Europe was not, in fact, the main reason for writing this book. Above all, the purpose—and challenge—was to cover more than three hundred years of European history and religion while doing justice to the aspects of durability *and* change, as well as to theoretical questions posed by the history of premodern religion. I have tried to come to terms with this challenge by attributing prominence to religion as a social and cultural force. This resulted in a conscious neglect of institutional aspects and their corollaries, which are usually covered by surveys concentrating on salient aspects of the history of early modern Europe. In this book, I do not look at early modern poor relief or at Baroque ecclesiastical architecture, to name only two examples. Likewise, I have not tried to cover all of Europe. What follows concentrates strongly on central and western Europe and excludes eastern Europe. In other words, this is not a survey. It is primarily an essay in interpretation. The conscious omissions noted above have afforded room, in turn, to connect my narrative and analysis with issues of methodological approach and of scholarly debate. In this respect, it is also a work that will familiarize the American reader with the most important European scholarly discussions of the last decades regarding the role and meaning of early modern religion as a cultural phenomenon.

Although seven years have passed since the original publication of this book, I continue to stand by the interpretations it offers. Given the vastness of the subject, it was (and is) not possible to include an exhaustive bibliography. For the same reason, I will not attempt here to cover all the important publications on aspects of early modern religion that have appeared since 2000. I will name only a handful, and no surveys or textbooks. Among approaches that lend more room to the institutional aspects of early modern religion than I have decided to, I want to mention Thomas Kaufmann's concentration on Lutheran *Konfessionskultur*, now highlighted in his *Konfession und Kultur: Lutherischer Protestantismus in der zweiten Hälfte des Reformationsjahrhunderts* (Tübingen, 2006), as well as Philip Benedict's *Christ's Churches Purely Reformed: A Social History of Calvinism* (New Haven and London, 2002). Diarmaid MacCulloch's *Reformation: Europe's House Divided, 1490–1700* (London, 2003) offers a new and lengthy interpretation of the Reformation and its aftermath on a broad European scale. Aspects of religion and violence are treated by Peter Burschel in *Sterben und Unsterblichkeit: Zur Kultur des Martyriums in der Frühen Neuzeit* (Munich, 2004) and in a collection of essays I recently edited jointly with Kim Siebenhüner, *Religion und Gewalt: Konflikte, Rituale, Deutungen (1500–1800)* (Göttingen, 2006), with German, American, and French contributions. Peter Hersche, whose work I frequently refer to in the following pages, has published a large interpretative synthesis of his research on European Baroque Catholicism in the two-volume study *Musse und Verschwendung: Europäische Gesellschaft und Kultur im Barockzeitalter* (Freiburg im Breisgau, 2006). Finally, H. C. Erik Midelfort has addressed central aspects of the ambivalence of the era of the Enlightenment in *Exorcism and Enlightenment: Johann Joseph Gassner and the Demons of Eighteenth-Century Germany* (New Haven, 2005).

I owe particular thanks to Kathy Brady, Tom Brady, Peter Hersche, Heidrun Homburg, Josef Mooser, and Patrice Veit, who have helped me in one way or another to come to terms with the original German manuscript. I am very grateful to Tom Brady, Mark A. Forster, Frank Roberts, Thomas Robisheaux, and to an anonymous reader, who all encouraged me to pursue, and Oxford

University Press to publish, a translation of *Religion und Kultur*. Thomas Dunlap has not only provided an excellent translation, but has also made contact with me whenever questions arose. I would like to thank him for both. The translation was made possible by a grant from the Freiwillige Akademische Gesellschaft, Basel. I also want to thank Cynthia Read, Daniel Gonzalez, and Sara Needles of Oxford University Press, as well as Mary Bellino, for their assistance and proficiency.

This book is based on many years of research and teaching. It owes more than they are probably aware of to my assistants and students in Kiel (1988–91), Zürich (1993–97), and Basel (from 1997 onward). They have my special gratitude. It finally owes a great deal to Maya Widmer, who helps me to keep my head above water in an academic environment ever more inundated by administrative demands.

Basel and Bern   April 2007

Contents

Religion and Culture in Early Modern Europe, 1500–1800

Introduction

*Religion and Culture: Popular Culture
and Religiosity*

Few historians question that the late Middle Ages was an era
profoundly marked by religiousness and piety. But the scholarly
consensus is not so clear when it comes to the religious life of the early
modern period (ca. 1500–1800). What is one to make of French
Enlightenment thinkers like Voltaire, who subjected religion and the
church to trenchant criticism, or LaMettrie and Diderot, who fully
embraced atheism? What about the Italian humanists of the fifteenth
and sixteenth centuries, whom historians—beginning with Jacob
Burckhardt and extending into the late twentieth century—saw as
unbelievers who made a radical break with the medieval past also in
their religious beliefs?

Scholarship has now corrected the image of humanism in this
particular respect: there is broad agreement among historians that
humanism all across Europe was a phenomenon rooted in Christianity,
its embrace of pre-Christian classical authorities notwithstanding. But can the same be said of the eighteenth-century Enlightenment, which was, at times, unsparingly critical of ecclesiastico-
religious traditions? Any answer must begin by acknowledging that
the movement was not everywhere as critical of religion and the
church as it was in France. In England, Scotland, Germany, Switzerland, Austria, and Italy, we are dealing with an essentially Christian
Enlightenment. Still, the Enlightenment does represent a break in
that its rationalism powerfully reinforced the trend toward the separation of religion and daily life that had begun among the educated

classes in the late-seventeenth century. This is indirectly confirmed by the reaction to this trend in the form of the Protestant movement of awakening and Catholic ultramontanism at the turn of the eighteenth century. Incidentally, in part this reaction is also an indication that the Enlightenment accentuated existing disparities between different sociocultural worlds: when it comes to the different mentalities of the educated and lower social strata, the Enlightenment accelerated the potential for change in the former, while contributing little to a corresponding change in the latter, whose exposure to the Enlightenment was slight.

It is undoubtedly correct that the eighteenth-century Enlightenment made essential contributions to the individualization of religious experience and thus to the secularization of the relationship between religion and society, even if in some instances the beginnings of these currents predated the eighteenth century. However, it would be wrong to claim that it promoted individualization and secularization *in general*—in other words, that it took hold of all social strata.

Let me posit two assumptions: first, religion in history must be seen and understood, always and without exception, as a cultural phenomenon; second, cultural experience in premodern, estate-based society always has a specific social locus. What this means for the sixteenth and seventeenth centuries is that we can speak only in a qualified sense of a religiosity that transcended social strata and was valid at a particular time for the entire society of a region or a country. And yet, as we will see, it is possible to identify certain contexts that transcended social strata in the sixteenth and seventeenth centuries, though these contexts fractured again radically under the influence of the Enlightenment. And from that time until the late twentieth century, profound differences existed between the top and the bottom—that is to say, clear distinctions between the religiosity of the higher, educated strata and the religiosity of the common people. In that respect the "concurrence of non-contemporaneous elements," to use a phrase of Reinhard Koselleck's, is indeed a truism for the history of the eighteenth century.

At this point, however, one question demands to be answered: How does one define "religion"? Following Thomas Luckmann, I see religion as a "socially constructed, more or less solidified, more or less obligatory system of symbols" that combines "a stance toward the world, the legitimization of natural and social orders, and meanings ... that transcend the individual with practical instructions on how to live and with personal obligations."[1] The fact that religion figures in this definition as a "socially constructed ... system of symbols" is useful for my purposes, in two respects. First, as a cultural phenomenon, religion is, in its origins, always embedded within a specific social context: religion is not conceivable without society.[2] Second, this part of the definition fits the pre-Enlightenment situation especially well, because in an era in which religion still played a central role in the daily life of Europeans, it was experienced primarily in everyday settings. "Socially constructed" does not mean, of course, that the content of a religion can be reduced, in the final analysis, to its social origins. I will presently clarify this point further in the course of looking at functionalist models, for example that of Émile Durkheim.

First, however, I will take a critical look at Luckmann's conception of religion as a "more or less obligatory system of symbols." When considering the early modern period, one should expand upon this notion by speaking of a system of symbols *and* rituals, since the ritual aspect of the religiosity of the early modern period is readily apparent. What I have in mind here are not only the rituals of the Church year with its high points at Christmas, Easter, Ascension, Pentecost, and the great saints' days; I am also thinking of the Protestant family ritual of devotion, of prayer (especially strongly ritualized in the customary practices of the Catholic Church and Catholic piety), and, finally, of the ritual character of early modern magic. By contrast, externally visible religious symbols were such things as baptismal names, rosaries, and the Protestant Psalter. Probably the most significant fusion of ritualistic and symbolic content occurred in the celebration of the Eucharist as part of the Catholic Mass or the Lord's Supper in Protestantism. As a system of symbols and rituals, religion was *more or less* obligatory because the churches did not make the symbols and rituals equally obligatory at all times for their members, and because, from the perspective of both the churches and the laity, not all symbols and rituals carried equal weight.

As for the final element of Luckmann's definition, it requires no further explanation that religion served as a system that provided a value-orientation to individuals and the collective, and—simultaneously—legitimized the existing natural and sociopolitical orders. All political orders of the early modern period, from absolutist monarchy in France and Spain, to the Swiss Confederation, to the Anabaptists in Münster in 1534/35, were eager to legitimize themselves politically. And the same holds true for the justification of theories of resistance in the seventeenth and eighteenth centuries. When it came to the legitimization of natural order, the people of pre-Enlightenment Europe strove to understand unusual natural events, such as earthquakes, floods, crop failures, monstrous births, and the appearance of comets, as God's punishment for sins or as a divine threat of judgment. The religious legitimization of the secular and natural order was thus common and exceedingly varied in this period.

Diseases, however, are one example of phenomena that were not seen exclusively as divine punishment; rather, they could also be attributed quite readily to the magical influence of witches or sorcerers. For us this raises the question of how to distinguish religion from magic. One could define magic as "the exercise of a preternatural control over nature by human beings, with the assistance of forces more powerful than they."[3] Magic is thus clearly distinct from religion in its manipulative aspect. Of course, this is pure theory. As I will show in the following section, in practice, that is to say, in the history of religion and piety, at least of the pre-Enlightenment period, it is by no means possible to distinguish clearly between religion, magic, and astrology (which, in the final analysis, was based on magical ideas).

Preliminary Methodological and Theoretical Reflections

Against Dogmatism and Functionalism

Modern historians of religion would do well to beware of both dogmatism and reductionism. To my mind, one can speak of dogmatism if, for example, certain aspects of the religiosity of our forebears in the early modern period are described, from a modern perspective, as "irrational" or "superstitious." Such labels, which spring from our own understanding of life and religion, are useless in reconstructing past worlds. It was precisely such dubious labels that the British historian E. P. Thompson had in mind when he spoke of the "enormous condescension of posterity" toward the worlds of its ancestors.[4] For us, the only promising strategy for at least beginning to understand the significance that the worlds of everyday life, imagination, and faith held for our ancestors lies in "anthropologizing" or "ethnologizing" our epistemological methods. What this implies is that one must try to understand these worlds of the past from the inside before making any scholarly statements about them. To give one example: to theologians, the notion of God may be a universal idea with corresponding abstract attributes. But for anthropologists, ethnologists, and historians, specific conceptions of God have their specific cultural loci, which means that they can be truly understood only from the perspective of their respective cultural contexts.[5] For epistemological reasons, we should therefore seek to work primarily from the perspective of the individuals and groups we are studying, instead of imposing our contemporary categories upon them a priori.[6]

The programmatic demand articulated in this context by the American anthropologist Clifford Geertz, that we proceed "from the native's point of view," is directed not least against a functionalist understanding of religion. What do we mean by a functionalist understanding? Karl Marx, Max Weber, and Émile Durkheim, to mention only three thinkers among the intellectual giants of the nineteenth and twentieth centuries, propagated functionalist theories of religion and religiosity, though one needs to distinguish between a functionalist super-elevation of religion and a functionalist reduction of the religious.

Most widely known today is surely the functionalist reduction of the religious by Karl Marx (1818–83). It is already adumbrated in his early writings, especially in his treatise *The German Ideology* (1845/46), which, among other things, stated programmatically: "Life is not determined by consciousness, but consciousness by life."[7] In Marx's "Theses on Feuerbach" we read that

> Feuerbach starts out from the fact of religious self-alienation, of the duplication of the world into a religious world and a secular one. His work consists in resolving the religious world into its secular basis. But that the secular basis detaches itself from itself and establishes itself as an independent realm in the clouds can only be explained by the cleavages and self-contradictions within this secular basis. The latter must, therefore, in itself be both understood in its contradiction and revolutionized in practice. Thus, for instance, after the earthly family is discovered to be the secret of the holy family, the former must then itself be destroyed in theory and in practice.[8]

Marx's later remark that religion was merely the "opium of the masses," which the ruling class used to keep the ruled from perceiving their true condition, flowed logically and consistently from these earlier reflections. These ideas of Marx's may be described as functionalist reductionism, because they reduce religion one-sidedly to its function as a sociopolitical instrument of domination, to its legitimizing function.

The conception of religion articulated by the sociologist Émile Durkheim (1885–1917) can also be labeled reductionist—based, of course, on very different premises—because he connected the idea of religion inseparably with the idea of the church. He defined "church" as a community of those who feel bound together by "a unified system of beliefs and practices relative to sacred things."[9] This emphatically reduces religion to its social, community-generating function. Durkheim was thus only being consistent when, in his well-known studies of the totemism of Australia and North America as elementary forms of religious life, he interpreted individual religion or individual totemism as manifestations of decadence.[10] Since one of the basic trends in early modern religiosity in Europe was at least some tendency toward an individualization and "privatization" of faith and—to some extent—of religious practice as well, Durkheim's theory offers little to the questions at the center of this inquiry, unless we too are willing to regard these individualizing tendencies a priori as signs of decay.

Max Weber, for example, simultaneously fascinated with the accomplishments of his time and deeply pessimistic about the sociocultural burdens of modernity, sought to understand the European individualization of faith and religious practice in the sixteenth century as "occidental rationalism." In the process, however, the role he assumed was not that of a reductionist, but that of someone who carried out a functionalist super-elevation of religion, most clearly in his essay *The Protestant Ethic and the Spirit of Capitalism* (1904–05), which I will examine more closely later.[11] Suffice it to note for now that while religion stands in a functional relationship to society also in Weber, it is not primarily society that dictates the conditions of religious life; rather, it is the ethic grounded in religious belief that has important repercussions for social behavior, one example of which, according to Weber, is the fact that the ethic of Calvinism as well as that of Pietism promotes the spirit of capitalism.

A brief interim conclusion is therefore that a modern social and cultural history of religion should make every effort to avoid the kind of dogmatism and functionalism I have described, because they mislead one into distorting the scholarly results of relevant studies through a priori determinations. Ideally, given the current state of scholarship in religious history, pertinent analyses for the period under discussion should thus focus especially on microhistorical studies. However, this methodological postulate cannot be met in the kind of study that the present book seeks to offer.

A Survey Between Microhistory and Macrohistory

"Microhistory" refers to an approach that is oriented primarily toward concrete action, which is why its usual starting point is the historical subject as the agent of history. By contrast, "macrohistory" can be characterized as a primarily structure-oriented approach to the past.[12] Examples of basic structures of early modern history are lordship, estate-based society, and patriarchy.

As a matter of fact, there are multifarious connections between *action* and *structure*. In German social history of the 1970s and 1980s, however, these connections were sacrificed to a kind of "reification" of structures, which meant that "structures and processes themselves took on the qualities of— anonymous—actors," although this came at the expense of a connection to the human being as the real agent of history.[13] The reification of structures created a situation in which scholars tended to regard them as a quality of history that is prior to the process of knowing and therefore "objective." But from the perspective of historical anthropology and the newer history of mentalities, the primary approaches to which I am committed, every form of historical writing is in the final analysis a work of construction. After all, historians are always chiefly interested in those phenomena and processes of the past to which they accord cultural significance in reference to their own time. This epistemological interest is not arbitrary, since it almost always remains tied to a concrete scholarly discourse within a specific scholarly community.

Max Weber's well-known saying that the "stream of immeasurable events flows unendingly towards eternity," and thus the "cultural problems which move men form themselves ever anew and in different colors, and the boundaries of that area in the infinite stream of concrete events which acquires meaning and significance for us ... are constantly subject to change,"[14] remains entirely true, even if I will not adopt Weber's complex methodology, which, in the final analysis, is not without its own contradictions. Indeed, "From the incomprehensible richness and complexity of past life, [the historian] isolates chains of events, threads of motives, and contexts of interaction. And from these, by positing beginnings and endpoints and imputing a meaningful connection, he constructs 'stories.' "[15] It is only on this basis that a survey of a specific thematic aspect of the past, as I have endeavored to offer here, can take shape.

Without question, surveys belong to the field of macrohistory. The dominant ordering principle of macrohistory is ideas about structures and processes. For example, the development of early modern religiosity is undoubtedly linked to mental structures that made it vastly more difficult—in pre-Enlightenment society—to question the religious meaning of the prevailing social and political orders. Few scholars in the sixteenth and seventeenth centuries dared to challenge the central sociopolitical status of religious patterns of interpretation. A survey of the religious history of Europe in the early modern period cannot get by without these ideas. To be sure, it is desirable "to connect the multifarious microstudies and expand them into a web of new interpretations of history, thereby allowing the distinct logical systems to emerge from their local context and be brought to bear on a description of the transformation of culture in its historical totality."[16] However, I believe that the idea of "circumventing" the problems of structural history by simply linking together and adding up microhistorical findings is illusory, for the simple reason that this idea is essentially the expression of a tendency to overestimate—on the basis of unspoken theoretically and often positivistic assumptions—the narrative capacity of empirical research within a larger framework:

Accordingly, further historical-anthropological research, no matter
how large the number of individuals and groups whose actions
and motivations it elucidates, cannot explain historical change on
a large scale. In other words, even historical anthropologists cannot dispense with the "systems level" if they regard the question of
cultural change as significant.[17]

But raising questions about the problems inherent in the topic of this book
in no way implies that I reject the historical-anthropological considerations
I have just sketched out: microhistory and macrohistory are not necessarily
mutually exclusive; on the contrary, each depends on the other. Of course, the
methodological perspective I have presented here assumes that structure and
process do not clandestinely take on a life of their own vis-à-vis human action and historical events; rather, structures must be understood as a kind of
framework for the actions of historical agents, a framework that is itself created and, at times, altered by the unfolding actions. That is certainly and un-
reservedly true for cultural change in the early modern period, which is the
primary focus of my inquiry.

In the centuries between 1500 and 1800, cultural change increasingly
acquired characteristics specific to social strata: in other words, it increasingly
adhered to "timetables" of change specific to different strata and groups. This
means, among other things, that from the perspective of change, the historical
manifestation of *culture* cannot be separated from that of *society*. The logical
implication for my methodological stance is that it would make no sense to
seek to construct a principled contradiction between a microhistorical and
a macrohistorical approach. Moreover, I assume that cultural as well as social
change constitute process-like phenomena—and by "processes" in cultural and
social terms I mean occurrences within specific social segments that are also
limited chronologically; in any case, I most certainly do not mean occurrences
that lead in some kind of linear fashion from Luther to Bismarck.

We are left with the question to what extent it still makes sense, from the
perspective of contemporary historical scholarship, to orient the content of
this book toward macrohistorical concepts such as "Reformation," "Counter-
Reformation," and "Enlightenment," to name only the three most important
ones. Especially within the framework of gender history, scholars have recently
raised the question of what sort of content in the grand narratives would do
justice to the category of "gender." In particular, historians have warned about
the power of a historical narrative that is aimed at modernity and its creation.
As Lynn Hunt has observed, even scholarship on women's history and gender
history has found it all but impossible to escape the seductive power of a

teleological narrative about nationalism, democracy, and the rise of the modern constitutional state.[18] I agree with Rudolf Schlögl when he emphasizes that historical scholarship cannot dispense with directional markers "as long as history remains related to a concept of development that means more than simply 'change.' "[19] Some kind of inherent teleology—a certain directional orientation—is a given in our practice of representation (that is, the way in which we communicate scientifically about the content of our scholarship). It is the product of the narrative structure we use, of the narrative nature of history. Yet under no circumstances must this unavoidable directional orientation be transformed clandestinely into determinism, when, for example, we turn the early modern period as a whole into a mere precursor to modernity or a modernity transfigured into something fascinating and mysterious.

Without a doubt, historical anthropology and with it the microhistorical approach make it incumbent upon us to question anew the received answers to the problems of continuity in the early modern period, answers we have grown fond of. In particular, the influence of these approaches challenges the notion of a linear and directional development of European history: as I see it, the process-like nature of early modern history gives rise also, and not least, to the gradual and particular (or sectoral) character of cultural and social change.

Religion as Culture

Religion as a Cultural Phenomenon

Religion was and is a cultural phenomenon. Here I will touch only tangentially upon the question of how to define culture, as that is an inexhaustible and therefore very tricky topic. Suffice it to say that Peter Burke's often-quoted definition calls for a critical engagement. Burke understands culture as "a system of shared meanings, attitudes and values, and the symbolic forms (performances, artifacts) in which they are expressed or embodied." Using this definition as his starting point, he observes that "popular culture" is perhaps best understood as "unofficial culture, the culture of the non-elite, the 'subordinate classes.' "[20] This notion of culture has been criticized—not without reason—for being somewhat narrow and excessively literary. However, when the counterproposal calls for an understanding of culture that allows us to trace the culture of a people "back to its economic-practical context of experience [*Erfahrenszusammenhänge*]," we find lurking in the background once again the specter of functional reductionism.[21]

While cultural processes are closely linked to social processes, they cannot be reduced to the latter. This is already apparent from the mere fact that the social elite of the sixteenth and seventeenth centuries participated actively in the popular culture of its day, whereas, conversely, the common people participated very little or not at all in the educated culture of the time. It is also evident in the fact that while cultural change could certainly be linked to specific social strata or estates, it was nevertheless subject to other laws of change than society, which was, by comparison, more static than culture. Revealing in this regard are the ways scholars have tried to describe modern popular culture, that is, popular culture of the nineteenth and twentieth centuries. Some have emphasized that what sets it apart from "the international culture that is subject to constant, rapid changes is its traditionalist nature, its group imprint, and its local forms of expression."[22]

The phrase "popular culture" (*Volkskultur*) is afflicted by the apparent inability of historians to reach even a provisional consensus about who the bearers of this culture were. The contributions to this vigorously debated question are by now legion. One criticism, voiced especially by German scholars, concerns the dubious history of the term *Volk* in the nineteenth and twentieth centuries, both its romanticizing obfuscation and its fascist instrumentalization. Another target of criticism is its vagueness. At the same time, culture and religiosity in the early modern period most certainly were not homogeneous and harmonious across social strata. We are thus left with the task of finding a terminology for the culture of the common people, the simple people, those strata and groups who had no meaningful share of the educated culture of their day and who, as subjects, were excluded from the exercise of political domination (with the exception of certain subordinate functions). This culture was, after all, not simply identical with the socially dominant culture of a particular era. I therefore prefer to retain the phrase "popular culture" as a heuristic category,[23] while simultaneously cautioning that we must not assume a model that posits a stark dichotomy between an elite culture and a popular culture. After all, whether there existed, in a particular place at a particular time, two dichotomous levels or multiple levels of collective cultural experience and articulation is not something we can decide a priori, but something that must always remain the object of concrete historical research.

The historian Bob Scribner has distinguished four conceptions of "popular culture":[24] first, "it can mean common social custom," for example the distinction between the dancing at a church feast and the dancing of the upper classes. Second, it can be understood more narrowly as the unofficial culture of those who do not participate in political power or in the corporative structures of the artisan guilds; that is, popular culture as the culture of "wayfaring folk, journeymen, of the plebeian lower strata." Third, there is the notion of popular culture as "superstitious" culture associated with the need to cope with life through magical means. Fourth, and finally, popular culture could be taken to mean a culture that is "related to elemental aspects of material life," as for example the recourse to belief in astrology. While one could certainly argue about the distinction between the third and fourth types, Scribner is right in emphasizing that the two are difficult to separate from "popular belief," which was often quite distinct from belief officially sanctioned by the church. Quod erat demonstrandum: popular culture and popular forms of religiosity were closely interconnected. Scribner's interlinking of popular culture with magic and the belief in astrology raises the general question about the relationship between religion (as a cultural phenomenon) and magic.

Religion and Magic: Is There a Difference?

There is still no consensus among historians as to what exactly we mean by "magic."[25] Richard Kieckhefer proposed to define it as

> That which makes an action magical is the type of power it invokes:
> if it relies on divine action or the manifest powers of nature it is
> not magical, while if it uses demonic aid or occult powers in nature
> it is magical.[26]

Although this definition promotes a distinction between religion and magic on the level of theory, it has the distinct disadvantage of foisting upon the many learned men who concerned themselves with natural magic right up to the end of the seventeenth century (and in some cases beyond) an understanding of the relationship between magic and religion that in no way corresponds to their own view of things. After all, to scholars in the tradition of Neoplatonism and Hermeticism as revived by fifteenth-century Florentine humanism, a concern with natural magic was, even in the sixteenth and seventeenth centuries, generally part of their attempt to comprehend God. On the basis of my own understanding of magic, I would like to highlight here especially the aspect of the manipulation of occult powers or demonic spirits.

To shed some light on this, I will take a brief look at the story of Goodwin Wharton (1653–1704), a member of the British upper class who left behind an autobiography written in the closing years of the seventeenth and the opening years of the eighteenth century. In it, he describes above all his endeavors in alchemy and magic, as well as the various phases of his relationship to his companion, Mary Parish. The latter had a medium named George, with whose help Wharton established contact with the netherworld of fairies—for quite pragmatic reasons, since the fairies guarded immense treasures in the netherworld and Wharton was chronically short of cash. In the end, the medium helped him not only to communicate directly with the archangels Michael and Gabriel, but also to speak directly to God. Told that he was destined for great tasks in the British state, Wharton took a summertime trip to Bath, where, loaded down with love amulets, he tried to catch the eye of the bathing Queen in order to bind her to himself forever after—unfortunately without any success. Goodwin Wharton described all this with the undiminished hope "that ye Lord will visit me with his grace and abundant favor."[27]

In Wharton's writings we find ideas that formed the foundation of most of the magical ideas of the sixteenth and seventeenth centuries. For one thing, there is the notion that all matter of any kind is animated and controlled by spirits; second, there is the belief in the possibility of remote action across empty space, as it were, in sympathetic magic, in manipulation at a distance; and, third, the notion that control of nature could be achieved by controlling the occult powers and benevolent spirits inherent in nature. This was distinguished from demonic magic, which sought to control *evil* spirits in an effort to attain worldly goals. Goodwin Wharton stuck exclusively to good spirits.

In a previous work I tried to show, on the basis of statements in sixteenth- and seventeenth-century autobiographies, that religious syncretism in the broadest sense, which also opens up a view onto the relationship between church-approved religion and the belief in magic or magical practices, was only in exceptional cases actually seen as such by contemporaries.[28] The conclusion we can draw from this is that religion and magic, as two categories referring to the world of people's lives, can hardly be distinguished with satisfactory precision in the pre-Enlightenment era. One important reason for this is that contemporary experiences, notions about, and applications of religion *and* magic by the people of the pre-Enlightenment age were in a sense regularly passed through the filter of the social and cultural experiences of their daily lives.

To be sure, in part the autobiographies of earlier centuries provide us with historical evidence that cannot be readily generalized. To some extent that is also true of the somewhat exalted Goodwin Wharton. At the same time, through his writings and the actions presented therein, he illustrated ideas and activities that were by no means untypical for many members of the Royal Society for the Promotion of Knowledge, the first academy of natural science, founded in 1660.

What is true of the world of science at that time—and not only in England—is that scientific, rational thinking in our modern sense and magical or alchemistical ideas were by no means as clearly separated as a traditional history of science, with its strong focus on the pioneering role of individual, eminent natural philosophers, would suggest. Far into the seventeenth century, demonology, the scientific investigation of the demonic in nature, which was in multifarious ways linked to contemporary witch persecutions, constituted an integral element of the scientific engagement with the mysteries of nature and the supernatural. The examination of unusual occurrences in nature, which until then had usually been regarded as divine portents, experienced a revival, especially in the late seventeenth century and not least in the setting of the English Royal Society, until the Enlightenment of the eighteenth century made a decisive break with the scientific fascination with miracles, wonders, and *mirabilia*.[29]

There are numerous indications that the final decades of the seventeenth and the first decades of the eighteenth century saw a profound cultural transformation. More clearly than before, the educated classes—a little faster here, somewhat more slowly there—began to distance themselves from the world as imagined by simpler folk: from faith in astrology and witches, and from the belief in miracles in general. What is true of miracles is also applicable to the magical and astrological imagination. Rebekka Habermas has emphasized that in the seventeenth century, the miraculous disappears "only from a particular cultural level, from the one we like to place at the center of historical scholarship as the only relevant level, so-called High Culture. 'Popular culture,' by contrast, would continue to speak of miracles for a long time to come."[30]

More recent scholarship on the history of science, which has lately begun to remember emphatically that it is an endeavor of cultural history, has shown how slow and gradual these shifts actually were, even on the level of educated culture.

Religion and Science: History of Science and History of Religion

The historian of science can not devote much attention to the study of superstition and magic, that is, of unreason, because this does not help him very much to understand human progress. Magic is essentially unprogressive and conservative; science is essentially progressive; the former goes backward; the latter, forward. We can not possibly deal with both movements at once except to indicate their constant strife, and even that is not very instructive, because that strife has hardly varied throughout the ages. Human folly being at once unprogressive, unchangeable, and unlimited, its study is a hopeless undertaking. There can not be much incentive to encompass that which is indefinite and to investigate the history of something which did not develop.[31]

This is how George Sarton, one of the founders of the modern historical study of the development of the natural sciences, began his three-volume introduction to the history of science, published between 1927 and 1947. Although younger historians of science in the postwar period tended to keep a critical distance from Sarton's dogmatic positivism, they did agree with his contention that the history of science was to be essentially a history of progress. The embrace of this premise was especially absolute among historians of science in the 1960s and 1970s who were under the influence of Karl Popper, a theorist of science. Among them was the English historian Mary Hesse, who emphasized in a programmatic essay written in 1973 that "natural science is just the arena of man's rational commerce with the world."[32] For a historian who was concerned with the development of the natural sciences, it was therefore legitimate and appropriate to classify and describe her subject matter according to rational categories. In looking at the development of science in the seventeenth century, it was not worth the trouble to deal with magical-hermetical or alchemistical currents, since these contributed nothing to scientific progress. Hesse even warned against overloading the picture that had already been drawn of the course of seventeenth-century science: "But even the suggestion that it is possible to get nearer the true picture by accumulating factors should be treated with caution. Throwing more light on a picture may distort what has already been seen."[33]

Of course these comments, thoroughly committed to the tradition of scientific positivism, came at a time when the well-known American theorist of science Thomas Kuhn had long since introduced a more differentiated approach into the discussion. Against Popper and his successors in the theory and history of science, Kuhn's theory of the paradigm and what he called "normal science" demonstrated that even paradigms that are contested and refuted in some of their details can have a long life if that is what the scientific community wants. In other words, he showed that the scientific discourse is by no means defined, in the Popperian sense, by a progress that is in some way inherent in a new paradigm. Incidentally, Kuhn also rejected Popper's presumption of dismissing entire branches of science—astrology or psychoanalysis, for example—from the outset as pseudo-science.[34] Still, Kuhn is undoubtedly a so-called internalist, that is, a proponent of an "internalist history of science."[35]

By contrast, during the last few decades, proponents of a historiography *external* to science have presented us emphatically with a contextual history of science, one that pays full attention to the basic social and especially cultural conditions for the production of knowledge and the development of science. Their starting point is the existence of a dialectical relationship between the production of scientific knowledge and a given cultural environment. This approach, strongly influenced by ideas from the sociology of knowledge, has so far been programmatically asserted and propagated most vigorously by Stephen Shapin and Simon Schaffer in their 1987 study of the controversy between Thomas Hobbes and Robert Boyle in the 1650s and 1660s and its subsequent implications for the history of science.[36] Here the problem of translating scientific understanding onto the social and political level, and the role of rhetoric in that process, are explicitly addressed. And since the publication of their book, these themes have become the topic of other studies on the history of science in the seventeenth and eighteenth centuries, in particular those by Anglo-American scholars—which is not to say that there are not also comparable contemporary phenomena.

Edward P. Thompson's criticism that many historians approached the culture of the common folk of times past, in particular, with the dubious and arrogant condescension of posterity applies in some sense also to the various proponents of an "internalist" theory and history of science. For example, when Imre Lakatos dismisses the English natural philosopher Francis Bacon (1561–1626) as "a confused and inconsistent thinker" who appealed only to "provincial and illiterate scholars,"[37] he is essentially disqualifying—unjustly— in hindsight an entire circle of scientists of the late seventeenth (and in part even the early eighteenth) century who focused on gathering empirical facts and institutionalizing the scientific enterprise. Today, against the backdrop of the enormous differentiation of fields of study within the discipline of history during the last two decades, this kind of stance is thoroughly unsatisfying, as it reinforces especially the traditional and—from the perspective of social and cultural history—outdated picture of the history of science as a pantheon of great thinkers.[38] The history of science, too, is connected to the real world.

Let me draw the following interim conclusions:

1. The history of early modern science was dominated until the 1980s by a one-sided scholarly orientation, one that led in some cases to a deterministic, a priori selection of scientific currents from the sixteenth to the eighteenth centuries that were worth studying, and other currents that were not.

2. This research focus was interlocked with a more or less exclusive "great thinkers perspective.'" Since genius towers above its time in any case, and thus does not necessarily require a grounding in its sociocultural soil when it comes to scientific achievements, a scientist's

sociocultural environment often entered into the discussion only selectively. What fell by the wayside in the process was frequently religion—at least those aspects of contemporary religiosity that could not be readily incorporated into the focus on progress. Here I am thinking especially of fields such as magic and alchemy.

3. Because of this self-imposed, dual limitation, traditional history of science is not entirely blameless for the fact that the *popular* perception of the complex relationship between early modern science and religion is still widely reduced to the construction of an almost a priori opposition between the Church and science.

Sixteenth- and Seventeenth-century Science as Knowledge of God

The case of the Zurich physician and scientist Johann Jakob Scheuchzer (1672–1733) shows that even a science that (unlike the work of Galileo Galilei, for example) was regarded emphatically as serving the knowledge of God was not automatically applauded by the Church.[39]

Scheuchzer was born in Zurich in 1672 and lived there throughout his life—although he was offered, as a result of Leibniz's efforts, the post of personal physician at the court of the Czar, he turned it down in 1714. Beginning in 1694 he held the position of the second city physician in Zurich; later he was also professor of mathematics at Zurich's Hohe Schule. However, it was only a few months before his death in 1733 that he attained what he had yearned for for so long: the position as the first city physician and the professorship of physics at the Carolinum.

Scheuchzer is regarded as, among other things, the founder of the scientific geography of the Swiss Alps, for which he quite literally did the footwork in the first two decades of the eighteenth century on several long trips into the mountains—equipped with a thermometer, a barometer, and a protractor. These trips and the measurements he took along the way are documented in his travel reports, which he published as an appendix to his three-volume *Natural History of Switzerland*.[40] In the area of geology and paleontology, he was an ardent proponent of a flood theory that—in contrast to other flood theories, as for example that of the Englishman Thomas Burnet—regarded the *diluvium* as an expression of the divine harmony of nature.[41]

In essence, all of Scheuchzer's scientific work was done in the service of the knowledge of God and to furnish physico-theological proof of God's existence. The most impressive testimony to that motivation is his (partially posthumous) four-volume work *Copper Bible* or *Physica Sacra*, published in Ulm and Augsburg in folio format between 1731 and 1735. In purely aesthetic terms, it is a stunning demonstration of the convergence and harmony of Biblical and scientific understanding. Scheuchzer derived the Biblical legitimization for this work from Romans 1:20, which states, in Scheuchzer's words, "that God's invisible nature, that is, His everlasting power and deity, will be seen from the perception of His works, that is, the creation of the world."[42]

Notwithstanding his unquestioned religiosity, and his tireless efforts to offer to a broader public a visual demonstration of the mutual compatibility of science and Biblical piety (for example, in his Zurich inaugural address of 1710 on the usefulness of mathematics for theology),[43] Scheuchzer had a number of run-ins with censorship by the council, which was largely controlled by the city's clergy. In his correspondence with the famous Basle mathematician Johannes Bernoulli, he complained bitterly from time to time about the difficulties the censorship caused him. As late as 1721, the Zurich clergy regarded it as expedient to denounce the Copernican system as heretical and, evidently, to castigate Swammerdam's discovery of spermatozoa as indecent.[44]

Of course, these were battles of retreat. The great defensive front— reinforced one more time by the German and French-speaking Swiss reformed theologians in 1674 with the *Formula Consensus*, which reasserted the dogma of predestination, and their systematic campaign against Cartesianism— had long since been riddled with holes, and it eventually collapsed for good in the 1720s and 1730s.

In the years prior to that, the relationship between natural science and theology in Zurich remained tense, as did Scheuchzer's relationship to the Reformed canons of the Great Minster of Zurich. A contemporary recorded the following on July 6, 1714:

> Herr Dr. Scheuchzer had a white crow, it got away on Saturday
> and onto the roof of Herr Baptisten [a neighbor]. Herr Dr. climbed
> onto the roof without shoes, lured and captured the bird, slipped
> and went down as far as the gutter, but was able to stem his foot
> against it, stand up and save himself, all the while holding the crow
> in his hand. People are saying that if he had fallen to his death, the
> canons would have given the crow a lifetime annuity [*leibgeding*].[45]

The example of Scheuchzer demonstrates three things: first, the truism— often overlooked in scholarship on the early modern period—that "church" is not automatically synonymous with "religion"; second, that the study of nature and knowledge of God could still be closely interconnected in the early eighteenth century; and, third, the evident need on the part of natural philosophers, at least of the sixteenth and seventeenth centuries, to justify what they were doing to pious or ecclesiastical critics.

The rhetoric of legitimization in the natural sciences is not a novelty of the late twentieth century, but a pervasive phenomenon as early as the seventeenth and early eighteenth centuries, from Francis Bacon to Isaac Newton. Bacon, who in his natural philosophy deliberately distinguished between God as *prima causa* and what he called the "second causes," that is, the divinely established, inherent laws of nature, wrote in his *Advancement of Learning* (1605):

> And as for the conceit that too much knowledge should incline a man
> to Atheism, and that the ignorance of second causes should make
> a more devout dependence upon God, which is the first cause; first,
> it is good to ask the question which Job asked of his friends: *Will
> you lie for God, as one man will do for another, to gratify him?*

There then follows the famous statement, "For certain it is that God worketh nothing in nature but by second causes." But if one reads on, one also en-counters Bacon's assertion that "a little or superficial knowledge of Philoso-phy [i.e., natural philosophy] may incline the mind of man to Atheism"; a deeper and continued study of natural philosophy, however, "doth bring the mind back again to Religion."[46]

Posterity has stylized Isaac Newton into the "architect of the mecha-nistically determined edifice of 'classical physics,' "[47] but Newton himself, throughout his life, clung firmly to his idea of a specifically divine providence (*providentia specialis*), that is, of a God who, in the final analysis, intervened directly in natural history, even if—from Newton's perspective—he did so very sporadically. To justify as well as to illustrate his special linkage of faith in providence with his effort to ground the understanding of nature in science, Newton stated in 1706, in the Latin edition of his work on optics, as always with a critical glance at Cartesian physics, that God used comets to periodi-cally reestablish the harmony of the universe.[48]

Moreover, in the same work he went so far as to make the following physico-theological pronouncement:

> And all this being so well arranged, it is not apparent from the
> phenomena of nature that there must exist an incorporeal, living,
> intelligent, and omnipresent Being which in infinite space—its
> sensory organ, as it were—sees through to the innermost nature of
> all things and comprehends them completely in their immediate
> presence. . . . Certainly there is in all of this nothing that would con-
> tradict itself or reason.[49]

The link between knowledge of nature and knowledge of God began to loosen only in the eighteenth century under the influence of the Enlightenment. The

Voltaire-inspired Enlightenment reception of Newton, in which little was left of Newton's belief in providence or of his intense study of the apocalyptic books of the Bible, is a good example of this development. But lest I make Newton out to be a model student of theological orthodoxy, we should remind ourselves of his secret Arianism[50] and his fascination with alchemy.

Religion, Natural Philosophy, and Alchemy

Over the past few decades, Newton's passionate interest in alchemy has given rise to new discussions in the history of science. Recently, scholarship has also cast a new light on Robert Boyle, long regarded exclusively as someone who transcended alchemy.

Today, as a growing number of historians of science are questioning the often deterministic faith in progress that characterized the traditional history of science, there is no longer a historiographical necessity to see Robert Boyle as some heroic conqueror of alchemy and thus of the occult sciences, even though it is possible to read some of Boyle's works—for example, *The Sceptical Chymist* of 1661—in this way.[51] In this tract, Boyle was particularly severe in his criticism of Paracelsus as the founder of the tradition of iatrochemically-oriented alchemy that still existed in the seventeenth century. But we also read statements like the following: "I distinguish betwixt those chymists that are either cheats, or but laborants, and the true *adepti*; by whom, could I enjoy their conversation, I would both willingly and thankfully be instructed especially concerning the nature and generation of metals."[52]

A fascination with an alchemistic understanding of things is unmistakable in these words, especially in the phrase "the true *adepti*," which has alchemistic connotations. In any case, only a few years later, Boyle saw no contradiction in his effort to explain an alchemistic transformation with concepts from mechanistic natural philosophy.[53]

One expert on the subject recently emphasized that "neither the emergence of chemistry nor the demise of alchemy" was as tidy a process as the older historiography made it out to be—and Boyle's role was, accordingly, more complex:

> Boyle's works and papers teem with alchemistic references, theories, practices and processes. Until Boyle's alchemistic pursuits are incorporated into his historical image, that image will remain distorted by a magnification of his work on "modern, reputable" topics of atomics, pneumatics and such like, at the expense of "archaic, disreputable" topics like alchemy.[54]

Betty Jo Teeter Dobbs, who spent her scholarly life studying Newton's alchemy, pointed out repeatedly that Newton's alchemistic penchant was centrally important to the formulation of his theory of gravity: the ideas of sympathetic influence underlying magic and alchemy helped Newton to distance himself from the principle of the theory of motion that dominated both traditional Aristotelian and the newer Cartesian physics, namely that any object that moves is set in motion through the direct, physical effect of force. In any case, there is simply no denying a certain affinity between alchemistic-magical ideas about sympathetic influence and the radically new postulate advanced by Newton in his theory of gravity, that there existed a physical effect of force between two bodies that did not touch each other.

In her last monograph on Newton, Dobbs tried to bring out the unity of all his work by way of his theology—a holistic interpretation, so to speak, of the life of this great Englishman.[55] Initially, I found this perspective persuasive.[56] Now, however, I am no longer convinced by the demand for a holistic understanding of sixteenth- and seventeenth-century scientists, because our modern cultural and social ideas of what is holistic must not be imposed upon the different worlds of earlier centuries.

From where I stand, there is simply no doubt that alchemy (and thus also magical ideas) played an important role in the development of European sciences into the late seventeenth century. What scholars have demonstrated for Boyle and Newton applies equally to Robert Hooke and to less well-known English scientists and scientific enthusiasts of the late seventeenth century, men like Elias Ashmole, John Aubrey, and others.[57] And evidence has been presented that a comparable development occurred in Germany.

In her critique of Keith Thomas's monumental study *Religion and the Decline of Magic* (1971), the cultural anthropologist Hildred Geertz emphasized that the real issue, from a historical-anthropological perspective, was not to explain the decline of magic in the early modern period, but to explain the emergence of a concept of magic as the opposite of religion and of enlightened reason.[58] In other words, it would be entirely false to question, in principle, the link between early modern religion, magic, and alchemy.

Stuart Clark has rightly defended the scientific status of the demonological tracts of the sixteenth and early seventeenth centuries against historians who wish to accept, in the history of science, only that which demonstrably promoted progress.[59] The relevant works of the skeptics Johann Weyer and Friedrich Spee, as well as those of the anti-Paracelsist and Weyer opponent Thomas Erastus, of the great French scholar Jean Bodin, the Scottish king James VI, the English hermeticist Robert Fludd, and many others, were as much an integral element of the scientific discourse about the mysteries of nature and the supernatural as were contemporary tracts on *magia naturalis* and *magia artificialis*. It was only in the fourth and fifth decades of the seventeenth century that a change began to take shape among scholars in this regard—though, needless to say, that change did not occur overnight, certainly not as abruptly as theorists such as Michel Foucault would seem to suggest.[60]

On the Relationship Between the History of Science and the History of Religion in the Early Modern Period

In his very fruitful discussion of the connections between magic, science, religion, and rationality, the social anthropologist Stanley J. Tambiah cautioned against drawing firm distinctions between "primitive" and "modern mentalities," based on the erroneous assumption that members of modern, western societies were "thinking scientifically all the time"; we know, after all, that "scientific activity is a special one practiced in very circumscribed circumstances."[61] Looking at the period of the so-called scientific revolution of the sixteenth and seventeenth centuries, Tambiah notes that "it is possible to separate analytically at least two orientations to our cosmos . . . *participation* versus *causality*." These two different perspectives of knowing could be assigned to religion and science, respectively, as complementary views of the world.[62]

What is important to me here is not so much this statement per se, but rather the thesis that Tambiah postulates in connection with it: namely, that a scientist of the seventeenth century could work simultaneously from two orientations—or, I would propose, perhaps even several, from our perspective incompatible, orientations—without perceiving a contradiction in doing so.[63]

The natural sciences have been called the "state religion" of the twentieth century.[64] This label, though sharpened to a polemical edge, is not entirely without truth. At any rate, it reinforces my belief that the history of early modern science, seriously neglected by the historical profession, could make substantial contributions to a better understanding of the culture of modernity. I believe that would be possible without invoking deterministic models about the relationship between the early modern period and modernity.[65] A history of the science of early modern Europe that wishes to be taken seriously, whose orientation is not merely forward-looking, and that seeks to be also a cultural history, must pay adequate attention to discontinuities and non-linear developments.

PART I

Upheaval and Renewal

I

The Ripple Effects of the Reformation

Reformation

An intense piety characterized the late fifteenth century. Penitential preachers from the mendicant orders crisscrossed the land, inspiring large audiences with their sermons delivered from the pulpit. Many people were keenly preoccupied with salvation. And yet, the Reformation was initially triggered by the actions of a single individual. Religious doubts led Martin Luther, an Augustinian monk and professor of theology at Wittenberg, to articulate, on the basis of his study of the Bible, radically novel views on a question that troubled him deeply: justification before God.

What was especially radical in Luther's stance was his denial of any possibility that human beings could be justified before God through their own merits. In Luther's view, the only thing that justified the believer was faith in the exclusive efficacy of divine grace. The sole means to that end was the understanding of faith on the basis of the Bible. That was the origin of Luther's public opposition, in 1517 and later, to any form of indulgence issued by the Church: according to the common understanding at the time, a person who acquired an indulgence could shorten his own stay in purgatory, or that of deceased family members, by bestowing material benefits on the Church.

It was the urban humanists (among them no small number of clerics) who ensured the rapid and astonishing diffusion of

Luther's first theses and writings. Thus the church reform that Luther had triggered took hold in the urban areas—at first among humanists as the representatives of the comparatively small urban educated class.[1] But what made the reform of the church into a true Reformation, into a socioreligious mass movement, was the fact that clerics, as preachers, began to adopt the Wittenberg reformer's ideas, in some cases perhaps merely his call for resistance to the existing conditions within the church. This mass movement was carried by local reformist currents that had deep roots in the urban artisanal class, and in which the zeal for religious reform not infrequently merged with anticlericalism and political resentment of the governing class of councilors.[2] In Germany and Switzerland, the cities became, in the words of H.-C. Rublack, the real "pacesetters of the Reformation," although the movement quickly gained numerous supporters in the countryside, as the Peasants' War of 1525 would demonstrate.[3]

Alongside sermons, printing played a fundamental role in the early spread of the Reformation in Germany and Switzerland. Within a single year, between 1518 and 1519 (that is, even before the Reformation became a mass movement), the annual production of pamphlets in Germany surged from 200 to 900 titles; thereafter this enormous output continued unabated for several years, primarily the printing of Luther's writings. By 1521, when Luther was summoned before the emperor at the Diet of Worms to explain himself, half a million copies of his writings were already in circulation.[4] To this we must add the tremendous rise in the number of Bibles printed in vernacular languages, even though many people—even among Protestants—continued to owe their knowledge of the Bible largely to church sermons.

Looking at the carriers of the reformist movements in the 1520s, it is not possible, in retrospect, to distinguish clearly between motives that were genuinely religious and those that were socioeconomic and political; that is true for both the cities and the countryside. The Reformation was an exclusively religious event in the beginning, but not so as it unfolded.

In contrast to Germany and Switzerland, the Reformation in France remained largely restricted to the cities and the nobility. With the exception of southern France, and especially Languedoc, the Reformation was not able to recruit followers from the rural population. Moreover, from the very beginning, the French crown placed considerable obstacles in its path, exemplified, for instance, by the Edict of 1562 that followed the Colloquy of Poissy in 1561. By this edict, the crown, while forced to officially recognize the existence of Protestantism in the cities, granted permission only to Huguenot worship in private houses.[5] The French Huguenots thus remained a minority movement.

Likewise, the supporters of the Reformation in the Habsburg Nether-lands, long persecuted, were able to gain some maneuvering room only in the second half of the sixteenth century, especially in the wake of the long war of independence against Spain that broke out in the 1560s and led to a split between a north that turned Calvinist and a south that remained Catholic.

In Denmark, the Reformation began to spread in the royal duchies of Schleswig and Holstein as early as the 1520s, but resistance from the conser-vative nobility delayed its official introduction in the rest of the monarchy until 1536, under Christian III (1533–59). From Denmark it crossed into Sweden and Finland.[6] In Sweden, it was from the beginning linked with the war of independence waged by Gustavus Vasa against Danish domination of the Union of Kalmar, the brittle alliance of the three Scandinavian kingdoms. Still, in this country, as in Finland and Norway with their low level of urban-ization, the Reformation took on decidedly authoritarian, governmental traits. The unrest and disturbances in Sweden and Finland in the 1520s were driven by the desire to preserve the old faith. In Denmark, by contrast, the Reforma-tion was carried also by a movement within the cities and by segments of the nobility. Norway, which was dominated by Denmark, saw the official intro-duction of the Reformation in 1539, with the crown also displaying an interest in the profits to be made from secularizing Church property.

In England, King Henry VIII (1509–47) used the Reformation to achieve complete independence from Rome, and with it also the possibility of a divorce from Catherine of Aragon. By the Act of Supremacy (1534) he appointed him-self and his successors the supreme head of the English church.[7] Of course, much remained unchanged in terms of church dogma. It was only under Elizabeth I (1558–1603) that the Reformation was able to establish itself among broader segments of the population.[8]

In Protestantism, Ernst Troeltsch has written, "the heart of the religion consists in the spirit of faith which is ... effected by the 'Word,' just as for Catholicism it consists in priesthood and sacrament, in obedience and in mys-ticism."[9] And because the trans-regional and supra-national hierarchies of the Roman Church were abolished by the Reformation, the local church commu-nity was invested with an entirely new, central importance in the religious life of the Protestants.[10] Needless to say, this happened also with respect to the organization of communal life under new conditions: the Reformation elimi-nated the worship of saints, which also meant that local processions during the church year and pilgrimages beyond the locality were abolished. The re-duction in the number of sacraments from seven to two (baptism and the Lord's Supper), as well as the abolition of the sacramentals, may have made Protestants even more inclined to resort to magical practices not approved of by the church as they sought to cope with the difficulties of life.[11] In the absence of church-consecrated objects (the so-called sacramentals), Bibles, hymnals, and prayer books were credited with almost talismanic powers in many places in the Protestant realms.[12]

Since the early Reformation in central Europe was primarily an urban phenomenon in its initial stages, its most powerful impact was in the most strongly urbanized regions of the old empire, in southern Germany and the Swiss Confederation. Alongside Martin Luther, a series of other preachers became regionally important and influential reformers, among them Martin Bucer (1491–1551) in Strasbourg, Johannes Oecolampadius (1482–1531) in Basel, and especially Huldrych Zwingli (1484–1531) in Zurich. Not a few of the reformers were motivated by strong apocalyptic beliefs. These beliefs were particularly pronounced in Martin Luther, whose actions were repeatedly dominated by the conviction that the end times had arrived, that the decisive battle against the rule of the Antichrist, whom he identified with the pope in Rome, had begun.[13]

Already by the early 1520s, the Reformation had ceased to be a uniform movement. The Anabaptist movement split off from the official Reformation, the Reformation protected from the top, as a separate, comparatively radical current of reform, initially in Zurich and its environs, in the Netherlands, and in Thuringia.[14] Beginning in the middle of the 1520s, we see a succession of cleavages of the reform movement in Germany and Switzerland over different doctrinal positions on the question of the Lord's Supper. While Zwingli and many of his southern German followers saw the Lord's Supper merely as the community's remembrance of Christ's sacrificial atonement, Martin Luther clung to the idea of Christ's presence in this sacrament. This split, enshrined for generations after the Colloquy of Marburg in 1529, was, first of all, an expression of the fact that Luther and the central and northern German reformers, on the one hand, and the southern German and Swiss reformers, on the other, came from divergent philosophical and theological traditions. Secondly, it was a manifestation of the strong communal imprint born by the Reformation in southern Germany and Switzerland.

The Reformation as a socioreligious movement began in the early 1520s in Wittenberg and Zurich, the first two urban centers of church reform. In the period after 1525, it is already imperative that we distinguish between the radical Reformation, which would become a catch-basin for Anabaptists, Spiritualists, and Antitrinitarians, and the "established" Reformation, with the latter divided once again into a Lutheran and a Zwinglian movement. These currents were joined in the 1540s by Calvinism, which radiated outward from Geneva, and which, needless to say, had much in common with Zwinglianism. That is why scholars today describe Zwinglianism and Calvinism together as the Reformed Confession, as distinct from Lutheranism.

From the very outset, the notion of the church of the true believers played a central role in Zwingli, Bucer, and Calvin, that is, the founders of Reformed Protestantism. The goal was to make this church visible in the world. For Luther, by contrast, the church of the true believers was a community which, in the final analysis, could not but remain invisible: against the backdrop of his "doctrine of the two kingdoms," the church of faith and the church as a communal institution were not a single entity. Zwingli, Bucer, and Calvin saw the matter differently. From the beginning, they strove to keep the church community (and thereby also access to the Lord's Supper as a community-creating sacrament) as pure as possible. That explains the importance accorded to moral discipline in the southern German/Swiss Reformed tradition. In this regard, as in its view of the Lord's Supper, this tradition was distinct from Lutheranism almost from the very outset. Beginning in Zurich, the marriage court, as a new, reformist institution, became a central instrument for implementing the Reformation.[15]

In Geneva, under the leadership of John Calvin, the *consistoire* was set up in 1540 as a specifically Calvinist expression of the communal morals court. Those who would speak of Calvin's alleged theocracy in Geneva must bear in mind that the consistory had close ties with the city's ruling class. It was presided over by a *syndic*, that is, a member of the small council. Only beginning in 1564, the year of Calvin's death, did the consistory have a majority of clergy. In addition to the city's pastors, the body included a group of community elders and lay people elected by the great council.[16] The Geneva consistory had the power to investigate the personal conduct of anyone who was morally suspect.

The example of the Genevan morals court was emulated in Biel and in the Reformed communities of Graubünden, and outside Switzerland among the French Huguenots of the sixteenth and seventeenth centuries, in Dutch Calvinism, and in the Calvinist communities of North America. The institution of the church consistory that was set up in the Duchy of Württemberg after the Thirty Years' War was also substantially influenced by this model. To the very end of the old empire, the church consistory placed into the hands of the Lutheran clergy an effective instrument for exerting moral discipline. In the Swiss Confederation, by contrast, the influence of Zwinglianism prevailed in the territories of Zurich and Bern and in Basel: that is to say, the marriage or morals court (*Chorgericht*) remained subject to close supervision by the state and practiced only a tempered form of the church ban (*Kirchenbann*).[17]

What transgressions were placed under the threat of ban? The Ban Ordinance (*Bannordnung*) of Basel in 1530 listed the following behaviors:

1. The worship of idols and images, pilgrimages, the practice of popish customs, soothsaying, magic, alliances with the devil, heresy, and Anabaptism;
2. Swearing and cursing;
3. Fishing, hunting, and working on Sunday, missing the sermon, not being willing to receive the sacraments;
4. Scorning or threatening parents, raising children poorly, not paying rents (*Zins*) and debts (*Gülten*) to the authorities, showing contempt for the church or the community;
5. Manslaughter, openly showing envy and hatred, receiving annual payments (*Pensionen*),[18] incitement;
6. Whoring and adultery;
7. Theft, usury, gambling, fraud;
8. Vilification, printing insulting booklets (*Schmähbüchlein*), perjury, lying to the detriment of others.[19]

The same thrust is found in the Bern mandates of the morals courts (*Chorgerichtsmandate*) of the seventeenth and eighteenth centuries. The Basel Ban Ordinance of 1530 shows clearly that these morals courts, by the terms of their mandate, had to concern themselves with far more than merely marital matters.

It was not only the ban as imposed by the Reformed morals courts, by which morally transgressive members of the community were excluded from the community of the Lord's Supper for a specified period of time, that ensured obedience toward these judicial bodies. Such obedience rested in equal measure on the widespread notion, rooted in the popular belief in providence, that God would punish communities with epidemics, natural catastrophes, or war for tolerating blatant sinners in their midst. Moral discipline was thus seen not only by theologians, but also by lay people, as the indispensable instrument for averting divine punishment, and this was the source of a good deal of its legitimacy.

Just how radical the reformist break with the ecclesiastical past could be in some cases is evident from the outbreaks of iconoclasm in the sixteenth century. Today we know much about individual episodes, for example in Zurich and Basel;[20] in its totality, however, the phenomenon is still in need of study and analysis.

A Carthusian monk from Basel noted in his chronicle of the Reformation period that the followers of the Reformation had become "quite unruly" beginning in the middle of January 1529. On February 9, 1529, we are told, they marched on the cathedral

> and stormed and smashed all the images with great anger [*ungestymmigkeit*] and with many blasphemous insults. Specifically, they took a large crucifix at the Episcopal church [*hohen stifft*] and tied a long rope to it, and many young boys, 8, 10, and 12 years old, dragged it to the grain market and sang "Oh you poor Judas," with many other words of ignominy; among other things they said, "If you are God, defend yourself, but if you are human, then bleed." Afterwards they hauled the crucifix into the city's workshop and burned it.[21]

Thus begins what is undoubtedly the most dramatic of the various—and certainly not consistent—accounts of the iconoclastic incident in Basel on February 9, 1529. The city council, which until then had put off a final decision on the Reformation question, was sufficiently intimidated to consent to the dismissal of councilors adhering to the old faith. The Reformation mandate of February 10, 1529, proclaimed the official abolition of the Mass in the city and its territory and the introduction of the Protestant service.

An exclusively sociopolitical explanation of the iconoclasm in Basel would be inadequate. To be sure, this action was also directed against the public self-display of rich council families, but the destruction involved "at the same time and primarily objects of the traditional salvific faith, now seen as false and pernicious."[22] The prohibition against images in the Ten Commandments surely played a role in this; yet the act of desecrating and profaning objects once regarded as sacral was also a kind of collective catharsis, a sort of collective exorcism.[23]

We encounter iconoclastic episodes not only during the early Reformation period, but also in the second half of the sixteenth century—in France, for example, during the religious wars that broke out in 1662, and in the Netherlands in 1666–67.[24] No matter how radical the break with the past as symbolized by Reformation iconoclasm may appear to have been, we must not overlook the continuities that linked the religious life of the late Middle Ages with that of the early modern period in the regions of Europe that turned Protestant, the Reformation notwithstanding.

Heinrich R. Schmidt, noting the parallels between the practice of morals courts in Reformed and mixed confessional communities in Graubünden and communities of Catholic central Switzerland, concluded that the moral codes in the rural communities he examined had pre-Reformation roots: "The social disciplining in the wake of the Reformation carried on an effort that the rural

Christian communities had begun on their own accord on the eve of the Reformation."[25] Moreover, rituals that had initially been abolished by the Reformation were later authorized again by Protestant clergy in response to pressure from below, one example being "churching," the ritual readmission of new mothers into the bosom of the church.[26] What is more, the assumption that the separation of certain consecrated, sacred spaces was given up in Protestantism as a result of the Reformation does not accord with the facts. The practice of blessing church foundation stones, church spaces, pulpits, baptismal fonts, altars, organs, bells, and cemeteries was resumed in German Lutheranism after a certain period and continued in many places.[27] Much the same holds true in general terms for the pious practices of early modern Protestants.

Before we turn to the Counter-Reformation, it should be noted that the Reformation was by no means a success story wherever preachers and laymen agitated on its behalf. We would be well advised to be cautious when reading the confessional apologetics of Protestant historiography of the nineteenth and in part even the first half of the twentieth centuries, for example when it implies that the Reformation in the German part of Switzerland would have continued its triumphal march had the Protestants not suffered a momentous military defeat in October 1531. More recent research has shown that a closer examination of the failure of reformist movements in Switzerland—especially in the cities of Lucerne, Zug, Freiburg, and Solothurn—leads to more careful assessments of the situation of confessional politics in the Swiss Confederation in the early 1530s.[28] Thus the *failure* of Reformation movements has rightly become a topic of historical research.

Counter-Reformation

The term "Counter-Reformation" is simply shorthand. I will discuss not only the Counter-Reformation as a delayed reaction of the Roman Church to the challenges of the Reformation, but also Catholic reforms, efforts toward renewal within the Church in the sixteenth century. These efforts began as early as the first half of the century, that is, before the Council of Trent in 1545 inaugurated the period of the Counter-Reformation.

In contrast to the older historiography, particularly that of the nineteenth and early twentieth centuries, scholars today look for the roots of the Reformation primarily in the religious sphere, and not chiefly in the defects of the church at the time. Still, it is necessary to note one problem that aroused anticlerical sentiments among the laity as early as the fifteenth century, resentments that reverberated into the Reformation period:[29] pluralism (the simul-taneous holding of multiple benefices) and the non-residency of the clergy. This was a common practice on the eve of the Reformation, and the all-too-frequent result was that some communities were less than suitably cared for spiritually by some vicar who was poorly or utterly untrained. Peter Blickle has shown that in both the urban and rural settings, the call for "appropriate" (*wohlfeile*) pastoral care—that is, for a resident priest of one's own—in south-ern Germany and in the Swiss Confederation was one of the standard de-mands urban and rural communities addressed to the Church as early as the fifteenth century.[30]

But there were also forces inside the Church that had been trying—in some cases decades before the Council of Trent—to rectify these deplorable conditions, although I will not discuss here in any greater detail the fifteenth-century reform movements within the church (the Brothers of the Common Life, the various monastic reforms, the mendicant orders, and so forth). A number of these efforts continued in the first decades of the sixteenth century, especially among the so-called *spirituali* in Italy, who sought to put into prac-tice a new kind of religiosity cleansed of all externalities. They remained a small minority, however, and around the middle of the century they were even persecuted for a time by the traditionalist pope Paul IV.

Within the milieu of the *spirituali* the new order of the Capuchins (founded 1526) emerged as a breakaway group from the Franciscans; fol-lowing the Council of Trent, it became, along with the Jesuits, one of the chief pillars of the Counter-Reformation. Two years earlier, the spiritual congrega-tion of the Theatines, an organization of secular clergy committed to reform, had been established. Among other events that followed, the Jesuit order was founded in 1534 by Ignatius of Loyola (1491–1556); a year later, Angela Merici (1474–1540) set up the society of the Ursulines in Brescia.

Although the pope could not ignore the variegated Catholic reform efforts of the pre-Tridentine period, the Roman curia was exceedingly slow, partic-ularly in calling for the general council demanded by Emperor Charles V, which was to address the ecclesiastical problems stirred up by the Reforma-tion. Rome feared a defeat for the papacy. Moreover, the various wars between France and the Holy Roman Empire or Habsburg Spain did their part to delay any action.

The Council of Trent met for a first session in 1545, which lasted until 1547. Another session followed in 1551–52, and the last one from 1561 to 1563. The choice of the location was dictated by Charles V's demand that the council take place within the empire. Trent met that criterion, and at the same time, the city was—from a Roman perspective—south of the Alps and thus close enough to Rome. Cardinal legates ensured contact between Rome and Trent during the sessions. In contrast to the councils of the fifteenth century (Constance and Basel), the Roman pope was very much present in Trent, not physically but in spirit.[31]

Of course, the Roman Catholic doctrinal decrees of faith and other reform texts were published only in the decades after the conclusion of the Council: in 1564 the *Professio fidei tridentina*, a summary of the basic articles of faith, following the model of the contemporary creeds; in 1566 the *Catechismus Romanus* as the foundation for teaching the flock of the faithful; and, finally, in 1593 the *Vulgata Clementina*, a revised edition of the Latin Bible—to name only three Tridentine reform texts. These processes illustrate the high degree to which Trent and the reforms connected with the Council reinforced the centralist, Rome-oriented structures of the Catholic Church.[32]

What were the fundamental theological positions of the Council of Trent? In opposition to the basic Protestant principle of *sola scriptura* (true faith must be based solely on the word of the Bible), the council fathers reaffirmed the traditional stance that the Vulgata *and* ecclesiastical tradition formed the foundation of faith. The overzealous Pope Paul IV, in no sense a reformer himself, went so far as to place the vernacular Bibles on the *Index librorum prohibitorum*, the papal list of prohibited books. More difficult to resolve were the questions connected with the other two Protestant basic principles—*sola gratia* and *sola fide*.[33] In essence, the Council was unwilling, when it came to the doctrine of justification, to entertain the strict Augustinian interpretation advocated by Luther, Zwingli, Bucer, and others, which denied that sinful humanity had free will. Against the doctrines of justification as taught by the reformers, the Council emphasized that baptism restored to the individual, sinful person part of his capacity of discernment, which meant that his actions were not automatically tainted by original sin. Unlike the reformers, the council fathers did not radically reject the possibility that each individual believer could contribute to salvation through personal merit. On the contrary: cautiously yet firmly, they reaffirmed the possibility of personal merit in questions of justification.[34]

In opposition to the Protestant reduction of the number of sacraments to two (baptism and the Eucharist), the Council asserted the central importance of all seven sacraments in Catholic doctrine. The sacraments were not merely a source of faith in the Lutheran sense, or a sign of membership in the Christian community in the Zwinglian sense; rather, they possessed an inner power of grace *ex opere operato*, which was bestowed upon the believer in the performance of the sacraments by the priest.

In addition to these fundamental decisions of doctrine, the Council of Trent had to deal with questions concerning the reform of the clergy. Bishops were required to make yearly visitations to each parish in their diocese. In fact, the position of the bishops was generally strengthened, including vis-à-vis individual priests and parishes. Priests living in a state of concubinage, a widespread phenomenon at the time, would lose their benefices if they refused to give up their way of life. In general, priests were urged to live up the dignity of their estate in their everyday conduct.

Without a doubt, the Council of Trent initiated a new era in Catholicism, but certainly not overnight. Its earliest implementation occurred in northern Italy, where Carlo Borromeo was archbishop of Milan from 1565 until his death in 1584. The Milanese archbishop and cardinal, who was canonized in the early seventeenth century, was deeply committed to his mission, which he sought to accomplish above all through pastoral care and the countless visitations it entailed.[35] With truly ascetic devotion, Borromeo shied away from no visitation, no matter how arduous the journey.

Borromeo also became the energetic promoter of Catholic reform and Counter-Reformation in Switzerland. In a lengthy letter to the pope, dated September 30, 1570, he urged the head of the Catholic Church to dispatch a nuncio to Catholic Switzerland. The task of this papal legate, as Borromeo saw it, was "to encourage the servants of the church to fulfill their duties and to improve their deplorable practices" with the help of the secular authorities, and to reverse the "usurpation of spiritual rights and offices" by the laity.[36] The mission of the first nuncio to Switzerland did not take place until 1579, however, and a permanent papal nunciature was not established in the Swiss Confederation until 1586, in Lucerne.

The reform of the training of priests and of the educational system was comparatively more successful. In close collaboration with Ludwig Pfyffer, the *Schultheiß* (mayor) of Lucerne and an entrepreunerial organizer of mercenary troops, Carlo Borromeo was able to open the first Jesuit college in Switzerland in Lucerne in 1574. The establishment of the Jesuit college in the Swiss city of Freiburg six years later was the result of the dedicated efforts of the nuncio Giovanni Francesco Bonhomini: the city council was anything but convinced of the matter, and the provincial of the Society of Jesus had to be actually compelled by an explicit command from Rome to consent to the foundation of the Freiburg college. This is yet another example of the considerable resistance that had to be overcome in some places before the decisions of the Council of Trent could be implemented. Additional Jesuit colleges were established in Switzerland in Porrentruy (1604), at the seat of the prince-bishop of Basel, and in Solothurn (1646).

North of Switzerland, in the Holy Roman Empire of the German Nation, the efforts to implement the Tridentine reforms dragged on at least until the middle of the seventeenth century, with substantial differences from region to region, and between one territorial state and the next. Early attempts were made particularly in Bavaria, where the Jesuits began to set up colleges even before the conclusion of the Council of Trent in 1563. They were followed, beginning in 1600, by the Capuchins, who founded a total of twenty Bavarian monasteries alongside the eight Jesuit colleges, and, finally, by the Ursulines.

At the other end of the spectrum we encounter a very different situation in the Rhenish-Westphalian prince-bishopric of Münster. There, Tridentine Catholicism did not truly establish itself until the decades following the Thirty Years' War.[37] In general, one should assume that this war, a disastrous con-flagration that flared up repeatedly and afflicted all of central Europe, brought some reform efforts initiated by the Church and the authorities to a halt, if it did not quash them altogether. Only the period after the Thirty Years' War saw the full and rich flowering of Baroque Catholicism in all the Catholic territories of the old empire, though within that current only some of the Tri-dentine reform endeavors were able to come to full fruition.

A renewed Catholicism entered Austria, at that time part of the old em-pire along with Bohemia and Moravia, along circuitous routes, so to speak. In the course of the sixteenth century, no small number of noble families in this region embraced Protestantism. The not insignificant support that Protes-tantism enjoyed among the Austrian nobility was not fundamentally chal-lenged until the 1580s, when the Counter-Reformation entered the Habsburg lands under Rudolf II. Only on the basis of a coerced Catholic religious unity, in part enforced with drastic measures, was it possible to renew the state on an absolutist foundation and without regard for special rights pertaining to estates or regions. More so than anywhere else, Catholicism became the state religion, especially since it constituted the only effective and therefore indis-pensable basis for the urgently needed renewal of the state in the Habsburg territories in the first half of the seventeenth century.[38]

Yet here, too, the full implementation of the process of re-Catholicization showed regional variations. In Bohemia, where broad segments of the popu-lation had also embraced Protestantism just as the nobility had, it was not possible to complete the thorough re-Catholicization, which was begun after 1620, until after the Peace of Westphalia. In the Kingdom of Hungary, by contrast, which in any case long resisted complete Habsburg control owing to the Turkish presence in parts of the kingdom, re-Catholicization was never completed. Protestantism was able to maintain itself into the modern period, especially among the nobility as well as in some cities.

From the end of the sixteenth century, the monarchy was successful in confessionally domesticating the nobility in the remaining Austrian lands by confessionalizing court patronage in the distribution of land and titles as well as the Church's allocation of benefices, and by establishing and expanding a princely monopoly on education with a Catholic imprint.[39] By curtailing the nobility's freedom of education, the Habsburgs were able to slowly bind the nobility once more to the state and the Church.

Protestantism was able to make special inroads into the Salzburg region—today part of Austria, at that time an independent ecclesiastical principality. Here, the archbishop used troops to support the Capuchins' missionary work among the rural population. This forced many back into the fold of Catholicism, but more than 1,200 Protestant peasants, especially in the mountain regions, clung to their faith and were forced to emigrate.[40] Of course, that in itself did not defeat Protestantism in Salzburg. Another expulsion of Protestants would occur a hundred years later.[41]

In Italy, particularly in the sphere of influence of the Archbishopric of Milan, the Tridentine renewal gained a foothold in large part through the foundation of seminaries, though subsequently, as we will presently see, it flagged rapidly. By contrast, in France, internally riven by the religious wars of the last decades of the sixteenth century, this process was delayed. On the whole, the Tridentine reforms did not take solid root in France until after 1650. Of course, the ground was prepared already in the first half of the seventeenth century, namely by the Jesuits, who had a total of 109 establishments in France by 1643. On the Catholic side, the Jesuits and the Capuchins were, comparatively, the most dynamic advocates and bearers of confessionalization, with the leading role falling to the Jesuits.

At the death of Ignatius of Loyola in 1556, the Society of Jesus had no fewer than a thousand members. A hundred years later there were 15,000 Jesuits and a total of 550 establishments scattered around the globe. The activities of the Jesuits extended far beyond Europe into North and South America and China. No other order in the seventeenth century symbolized so clearly the geographic reach of post-Tridentine Catholicism. In 1773, the year Pope Clement XIV disbanded the order, it counted 23,000 members and 1,600 establishments, 800 of which were colleges.[42]

But it was not only the reform orders that played an important role in the diffusion of a renewed Catholicism. In Spain in the second half of the sixteenth century, the Inquisition was placed in the service of the Counter-Reformation. This is evident from the files of the courts of Toledo and Cuenca, where, in the period in question, the largest number of cases dealing with bigamy, blasphemy, so-called superstitious practices and heretical beliefs, as well as nonconformity in sexual matters, were prosecuted.[43] In the process, the newly created network of "comisarios"—most of whom belonged to the parish clergy—represented a kind of extended arm of the regional Inquisition reaching down to the level of the individual village. This was a uniquely Spanish arrangement, however, for in Italy, where the Inquisition was also active, the local clergy as a rule did not perform the mediating function that Tridentine Catholicism had envisioned for it.[44] These observations might lead one to believe that the efforts of the Inquisition to enforce conformity were merely the result of church and royal politics at the highest level. But as Hsia reminds us, "it was Spanish Catholicism that created the Inquisition and not the other way round. Until the end of the old regime, Spain remained a deeply religious society."[45] That was more true of Castile, however, than in Spain as a whole, where, much as in France, the periphery was touched far less by Tridentine reform efforts.

It would appear that a good deal of the ecclesiastical and religious mood of renewal that existed in Castile was passed on to the southern Netherlands (the area of Belgium, Luxembourg, and the modern-day region of Artois in France). This was the largely French-speaking part of the Netherlands, which remained loyal to the Habsburgs. Sealing itself off from the officially Calvinist States General of the Netherlands in the north, Catholicism in the southern Netherlands became an important part of the collective identity in the late sixteenth and seventeenth centuries. The region that is modern-day Belgium "became an export land of Catholic renewal," involving, specifically, the print shops of Antwerp and the universities of Louvain and Douai. Next to Salamanca, Douai was the town from which most of the newly trained priests were sent to Ireland in the second half of the sixteenth century. Theological and devotional literature in Gaelic was printed in Antwerp, Brussels, and Louvain. Thanks to the initiative of Irish monks, the University of Louvain became a center for Catholic Gaelic literature.[46]

Confessionalization and Pressure on Popular Culture

In recent years, scholarship on confessionalization, more emphatically than any other field of research in early modern European history, has raised the question what a religious history in the modern sense can contribute to a better understanding of macrohistorical events—in this case, primarily a better understanding of the great historical transformations since the late Middle Ages and the sixteenth century that gave rise, over many centuries, to the culture and society of the modern world. These questions remain legitimate as long as we do not elevate them into the guiding questions for the study of early modern history as a whole. The study of early modern Europe must not

be forced onto the procrustean bed of deterministic ideas, of whatever provenance. In this regard, the microhistorical research that has been undertaken
recently in early modern studies is a salutary corrective. The results of its
labors point also to the forgotten, the strange, the seemingly unrepresentative.
Conversely, it would be wrong to assume that microhistory has simply swept
aside the great macrohistorical explanatory approaches, such as Norbert Elias's
theory of the civilizing process, or Max Weber's notion of the inner kinship
between ascetic Protestantism and the spirit of capitalism. The large questions
can and should continue to draw our attention. We must be aware, however,
that the reach of these approaches, and newer ones like it (including the concept of confessionalization), remains invariably limited, especially on the small
scale and in local and regional contexts, but also with respect to perspectives
that embrace whole societies and cut across social classes.[47]

The Intractability of Historical-Anthropological Findings

"Confessionalization," according to Heinz Schilling,

> refers to a fundamental social process that profoundly altered pub-
> lic and private life in Europe. It did so usually interlocked with, but
> at times also running counter to, the creation of the early modern
> states, and with the formation of an early modern, disciplined soci-
> ety of subjects. Unlike medieval society, this society was not orga-
> nized in a personal and fragmented manner, but institutionally and
> territorially. In addition, there were certain interactions with the
> simultaneous emergence of the modern economic systems.[48]

In his essay "National Identity and Confession," Schilling articulated the thesis
that "the early modern creation of the state as well as the emergence of national identities were also shaped in crucial ways by religious or confessional
facts." State formation and national identity were "the two most important,
systematically distinguishable though closely interconnected consequences"
of the principle that religion was to provide the glue that held early modern
society together:

> The *instrumental* side, which turned religion and confession into
> instruments in the hand of the state, with the goal of creating peace
> and order, and, above all, the voluntary obedience of the subjects and
> harmony between different estates and social groups; and the *inte-*
> *grative* side, which produced emotionally directed, unity-creating
> self-association and voluntary consensus, without which individual

or collective identity are hard to conceive, at least on a lasting basis.[49]

Elsewhere, Schilling makes clear what kind of importance he claims for his perspective. It was to supplement and modify, if not entirely replace, the well-known theory of the civilizing process developed by Elias:

> If one follows the sociologist Norbert Elias in grasping this funda-mental transformation from the medieval personal state [*Perso-nenverbandsstaat*] to the modern, institutional territorial state as the gradual monopolization of the key positions in public affairs by the sovereign state power, the analysis in terms of confessional his-tory and the sociology of religion reveals the following: at the be-ginning was not, as Elias postulated, the monopoly of taxation and military force, but the monopoly over religion and over the church that was dominant, or at least prevalent, in the respective state territory, a monopoly the early modern state secured for itself in the wake of confessionalization.[50]

This view of the process of confessionalization is oriented primarily toward the early modern process of state-formation. It is a view that is predominantly statist and shaped on the whole by a rather one-sided "forward-looking per-spective" (W. Brückner). If we look at matters also from below, that is, from the everyday piety and religious practice of common folk, we will arrive at a more differentiated interpretation of the processes of confessionalization, one that does justice also to the experiences of the groups in question.

Bernd Roeck summarized his observations on the situation in Augsburg in the age of the Thirty Years' War:

> Some patterns of behavior, manifestations of a certain indifference, seem to indicate that for many individuals at the time, confession was more of a way of life rather than something determined by doctrines of faith. Conversely, one encounters forms of religiosity that either stood in a problematic relationship to the doctrines of the established confessions, or were actually regarded as outright heret-ical: "superstitious" practices to which the authorities responded with suspicion or repression.[51]

A 1662 diocesan statute from Cologne condemned astrological prediction (*astrologia divinatoria*) as superstitious and forbidden by the Church. Also ruled superstitious were the interpretation of dreams and so-called confer-ences and bindings, "to counter disease and injuries to humans and animals,

to preserve life, to allay pain and staunch bleeding wounds," and to attain invul-
nerability. "The [magical] use of characters and astronomical pictures, prayers
of a specific length and order, amulets, saints' names, and relics for purposes
they could not possess inherently or in accordance with the will of God, and a
good deal more was also superstitious."[52]

That this statute was still necessary nearly a century after the conclusion
of the Council of Trent shows that, even at this time, pious practices that were
in no way approved of by the Catholic Church were common in the archbishopric of Cologne. My use of the term "pious practices" here is quite deliberate:
from everything we know today it would not appear that a meaningful number of laypeople at the time saw astrology and magic as openly opposed to
Christian views sanctioned by the Church. I believe that Roeck was correct in
concluding that the activities and popularity of sorcerers inside and outside
Augsburg in the late sixteenth century and in the period of the Thirty Years'
War confirms "the existence of an attitude that could be activated in certain cases, was present 'below' the Christian-confessional thinking, and . . .
combined with the latter in a way that made it hard to tell the two apart."[53] It
is precisely this that makes the use of historiographical categories such as
"superstition" to characterize certain early modern ideas and practices of faith
so dubious. In essence, scholars of piety who employ this term in an undif-
ferentiated way adopt the categories of the early modern confessional churches
without questioning them in accordance with the accepted rules of historical
source criticism.

There was, then, first of all, disagreement between the confessional
churches and many laypeople over their respective views of what should
be regarded, from a religious perspective, as acceptable beliefs and practices
of faith—the numerous mandates of faith from Catholic and Protestant
churches and authorities in the early modern period is sufficient evidence. The
diocesan statute from Cologne that I have cited is only one example of many.

Second, we must be very clear about the fact that the relationship between
pastor and village was, for a variety of reasons, by no means always unprob-
lematic. In the Protestant regions and territories of Switzerland and Germany,
the village clergy increasingly became, in the wake of confessionalization, the
voice of the authorities in the countryside. If there were tensions between the
authorities and their subjects, the clergy sometimes found itself in a very difficult position. For example, it has been argued that the reason why the rural
population remained aloof from the Reformed churches in the territories of
Bern and Basel following the crushing of the Swiss Peasants' War in 1653 had
to do with the alienation of rural folk from its clergy.[54] During the Peasants'
War, the latter had decidedly thrown its support behind the authorities. What

has been said about early modern Lutheranism is even more true for the Reformed Confession: both were urban confessions; almost without exception, the clergy hailed from urban environments, and they were thus not only representatives of the authorities in the countryside, but at the same time also ambassadors of a specifically urban culture.[55] By contrast, the Catholic clergy was by no means recruited solely from the urban milieu. Catholic priests were therefore more willing and able to accommodate themselves to practices of faith in the countryside and the villages. At the same time, however, these rather better chances of being integrated within the village placed limitations on the reach of their reformist ambitions.

Added to this was the fact that the priest or pastor interacted with his fellow villagers not merely as a "cleric" in the narrower sense of the word. Multifarious economic relations existed between him and his community: first and foremost, in both Protestantism and Catholicism, by means of the tithe, which villagers had to pay to their clergy, and which was the object of countless quarrels between peasants and tithe-lords in early modern Europe. In the case of the Catholic priest, there were also various surplice fees for ritual acts, offerings, and endowments for masses. Pastoral care and the liturgy, as Rainer Beck has observed with regard to the Bavarian village of the late seventeenth and eighteenth centuries,

> always had to do with money and goods. That may appear trivial, but it implies for the social history of religious life that the encounter between priest and village, between the representative of the church and the faithful, was two-fold: a spiritual and a material encounter— and that there was an inherent correspondence between the two.[56]

Third, and finally, there were always frictions concerning the disciplining pursued by the church and the secular authorities. In any case, the population certainly did not accept this without opposition. There were multifarious facets to social disciplining: it involved a stepped-up fight against crime, the repression of begging, a heightened supervision of young people and their celebrations, and an expansion of the school system—to name only the four most important areas.[57]

Baroque Catholicism and Confessionalization

Over the course of two decades of scholarship that began in the mid-1970s, scholars tended to assume that the processes of confessionalization in the Protestant and Catholic territories of the old empire were essentially comparable, parallel events. In particular, Wolfgang Reinhard, in a number of essays

spanning twenty years, tried to make clear that the confessionalization efforts
within Tridentine Catholicism were not fundamentally different, in terms of
their goals and tendencies, from what he regarded as parallel processes on the
Protestant side.[58] The thrust of Heinz Schilling's studies on confessionalization in German and Dutch Protestantism was very much the same. In recent
years, however, scholars have increasingly voiced their doubts about this thesis
of parallelism. The Bern historian Peter Hersche, in particular, propounds the
view that from the very beginning, Catholic confessionalization did not pursue the same goals and certainly did not have the same success as Protestant
confessionalization—which is why one should speak about relatively separate
processes that were by no means parallel. He is especially critical—and not
without reason—of those who speak about early modern Catholicism in Europe
as a monolithic entity, as though it were not necessary to distinguish different
forms of concrete, religio-social and cultural expressions within Catholicism
across Europe.[59] From this perspective, the development of French Catholicism
would fit most readily into the previously mentioned interpretive scheme of confessionalization, while that is not true for Catholicism in a more general respect.

French Catholicism in the seventeenth and eighteenth centuries was characterized by strong tensions between two—in part very different—spheres of
activity, that of the Jesuits and that of the clergy and laity oriented toward
Jansenism. Hersche sees France, very much in contrast to the other Catholic
countries of Europe, as *the* country in which the claims of reform put forth by
Tridentine Catholicism were implemented most thoroughly in practice:

> The reform was initially one of the entire clergy. Unlike in Italy or
> Spain, the clergy in France declined in quantity, but increased in
> quality. . . . It was here that a disciplined, well trained, and broadly
> educated clergy was formed, which already in its external conduct,
> dressed in a cassock, well mannered, with no penchant for women,
> alcohol, or gambling—of course, there were always exceptions—
> set itself distinctly apart from the mass of the people.[60]

Needless to say, even here the reforms took effect only slowly and gradually.
A more thoroughgoing reform of the clergy had barely gotten under way by
around 1640.[61] After that, the renewed clergy deliberately endeavored to spread
its modes of conduct to wider segments of the population through periodic
missionary work among the people. It is only against this background that
one can really explain the broad appeal of Jansenism, a usually fairly ascetic
form of Catholicism.

The kind of Baroque Catholicism that was able to spread in the Holy
Roman Empire, Switzerland, Italy, and Spain, with its opulent processions,

clerical plays, and translations of relics, hardly resonated in France. On the whole, French Catholicism of the seventeenth and eighteenth centuries was more sober than Baroque Catholicism. It was, as Hersche has suggested, a "classicist" Catholicism. That was true at least for the core region of the French monarchy, whereas the periphery, especially Provence, Brittany, and Lorraine, must be accorded a special role of sorts.[62]

In all of this, one must remember that in France the Tridentine calls for reform were not implemented simply in quiet obedience to Rome. Instead, the specifically Gallic manifestation of French Catholicism, which had existed since the early sixteenth century and was not infrequently critical of Rome, received additional accents. It is revealing for this special situation that while the French clergy officially adopted the Tridentine conciliar decrees in the early seventeenth century, the crown and its institutions of state ignored them—at least officially.[63] The entire early modern period is characterized by a specifically French church policy on the part of the French kings—that is to say, a Gallican policy that was at no time truly faithful to Rome. This assessment is not altered by the suppression of the Calvinist minority of the Huguenots by Louis XIV—we recall his revocation of the Edict of Nantes in 1685. This was a largely politically motivated move by the Sun King, through which he was hoping to improve relations with the pope at least temporarily.

Outside France, post-Tridentine Catholicism took on primarily Baroque trappings. One well-known element of Baroque Catholicism is its sensuality, visibly and tellingly expressed in the veneration of saints (especially within the framework of the cult of Mary), the Church's enthusiasm for building projects, processions, ecclesiastical theater, and much more. It was an emphatic demonstration of the degree to which everyday life in the seventeenth century was religiously imprinted, indeed pervaded, by religiosity. At the center of this religiosity stood the intense veneration of Mary. Its special importance is evident, for example, in the contemporary Catholic calendar, with its many feast days commemorating the stages in the life of the Mother of God. In the post-Tridentine era, the Marian cult inspired a new surge in the practice of pilgrimages, though it would not reach its peak until the eighteenth century.[64]

New confraternities and congregations arose in conjunction with both the intensified veneration of Mary and the Tridentine revaluation of the sacrament of the Eucharist. First and foremost were the very numerous Marian congregations in western and central Europe, which came to play a crucial role in the diffusion of Jesuit, post-Tridentine piety.[65] Frequent Communion and, connected with it, weekly confession were made absolutely obligatory for the members of these congregations—in addition to other self-imposed disciplines.[66] Of course, it should be emphasized that congregations and fraternities cannot be equated. The latter rarely put forth comparable pretensions; their rituals were usually more tradition-bound, concerned less with innovation than conservation.

Early Marian congregations appeared in the second half of the sixteenth century in towns that were home to nuncios or papal legates (Cologne, Munich, Vienna, Lucerne, and Avignon), and in university towns (Cologne, Louvain, Dôle, Toulouse, Pont-à-Mousson in Lorraine, and Ingolstadt in Bavaria).[67] Membership figures indicate just how considerable the reformist influence of these congregations must have been on religious and ecclesiastical life. Cologne and Lille in northern France each had around 2,000 members, predominantly male, around the middle of the seventeenth century, in each instance equivalent to about 4.4% of the city population. In Antwerp at around the same time, membership amounted to nearly 7.3% of the city's residents. The ratios were higher still in a number of smaller towns: 3,000 members in Ingolstadt, 1,000 in Nancy. If the figure of 2,000 members in the Swiss city of Freiburg is accurate, it would mean that nearly half of its population— including 900 women—participated in the activities of the Marian congregation.[68] Europe-wide, however, such a high ratio of women was the exception rather than the rule. Yet we must not overlook the fact that women took their cues in other forms as well from the reform efforts of the Jesuit order: for example, within the women's congregations that began to emerge in the 1530s, such as the Ursulines and the English Ladies.[69]

The observations regarding the special role of French Catholicism hold true also when it comes to the participation of the European courts in the Jesuit Marian congregations. A closer look at the way in which Marian congregations spread reveals two conceptions of the Christian state: a Bavarian one, in which the duke—as the Elector—and a large segment of his court participated actively and enthusiastically in the Munich Marian congregation; and a French one, in which the king kept his distance from Rome, while many of his courtiers were involved.[70]

In addition to the veneration of new saints like Francis Xavier, Filippo Neri, and Francesco Borgia, as well as the newly emerging cult of Joseph, the catacomb saints attracted a good deal of attention (particularly in the southern German-Swiss region and in parts of Austria).[71] In the seventeenth century, their translation feasts provided the occasion for some magnificent performances of Baroque ecclesiasticism and religiosity.[72] The *Engelweihfeier* of Einsiedeln in 1659, which was combined with the solemn translation of the relics of the Roman martyr Placidus, lasted a total of fourteen days. All the ecclesiastical and secular dignitaries who mattered were invited to the celebration, from the papal nuncio and the bishop of Constance to Mayor Fleckstein of Lucerne. The climax of the festivities was the monumental, colorful relic procession, followed the same evening by the performance of an ecclesiastical play.[73] Of the five sections that made up the procession, the fourth was the high point:

> Out in front, dressed in a red robe, strode the guardian angel of the Catholic Church, on his head a helmet, in the right hand a red cross banner, in the left the escutcheon with the inscription: *Pro Ecclesia Catholica*. Behind him was carried a new red flag bearing the likeness of Saint Placidus. It was flanked by mail clad men in gleaming armor. Next came the processional cross of the convent of Einsiedeln with the two candle bearers, followed by two silver statues of the Virgin Mary, then the fathers of the convent and the attending Jesuits, dressed in dalmatics, chasubles, or pluvials. Behind them walked the nine abbots [of Einsiedeln and other Benedictine convents of Switzerland and southern Germany] in their pontifical vestments, bearing relics on precious pillows. They were followed by a red labarum bearing the inscription: *Corpus S. Placidi mart.* Two angels with palm fronds and cymbals, censer, and incense boat walked in front of the body of Saint Placidus. Four men carried the baldachin that covered the reliquary, four others carried the heavy reliquary, six men clad in armor marched by their side.[74]

Now, Baroque-era Einsiedeln's display of Catholic pageantry was undoubtedly exceptional. But in Wil, which was part of the princely abbey of St. Gall, 56 members of the clergy and 5,000 people participated in the festive translation of the relics of Pancratius in 1672; on this occasion the surrounding villages were all but deserted.[75]

It is well known that the Jesuits developed theater into a high art, one that effectively supported the formation of a confessional identity among the audience, though not always without engaging in polemics. In Germany, between 1555 and 1665, Jesuit authors put on a total of 323 ecclesiastical plays. For generations of students at the Jesuit colleges, the spiritual theater was an integral part of their religious education.[76] The Benedictines, in for example, Einsiedeln and Salzburg, also devoted themselves to the ecclesiastical theater of the Baroque, though not nearly on the same scale. Most plays drew their subject matter from the lives of the saints. By the final decades of the seventeenth century, however, the strictly religious play was exhausted. Its place was increasingly taken by the courtly secular heroic play. From this time on, one scholar of the subject has noted, "the psychological locus [*Seelenzustand*] of the play" was "no longer the religious but the ethical system of Catholicism."[77]

A court-dominated culture replaced the church-dominated culture as the exemplar.

Not all of the changes I have touched on in the preceding discussion can be assigned to a process of confessionalization shaped by Tridentine Catholicism. For example, it is questionable whether the translations of saints in the Baroque era belong in this category. Moreover, the attempts to implement the reform plans of Tridentine Catholicism were at best only partially successful in the Romanistic world outside of France. As for Italy in the Baroque (1600–1750), Peter Hersche recently laid out sound arguments for his conclusion that "the Tridentine reform movement failed."[78] With regard to southern Italy, he finds support in the work of Gabriel de Rosa and his school, who have, among other things, pointed to the high degree of autonomy of the lower clergy, which allowed them to escape episcopal control and supervision. With regard to central and northern Italy, the definite impression we get is that the initial reformist vigor had already evaporated in the seventeenth century and in fact did not pick up again until the end of the eighteenth century—now, of course, under the banner of the Enlightenment. Moreover, it is quite clear that the era of the genuine reform papacy already came to an end with Paul V (1605–21)— and against the background of the costly, Baroque display of splendor and pageantry by the Roman Church, "the financial bleeding of the provinces by the central ecclesiastical authorities" may constitute "Rome's greatest responsibility for the failure to implement the reform."[79]

The Limits of Ecclesiastical Discipline

It would be wrong, however, to think of the process of confessionalization solely as the result of activities by the courts and governments of various European princes and the leaders of the respective churches who cooperated with them. We must not overlook the active role of local "middlemen." In addition to the local clergy, they included teachers, urban councilors, merchants, and village notables. Given the utter absence of policing forces in the modern sense, it was they who ensured that the ecclesiastical regulations and ordinances of faith issued by the secular authorities were in fact observed and that violators were punished.

Confessionalization was not merely a process of establishing a creed on the basis of the church's teaching of the catechism and periodic ecclesiastical visitations. As a rule, the formation of a creed was accompanied not only by the attempt to increase state control over the local administration of church property and the system of charity, but also by ecclesiastical *and* moral discipline enforced by the authorities. For example, within the framework of ecclesiastical discipline, regular attendance at Mass was made obligatory, and in Catholic regions also confession, which was now confirmed in writing by priests on "confession certificates" (*Beichtzettel*) if it was not administered by the penitent's own priest. The framework of moral discipline, however, extended far beyond these ecclesiastical concerns and encompassed, among other things, the battle against so-called *Zutrinken* (public drunkenness), gambling, idleness, prostitution, cursing and blasphemy, the disobedience of children toward their parents, the regulation of engagements and marriage, and much more. The contemporary regulations of public order in the territorial states of the Holy Roman Empire are eloquent testimony to the wide reach of the moral discipline ordained by the secular authorities.

The process of confessionalization in the wider sense included, first, at its core, the formation of a confession on the basis of printed ecclesiastical doctrinal tracts—for example, the *Formula of Concord* (1577) of the Lutherans, the *Heidelberg Catechism* of the Reformed confessions (1563), or the *Catechismus Romanus* (1566) of the Roman Catholic Church. These tracts served as the guidelines for teaching the faithful, carrying out missionary work among them, and, if need be, indoctrinating them.

In the period under discussion, confessional pluralism constituted a fundamental factor of the history of the old empire, both on the level of high politics and, not infrequently, on the level of daily life, at least in the confessionally mixed regions of southwestern Germany. However, this pluralism does not mean that any one of the three confessional churches I have mentioned moderated in the least its exclusive claim to be in possession of the sole truth. On the contrary: from the late sixteenth century on, the Protestant clergy on all sides entrenched itself increasingly behind the walls of orthodoxy. The Saxon universities in Leipzig and Wittenberg became bastions of orthodoxy in German Lutheranism, while the centers of Reformed and Calvinist orthodoxy emerged outside the borders of the empire, at the universities and colleges of Basel, Geneva, and Leiden in the Netherlands. The universities in Ingolstadt, Cologne, and Louvain became comparable centers for Catholicism north of the Alps.

There is no need to discuss in detail here the doctrinal differences between Lutheranism and Calvinism, such as those concerning the Lord's Supper and predestination, and I will confine myself to external differences. Apart from the liturgy of divine services, these differences became evident in the divergent organization of the churches, in particular on the parish level. In German Lutheranism, decision-making power and supervisory functions lay nearly exclusively with the territorial functionaries, whereas among the Reformed, the entire parish, as a corporate body, traditionally held considerable decision-making authority. By delegating so-called Elders to the communal morals court, that is, to the consistory or the presbytery, the community as a corporate body exercised considerable influence on the life of individual parishioners—at least in theory, for in the German territorial states in which Calvinism found a reception between the 1560s and the beginning of the Thirty Years' War, this Genevan model of church organization rarely took hold in its pure form. The reason for this was that the German princes of the Reformed Confessions in no way lagged behind their Lutheran colleagues in their claim to exercise power over the territorial churches. Still, it can be said that German Calvinism placed a greater emphasis on the need for moral discipline than did Lutheranism.

Before Pietism and the Enlightenment began to relativize the rigid confessional thinking of the previous generations in the eighteenth century, the confessionalism cultivated especially by the clergy constituted a fixed element, as it were, of the way in which the confessions interacted. Not infrequently, this confessionalism expressed a good deal of arrogance and even contempt for those who held a different faith. This attitude was, however, by no means shared by all the laity.

This difference in the confessionalism of the clergy and the laity was recently confirmed by two outstanding studies on the coexistence of Catholic and Lutheran communities in Augsburg in the seventeenth and eighteenth centuries.[80] To be sure, one study maintained that the tendency by the artisans of both confessions to close themselves off as corporations was inevitable over the long run. The other study, however, pointed emphatically to those areas of everyday life that continued to unite the city's inhabitants socially and economically, in spite of the tendencies of both confessions to isolate themselves. A similarly pragmatic spirit of cooperation prevailed in Oppenheim on the Rhine, where no fewer than three confessions and a small Jewish community coexisted in the eighteenth century.[81] In the confessionally mixed Thurgau, as well, we find repeated demonstrations of trans-confessional unity, all the mutual demarcations among the laity notwithstanding.[82] One example is the village of Üsslingen. Renward Cysat, the town clerk of Lucerne and a contemporary witness, reports that the Reformed citizens of Üsslingen protested when their prior sought to divide the community's cemetery on a confessional basis. The deceased Catholics, they argued, "had been their good friends and relatives, wherefore they wish to remain in the same place [so wöllen sie in demselben nochmahlen verharren], and do not wish to be excluded after death from the community of those who, during their lifetime, had been their good and dear friends."[83]

At the turn of the seventeenth century, the Catholics of Bietingen continued to do what they had done in pre-Reformation times, visiting the now Reformed church in the neighboring town of Thayngen, which was part of Schaffhausen's territory. The council of Schaffhausen objected when the cathedral chapter of Constance tried to cut off Bietingen's filial church by arguing that

> the people of Bietingen, living and dead, have always been part of Thayngen, seeing that for many years now, indeed for as long as anyone can remember, they have visited their church without any hardship, complaints, or demonstrated malice [bewisenen Truzens], listened to God's word, had their children baptized at that very church [ire Kinder mit dem christenlichen Touff der Kirchen daselbst inverleben lassen], thus they get along with each other without any trouble.[84]

The attitude reflected in these examples is a pleasant departure from the confessional polemics uttered by many clerics on both sides. Of course, these polemics were not entirely without effect. We can see this, for example, in a number of territories in Germany in the last decades of the eighteenth century, when a front of opposition arose among the faithful to the new hymnal inspired by the Enlightenment. The opposition was justified by, among other things, the argument that the new hymnal betrayed the secret re-Catholicization tendency of the hitherto Protestant authorities or the desire of the Catholic clergy for a rapprochement with the Lutherans.[85]

One essential instrument of ecclesiastical discipline—as distinct from the more broadly conceived notion of moral discipline—in the wake of the Reformation and the Tridentine reform movement was the teaching of the catechism to both children and the adult members of the parish. To that end, clerics of both confessions, following in the footsteps of Martin Luther's *Small* and *Large Catechism* from the late 1520s, composed a whole series of catechisms as introductions to the basic principles of the true faith. Priests and pastors were required to give regular catechism lessons, especially to children and adolescents. However, the effect of this instruction was limited, for two, or possibly three, reasons. First, not infrequently the discipline of the clergy itself left much to be desired. Second, there were repeated expressions of resistance among the population. In the territory of the city of Zurich, parents who were not sending their children to catechism class even had to be threatened with a monetary fine.[86] Third, there is the controversial thesis that the teaching of catechism amounted essentially to mere indoctrination, which had only superficial results: at best, the population instructed in this way was able to recite the maxims of faith it had supposedly learned in a mechanical fashion, without any deeper understanding.[87]

Within Reformation scholarship, in the 1970s this last thesis led to a debate, especially among American scholars and sometimes carried on with

great apologetic effort, about the breadth and depth of the impact of the Reformation. Today, it appears that a consensus on the matter is slowly beginning
to emerge. For Heiko A. Oberman, there was no doubt that in many places
throughout Europe, the Reformation deprived itself early on of the chance to
have a broad impact because it allowed itself to be turned into an affair
controlled and imposed "from above," which alienated many potential supporters.[88] At any rate, within this context, the fact that even in Reformed territories, where social discipline is known to have been the most rigorous, complaints about the so-called superstition of the simple folk were widespread as
late as the seventeenth century should give us pause. In the Reformed Pays de
Vaud in Switzerland, for example, there were repeated complaints between
1630 and 1670—that is, more than a hundred years after the introduction of
the Reformation—about rural folk venerating a tree trunk they regarded as
sacred because it was believed to have the power to heal gout, or about the
religious veneration of a certain fountain, whose waters were said to exorcise
"evil spirits."[89] When introduced as an act of state, the Reformation had a difficult time taking root and establishing itself on the ground, and in this respect
there was no essential difference between the Reformed Pays de Vaud and
Lutheran Scandinavia. In Lutheran Norway, for example, the veneration of
saints persisted into the seventeenth century. As late as 1622, the King felt
compelled to issue yet another prohibition of pilgrimages.[90]

Moreover, a growing chorus of skeptical voices is now making itself heard
about the effect of disciplining and catechism in post-Tridentine Catholicism.
For example, in reference to the re-Catholicization of the late sixteenth and
seventeenth centuries, a study of baptismal names in villages of Upper Austria
concluded that

> the development of Catholic attitudes among the population pro-
> gressed very slowly. In particular, the idea that the installation of
> Catholic clergy in this area automatically guaranteed an inner re-
> Catholicization will need to be considerably revised. At least the prac-
> tice of baptismal name-giving—though an indicator of only lim-
> ited, regional reliability—provides a clear demonstration, first, that
> these priests were hardly able or willing to exert any real influence on
> the population, and, second, that attitudes from the Reformation
> period continued to shape the parish members for generations.[91]

Even in Bavaria, Protestantism was able to persist into the seventeenth
century in some areas, in spite of the early and, it would seem, broadly-based
counter-reformationist missionary work among the rural population.[92] With
respect to Protestantism in the mountainous regions of Salzburg, I have already

mentioned the expulsion of peasants in the 1630s, when they were forced to leave the land because they clung tenaciously to their Protestant faith. Still, Protestantism survived even here, and a missionary campaign undertaken by the Jesuits in the early eighteenth century had little to show for itself. When the Protestant peasants began to organize in 1731 in the wake of spontaneous gatherings in opposition to the growing attempts by the authorities to suppress the Protestant faith, archbishop Leopold Anton Firmian smelled a potential revolt of the subjects. He dispatched troops into the mountain valleys, eventually forcing thousands of Protestants to emigrate in the middle of winter—the last great, confessionally legitimated expulsion in Europe in the wake of the revocation of the Edict of Nantes in France in 1685.[93] The general assumption should be that Tridentine reforms in the region of central Europe achieved real successes only after the Thirty Years' War, and that these successes in turn began to bear fruit only in the eighteenth century. In addition, it must be noted that they were partial and regionally limited, which means that they were not able to truly replace let alone overcome the traditional Catholicism that was not reform-oriented.[94]

Of course, the warnings by modern historians not to overestimate the effects especially of the Catholic Counter-Reformation must not obscure the fact that there were also successes from the perspective of the Church and the secular rulers. This is true primarily for the reform of the clergy, for the implementation of the new doctrine of marriage and the Church's claim of control it entailed, as well as for new forms of devotion. In some places, regular catechization was also institutionalized. But based on the current state of scholarship, it appears rather more doubtful whether, for example, the so-called *Osterzettel* that was introduced throughout Catholicism by the Council of Trent, on which a priest confirmed in writing a parishioner's confession and Communion at Easter, proved everywhere as effective an instrument of discipline as it did in the Electorate of Cologne, where "the number of negligent communicants" showed a "strong decline." One thing that should give us pause, however, is the conclusion that the reception of Communion, in particular, showed "that Catholic reform was most likely to be successful when it made use of effective and tough instruments of supervision and punishment."[95] And where this supervision was implemented in a rather lackluster manner and "largely ground to a halt in the eighteenth century," as it did in Italy and in the countryside, the disciplinary effect of the *Osterzettel* remained limited.[96]

The broad introduction of the *Osterzettel* belongs in the context of ecclesiastical record-keeping, which was systematized by the Reformation and the Counter-Reformation. Registers of baptisms and deaths were now set up, along with records of marriages—though far into the seventeenth century, especially within Catholicism, the quality and thoroughness of these records depended, of course, on the discipline of the responsible clergy. To some extent, pre-Reformation practices were continued and systematized, for baptismal registers existed in Italy and southern France as early as the fourteenth century. The first parish register in German-speaking lands was begun in 1490 in Basel in the parish of St. Theodor.[97] The baptismal and marriage registers "served as proof of infant baptism and the—confessionally 'correct'—ecclesiastical marriage. Given the persecution of the Anabaptists, who refused infant baptism, the different conceptions of marriage (in terms of church law and doctrine) held by the various confessions, and the absence of a non-ecclesiastical (state) marriage, this allowed for a high degree of social control and disciplining."[98] That the new registers had no small measure of success in helping to combat concubinage and reduce the number of extramarital births is obvious, but I think it is rather doubtful that they also led to a decline in pre- and extramarital sexual activity, given the broad ineffectiveness (at least in the countryside) of other measures in this area by the church and the authorities.[99]

Ecclesiastical discipline and moral discipline were mutually complementary. For this reason, confessionalization was an integral element of what Gerhard Oestreich called "social disciplining" (*Sozialdisziplinierung*), the sociocultural manifestation of the process by which secular authority became more intense and pervasive in the early modern period.[100] It would be wrong, however, to link the process of social disciplining in its entirety to confessionalization. The latter was a product of Reformation and Counter-Reformation, while the pretensions of ethical reform on the part of some German states reach back before this period and thus had largely secular roots. Two examples are Bavaria and Württemberg, where such efforts by the state are already apparent in the fifteenth century. The same holds true for the communal reform efforts on the territory of what is today Switzerland.

The more recent Reformation scholarship is also inclined to pay due attention to aspects of continuity between the late Middle Ages and the early modern period, alongside the unquestioned innovations that followed in the wake of Reformation, Counter-Reformation, and the efforts at confessionalization.[101] If we look at this continuity less from the normative perspective and more from the perspective of the history of *mentalités*, what comes into view are aspects of piety, religiosity, and worldview that resisted the very efforts at disciplining and uniformization over a longer period of time. These include the elements of continuity in the belief in astrology—which cut across social classes—from the Middle Ages into the seventeenth century. It includes also the continuity in the belief in magic and magical practices, as well such phenomena as the elements of traditional saint worship, that were preserved in the pious practices of the Protestants.[102]

The School as a Sphere of Confessional Renewal

Among the areas in which the confessional efforts in the early modern period undoubtedly had some effect was the school system, which, by way of example, I will examine in closer detail. The Protestant side recognized the central role of the school in confessional politics early on: without an improved and, especially from an ecclesiastical point of view, reliable educational system, the recruitment of future clergy was acutely threatened. For that reason, as early as 1523 Martin Luther addressed the councilors of the German city, urging them to send children to school. "Children" referred here primarily to boys, however, even though the education of girls would receive a (comparatively modest) boost from both the Reformation and the Counter-Reformation.[103]

For the beginnings of school reform under the banner of the Reformation we can look to the example of Zurich, where Heinrich Bullinger, Zwingli's successor and head of the Zurich church after 1532, at a time when the problem of recruiting the next generation of leaders was starting to become more pressing, began to refashion the Zurich schools into a comprehensive educational system.[104] The city's two Latin schools were reformed and restructured into the preliminary level for the study of theology proper within the framework of the so-called Prophecy (*Prophezei*). At the same time, the system of scholarships was expanded. After the middle of the century there were plans to establish, at the lower school level, two German schools financed by the council as the preliminary grade to the two Latin schools. These plans were not realized, however; the city was left with the already existing, privately run German schools that taught reading, writing, and some arithmetic. Needless to say, though, they now came under closer supervision by the authorities.[105]

The effort to promote schooling among the rural population was not undertaken on a broader basis until the seventeenth century. But when it did come, the *Antistes* Johann Jakob Breitinger in Zurich made a very determined push, with the result that remarkably high rates of literacy were recorded in the Zurich countryside in the seventeenth century.[106] Sweden is probably the only other comparable example, a country where the wish of the authorities for literacy was also implemented with a good deal of pressure by the Lutheran clergy on the rural population. In the territory of Bern, the *Volksschule* (elementary school) was established in the countryside by a decree of April 12, 1616:

> Having recognized the duty of our office to strive not only for the worldly welfare of our subjects entrusted to us by God, but also for the salvation of their souls, we have thus pondered means by which our subjects, especially young people, shall be raised, guided, and

instructed in greater fear of God, a better knowledge of His holy word and the mystery of the holy sacraments.... To that end, we have found no better method than having schoolmasters hired and maintained wherever there are large parishes, for the purpose of teaching and instructing the young.[107]

The same intent lay behind the Gotha school decree of 1642, in which the elementary school for girls was in fact put on equal footing with that for boys. It stipulated

that the boys and girls throughout this praiseworthy principality shall be gradually instructed in good order, by means of God's help and the application of the requisite diligence, in catechism and the understanding thereof, selected Biblical sayings, Psalms, and prayers, as well as in reading, writing, singing, arithmetic, and, where there is more than one preceptor, in the knowledge of several useful things, some natural, some worldly, and others, in addition to which they shall be guided toward Christian discipline and good morals.[108]

Evidently there were considerable regional differences within both Protestantism and Catholicism when it came to the promotion of rural schools in the framework of early modern confessionalization. In France, the state and the church did not make a concerted effort to promote the system of elementary schools until after the Edict of Nantes: in the wake of the forced conversion of the Huguenots as a result of the Edict, the school was recognized as an important instrument in the fight against crypto-Protestantism.[109] We are told that the number of parish schools in the Electorate of Cologne began to rise significantly only in the eighteenth century. In the sixteenth century, less than 10% of the parishes had such a school. This means that in Electoral Cologne, on average only one parish in ten had a public elementary school in the sixteenth century; in the neighboring Duchy of Jülich, the average at that time was already 20%.[110] A complaint by the archiepiscopal schoolmaster in Cologne in 1786 reveals that in many places, in both Catholic and Protestant regions, the problem of school reform was truly recognized only in the wake of the Enlightenment, and thus not as a part of early modern confessionalization:

Most teachers are unable to manage even adequate lessons in the subjects of instructions. In the countryside, a tailor or cobbler will take on the school as a side job; in the cities it is an organ player or errant [verlaufener] student. The entire instruction is devoid of teaching style and method. Disorder prevails in the entire school system; students are sent to school as one sees fit. Any separation

into classes is unknown; the school houses and classrooms resemble a gloomy prison, where shabbiness and horror rule, where
spirit and health are ruined.[111]

Within Catholicism, the system of elementary schools took shape largely
around religious instruction, by means of catechism lessons for children and
adolescents. The crucial role in this process was played by the Ursulines, the
Jesuits, and the so-called Christian Teaching Societies (*Christenlehrgesellschaften*),
largely shaped by Carlo Borromeo, as new, post-Tridentine brotherhoods.[112]
In addition, smaller women's orders, organized on the model of the Jesuits,
such as the English Ladies founded by Mary Ward, also participated in this
educational mission.

Distinct differences between the confessions existed with regard to higher
education for girls and women, because the Protestant Reformation consigned
women more strongly to the realm of home and family as their primary field of
activity.[113] A broader interest in the education of girls and women can be attested
within Protestantism only since around the middle of the seventeenth century,
while Catholicism, drawing on the ascetic-monastic tradition that reached back
into the Middle Ages and was by no means abolished through the Counter-
Reformation, offered other options much earlier.

Within the Catholic Church, the implicit claims to an education that was in
principle equal for boys and girls gave rise to controversy, as a result of which
the houses of the English Ladies were dissolved in 1630–31 on orders from the
Pope. Thereafter, under the impact of this development, the way in which the
Ursulines, Augustinian Nuns (*Welschnonnen*), and Catherine nuns thought of
themselves seems to have changed:

> The starting point was no longer the principled equality of the sexes,
> but rather a cultivation of inequality: "higher daughters" are edu-
> cated for the . . . role of the wife and mistress of the house, as at-
> tractive as she is modest. Languages—especially French, the new
> vernacular—were part of the curriculum. Latin moved into the
> background; instruction in etiquette and dancing lessons were added.
> The difference between the education of girls and the education
> of boys became more glaring again.[114]

To be sure, I would not go so far as to speak of an "education explosion in the
period between the Reformation and the Enlightenment."[115] We are dealing
with far too long a period to apply the phrase "education revolution"—coined
to describe England between the middle of the sixteenth and the middle of the
seventeenth centuries—to the German-speaking lands. However, there can be

no doubt that between the sixteenth century and the Enlightenment, the school became, in the words of Richard van Dülmen, the "decisive institution of socialization."

Popular Culture Under Pressure

From the perspective of the development in the German territorial states, Heinz Schilling has tried to define the process of "social disciplining" (*Sozialdisziplinierung*) as follows:

> Social disciplining refers to the incorporation of the individual and of social groups into the uniform body of subjects, and to the leveling of regional and particularistic interests in favor of a "common good" defined by way of the territorial state; the content of this 'common good' was determined by the prince and his officials. The early modern confessions were involved in this process in a multitude of ways.[116]

As I see it, social disciplining was not confined to the process of confessionalization. In areas where the two processes overlapped during the sixteenth and seventeenth centuries, we can define as part of confessionalization what Peter Burke has described as attempts by the authorities and the church to "reform popular culture," in the sense of suppressing it. The guiding stars of this reform were values like "decency, diligence, gravity, modesty, orderliness, prudence, reason, self-control, sobriety, and thrift," which were now to be implanted also in the lower strata of the population. In other words, values that would later constitute "the petty-bourgeois ethic," as Peter Burke remarks with a touch of disdain.[117]

In Bavaria in the wake of this "reform of popular culture," specifically in the first half of the seventeenth century, a concerted effort was made to combat swearing and blasphemy; the authorities also prohibited fortune-telling, card reading, and other such arts. This process bears a strong resemblance to the 1662 diocesan statute from Cologne quoted above. An attempt was made "to cure the subjects by force of their so-called superstition and their unorthodox, magico-religious practices."[118] Added to this were decrees and ordinances that regulated separate bathing hours for men and women and abolished certain popular dances for moral reasons. Then there were rules governing tavern visits and restrictive measures concerning games, masquerades, and competitions, and legal restrictions—based once again on new, more rigid notions of morality—of the traditional bride-wooing practices of rural folk.[119]

Johannes Kessler, the Reformed chronicler of St. Gall, described the ramifications that flowed from the new ideas of morality down to the level of everyday clothes:

> Until now it has also been an abuse among rich and common
> daughters that they uncover themselves in front and sideways down
> to the breast, one more shamefully than the next, in the churches,
> in alleyways, at weddings, and when they dress festively, and it was so
> common that it was regarded as honorable and daughterly. But
> now [1526, shortly before the introduction of the Reformation in the
> city of St. Gall], this is considered shameful before God, his angels,
> and the world, when coming before the community, as is proper for
> pure unmarried women, very neatly covered up everywhere.[120]

The fact that the public brothels were abolished in many Protestant cities following the introduction of the Reformation is part of the same story. Of course we should not be misled into thinking that this got rid of prostitution altogether. In Basel, for example, the public brothel was closed down in 1531, and yet in Christian Wurstisen's *Chronicle of Basel* as continued by Daniel Bruckner, we find a reference in the year 1619 to a passage in the new Basel church statutes according to which "indecent women and public whores, so as to avoid nuisance and sexual immorality, shall be removed not only from the taverns, but also from the streets."[121] The Jesuit priest Julien Maunoir, who was engaged in a mission to the people in Brittany in the 1640s, reports in his account that he struggled against the dances held by the young people of Plougastel at night and on Sundays, and how he tried to displace their "obscene songs" by introducing Christian hymns.[122]

This sphere of regulation and regimentation, expansively defined throughout Europe, saw frequent conflicts between the authorities or the church and the subjects, conflicts that were carried out chiefly at the village level and strained, not least in the relationship between the priest or pastor and his fellow villagers. One well-known example was the repeated attempts by Catholic bishops, beginning around the middle of the seventeenth century, to reduce the number of feast days, and especially the so-called *Gelöbnistage* (vow days), which in some parishes had been spontaneously turned into saints' feast days in response to some immediate occurrence—for example, if a storm had spared the community. This kind of reduction in the number of feast days ran into popular opposition in the archbishopric of Mainz.[123] The people of Zug responded in a similar manner in 1646 after the city council had prevailed upon the bishop to abolish a number of feast days. The community forced the council to revoke its measures, which meant that the episcopal vicar-general was compelled to confirm the reduction of the feast days a year later ex officio against the will of the population.[124] As we will see, the same insubordinate behaviors would continue during the period of the Enlightenment in the late eighteenth century.[125]

The Zwinglian and Calvinist clergy—in short, the official Reformed religion—undoubtedly proceeded in the most radical fashion when it came to restructuring the traditional, pre-Reformation calendar of feast days. After the Reformation, the rigorous reduction of feast days with the consent of the secular authorities led to "a radical change in the traditional rhythm of the week, month, and year in the Reformed territories. Here . . . only a few feast days were left in place besides Sunday: Christmas, Easter, and Pentecost as two-day feasts, and in addition New Year's and Christ's Ascension. By contrast, the structure of the old church year was, on the whole, left unchanged."[126]

Moreover, the reduction in feast days in Reformed regions went hand in hand with a "rigorous sanctification of the remaining Sundays and feast days," which was watched over by the Reformed morals court (*Sittengericht*), especially the community elders. The old forms of sociability practiced on the feast days were thereby severely curtailed, if not entirely prohibited.[127]

The reformers and their successors were locked in a virtually permanent conflict over *Kirchweih* (church dedication day) festivals, which in their eyes led all too frequently to excessive exuberance, drinking, brawling, and promiscuity. One particular sore point was the regular participation of boys' association (*Knabenschaften*) in the *Kirchweih* festivals. From the perspective of the defenders of a new moral code, the *Knabenschaften* were perhaps their fiercest opponents, because they made the most strenuous and frequent efforts to evade the attempted cultural reforms by the church and the authorities. Needless to say, there were characteristic differences in this regard between Protestant—especially Reformed—and Catholic regions. In Geneva, the initial attempts to suppress the *Abbayes de Jeunesse*, an annual event when boys and teenagers elected an "abbot" for one day, were already made before Calvin's definitive arrival in the city on the Rhône (1540): "Ever since the reception of the Gospel, games, dances, mask-wearing, and the like have been prohibited, and only exercises in the use of weapons are still allowed," wrote the contemporary Genevan chronicler François Bonivard.[128] By contrast, in the Catholic city of Zug in central Switzerland, the election of a child bishop by the students on St. Nicholas Day continued throughout the sixteenth and seventeenth centuries.[129]

It was not only the church dedication feasts that were scaled back, if not completely abolished. *Fasnacht* (Shrovetide) also came under attack. In the Protestant cities of the Swiss Confederation it fell victim to the Reformation entirely—though in Basel, as further reports during the Reformation century reveal, the defeat was only partial. Still, it was only much later that *Fasnacht* returned in all its glory. In Zurich, where *Fasnacht* had been abolished in 1529, Zwingli's successor Heinrich Bullinger reported in his history of the Reformation: "Since much immorality occurred in conjunction with *fassnacht*, all this was abolished in Zurich."[130] In Catholic Lucerne, as well, the existing *Fasnacht* customs were curtailed in the later sixteenth century. In Cologne, the church took steps against carnival, though not until 1617 and 1644, which reflects the characteristically late period at which the Counter-Reformation took root in the region of the lower Rhine.[131] In Protestant Nuremberg, *Fasnacht* was completely abolished between 1525 and 1538; when it was celebrated again in 1539, after a nineteen-year hiatus, the council immediately prohibited it once more. The reason for the renewed prohibition was a float that had been aimed satirically at the Lutheran pastor Andreas Osiander, whom the people of Nuremberg saw as the man chiefly responsible for the official constraints on traditional *Fasnacht* customs. Following the proclamation of the renewed prohibition, the crowd stormed Osiander's house.[132]

A large number of other popular customs also came under pressure in the course of the so-called reform of popular culture. They included, for example, the pulling of the plow (*Pflug- und Blochziehen*) on Ash Wednesday, when young men harnessed girls and young women to the plough, which they then had to pull through the village or town—undoubtedly a very symbolically loaded event. In the wake of the reforms of the sixteenth century, this custom was suppressed not only in Protestant but also in Catholic territories; it survived only in scattered locations in Tyrol and Switzerland as a practice engaged in almost exclusively by fraternities.[133]

In essence, many of the regulatory efforts described here reflect the slow but steady growth of official control over public times and spaces, the sort of control that was also manifested in the Catholic reduction of feast days in the seventeenth and eighteenth centuries. To protect the sphere of work, public entertainment was assigned more precisely defined temporal frameworks, while public space was increasingly removed from expressions of popular spontaneity and declared a stage for official events. Regional differences in these efforts existed not only with respect to confessional politics, but also for simple climatic reasons.[134] In Scandinavia, the public space was far less important as the site of large and elaborate feasts than was the case elsewhere in Europe.

Confessionalization as Christianization?

The French historian Jean Delumeau used the continuities between the Middle Ages and the early modern period that I have mentioned to advance a radical version of the concept of confessionalization. As he sees it, the Middle Ages

THE RIPPLE EFFECTS OF THE REFORMATION 63

was essentially an un-Christian, pagan era, and the mass of the population had by no means been Christianized. Delumeau postulated that "on the eve of the Reformation, the average European was only superficially Christianized. Under these conditions, the two reforms, that of Luther and that of Rome, were in the end merely two ostensibly competing, though in the final analysis converging, processes of Christianizing the masses and spiritualizing religious sensibilities."[135] He then goes on to list—of course, primarily on the basis of French sources—everything in the religiosity of the masses that was supposedly not Christian and was therefore opposed by the reformers, both Protestant and Catholics. The non-Christian aspects fall under the collective concept of an animistic magical mindset. In this context, the philosophy of the Neoplatonists of the sixteenth and seventeenth centuries, though surely not a popular philosophy, is invested with an unmistakable connotation:

> The vitalistic philosophy of the Neoplatonists was merely the conscious expression of a synthetic mindset that was fundamentally primitive [*fondamentalement primitive*] and did not distinguish clearly between nature and the supernatural.... Since it is hardly capable of analytical examination, the archaic gaze distinguished imperfectly between the visible and the invisible, between the part and the whole, between the reflection and the model.[136]

Delumeau's conclusion is obvious:

> Deep ignorance of essential elements of Christianity, and the occasional persistence of pre-Christian ceremonies and quite frequently of a pagan mentality are the two faces of the same intellectual and psychological reality in France—and surely also in Europe—at the beginning of the "classic" period, which dates in France from around the middle of the seventeenth century with Louis XIV's ascension to the throne.[137]

This, in a sense, is the background against which Delumeau describes the missionary efforts, in particular, of the Catholic clergy in the seventeenth and eighteenth centuries.

Delumeau's interpretation has found only a limited following outside France.[138] Some time ago, Natalie Zemon Davis made the criticism (rightly, I believe) that the attempt to draw what is, in the final analysis, an artificial boundary between so-called superstition and church-approved religiosity blocks an understanding of the importance of the "*meaning, modes* and *uses* of popular religion to peasants and city dwellers." Such a view leads to distortions if popular religion is seen today exclusively through the eyes of a Jean Gerson,

Carlo Borromeo, or Erasmus of Rotterdam. Moreover, Delumeau's approach fixed the relationship between clergy and laity in a very questionable way, since the consistent assumption is that only the "spiritual elite" had been able to preserve for itself an authentic religiosity and unadulterated religious sensibility.[139] Such dubious schematizations are also hinted at now and then in more recent works by other French historians.[140]

Another French historian, however, has made the ironically critical comment that Delumeau—just like the post-Tridentine bishops of the seventeenth century—is spontaneously opposed to the mixing of the "religious" and the "non-religious."[141] Jean-Claude Schmitt has argued, against Delumeau and religious historians with a similar bent, that we would do best to dispense with the theory that certain "remnants" of paganism had persisted within European religiosity in certain periods or centuries: after all, in a living culture there is no such thing as "remnants." Whatever is not actively lived does not exist as a cultural factor. There are no circumstances under which a given faith or a specific ritual could be described as some kind of heterogeneous combination of leftovers and new elements. Rather, such a faith or ritual constitutes an experience that draws "its meaning solely from its coherence in the present."[142]

Confessionalization and Modernization

To its discoverers in the 1970s, the process of early modern confessionalization constituted *the* essential link between the Reformation, the Counter-Reformation, and modernity. What characterizes modernity?

> There is the whole phenomenon of the formation of giant states with their vast military power, which shatters the dream of an ecclesiastical world-empire, the development of modern capitalistic business-organization, bringing everything under its sway, the growth of applied science, which has accomplished more in a couple of centuries than in the two previous millenniums, the immense increase in the figures of population, which has become possible through all this and in turn creates the necessity of it all, the bringing of the whole world within our mental horizon and the contact with immense non-Christian empires, the struggles of the nations without, in the arena of world-politics, and the struggle within of the new social classes created by this development.[143]

This was Ernst Troeltsch's answer at the beginning of the last century, and it is not without a critical undertone.

German-language historiography of the postwar period was deeply influenced by Troeltsch's picture of modernity, as well as by Max Weber's comparable image. Notwithstanding all the criticism that is now leveled against
German structural history of the 1970s and 1980s, the so-called Bielefeld
School (Hans-Ulrich Wehler, Jürgen Kocka, and others) surely deserves credit
for the fact that a more differentiated view of modernity (in some parts going
beyond the original Bielefeld approaches) has established itself among historians since then. Anyone who imagines the emergence of modernity as a
process-like event that was specific to social class and gender can no longer
proceed from a kind of monolithic picture of modernity, which is what Weber
and Troeltsch had still done.

More recently, modernity has been described, from a perspective more
critical of progress, as

> that phase in the historical evolution of the European-Atlantic world
> which is characterized by the continuously necessary reconciliation
> of two fundamental problems. On the one side is the necessary rec-
> ognition of individualization and rationalization as the driving and—
> in my view—indispensable forces of social development. On the
> other side, however, is the ongoing search for new normative and
> ordering systems capable of giving an acceptable form to the social
> consequences of individualization and rationalization, and to
> make coexistence and survival possible.

This also means that "the history of modernity, even in its most fortunate
phase, is always also the implicit history of its failure; indeed, the possibility of
failure is the core of modernity itself."[144]

The question we need to examine in greater detail here is this: How can
the scholarship of the early modern period, and especially the study of confessionalization, do justice to such a differentiated view of modernity? Ever
since Heinz Schilling and Wolfgang Reinhard introduced their influential
notion of parallel Catholic and Protestant processes of confessionalization into
the scholarly debate in the 1970s, German scholarship has made the link between Reformation, the Counter-Reformation, and modernity essentially on
the basis of considerations borrowed from modernization theories.

In 1977, Wolfgang Reinhard gave one of his programmatic contributions
to the new interpretation of the Catholic Counter-Reformation the interroga-
tory title "Counter-Reformation as Modernization?" He then hastened to answer his own question in the affirmative: "Methodical, planned, and organized
action is especially characteristic of the formation of confession from above.
In this regard the Tridentine reforms constitute a fundamental modernization

of the old church."[145] Later he elaborated further: "By disciplining and individualizing the believers, post-Tridentine Catholicism was thus moving in the same direction as the Protestant confessions, with one exception: when it comes to literacy, Protestantism retained its modernizing lead."[146]

The postwar sociological theories of modernization go back to the social theories of the nineteenth century. Those theories found a particularly striking articulation in the historical materialism of Karl Marx, and their bourgeois-liberal counterpart, as it were, in Max Weber's conception of western rationalization. The modernization theory developed since World War II, at first primarily in the United States, was used above all in the comparative explanation of the "great transformation" in the western world, which has been summarily described as the "transition from the estatist-corporative to the centralistic-bureaucratic state, from a society of agrarian privileges to a society of civic classes, and from a pre-capitalist and pre-industrial to a capitalist-industrial economy."[147] In a specific Eurocentric narrowing, elements borrowed from this theory made their way into German-language historiography beginning in the 1970s through the previously mentioned Bielefeld School, and thus also into attempts to explain fundamental processes of transformation that occurred in the early modern period.

A 1995 essay by Heinz Schilling on "confessional Europe" in the sixteenth and seventeenth centuries visibly strengthened the connection between scholarship on confessionalization and modernization theory.[148] The Reformation is here seen as a kind of "crisis of modernization," namely as the response to the attempts at organizational renewal on the part of the Roman curia in the fifteenth century. The Archimedean point in this conception of the Reformation is the thesis of a "warm-up time of modernity": According to Schilling, the coincidence of the emergence of the confessional churches "with the fundamental political, legal, and administrative transformation that produced the early modern state justifies our speaking of confessional Europe as the 'warm-up time of modernity.' "[149]

The emphasis on the signal importance of the early modern process of state formation is intended to imbue this blending of the confessionalization process and theoretical approaches to modernization with persuasive power. Schilling's perspective is much too subtle and differentiated for him to posit a kind of linear progression of early modern modernization. Instead, he also notes resistance and setbacks. Still, to my mind he is not able, in the end, to avoid the impression that an evolutionary inevitability attaches to his model of confessionalization. Criticism has also been aimed at the statism within scholarship on confessionalization in Catholicism: "Until now, research on

Catholic reform has been fixated on the top: on popes, religiously zealous princes, nuncios, bishops, and the founders of religious orders."[150]

It is now widely understood that the perception of the sacral and the individual appropriation of this perception in the early modern period were substantially filtered and shaped by the social and cultural experiences of everyday life. Against this backdrop, it is imperative to question the far-too-smooth and teleological notion of a kind of linear–progressive course to the process of confessionalization, a notion that was oriented primarily to the developmental stage of the state in the nineteenth century. We now know that forms of saint worship existed both in Lutheranism and among the Reformed; that Catholic exorcists were also sought out by Protestants; that the conversion of the Presbyterian theologian Richard Baxter—a star witness for Max Weber—was strongly influenced by a Jesuit devotional tract which had been given a makeshift Protestant veneer; that the Huguenot resistance theories of the 1570s were articulated almost entirely in the legal and moral language of their Catholic adversaries.[151] We also know (I am thinking of the scholarship on bi-confessional cities of the old empire)[152] that within the bi-confessional urban environment, there was a good deal more mutual social interweaving among the various confessional groups than one would be led to believe by conceptions of confessionalization oriented chiefly toward normative source material.

Without a doubt, we must not underestimate the role played by a professed adherence to a particular confession out of an inner conviction of faith. Yet in the autobiographical sources of the time, the confessional self-understanding reflects in many cases a religious conviction that was by no means derived only from catechesis and ecclesiastical instructions, a conviction that often expresses, in confessional terms, merely a vague socioreligious sense of belonging. This kind of confessional self-understanding was frequently oriented more toward symbols and external rituals than toward genuine questions of faith.

If we examine other, non-normative types of sources, it becomes evident, for example, that this confessional self-understanding in the countryside corresponded—in its way—to the manner in which peasant communities in central Alsace in the first half of the sixteenth century adopted the concerns of the Strasbourg reformers and translated them into their own world: their preoccupations were understood by the peasants in Old Testament terms—in the sense of the Ten Commandments—and interpreted primarily from a communal and neighborly point of view.[153] Something similar is also true of the reception of the Tridentine reforms in Catholic regions in the late sixteenth and seventeenth centuries. Visitation protocols from the bishopric of Speyer and the diocese of Würzburg reveal the extent to which the individual priest was embedded within the traditional value-community of the village and was therefore, contrary to the expectations of the ecclesiastical hierarchy, incapable of acting as the reformer of religious life.[154] In most of the rest of Catholic Europe, with the exception of France, the Tridentine will toward renewal often evaporated within a few short decades. Incidentally, Protestant visitation records from the late sixteenth century indicate that the reformist concerns within the Alsace peasantry mentioned earlier had lost much of their original attraction.

Closely connected with the question of the diffusion and reception of evangelical teachings is the striking tendency (previously noted) within Reformation historiography during the last decade or so to reveal the elements of continuity between the late Middle Ages and the sixteenth century. In a comparable sense this is also true of scholarship dealing with the issue of secularization. We are beginning to recognize the full extent to which the secularization process between the seventeenth and the nineteenth centuries was a socially and culturally differentiated event, the full extent to which varied historical layers existed side by side, and just how much the secularization and—to follow Weber—the rationalization of mentalities and of thought and behavior differed, depending on social class and cultural environment. If we are forced to realize that there is no scheme of historical periodization that is equally valid for all social strata, what, precisely, constitutes the specific character of early modern religiosity? And when all else fails, is the dynamic of the process of state-creation the only crucial factor?

To be sure, the sort of blueprints of a more or less linear course of history from Luther to the *Kaiserreich* that were propounded in the late nineteenth and early twentieth centuries have been abandoned, since there is now a broad consensus within the historical discipline that the road to modernity was a process.[155] In principle, this would offer a great opportunity to combine under one roof different approaches to the phenomenon of confessionalization—macrohistorical and microhistorical studies, as well as political history and the history of mentalities. Yet this opportunity has to a certain extent been squandered, because the process of state formation in the early modern period has been invested with central conceptual importance as the primary expression and chief goal of confessionalization, an approach that has been proved influential. Let me note, merely as an aside, that this pattern of argumentation is oriented far too much toward the development of German territorial states: in pre-Enlightenment Italy, for example, with the exception of Savoy-Piedmont, the development toward the modern state "occurred, if at all, only in a rudimentary, fragmentary, and limited way."[156]

Wolfgang Schieder has related what I just referred to as the process-character of the path to modernity to the religious development. From the sixteenth century to the end of the nineteenth century, he sees a "continuity of repeated, wave-like efforts at confessional re-Christianization." This raises the question of "whether the confessional modernizations of the early modern period were not after all merely partial modernizations."[157] The question implies a far-reaching decoupling of state-formation processes and confessionalization processes. The trend toward making state-formation the foundation of research on confessionalization foists a basic evolutionary pattern upon the course of European history between the Reformation and modernity, a pattern that is now being increasingly qualified and relativized by a steadily rising tide of historical-anthropological research and scholarship on the history of *mentalités*.

To be sure, a narrative account of the findings of research into fundamental processes of Reformation and confessionalization, like all historical writing, cannot do without a certain internal directedness. But that would also be possible if it were guided merely by a "weak" modernization theory.[158] By that I mean theoretical borrowings that are not decided a priori when it comes to the question of determining causality. This makes them different not only from the classical modernization theory with its evolutionistic and even deterministic tendencies, but also from other universalistic approaches, like the Weberian sociology of religion and domination and historical materialism.

A religious history of the early modern period that is guided by nonevolutionary conceptions of historical change and is, in a sense, saturated with the history of mentalities, would have two effects: first, it would qualify readily employed epochal boundaries of the early modern period, and, equally important, the role of the Reformation as a profound rupture; second, it would relativize the notion of the early modern period as a "pattern book"[159] for understanding and explaining the fundamental processes of modernity.

The So-called Second Reformation

Scholars use the term "Second Reformation" to refer to the transition from Lutheranism to Calvinism or the Reformed Confession in a number of German territorial states, in the free Hanseatic city of Bremen, and in the imperial city of Colmar in the Alsace in the years between the Peace of Augsburg in 1555 and the outbreak of the Thirty Years' War in 1618. The term is not uncontroversial, primarily because the Pietists, too, claimed to have undergone a second Reformation, and because one can, in good faith, argue whether or not "Reformation" is in any way a suitable word to describe a collective conversion from one Protestant confession to another. For that reason one occasionally encounters in the scholarly debate the more cautious reference to the mere phenomenon of the "Reformed confessionalization" in the old empire.[160] I will retain the phrase "Second Reformation" here, though I do not wish to gloss over the fact that it is controversial.

The process of the Second Reformation is a phenomenon limited exclusively to the German Empire.[161] Elsewhere, in France or England, for example, there was no comparable transition from Lutheranism to the Reformed faith. The French Huguenots were from the outset dogmatically oriented toward Geneva, and thus without a doubt Calvinist. The situation was somewhat more complicated in England, where in the early phase of the Reformation, under Henry VIII, individual reform-minded clerics still maintained contact with Wittenberg and Lutheranism. Subsequently, during the reign of Edward VI (1547–53), the Zwinglian influence was clearly predominant under the archbishop Thomas Cranmer—the Zurich *Antistes* Heinrich Bullinger was an important authority in England in those years. When Elizabeth I, following the brief Catholic interlude under Mary Tudor, declared Protestantism once again the state religion in 1559, the leading men of the church had good contacts to Zurich and Geneva, as well as Heidelberg, which had by then become Reformed. And so in the case of England as well, looking at the development of church policy in the sixteenth century, one can hardly speak of a confessional change within Protestantism. After its official break with Rome in 1534, the English state church was virtually from the beginning oriented toward the Reformed faith. The same applies even more so to Scotland, where Lutheranism never played any role at all.[162]

Things were very different in the Holy Roman Empire of the German Nation, even though the Peace of Augsburg (1555), which recognized the existence of Protestantism in terms of imperial law, mentioned, alongside the Catholics, only the "followers of the Augsburg confession." This referred to the followers of the *Confessio Augustana* of 1530, the first official confession of the German Lutherans. No mention was made in the Peace of Augsburg of Zwinglians, let alone Calvinists, which means that the Reformed Confession was not considered in the Peace and was therefore also not recognized by imperial law. This created, both politically and legally, a rather delicate situation for German princes who were attracted to the Reformed faith.

It is therefore no coincidence that the first entity to throw its weight behind the Reformed faith after 1555, thereby opposing the legal norms that were valid in the empire, was a relatively large and thus influential territorial state. This role fell to the Electorate of the Palatinate with its residential city of Heidelberg, that is to say, to Elector Frederick III and his councilors. The

Heidelberg Catechism of 1563 marked, in a sense, the Heidelberg court's open embrace of the Reformed Confession, a move that had been developing since 1559. Influential councilors of the Elector of the Palatinate supported this change. Another critical part was played by the theologian Pierre Boquin, and especially by the theologically very learned Heidelberg medical professor Thomas Erastus (1524–83).[163] Erastus was an ardent Zwinglian, a close confidant of Heinrich Bullinger in Zurich, and later, during the Church Quarrel of the Palatinate (*Pfälzer Kirchenstreit*), which was in essence about the relationship between church and state, a strict defender of state church notions based on the model of the Zurich Reformation, where the city council had, after all, played a part in determining the fate of the Protestant Church at an early stage (1523). The term "Erastianism"—which is especially common in English historiography and describes the kind of emphatic state church position advocated by the English kings of the sixteenth and seventeenth centuries—goes back to Thomas Erastus. After 1561, the newly appointed theologians Caspar Olevian and Zacharias Ursinus at the University of Heidelberg were among the decisive authors of the confessional turnaround. Ursinus was the most important author of the *Heidelberg Catechism*.

The Peace of Augsburg in 1555 stipulated the following, among other things:

> In order that the two above-mentioned, related religions [Catholics and Lutherans] may exist together and remain in lasting peace and good security, the ecclesiastical jurisdiction … over the Augsburg Confession, doctrine, appointment of ministers, church practices, ordinances, and ceremonies, as they are or will be established, shall from now cease and the Augsburg Confession shall be left to the free and untrammeled enjoyment of their religion, ceremonies, appointment of ministers, as is stated in a subsequent separate article, until the final reconciliation [*Vergleichung*] of religion will take place.[164]

It is interesting to note the importance that is accorded in this document to the religious reconciliation that is to be pursued in the future—after all, in 1555 the Council of Trent was still a long way from concluding. There was thus still hope (by now modest, to be sure) for a reconciliation between the confessions. At all times, though, the treaty of 1555 speaks only of two confessions.

In view of the events in the Palatinate, the question of the subsequent fate of the Reformed Confession was decided by the Diet of Augsburg in 1566. Here Frederick III of the Palatinate was able to achieve the de facto toleration of the Reformed faith, a toleration that was thereafter practiced throughout the empire. This success was possible because the inherently dangerous co-alition hostile to the Palatinate, which included Lutheran imperial princes along with the emperor and the Catholic imperial cities, fell apart at the critical moment.[165]

Needless to say, the full import that the resolutions of 1566 would have for the history of the empire could not be apparent to the participants at the time. It is only we who know that in the increasingly poisoned confessional climate at the turn of the sixteenth century, the Palatinate would become the great hope of the Reformed, especially of the Reformed nobility in the Habsburg lands. The election of Frederick V, the Elector of the Palatinate, as King of Bohemia was an immediate cause of the Thirty Years' War.

A first direct result of the negotiations at the Diet of Augsburg in 1566 was that a number of small imperial territories, following in the wake of the powerful Palatinate, also changed from the Lutheran to the Reformed faith in subsequent years and decades. The list includes a number of imperial counties, of which I will mention only the more important ones: initially the counties of Nassau-Dillenburg, Hanau-Münzenberg and Sayn-Wittgenstein, and a number of other Wetterau counties; next the Westphalian counties of Bentheim, Tecklenburg, and Steinfurt, and, finally (1605), among others, the county of Lippe in the border region between Northern Hesse and Westphalia, and in the same decade the landgraviates of Hesse-Cassel and Hesse-Marburg under Landgrave Moritz the Learned (1572–1632).

Yet efforts in that direction were not everywhere successful. In Electoral Saxony, members of the ruling elite who were trying to prepare the desired conversion as disguised followers of the Reformed faith—as so-called crypto-Calvinists or Philippists—were denounced, and some (including Melanchthon's son-in-law, the physician Caspar Peucer) were temporarily incarcerated. The theologian Christoph Pezel was expelled and would find a new home for his activities in Bremen. In the end, there would be no second Reformation in Electoral Saxony, where the University of Wittenberg was for a time entirely in the hands of the renewers. From 1574, it adhered to Lutheran orthodoxy.

While the meaning of the term "crypto-Calvinists" is fairly evident, the term "Philippism" calls for an explanation. It goes back to the Wittenberg reformer Philipp Melanchthon, who emerged, after Luther's death in 1546, as the leading caretaker of Lutheranism in Wittenberg and Electoral Saxony. As such, he was drawn into the theological factional struggles that at times threatened to split German Lutheranism between the late 1540s and the early 1570s. Melanchthon died in 1560. During the last years of his life, he had increasingly assumed a mediating role vis-à-vis followers of the Reformed faith on the question of the theology of the Eucharist. This rapprochement with the

Reformed camp was all the more explosive because the question of the Eucharist had become, since the first decade of the Reformation, the central touchstone of orthodoxy within Protestantism. The label "Philippists" was given to those who followed the teachings on the Eucharist of the late Melanchthon. From the larger perspective of the long-term confessional development, Philippism ends up looking like an ephemeral phenomenon limited approximately to the decades between 1560 and 1600.[166] The boundary between Philippism and clandestine Calvinism was, of course, fluid.

Among the important territorial states of the empire, Brandenburg-Prussia played a unique and special role within the framework of the changes I have been discussing, in two respects: on Christmas of 1613, the Elector of Brandenburg, Johann Sigismund, converted ceremoniously from Lutheranism to Calvinism, the last imperial prince to do so before the outbreak of the Thirty Years' War. However, unlike the imperial princes who had preceded him beginning in the 1560s, Johann Sigismund did not expect his subjects to follow suit and adopt the Reformed Confession. Despite the fact that Calvinism lacked deep roots in the territory, the elector's Reformed court preachers were able, in the following decades, to solidify a group of loyal Calvinists within the political and courtly elite, who would subsequently play a fundamental role in the consolidation of Brandenburgian-Prussian absolutism.[167] Through their confession, these men were, after all, more strongly bound to the territorial prince than were the other, Lutheran nobles of the land. As a result of the change of confession, a climate of religious tolerance became the indispensable foundation of domestic politics in this territorial state, which until then had had an exclusively Lutheran imprint. It was this pragmatic tolerance that allowed the Great Elector Frederick William, between 1640 and his death in 1688, to admit religious refugees from the Netherlands (especially Mennonites) immediately after the end of the Thirty Years' War, and larger numbers of Huguenots in 1685 after King Louis XIV of France had repealed the Edict of Nantes, in order to pursue a deliberate settlement policy with the help of these refugees. And it was the same spirit of pragmatic tolerance that drove King Frederick William I, the Soldier King, to admit into the Kingdom of Prussia the Protestants—largely peasants—expelled from the Archbishopric of Salzburg in 1731.

The second reason why Brandenburg-Prussia played a unique role among German territorial states of the seventeenth and eighteenth centuries in terms of confessional politics arises from the special form that Brandenburgian-Prussian absolutism took. In complete contrast to France, the expansion of state domination was based not on a special, politically and culturally integrative role of the court. In the Electorate of Brandenburg and in the Duchy (later the Kingdom) of Prussia, the domestication of the nobility and the consolidation of princely rule in general was achieved primarily through the intensive build-up and consolidation of the army. Unlike contemporary mercenary armies, this military force was composed largely of the prince's own subjects, a situation that was made possible through the simultaneous expansion of a recruiting system throughout the land.

This development accorded the territorial lords a relatively high degree of freedom to shape court life. That is why the first king of Prussia, Frederick I (reigned 1688–1713), could afford to permit the creation of an alliance between the court and leading exponents of Pietism, an alliance that would play a strong role in shaping the reign of his successor, the Soldier King Frederick William I.[168] Against this backdrop, the orphanage and the university at Halle became the center of German Pietism in those years. Under Frederick William I, Pietism became, as Carl Hinrich has put it, the "Prussian state religion," and thus, beyond purely religious concerns, the most important ideological foundation of state reforms.[169]

Life at the village level in Brandenburg-Prussia was undoubtedly dominated by the noble manorial lord—the *Junker*—and the pastor. In spite of the Reformed Confession of the princely house and the political elite of the land, here, as in the other territorial states, confessionalization assigned the clergy the role of the local bearers and exponents of the state's central administration.

As a rule, the pastors of German Lutheranism hailed from the urban bourgeois milieu and not infrequently tended to establish real pastoral dynasties, in which the clerical office passed from father to son to grandson—not to mention all the cross-connections to other pastoral dynasties that were created by marriages.[170] In Württemberg in the eighteenth century, more than 40% of pastors came from such dynasties. In eighteenth-century Pomerania, an average of 55% of pastors and 64% of pastors' wives had grown up in a parsonage. The parsonage thus became an important cultural mission for disseminating bourgeois culture in the countryside. Hundreds of the great minds of Germany (some well known, others less so) in the seventeenth and eighteenth centuries came from parsonages—Andreas Gryphius, Gotthold Ephraim Lessing, Matthias Claudius, Friedrich Schleiermacher, the historians Theodor Mommsen and Gustav Droysen, and many more.

But let us return to the Second Reformation. As I have already indicated, it was predominantly an event at the level of the territorial state, but not exclusively so. Here we must take a look at the free imperial city of Colmar in the Alsace and at the free Hanseatic city of Bremen.

The Reformation in Colmar was a late city-reformation, a phrase I use to describe the few Reformations in imperial cities that did not take place until the second half of the sixteenth century.[171] The Reformation was introduced in Colmar in 1575, although it was not the city's entire population that become Protestant. Thereafter, the city community was divided into a Protestant and a Catholic half. In the first decades after 1575, most of the pastors came from the region under the influence of the church in Basel. At the time that also included the margraviate of Baden-Durlach, which was officially Lutheran. But even in Basel itself, under *Antistes* Simon Sulzer (1508–85), the dogmatic orientation of the church was by no means clearly determined. Sulzer was close to Lutheranism. Reformed orthodoxy did not make its entrance into Basel until the 1580s.

This Basel "conversion," which cannot be described as a Second Reformation because Basel had never been officially Lutheran, was reenacted in Colmar in the 1580s.[172] The Protestant church of Colmar, no matter how strenuously it continued to invoke the Augsburg Confession for political reasons, was, from that time on, de facto a Reformed church, much like the neighboring churches in Mühlhausen and Basel, with whom it had intensive contacts. It was only during the Thirty Years' War, after 1632, that Lutheranism was able to gain a permanent foothold in Colmar. After the imperial troops had retaken the city from the Swedes in 1628, the Protestant rites were completely suppressed for four years. In response, a number of leading Reformed families left Colmar and went to Mühlhausen and Basel.

The 1580s also saw a conversion from Lutheranism to Calvinism in Bremen, under the aegis of Christoph Pezel, at one time a theologian in Electoral Saxony and pastor in Bremen from 1582 until his death in 1604. Much like in Colmar, the community's change of confession did not mean that the independence of the church toward the city council had simultaneously increased. In Bremen, as in Colmar, the council remained the dominant force in church matters even after the adoption of the Reformed Confession. The council quietly ignored Pezel's proposal to establish a consistory after the model of Geneva, "evidently because the attempt to strengthen clerical influence that appeared in this proposal was not welcome."[173]

What were the motives that drove the bearers of the Second Reformation? In all cases they were members of the clergy, princely courts, or city councils. With respect to Electoral Saxony, Ronnie Hsia speaks of a "small minority" of crypto-Calvinists that was composed mostly of humanists and lawyers.[174] A similar picture emerges in Colmar. Here the common faithful as a whole had hardly anything to do with the Second Reformation; rather, in a sense they were its victims, because they had to adapt to the new realities of the church following the "conversion." It goes without saying that this created a lot of confessional confusion among the common people. The charge that was leveled in the 1630s against the Protestants of Colmar, namely that after 1590 they did not know, in many cases, whether they were Reformed or Lutheran, was surely more than mere polemic. Moreover, something similar is presumably also true for some of the population in those imperial principalities in which the Second Reformation took place. On the other hand, in Electoral Saxony the resistance to the maneuver of the so-called crypto-Calvinists formed not only among the Lutheran clergy and within the nobility, but clearly also within the common people, among whom Lutheranism had taken deep roots.[175]

Among the theologians who acted as the opinion leaders in the Second Reformation, we can almost always identify religious motives. But why were the crucial exponents of the respective secular authorities ready and willing to follow them? In the territorial states of the old empire that I have mentioned, political motives surely played a not inconsequential role alongside theological considerations: the confessional change to the Reformed faith made it possible to intensify the disciplinary claims against one's subjects (for example, through moral discipline). But it was also a way to substantially consolidate and possibly even perfect princely rule, or the rule of a clique of councilor families.

To all of this we must add that a whole host of princely officials in the Old Reich during the last decades of the sixteenth and the beginning of the seventeenth centuries were part of the milieu of late humanism. And wherever one looks, in Silesia, at the Prague Court, along the Upper Rhine, and elsewhere, this humanism was in the final analysis closer to the Reformed Confession than it was to Lutheranism. This closeness of late humanism to the Reformed faith is a fact, notwithstanding the undeniable distance that many late humanists assumed toward the disciplinary pretensions of Zwinglianism and Calvinism.[176] In this respect Basel is an exception, because here the flourishing late humanism clearly fell victim to the introduction of Reformed orthodoxy beginning in the 1580s. But perhaps this was also, at least in part, due to the fact that late humanism and Paracelsism in Basel were deeply intertwined, which made late humanism, from the perspective of the church, suspect of being heretical.

At the beginning of the Thirty Years' War, the German Reformed Confession stood at the height of its political role within the empire. Yet the precipitous decline was not long in coming. It began in 1620 at the battle at the White Mountain near Prague, which cost Frederick V of the Palatinate not only the Bohemian crown but also his electoral principality. Although the Peace of Westphalia in 1648 at long last brought the recognition of the Reformed Confession in imperial law, the decline of the ecclesiastical and political influence of Calvinism in the empire, which had been sealed by the war, could not be reversed. After 1648, the crucial support for Calvinism or the

Reformed faith within the Reich was no longer the territorially much reduced Palatinate, but the court of Brandenburg-Prussia.

As we have already seen, in Bohemia the deep traces of Protestantism were radically erased by the Habsburgs after 1620. Within the Habsburg lands, Calvinism was able to survive only in Hungary, where it had taken root among the Magyars. Between 1561 and 1571, the city of Debrecen became the "Hungarian Geneva." The *Confessio Catholica Debrecinensis* in 1562 was a statement of Hungary's Reformed groups. Five years later, the Second Helvetic Confession, the work of Heinrich Bullinger, was officially adopted.[177] In the course of the first half of the seventeenth century, the Reformed church of Hungary was seized by an internal reform movement, which one scholar has described as the Hungarian Puritanism.[178] Close ties were established with English Puritanism, and a number of English devotional tracts were published in translation. Special attention was devoted to a rigorous reform of morals, to combating dancing and strengthening the church's morals courts. In Hungary, much as in England, an unusually rich, introspective autobiographical literature arose within the environment of Puritanism.[179]

2

Renewal Versus Ossification

> With the beginning of the seventeenth century, piety in
> all European lands underwent a profound transformation.
> Puritanism, Jansenism, and Pietism are only various na-
> tional manifestations (and various labels created by the
> scholarship of different countries) for the new piety. Shed-
> ding light on the preconditions, development, and variants
> of this piety is an urgent task of scholarship.[1]

In many respects, this thesis from the Göttingen historian Hartmut
Lehmann has remained a scholarly desideratum. Although I can
only begin to discuss this richly detailed program within the framework of the present survey, I must point emphatically to the commonalities shared by the four movements of renewal examined in this
chapter.

Nadere Reformatie and Pietism

The Dutch struggle of independence from Spanish rule began in 1566
with a massive series of spontaneous and violent assaults on monasteries and images. This led to ruthless military intervention by Spain,
and to a war of liberation that lasted—with long interruptions—
until the 1640s. The Peace of Westphalia finally recognized the independence of the United Provinces, that is, the northern part

of the Netherlands. The seven northern provinces had declared their independence from Spain in 1579. The southern provinces, in the area of modern-day Belgium, remained Spanish and thus also Catholic. The image-smashing and attacks on monasteries in 1566 were also accompanied by a revolt of the nobility, which demanded a political voice for itself as an estate and opposed the ecclesiastical and religious overlordship of Spain. Their leader was Count William of Nassau-Orange, who openly converted to Calvinism in 1573. There were obvious connections between the events in the Netherlands and the Second Reformation in the German counties of the Wetterau.

The older, confessionally oriented historiography, taking its cue from William of Orange's conversion to the Reformed Confession, linked the Dutch struggle for independence with this conversion. Thus the war of independence fought by the Dutch States General appeared not only as the struggle of the Dutch nobility and cities against Spanish policies, which categorically ignored the customary liberties of the estates, but also simultaneously as a campaign of the progressive Calvinists against the reactionary forces of darkness in league with the Inquisition. Quite apart from the fact that the Dutch Reformed were not nearly as close to Genevan Calvinism as the French Huguenots, which means one cannot simply lump all of them together as Calvinists, more recent scholarship has shown that this black and white version in no way corresponds to historical reality.[2]

When the States General abolished the Catholic Mass in 1581, two years after proclaiming their independence from Spain, this by no means meant that most of the population in the seven northern provinces had already become Reformed. Even at the turn of the sixteenth century, Catholics still constituted the majority. The growth of the Reformed communities was slow, for a variety of reasons. There were, for one, widespread Anabaptist currents in the Netherlands, which made a rapid spread of the Reformed faith more difficult. A certain religious eclecticism among considerable population groups, which made them unreceptive to the growing confessionalism of the churches, should also be mentioned.[3] But we should also emphasize that both the Estates General as well as the city magistrates—in modern parlance, the politicians and the authorities—certainly did not strive to promote the diffusion of the Reformed Confession. Their prime concern was the struggle against Spain, and for that reason they were not interested in driving the still considerable number of Catholics in their own ranks into the arms of Spain by engaging in confessional politics that was blatantly Reformed.[4]

Still, the Reformed faith spread rapidly within the upper strata and the educated classes, as is indicated by the number of Reformed universities that were founded, beginning with the University of Leiden. Franeker came next in 1585, followed, in the first half of the seventeenth century, by Groningen, Utrecht, and Harderwijk. This new university milieu, which had a Reformed imprint from the very outset, was the setting, at the beginning of the seventeenth century, for the Arminian controversy over the Calvinist doctrine of predestination. The word "Arminian" goes back to Jacobus Arminius, a professor of theology at the University of Leiden. He questioned the (really quite terrible) Calvinist notion that God, in his unfathomable will, had consigned the majority of humankind to eternal damnation while setting aside only a small minority for eternal salvation, emphasizing instead that Christ had died on the cross for all of humanity.[5]

At a time when both Lutheran and Reformed theologians began to take refuge behind increasingly orthodox doctrinal constructs, dogmatically spelled out in great detail, such religious doubts were bound to meet with opposition from the proponents of orthodoxy. Eventually, orthodoxy carried the day at the Reformed Synod of Dordrecht in 1618/19, which evolved into an international Reformed synod with Dutch, German, Swiss, English, and French participants. The doctrine of predestination remained a firmly entrenched element of the official teachings of the Reformed church. In the seventeenth century, the influence of orthodoxy led, both in the Reformed faith and in Lutheranism, to a strong formalization—if not an ossification—of religious life within the bosom of the official church. This is part of what characterizes the background against which the *Nadere Reformatie* would emerge in the Netherlands.[6]

Not long after the Synod of Dordrecht, Reformed clergy and theologians in the Netherlands issued the first calls for a "further" Reformation. Here, too, as would happen repeatedly in later German and Swiss Pietism, those eager for reform demanded a more thorough, second Reformation. Dutch historiography has adopted the term *Nadere Reformatie* to describe this reform movement, though one could just as well speak of a Dutch "Puritanism." In any case, English influences are impossible to overlook in the Nadere Reformatie of the seventeenth century.

One of the precursors of the Nadere Reformatie was the Walloon pastor Jean Taffin (1528–1602). For some years he was court preacher to William of Orange. Like the Puritan theologian William Perkins (d. 1603), Taffin was concerned above all with pastoral theology, that is, providing pastoral care to the laity on their questions regarding their personal, religious way of life. Like Perkins, he penned influential devotional tracts and books of solace that were animated by the spirit of moral and religious renewal of the life of the individual.[7] After his death, other Dutch theologians picked up these impulses from him and developed them further. From a large group of names I will mention only Gisbertus Voetius (1589–1676), one of the leading Dutch theologians of the seventeenth century. As professor at Utrecht, he made a name for himself as a staunch opponent not only of Arminianism, but later also of Cartesianism. He encouraged his students to live an ascetic life, and in other ways, too, he advocated Puritan rigor: Voetius opposed both luxury in dress and long hair on men (another parallel to the English Puritans, who were called Roundheads on account of their short hair), and he fought relentlessly against dancing and the new habit of using tobacco.[8]

Here we must add that the primary conduit for Puritan influences in the Netherlands (much as was the case subsequently in German Pietism) was the translation of English Puritan devotional tracts. This work of translation had already begun before the end of the sixteenth century, and it peaked in the first two decades of the seventeenth century. A total of 49 of Perkins's works were published in Dutch editions.[9]

Puritanism exerted a direct influence on the Nadere Reformatie in the person of the English theologian William Ames (1576–1633), who resided in the Netherlands beginning in 1610 after losing his post at the University of Cambridge on account of his Puritanism. We must add other English Puritan pastors who came to the Netherlands temporarily in the seventeenth century, and at least some of whom maintained closer ties with the Dutch and influenced them in the spirit of their own theology. These manifold English influences explain why the pious movement of the Nadere Reformatie, which initially took hold primarily of the clergy but then spread increasingly to the laity as well, "displays typical Puritan traits in devotional and moral terms."[10] An important role was played by the attempt to perfect and sanctify one's own life within a circle of the pious and the true believers. What emerges in this process as early as the later seventeenth century is a penchant toward what was primarily an introspective preoccupation with the religious state of one's own soul—a precursor to the changes that would lead, specifically within the environment of eighteenth century German Pietism, to the so-called *Erfahrungsseelenkunde* (empirical psychology) and thus to the psychologizing of religious experience. Yet in addition to the readily apparent influences from Puritanism, genuine Dutch roots played an important role in this reform movement, which means that it would be rash and wrong to describe the Nadere Reformatie as a mere import from neighboring England.

Huguenot influences were also brought to bear, especially in the person of the French cleric Jean de Labadie. When Labadie and his small, radical-mystical circle split off from the official church (1669), it signaled that the Nadere Reformatie was showing signs of dissolution in the last third of the seventeenth century.[11] The separatist Labadists included such well-known women as Anna Maria van Schurman (1607–78) and (for a while) Maria Sibylla Merian (1647–1717).

Similar to Puritanism, the Nadere Reformatie also seems to have found its reception primarily in a middle stratum of the population. Given its claims of moral reform, there was no bridge of any note that connected it with the traditional forms of piety in popular culture.

Pietism

In the past, no small number of historians sought to pinpoint the beginnings of Pietism in Germany in the Nadere Reformatie of the Netherlands. Like the Nadere Reformatie, however, Pietism in German-speaking lands had more than one root—although, needless to say, Dutch influences should not be underestimated, especially on lower Rhenish and Swiss-Reformed Pietism.[12] All seventeenth-century Protestant movements of renewal share an intellectual and mental climate of fear and uncertainty that was engendered by the economic and social crises—here I am thinking of the crises of subsistence, actual famines, and epidemics—and especially by the great wars of that century. Pietism, exactly like Puritanism at times, displayed traits that were clearly eschatological in nature. The successes of the Catholics in the Thirty Years' War, the advances of the Turks into Hungary and Austria, the appearance of comets, and other such events constituted, especially for pious Protestants, "signs of the times," unmistakable omens that the end times had begun.[13]

Over the years, scholarship has offered three attempts to pinpoint the chronological beginnings of Pietism in Germany. One common view links the beginnings of German Pietism with the activities of the pastor Philipp Jakob Spener, at the time a preacher in Frankfurt, either with the founding of a Circle of the Pious in 1670, or with the appearance of Spener's tract *Pia Desideria* in 1675, which would set the tone for the subsequent development of the renewal movement known as Pietism. Another school of thought among scholars of Pietism takes 1689 as the beginning, because the conflict between Lutheran orthodoxy and Pietism erupted openly in 1689/90.[14]

There is, however, a good deal that argues in favor of a third perspective, namely an early date, as was suggested by the church historian Johannes Wallmann. He posits a precursor and early phase of German Pietism that began between 1604 and 1610 with the publication of the *Vier Bücher vom wahren Christentum* (Four Books of True Christianity) by Johann Arndt (1555–1621). The reason, Wallmann argues, is that "Johann Arndt's influence on the Lutheran church of the seventeenth century ... surpasses that of all other scholastic theologians, and the ripple effects that emanate from him are the most significant in terms of the history of piety."[15] Johann Arndt's devotional work *Vom wahren Christentum*, which has a strong mystical imprint, was born of his sermons and went through countless editions after 1606. On the basis of Arndt's role and other considerations, Wallmann posits a dual beginning to German Pietism: Johann Arndt launched a precursor and early phase of Pietism as a "direction in piety that was embodied primarily in literary texts." A second phase of Pietism as a "socially discernible movement that placed itself in opposition to orthodoxy and brought forth new forms of ecclesiastical and religious communal life" began with Philipp Jacob Spener (1635–1705).[16]

The tremendous demand for Arndt's work can only be explained against the background that, as early as the beginning of the seventeenth century, circles began to form here and there on the margins and outside of the Lutheran church that rejected Protestant orthodoxy and pursued a renewal of piety. Such circles, recruited primarily from the middle and higher strata of burghers, existed in Schleswig-Holstein, for example. Their members were influenced by the mystical spiritualism of Valentin Weigel, Kaspar Schwenckfeld, and especially Jacob Böhme, spiritualistic authors of the sixteenth and seventeenth century who stood entirely outside the circle of writers approved by the church.[17]

It is certainly true that as a result of the fusion of such reformist currents in German Lutheranism with the idea of the perfection of the inner person (highlighted by the spiritualistic authors mentioned above), the more broadly conceived notion of a link between the perfection of man and a general reformation, which reappears time and again throughout the entire seventeenth century, entered into the mental world of early Pietism. We encounter here "a first source spring of the later optimistic belief in progress: the nature and goal of religion is no longer, as it was in Luther, absolute obedience to God, but the effort to find bliss; the human being is no longer a creature hopelessly mired in original sin, but the microcosm in whose spirit have been laid down the laws of the macrocosm, which he can therefore nurse into clear understanding and make use of."[18]

When it comes to the development of Pietism as a socially discernible lay movement, Spener's *Pia Desideria* was the founding manifesto and practical manual in one. The full title of this tract, published in 1675 as the preface to a new edition of Johann Arndt's Gospel postil, was "Pia Desideria or heartfelt longing for an improvement of the true Protestant Church pleasing to God." If this should not be considered to have been an all-out attack against orthodoxy in general, it was certainly a declaration of war aimed at its more obdurate representatives. They were primarily responsible for an ossified faith by the book and a lack of practical piety, which the Pietists believed characterized church

life in too many quarters and which had to be overcome through a new practice
of piety, a reformed *praxis pietatis*. Spener demanded that

> the Bible should unambiguously take its place of preeminence in
> church life, through both private reading and common discus-
> sions in small circles, whereby the crucial goal should be practi-
> cal application and the inner growth of faith.... Since Christianity
> was not knowledge but action, all-embracing love had to deter-
> mine and shape the life of the faithful. Debates over questions of
> faith should be put aside and reserved for experts, in favor of exer-
> cises of love [practical love of one's neighbor in education, care
> for the poor, missionary work, and the like].

Everything, Spener maintained, depended on the proper way of life pleasing
to God.[19]

In the demonstration of practical piety, and in its initiatives in the sphere of
schooling and education, early Pietism in Germany was without a doubt a force
for innovation. The Lutheran conception of justification as a process that took
place, in the final analysis, inside the individual believer, became in Spenerian
Pietism something that could also be grasped externally. Spener and his followers believed that the forgiveness of sins had to become visible in a "real,"
external transformation of a person's way of life. For many Pietists, the process
of justification became a rebirth; in this way the experience of conversion assumed a central place in a person's life, and its consequences were visible to
outsiders. The way in which a Pietist interacted with his environment "became,
in fact, the test of whether his rebirth is real and no delusion of the mind or the
emotions."[20] This explains some of the points of contact between the early
Enlightenment and Pietism. But when Enlightenment began to exert a broad
effect within the educated strata as the eighteenth century progressed, Pietism
and the Enlightenment parted ways. In the end, Pietism became a conservative,
socioreligious force. This change in attitude was also reflected in the movement's social composition: "Beginning at the end of the eighteenth century,
what had been an urban-bourgeois group with strong ties to the political elite
changed into a petty bourgeois movement that confronted the process of sociocultural change helplessly."[21]

The potential for ecclesiastical and social transformation inherent in early
Lutheran Pietism was rooted in the circles of the pious who met regularly
outside of the local church for devotional practices, which Spener called *collegia pietatis*. These groups were supposed to help create a vibrant new piety.
The hopes that Spener and other early Pietists entertained in this regard were
nourished by an intensive apocalyptic belief. The circles of the pious created

the indispensable spiritual preparation for Christ's imminent reign on earth. Apocalyptic beliefs, for example the expectation of the imminent Last Judgment, were already found in Luther. But it was only through Philipp Jacob Spener that chiliasm, the belief in the approaching thousand-year reign of Christ, which until then had been firmly rooted during certain phases primarily within Protestant fringe groups (such as the Anabaptists), found its way into Lutheran theology.[22] The so-called "hope for better times" thus became the constitutive element of the history of early Lutheran Pietism in Germany. In certain respects that is also true of Swiss Pietism. Samuel König (1671–1750), a Pietist pastor who was later expelled from Bern, expected the beginning of Christ's thousand-year reign during his own lifetime. König's chiliasm was for him not only "*the* key to understanding *all* of Holy Scripture, but at the same time also *the* key to understanding his time."[23] It should be noted, however, that König was close to radical Pietism, in which apocalyptic thinking and feeling played an even more central role.

Some scholars have also tried to use sociopsychological approaches to explain the success of Pietism in founding these *collegia pietatis*. In the view of Hartmut Lehmann, what made the collegia attractive was, among other things, the fact that the attempt was made, within their setting, to create new hopes to combat the existential and spiritual fear that was widespread in the crisis-ridden seventeenth century. The *collegia pietatis* provided a place where fear— a product of the times though undoubtedly manifested differently in each person—was "processed and transformed" into new confidence and a new courage to go on living. This process was possible "because in these conventicles, the doctrine of rebirth and, more importantly still, eschatology conveyed a new meaning to Christians concerned about the salvation of their souls."[24]

The great significance that attached to the spiritual rebirth of the individual believer led also in Pietism—as it already had in Puritanism—to a special appreciation of individual religious experience. It was within this context that the act of bearing witness by Pietists assumed an important role. Such witness-bearing took on a special form in autobiographical and biographical writings. This explains the appearance and in part the considerable success of a whole series of collections of biographical and autobiographical accounts, from Gottfried Arnold's *Unpartheyische Kirchen- und Ketzerhistorie* (Impartial History of the Church and of Heretics; 1699/1700) to Erdmann Graf Henckel's four-volume work *Die letzten Stunden einiger der evangelischen Lehre zugetaner Personen* (The Last Hours of Some Persons Devoted to Protestant Teachings), published between 1720 and 1733).

The real fathers of the German Pietism that emerged from Lutheranism (as we have seen, the roots of Reformed Pietism were more in the Netherlands) were Frankfurt pastor Philipp Jacob Spener, discussed above, who was from 1691 provost and member of the consistory in Brandenburg, and August Hermann Francke (1663–1727), professor of oriental languages and later also of theology at the newly established University of Halle and founder of the famous orphanage in that city. Francke built this orphanage into the center of a Pietist mission of global reach. Outside of Brandenburg-Prussia, a second stronghold of Pietism arose relatively early in Württemberg, where the Tübingen professor Johann Andreas Hochstetter (1637–1720), a close confidant and friend of Spener's and Francke's, became the first important exponent of the new movement.

In the space of a few decades, Pietism was able to develop into a powerful (initially chiefly urban-bourgeois) reform movement within German Protestantism. Of fundamental importance was the educational impulse in the movement, which was transmitted from Pietism to the development of the German bourgeoisie. What I am referring to here is the promotion—advocated above all by August Hermann Francke—of practical knowledge through elementary and secondary schools. Also important were the repercussions of the ascetic and anti-courtly ethic of Pietism, especially in Württemberg in the eighteenth century. The emphasis on the everyday ethics of thrift and diligence, and the Pietist battle against luxury—for example, in dress—were adopted by the Enlightenment in the course of the eighteenth century.[25]

Nadere Reformatie, Puritanism, and Pietism resemble each other with respect to this focus on ascetical ethics of daily life. The influence of Puritanism on the Pietism of the German-speaking lands is unmistakable here. In Switzerland, too, we find a number of translations of English tractates among the earliest Pietistic devotional writings in the last three decades of the seventeenth century.[26] It was also part of the nature of Pietism that its proponents were substantially more open and tolerant on doctrinal questions than were the champions of theological orthodoxy. Consistent with this attitude, for Samuel Lutz, Daniel Willi, and Hieronymus d'Annone, fundamental priority attached, under the banner of eschatology, "not to doctrine, but to penance, and to the rebirth and renewal of life in sanctification." And so it is not surprising that the reformer these three representatives of Swiss Pietism felt closest to was not a Reformed reformer, but Martin Luther.[27]

The history of Pietism in Switzerland is marked by a number of banishments and expulsions initiated by the authorities. The most tragic was undoubtedly the history of Pietism in Lucerne. In the Catholic environment of the Lucerne region, a number of locals with Protestant-Pietist leanings were arrested in 1739 and in 1746/47, incarcerated, and interrogated under torture. In the end, 45 adults and 26 children were sentenced to eternal banishment, two men were sent to the galleys, and Jakob Schmidlin, known as Sulzjoggi and the most prominent Pietist in the eyes of the authorities, was executed as a heretic and apostate.[28]

The Puritans

The word "Puritan"—like Whig, Tory, Quaker, and Methodist—was originally coined by opponents as a derogatory label. Sixteenth- and seventeenth-century Puritans, like the London artisan Nehemiah Wallington, for example, called themselves the "people of the Lord," "children of God," or simply "His people."[29] Also common was the self-description as "godly people," or occasionally also "saints." The "godlie should endeavour to express a cheerful spirit," wrote the jurist and parliamentarian Sir Simonds d'Ewes, "because by this they stopp the mouths of such as scandalize religion, alledging that it makes men and women sadd and melancholie."[30]

The terms "Puritans" and "Puritanism" first emerged out of the controversy that erupted in the winter of 1567/68 over the question of what pastors should wear during ritual acts. Those among the clergy of the official church who opposed the prescribed surplice justified their resistance by, among other things, calling for a "stainless religion"—a stance to which their opponents readily attached the derogatory label "Puritanism," which they understood as the translation of the Latin term *cathari*, "heretic."[31] Thereafter, the view was that "the hotter sort of protestants are called puritans," as a pamphlet writer put it in the 1580s.[32]

Generally speaking, the Puritans of the Elizabethan age and of the seventeenth century were not church separatists who sought to split off from the official church. It therefore needs to be emphasized that it would be anachronistic to set up "Anglicanism" as the opposite of "Puritanism" *prior* to the middle of the seventeenth century, for doing so creates a dichotomy that is historically false.[33] As I will presently show, it was only the discriminatory legislation of the 1660s that really forced Presbyterians and Independents (or Congregationalists), as representatives of the two chief currents of post-revolutionary Puritanism, to assume a separatist stance.

Historical Survey

It is, in point of fact, contradictory to speak of the "introduction of the Reformation" in a particular realm, since we associate far more with the process of Reformation than merely the abolition of the Mass. This observation

holds true especially for the Reformation process in England, which was grad-
uated from its very beginning (1529), and in which the establishment of
a state church disconnected from Rome was initially more important than
the question of its doctrinal orientation.[34] This clearly applies to the reign of
Henry VIII. It was only during the brief reign of Edward VI (1547–53) that the
English Reformation was given an unmistakably evangelical tenor through
the *Book of Common Prayer* of 1552, which leaned heavily on Martin Bucer's
later work: the Lord's Supper replaced the existing Mass and the surplice took
the place of the priestly stole.[35]

The six years of re-Catholicization of the country under Mary Tudor
(1552–58) are important to the history of Puritanism in two respects, above all:
first, the marriage of the Catholic queen to Philipp II of Spain led to a new
alliance between a national desire for independence and pro-reformationist
currents. Not only did anti-Catholicism become a factor in English politics
whose importance should not be underestimated, henceforth it also helped to
broaden the effect of Puritanism, which did not tire of invoking the Catholic
threat, sometimes in apocalyptic language. Second, re-Catholicization forced a
large number of Protestant clergy into temporary exile—in British scholarship
they are known as the "Marian exiles." In Emden, Frankfurt, Basel, Zurich,
and Geneva, they established direct contact especially with the Reformed
ecclesiastical-religious tradition of the continent. Influenced by their personal
experience of continental European Protestantism, not a few of them regarded
the English Reformation as an endeavor that was in many respects incomplete.

This impression persisted after their return to England, when the re-
Catholicization that had begun was reversed under Elizabeth I, while at the
same time only the Queen's claim to supremacy over the church was given a
clear expression, but not so her confessional policy, which, in the final analysis, sought to mediate between Catholic and Protestant traditions.[36] In the
agreement reached with Parliament in 1559, the Queen was referred to as "the
only supreme governor of this realm and of all other Her Highness's domin-
ions and countries, as well in all spiritual or ecclesiastical things or causes."
A pamphlet published in 1584 by Cardinal William Allen, the chief organizer
of resistance among Elizabethan Catholics to their oppression and persecution, questioned the oath of supremacy that was part of the Act of Supremacy
and was also demanded from all secular and ecclesiastical office holders under
Elizabeth. This oath, the Cardinal maintained, had already struck the Catholics as ridiculous under Henry VIII and Edward VI, since Henry had been a
layman and Edward a mere child. Now that it was supposed to be sworn upon
a woman, "it is accounted a thing most monstrous and unnatural and the very
gap to bring any realm to the thralldom of all sects, heresy, paganism, Turkism,

or atheism."[37] With this stance, William Allen—since 1568 the head of the Collegium Anglicum in Douai, a Jesuit seminary that, among other things, trained missionaries for the not undangerous missionary work in England—was in every way the equal of the Scottish reformer John Knox. As early as the 1550s, Knox had published a pamphlet with the title *The First Blast of the Trumpet against the Monstrous Regiment of Women*. Although this tract was aimed against the rule of the Catholic Mary Tudor, it made its author a persona non grata at the English court under Elizabeth I as well.[38]

The Marian exiles who returned after the death of Mary Tudor in 1558, along with no small number of bishops newly installed under Elizabeth, were dissatisfied by the doctrinally mediating position that was pursued in the following years.[39] In the winter of 1567–68 this led to the first organized protest of individual clergyman against the prescribed use of the surplice—and this, over the longer term, would eventually give rise to the ecclesiastical renewal movement of Puritanism.

When the exiles of the 1550s returned, they brought with them not only their specific experiences, especially with Reformed church ordinances and the Reformed service, but also the Geneva Bible, an English translation produced in exile in that Swiss city. Along with John Foxe's *Acts and Monuments of these Latter and Perilous Days*, it became the basic reading in Protestant homes during the Elizabethan and early Stuart periods. The Geneva Bible went through 70 new editions under Elizabeth alone, with an additional 30 editions of the New Testament.[40] John Foxe's *Act and Monuments*, soon referred to merely as the *Book of Martyrs*, was printed in large numbers between 1563, the year it first appeared, and the English Civil War. Like no other work during these years, this book of Protestant martyrs, strongly suffused with an apocalyptic faith, proclaimed the special divine mission of the English people as a "Protestant nation."[41] With the approaching end times, Foxe believed, England, as God's chosen nation, was especially called upon to testify to the Protestant faith. This mission, combined with the enormous popularity of the *Book of Martyrs*, is one reason why only a few radicals sought to break with the state church as separatists under Elizabeth: separatists implicitly challenged England's divine mission as the Protestant bastion against the attacks of Babylon (that is, Catholicism), especially in view of the threat from the Spanish Armada (1588), the destruction of which in turn seemed to confirm England's mission. The Separatists Henry Barrow and John Greenwood, leaders of a small radical group that rejected the state church, were consequently executed in 1593 after having spent several years in prison.[42]

Barrow and Greenwood were the leaders of a small minority. By contrast, the Presbyterian movement proved capable of drawing much broader support, thus posing a real challenge to the established ecclesiastical *and* political order. The theologian Thomas Cartwright (1535–1603) emerged as the spokesman of this movement in 1570 through a series of lectures on the Acts of the Apostles, a spokesman who had to be taken seriously. The appearance of the Presbyterian movement at this time should undoubtedly be seen in connection with a similar struggle that occurred in those years over the ecclesiastical constitution in the Electoral Palatinate. Within the framework of his Presbyterian calls for reform, Cartwright, who was expelled from the University of Cambridge in 1570, questioned not only the role of the bishops, but with equal vehemence also the crown's claim to leadership over the church. Under the banner of Calvinism, Cartwright demanded that the clergy, organized in synods, should be relatively independent from the secular arm, which included the call for the abolition of the episcopal offices and of the monarchy's supremacy within the church. On the level of the parishes, moral discipline was to be implemented following the model of Geneva. For the crown and the episcopacy, Cartwright's sally was an alarming demonstration that the Puritan movement had by then also penetrated the universities of the land and had become a threat—one not to be underestimated—to the existing state church system; this impression was further reinforced in 1588/89 by the appearance of the anonymous, so-called Marprelate Tracts, which also had a Presbyterian imprint.

The response by the leaders of the church was correspondingly harsh and uncompromising. That is especially true for the years after 1583, when archbishop John Whitgift (ca. 1533–1604) made a name for himself as a formidable foe of the Puritans.[43] It is revealing that Whitgift, in the year he assumed the post of archbishop of Canterbury, not only took resolute steps against Puritan-minded clergy, but at the same time also made all preaching, reading, and the teaching of catechism within a private framework punishable, on the explicit grounds that such activity was schismatic—an indication of how much of a foothold Puritanism had gained also among the laity within the short space of a few years.[44] Whitgift was unable or unwilling to recognize that such private gatherings were by no means subversive, since their purpose was the "repetition" within a circle of the pious of sermons that had been delivered in public. And since these circles were already firmly established, he was unable to do much against their continued existence.[45]

John Whitgift was one of the prime targets of the Marprelate Tracts. One example is *The Just Reproof and Censure* from 1589:

I, Martin Senior, gentleman, son and heir to the reverend and worthy Metropolitan Martin Marprelate the Great, do protest, affirm, say, propound, and object against John Canterbury and his brethren, in manner and form following.

First, I protest and affirm that the foresaid John Whitgift, alias Canterbury, which nameth himself Archbishop of Canterbury, is no minister at all in the Church of God, but hath and doth wrongfully usurp and invade the name and seat of the ministry, unto the great detriment of the Church of God, the utter spoil of the souls of men, and the likely ruin of this commonwealth, together with the dishonour of her Majesty and the State. And in this case do I affirm all the lord bishops in England to be.[46]

Although this and other anonymous protests could not be stopped, the measures taken by Whitgift, and largely backed by the Queen and the Royal Council, did much to create a situation where the party of the Puritans, by now represented not only at the universities but also in parliament, was no longer publicly visible as an especially vigorous reform movement during the closing dozen or so years of the sixteenth century. Next to Thomas Cartwright, it was William Perkins (1558–1602), in particular, who exerted considerable influence on English Puritanism at the turn of the sixteenth century. It is characteristic of a certain internal transformation of the movement that Perkins was less a man of external church reform, and much more an eminent pastoral theologian who was especially committed to trying to relieve the afflicted consciences of the pious.

As for the theological and doctrinal orientation of the Puritan churchmen during the age of Elizabeth and thereafter, it would we wrong to label all of them "Calvinists"—notwithstanding the fact that Thomas Cartwright, for example, drew on John Calvin. John Whitgift, the inveterate opponent of the Puritans, also never tired of invoking Calvin.[47] Alongside Calvin and his successor Theodor Beza, the Swiss theologians Heinrich Bullinger and Wolfgang Musculus also played an important role, if not the preeminent one, for the Puritan clerics as doctrinal authorities, as did Petrus Martyr Vermigli of Italy.[48]

Of course, the official direction of the English church remained Calvinist with respect to one issue on which the Puritans and their opponents within the church found agreement that lasted into the early part of the seventeenth century: the affirmation of Calvin's and Beza's doctrine of predestination before and after the Reformed synod of Dordrecht in 1618–19.[49] In other ways, however, the hopes of those Puritans who had believed that James I, who in 1603 became the first Stuart to ascend to the throne, would accommodate them on the question of the surplice, contested for more than three decades, and on the issue of the sign of the cross at baptism, regarded as equally offensive, were dashed. A meeting with a delegation of Puritan clergy at the Hampton Court Conference in 1604 brought no loosening of the status quo.[50] Still, open confrontation between Puritans and their enemies within the clergy was largely avoided under James I—a visible result of the skillful ecclesiastical policy of the first Stuart monarch, whose choice of bishops was usually moderate churchmen capable of reaching an understanding with the Puritans on basic questions of theology. That applies not least to the archbishops of Canterbury (George Abbot, in office 1611–33) and York (Tobie Matthew, in office 1606–28).[51]

Still, it was already during the reign of James I that a confrontation began to take shape within the state church, though it did not erupt into open conflict until Charles I, following his ascension to the throne in 1625, began to systematically promote a group of so-called Arminians within the higher clergy. This group included William Laud and Richard Neile, the future archbishops of Canterbury and York.[52] Like the Dutch Arminians of the early seventeenth century, the members of the group rejected the doctrine of predestination. Unlike their Dutch brethren, they simultaneously and emphatically pushed a program of church reform that sought to widen the distance between clergy and laity, to reassert and make visible the clergy's mediating function during the Lord's Supper, and to promote the splendid ornamentation of church space in the Baroque sense. Under Charles I this group quickly took over leadership in church affairs. In the end, it was partially responsible for the disastrous failure of the king's ecclesiastical policy in Scotland, which set in motion in 1637 the developments that eventually led to the Civil War.

It was not only the Puritans who felt put upon, sometimes intensely so, by the Arminians. Members of the gentry who were close to Puritanism, urban merchants, and laymen from the lower social strata also took offense at the aloof and occasionally rather arrogant way in which Arminians interacted with parishioners.[53] No small number of Puritans across all social strata regarded Arminianism as a disguised attempt at re-Catholicization, which in turn promoted among the faithful—as previously under Mary Tudor—the feeling of existential threat and the sense that they were living in the end times. Both factors played an important role in the outbreak of the civil war, revitalized, so to speak, by the revolt of the Catholic Irish in the fall of 1641.[54] Still, as we will see, it would be false to follow the older scholarship and continue to speak of the "*Puritan* revolution" that began in 1641.

When the Arminians rapidly lost their hold on the state church in the fall of 1640 with the opening of the Long Parliament, the Puritans, for the first time since the 1570s, saw another chance to carry out a fundamental reform of the church from top to bottom. Yet despite their common opposition to the civil war party of the king, the group of church reformers remained divided within. At any rate, they were unable to prevent the clear signs of disintegration within the ecclesiastical sphere in the 1640s, the appearance of new sects and free churches, as well as the formation of special groups at the margins of the official church. In the process, Puritanism failed, in the 1640s, to take advantage of the opportunity for a fundamental reordering of the church.[55] To be sure, a Presbyterian constitution was introduced in most parishes in London after the end of the first civil war in July 1646, and initial steps were also taken in Lancashire. Otherwise, however, the pace of reform in the countryside was very slow.

The long-cherished but barely begun project of national church reform collapsed after Presbyterianism permanently lost its political credibility in the eyes of many Englishmen and women when the Scots (most of whom were Presbyterians) joined forces with the king in the second civil war in 1648.[56] Presbyterianism—an organization of the church without bishops and with considerable authority vested in synods of the clergy and in marriage or morals courts in the parishes—had taken deep roots in Scotland since the beginnings of the Reformation there in the 1560s. But the cause of Presbyterianism south of Scotland was profoundly damaged when the Presbyterian Scots allied themselves with the king, who was being opposed by the supporters of Parliament in England, including not least the Puritans.

In the face of this development in the 1640s, one should no longer speak of Puritanism as such for the period after around 1645, but rather of the individual groups into which Puritanism began to split: Presbyterians and Independents or Congregationalists. Still, the identification with the state church persisted, except among the radical groups. This identification would only be destroyed—from the outside, so to speak—after the restoration of the Stuarts (1660), when Presbyterians and Independents, together with Quakers, were excluded from the state church as non-conformists and dissenters by the discriminatory legislation of the early 1660s, and suffered periodic persecution over the next two decades.[57]

Thematic Aspects

The discussion so far can be briefly summarized as follows:[58] with a few exceptions, Puritanism was a movement of renewal *within* the state church. Puritans differed from their fellow Englishmen and Englishwomen not in principle but only in degree, especially by virtue of their more intense piety. Even within Puritanism there were fluid distinctions between radical and moderate followers, distinctions that sometimes had a social basis. A Puritan member of the gentry was usually more deeply enmeshed within a web of sociocultural rules, for example those pertaining to festivities and dancing, than was a Puritan artisan.

The piety of the Puritans was a pronounced Biblical piety, a fact that is reflected, for example, in the extraordinarily large number of Geneva Bibles that were published. Puritans were also more rigorous than their contemporaries in setting themselves apart from Catholicism: in essence, Puritans did not accord Catholicism the status of a religion, regarding it chiefly as a form of papal and priestly despotism. That also explains the uncompromising opposition to everything that was regarded as papist remnants within their own church. Most Puritans were especially critical of the clergy of their day, for their own ideal was not only that of the pious pastor, but equally that of the learned, well-trained pastor. Finally, it is important to emphasize Patrick Collinson's observation that there "was probably no such creature as a puritan in the singular. Puritans were always plural, close with one another but careful to shun what they deplored as the 'company keeping' of others."[59] Collinson was pointing out the strong group cohesion among Puritans. As the community of the pious, they continually sought to set themselves apart from "ungodly company" and its expressions of sociability in inns and taverns.

Equal in importance to Bible piety was the sermon, which was held in extraordinarily high esteem. For Puritans, the establishment of the sermons was "in general and everywhere a principled demand."[60] That this demand concealed a fundamentally different conception of the church than that held by Queen Elizabeth is revealed by a statement the Queen made to her first archbishop, Edmund Grindal, to the effect that she would be quite content with a clergy "such as can read the scriptures and homilies well unto the people."[61] There is no question that the high regard for the sermon outranked the Puritan call for the observance of the Sabbath, which, incidentally, was also adopted by many non-Puritans in the course of the seventeenth century.[62] As early as the 1580s, Archbishop Whitgift felt compelled, as we have seen, to prohibit followers of Puritanism from holding private gatherings for the purpose of "repetition." Such meetings were devoted to intensive discussion of the most recent sermon in a small circle of the pious. The basis for these "repetitions" were sermon notes, and here the women—at least within the upper social strata—were no less active than the men; in fact they showed themselves to be particularly diligent.[63] In practice the line separating the "repetition" of a sermon from personal interpretation of the Bible was undoubtedly rather blurred. In that sense we are dealing with at least potential conventicles, gatherings of the pious outside of the church, of the sort that would become customary in Pietism.[64]

This alerts us once again to the fact that the renewal movement of Puritanism, as early as the 1580s, was by no means limited only to rebellious clergy, but already counted a considerable number of lay supporters in its ranks. And that number seems to have grown further into the early seventeenth century. Still, Puritanism remained a decided minority movement within the state church also in the seventeenth century, although we must not underestimate the number of sympathizers, especially, for example, on the eve of the Civil War.

Where Puritans found themselves in the majority on the local level, they generally attempted to enforce their own kind of strict discipline within the parish. The notion that these might have been primarily disciplinary efforts aimed by the local middle and upper strata against the common people and the poor has now been largely refuted. For example, a study of Earls Colne (Essex) has demonstrated that the measures of social discipline within the framework of the community were directed primarily at the segment of the population that was young and still unmarried.[65] Once again, it is the young who appear as particularly stubborn opponents of efforts to implement a strict moral regimen, and thus of efforts to "reform popular culture" from above.

We must not overlook the fact that the growing role of the laity in Puritanism—and thus also within the state church—had a corollary in the social rise of the clergy. Between 1559, when an accord was reached between Elizabeth I and Parliament about the status of the church in the Elizabethan Settlement, and the end of the reign of James I in 1625, the parish clergy emerged as the partner of the noble landowners at the local level. The Puritan call for an academically trained clergy found a positive echo to the extent that most clergyman, from this time on, had a university education.[66]

As we have seen, the official doctrine of the state church included, far into the seventeenth century, the teaching of double predestination, a legacy not only of Calvin but also, and especially, of the Strasbourg reformer Martin Bucer.[67] It received its last affirmation, against a backdrop of strong influence exerted by the Puritans, at the Westminster Assembly in 1647—but this came at a time when a series of prominent Puritan theologians, led by Richard Baxter, were already beginning to deviate from the previous line, not to mention the Anglican theologians of the second half of the seventeenth century.[68] In the first decades of the seventeenth century, the doctrine of divine election and damnation was still part of the basic stock of Puritan thinking, at least among Puritan-minded theologians. Not least for this very reason, the appearance of the Arminians after 1625 represented a provocative challenge.

Still, it must be emphasized that the federal theology adopted by Heinrich Bullinger and the Heidelberg theologians began to play an increasingly important role from the closing years of the sixteenth century, above all through the teachings of the leading Puritan theologian William Perkins. Federal or covenental theology was concerned with the covenant that existed between the individual believer and God, and it stood in a real relationship of tension to predestinarian theology. The latter emphasized the unknowability of God's decision and thus the majesty of God, which lay beyond the sphere of direct, everyday human experience. By contrast, federal theology had, since its inception in Heinrich Bullinger, a subterranean tendency—even if it was not explicitly stated in these terms—to conceive of God as a kind of covenental partner of humanity. Unlike predestinarian theology, it sought to bring God closer to the believer, to make Him accessible to direct experience. Since federal theology exerted a strong influence on Puritan pastoral care, its new picture of God was disseminated not only among theologians but also among the laity, contributing within the latter to a relativization of the dogma of predestination.

But the belief in predestination was also undermined among the laity by the faith in God's special providence (omnipresent in Puritan diaries and autobiographies), because this particular belief was essentially aimed at making God's presence visible in personal and collective history.[69] At any rate, the picture of God held by Puritans of the 1630s and 1640s (and even more so thereafter) was most definitely no longer that of Calvin's predestinarian theology. Hence the attempt to explain the special involvement of Puritans and their sympathizers on the side of the Long Parliament in the clashes of the 1640s by way of the Puritans' belief in predestination (as Michael Walzer sought to do some forty years ago), seems problematic from our perspective today.[70] In contrast to Walzer, the consensus today tends toward the view that at least up to the meeting of the Long Parliament in 1640, the innovators in church matters were not the Puritans but the king and his Arminian bishops.

A more likely argument would be that a combination of apocalyptic fears and hopes, given the Thirty Years' War on the continent and virulent anti-Catholicism at home, pushed many pious individuals to take decisive action on the side of the Long Parliament. The call for action seemed all the more urgent as the widespread anti-Catholicism was substantially nourished and intensified by William Laud's ecclesiastical policies, which, as we have already seen, were viewed by many (and not only Puritans) as a veiled attempt at re-Catholicization. This feeling was further reinforced in 1641 by the outbreak of the revolt of the Catholic Irish. Now it appeared that the apocalyptic battle of the Antichrist for world domination, as foretold in the Revelation of John, had indeed commenced—or at least that is how many believers saw the situation at the eve of the civil war. But these were impulses that took hold not only of the Puritans in the narrower sense of the word, spurring them to action. Still, the highlighting of these factors in recent scholarship provides a meaningful explanation for the radical change within the Puritanism of the early 1640s from the traditional justification of passive resistance only toward the legitimization of active resistance.

The comparatively much more widespread belief in England's special election, based on the ideas of John Foxe, bore merely an apocalyptic, but certainly not a chiliastic, imprint. And yet, we know today that within the educated circles of English society at the time, and not least among the future Independents (that is, among the uncompromising Calvinists), who had strictly rejected the Episcopal constitution of the English church since the early 1640s, chiliastic thinking derived from the relevant writings of Thomas Brightman, Johann Alsted, and Joseph Mede, was quite widespread.[71] Chiliasm entails the belief in a thousand-year reign by Christ that will follow upon the end of our own collective history, whereas the apocalyptic belief at the time was not necessarily chiliastic as well, but could be limited to the belief in or the fearful anticipation of the imminent Last Judgment.

Following Max Weber, scholars have repeatedly referred to the special occupational ethic of Puritanism. Weber connected this ethic (along with other forms of what he called ascetic Protestantism) not only with the "spirit of capitalism," but also, and especially, with the belief in predestination.[72] He imagined that the Puritans, motivated by the strong inner pressure of uncertainty regarding the fate of their soul, sought to demonstrate to themselves that they were among the elect by engaging in external behavior that was deemed pleasing to God. His main witness in making this connection was the Presbyterian pastor and theologian Richard Baxter (b. 1615). Baxter, however, unlike his predecessors, was no longer an adherent of the doctrine of dual predestination. Although he retained the notion of divine election, he dismissed the idea that a large majority of humanity would be consigned to eternal damnation.[73]

At the conclusion of this section, I would like to return once more to the rich and extraordinarily widely diffused autobiographical writings spawned by English Puritanism. A large number of these diaries and autobiographies are spiritual self-testimonials that served a variety of purposes: as diaries they served the daily check on one's conscience; as autobiographies they served the control over the path of one's own life; as final reckonings they served the urge to offer a testimonial at the end of one's life. English Puritanism, just as later Pietism, placed importance on the personal, individual experience of conscience that was, in this emphatic form, entirely new within the Protestantism of the time. Until then, the only similar phenomenon had been found in the realm of the mystically inspired asceticism of sixteenth-century Spanish

Catholicism—not only in Ignatius of Loyola, whose *Spiritual Exercises* became the guide for a strict, individual examination of faith and conscience for generations of Jesuits, but also in Teresa of Avila. Yet in contrast to these efforts, which, in the final analysis, remained deeply rooted in late medieval mysticism, the comparable tendencies in Puritanism stood much more under the banner of proving oneself in one's vocation and in the world.

The spiritual diary, as Gerd Birkner has said in his excellent literary study, "is the treasury of the demonstrations of God's favor.... The person who has mastered the form of the spiritual diary has been given the opportunity to overcome the troubling uncertainty of grace. The effect of the accumulated signs of grace is more than the sum of their addition."[74] As we have seen from the of Pietism, systematic self-examination in autobiographical writings could lead in the end to what one might call—encapsulating a complex process in a somewhat simplified description—the psychologization of questions of faith, and thus to the secularization of what began as religious self-examination. Can the same be said of the Puritan autobiographical texts of the seventeenth century? Were they in a sense the precursors of a modern, secular individualism? In opposition to this approach, some scholars have rightly emphasized that these Puritan writers—both men and women—understood themselves at all times as nothing more than the instruments of God. For that reason, we can speak at most of a "secondary voluntarism," which, needless to say, always expressed itself in collectively established forms.[75]

Still, there is no denying that the doctrine of Puritanism, especially in the first half of the seventeenth century, contained elements—with respect to both covenental and pastoral theology—that emphatically promoted the individualization process. The ambivalence I have touched on here between the respective weight placed on self-experience and self-discipline and the merging of the individual into collective contexts finds expression, among other places, in various passages of the voluminous diary of the Puritan pastor Ralph Josselin from the Civil War period, who wrote on August 16, 1648, "And in respect of my soule, my heart is full of sinfull and vain meditacions, not being cleane in the eyes of god.... Oh, give me a cleane heart; and keep me in uprightness: oh, make this nacion happy in peace and truth."[76]

Jansenism

No Counter-Reformation, no Jansenism. This succinct statement has a twofold meaning. First, without the intensification of religious life intended and (in France actually) initiated by the Counter-Reformation, the reform movement of

Jansenism would most likely never have arisen. Second, without the decision by the Council of Trent on the questions that had remained open regarding the doctrine of justification, Jansenism would not have had its theological starting point.

As has already become clear,[77] the decision of Tridentine Catholicism on the matter of justification was based on a compromise. To be sure, in the end the Spanish Jesuits were able to prevail over those members of the Council who leaned more heavily on St. Augustine's doctrine of grace. In other words, a doctrine of justification in the Augustinian sense, which in the end reduced the share of the individual believer in his own salvation to a minimum (if it did not deny it outright) as a way of further elevating God's omnipotence and grace, was unable to carry the day in Trent. However, the corresponding conciliar decree left the question of the relationship between divine grace and human will in a peculiar and, in the final analysis, unresolved limbo. Here lay the theological starting point of Jansenism, which initially represented a movement exclusively within the Dutch-Walloon and French clergy; later, in the eighteenth century, it found numerous supporters in the rest of Catholic Europe, especially in Italy and Austria. Of course, Peter Hersche has rightly emphasized in this context that Jansenism as a whole was "not an exclusively theological problem," but also, especially in its late phase (that is, chiefly the eighteenth century), "a political, intellectual, and cultural phenomenon."[78]

The decree by the Council of Trent on the doctrine of justification thus remained in need of interpretation. In a treatise published in Lisbon in 1588, the Jesuit Luis de Molina offered a new take on the question of justification. He placed a strong emphasis on the role of free will, while reducing the role of God in the justification of the individual human being by maintaining that predestination would reduce the human will to nothing more than divine foreknowledge. Although the Roman curia was not pleased with this new viewpoint, it shied away from condemning it publicly, because it did not wish to make an enemy of the Jesuit order, and because the new theory of Molinism— as Molina's teachings were soon called—indirectly emphasized the special status of the Church sacraments very much in the Tridentine spirit.[79]

The theological beginnings of Jansenism are connected with the fight against Molinism. The Dutch theologian Cornelis Jansen (1585–1638) wrote a treatise opposing the teachings of the Spanish Jesuit; it was published two years after his death with the programmatic title *Augustinus*. The human being, Jansen wrote, has an indispensable need for God's grace to accomplish the good, for given Original Sin, his will tends exclusively toward evil. In this voluminous work of some 1,300 pages, Jansen thus imparted an Augustinian spin to the doctrine of justification, although, needless to say, without according the notion of predestination the same rank it held among Protestant reformers.[80]

It did not take long for a response from the Jesuits and the first condemnation from Rome in 1642. Within a few short years after the publication of *Augustinus*, the controversy was in full swing. Cornelis Jansen was not there to witness it, having succumbed to the plague in 1638 as the newly appointed bishop of Ypres. The French theologian Antoine Arnauld (1612–94) was one of his first public defenders, a stance that cost him his chair at the Sorbonne in 1656, after a papal bull had publicly condemned five of Jansen's teachings. There followed Blaise Pascal's *Lettres provinciales* (1656/57) as a further defense of Jansenist positions. The strong demand for this work alone demonstrates that the controversy was continuing to spread. This was increasingly an open confrontation between Jansenists and their sympathizers and the camp of the Jesuits, whereby individual Jesuits, through their risky casuistry, indirectly reinforced the position of the Jansenists even more.

Jesuit casuistry dealt with the judgment of individual acts of sin by the confessor, and thus implicitly also with the question of justification. On this question, Jesuits who were especially willing to strike a compromise tended to grant the sacraments of confession and Mass a purifying effect even in case of moral sins. Their opponents denounced them as laxists. And their opponents in France in the second half of the seventeenth century included not only Jansenists, but also a growing number of so-called rigorists among the clergy. The latter rejected—as did the *dévots* (i.e., the "pious") among the French laity—the specifically Baroque, exuberantly sensual Catholicism that was propagated and promoted by the majority of the Jesuits. Most rigorists echoed the widespread demand that the Catholic Church of France become largely independent from Rome—they were thus Gallicans. With their aloof detachment from the papal curia they supported Louis XIV in his clashes with the pope over the latter's régale within the church of France. Among the Gallican-inspired *Four Articles* published in 1682, which dealt with the relationship between secular and ecclesiastical power and was signed by most of the higher clergy in France, Article 4 stated unequivocally that although the pope holds chief authority in questions of faith, and although the papal decrees apply to all churches of the land, the decisions of the pope are not infallible, but depend on the consent of the church, which in this case probably meant the higher clergy.[81] Louis XIV (1643–1715), however, was locked in a struggle not only with the pope, but also with the Jansenists. Still, the rigorism that was promoted inside and outside the court during the last two decades of the Sun King's reign by Madam de Maintenon, the king's mistress, promoted the

102 UPHEAVAL AND RENEWAL

critical distance of the court and the upper ranks of the clergy toward the
Jesuits, thus indirectly helping Jansenism to spread further.[82]

Against this background, the Jansenists were increasingly successful in
shifting the controversy with their opponents away from the dogmatic con-
fines of the doctrine of justification and original sin, and into the much wider
terrain of piety and morality, a development to which I will presently return.
And from this perspective it is indeed possible to assign Jansen and the abbot
of Saint-Cyran, Jean Duvergier de Hauranne (1581–1643), an ally of the first
hour, to one of the main currents of Catholic reform.[83] One expert on the subject has explained in more detail what that means:

> If one had to characterize Jansenism in one sentence, one could
> describe its essence as "anti-Baroque." It was a countermovement to
> everything that came out of Rome under this banner and shaped
> the Catholic world decisively, beginning in the sixteenth century and
> extending far into the eighteenth. Yet one has to beware of over-
> simplifications: like Catholicism itself, Jansenism was not a uni-
> form, coherent movement. Moreover, in spite of its latent and
> virulent anti-Romism and anti-curialism, one cannot place it in
> opposition to the Council of Trent. Rather, Jansenism and Baroque
> Catholicism were two, mutually opposed consequences of Trent:
> the former was characteristic of "classicistic" Catholicism (in France),
> the latter prevailed outside of France.[84]

With a view toward the eighteenth century, French scholarship usually speaks
of a Second Jansenism.[85] Assuming that this was still a unified movement,
the laity played a comparatively large role in it by this time. The chronological
beginning of the movement known as Second Jansenism coincides with the
publication of a treatise by Pasquier Quesnel—a member of the congregation
of the Oratory—which became known under the shortened title *Réflexions
morales*. The Oratory was a reform order that was close to Jansenism from the
very beginning. In his tractate, Quesnel adopted some of Jansenius's reflections on divine grace and combined them with, among other things, Gallican
ideas (that is, those critical of Rome).[86] The Second Jansenism of the 1690s
and of the eighteenth century was thus from the outset closely interlaced with
Gallicanism. Moreover, as a movement that was increasingly outside of the
church, it was—from the middle of the eighteenth century, at the latest—also
connected with the growing opposition of the parliaments (the "sovereign"
courts of the land) toward the court and the government. In league with the
Gallican-oriented parliaments, the secular clergy, and other enemies of the
Compagnie de Jésus, the Jansenists succeeded in the early 1760s in driving

the Jesuits out of France, a decade before the order was dissolved by a papal decree in 1773.[87]

Thus, at the threshold of the Second Jansenism there stood, chronologically and in terms of content, the public debate over the *Réflexions morales* by the prominent Jansenist Pasquier Quesnel.[88] The condemnation by Rome, which was also supported by Louis XIV for reasons of domestic politics, came in the papal bulls *Vineam Domini* (1705) and *Unigenitus* (1713). Many Jansenists appealed *Unigenitus* to a general council and were henceforth known as the "appellants." Some of them refused to sign the anti-Jansenist declaration that was now introduced and in the future had to be signed by every member of the clergy; the resisters included the nuns of the Paris stronghold of Jansenism, the convent of Port Royal. In a coup-like action in 1709, on orders from the French king, the nuns were dispersed to other Cistercian convents and the Port Royal was razed to the ground. Yet even these drastic measures by the old Sun King were by no means able to put an end to the movement. Instead, the "Second Jansenism," in its links to rigorist and Gallican currents, blossomed into a "veritable party of opposition to Rome and the King."[89]

Let me try to sketch the essential aspects of the piety of the followers of Jansenism. It was marked by an assiduous reading of the Bible, but also of the Church Fathers, especially, of course, the writings of Saint Augustine. When it came to the doctrine of the sacraments, confession was paramount, in keeping with their critical and negative view of humanity. Their ideas about the ideal church space were anti-Baroque par excellence and exceedingly ascetic, a stance that was manifested, for example, in their reservations about pictorial decorations in the church. They were equally critical of church music, though like the Huguenots they enjoyed singing Psalms. They looked askance at the veneration of the saints—and especially the cult of Mary—that was promoted by the Jesuits. As for everyday life,

> a strict schedule regulated the course of the day for Jansenists; useless entertainments, dangerous diversions, comedies, dancing, and other pleasures were scorned among them. A special chapter concerns their rigorous position on sexual ethics.... A true Jansenist remained modest when it came to his needs of daily life—living space, food, clothing, servants—and rejected any and all luxury. With this conduct of life, the Jansenists resembled the Puritans. In contrast to the latter, however, they lacked any interest in acquiring riches through work pleasing to God; instead, they advocated the prohibition of interest and restricted their economic activities to what was minimally necessary. That is especially true of early

Jansenism, where we occasionally find an attitude of withdrawal from the world that sometimes assumed extreme forms.[90]

Blaise Pascal, for example, invoked original Christianity in language full of yearning, a time when there had still been a clear separation between the church and the world: "Back then one had to leave the world in order to be admitted into the church.... The two were regarded as opposites, as two irreconcilable enemies, each of which persecuted the other without pause."[91]

Still, the Jansenists were often denounced by their enemies as Protestants in disguise. One thing that set them starkly apart from Puritanism and Pietism, however, was an evident lack of interest in eschatological speculations or chiliastic visions. To be sure, in their theology of justification, their veneration of the Bible, their aloofness from the Baroque cult of the saints, and more, they were in fact close to contemporary Protestantism. But on the whole, there is no doubt that the elements separating them predominated.

With its rigorous demands on everyday ethics and on the spiritual asceticism of the individual, Jansenism in France never became a popular movement. Its influence was limited not only on the level of the village parishes, but also within urban society.[92] Many Parisians were little inclined to give up the theater, dancing, and gambling. Here, as well as among the common people and the lower classes in the countryside, the appeals and ethical measures of the rigorists among the bishops were able to achieve little.

In the course of the eighteenth century, the effect of Jansenism radiated far beyond the borders of the southern Netherlands and France. Blaise Pascal's *Pensées* appeared in translation in England as early as 1688, the first of a number of translations of the work of this prominent Jansenist. John Wesley, the founder of eighteenth-century English Methodism, an early form of the Protestant Awakening, pronounced the *Pensées* to be obligatory reading for future Methodist pastors.[93] Italy experienced an intensive reception of Jansenist ideas, particularly in the second half of the eighteenth century, within the educated class, that is to say, especially in the higher clergy.[94] But undoubtedly the most important reverberations occurred in Austria. Here the contacts between Jansenism and Enlightenment were the most vigorous, which is already evident in the fact that Austrian late Jansenism provided the theological basis for the Josephinian reforms of the late eighteenth century.[95]

In the eighteenth century, the House of Austria was composed chiefly of the great Habsburg landholdings, which stretched from Bohemia to modern-day Slovakia, from Transylvania to Tyrol, and from there—of course not in a contiguous block—into the Breisgau, the southern Netherlands in the west (after 1713), and in the European south right up to the Mediterranean coast in the Grand Duchy of Tuscany (after 1737). Much more so than in Brandenburg-Prussia, the poor possibilities of communication set limits from the very outset to absolutist harmonization and centralization in the vast complex of Austrian lands, as did the great regional differences in the mentalities and political consciousness of the population.

One basic precondition for the consolidation and renewal of the polity, at least in the core lands of Habsburg rule, was Catholicism as the shared confession of rulers and subjects alike. The not inconsiderable support that Protestantism enjoyed in the sixteenth century, especially among the Austrian nobility, was not fundamentally questioned until the Counter-Reformation entered the Habsburg lands beginning in the 1580s under Emperor Rudolf II. Only on the basis of the Catholic unity of faith, which was in part compelled, would it become possible to renew the state without consideration for special rights connected with estates and different regions. We have already seen, however, that the re-Catholicization process produced results that varied from region to region.

Even the state-sponsored, specifically Austrian form of ecclesiastical religiosity was not able to stop the lifestyle within the leading political strata from becoming increasingly secularized in the course of the eighteenth century. In this process, the secularization of the polity emanated principally from late Jansenism, which found a number of influential supporters in Austria's leading strata, and especially within the higher clergy. These supporters included, among many others, above all Archbishop Christoph Anton Count Migazzi (1714–1803), one of the most important early promoters of Austrian late Jansenism, Ambros Simon Edler von Stock (1710–72), an influential theologian from the University of Vienna, and Ignaz Müller (1713–82), the provost of Vienna's Augustinian Abbey of Saint Dorothea and the confessor of Maria Theresa. The Viennese medical professor Anton de Haen—and not the imperial personal physician Gerard van Swieten, as is repeatedly claimed—functioned as an important intermediary to the ecclesiastical-theological center of European late Jansenism in Utrecht.[96] The occupation of influential positions by men who felt committed to the *sana doctrina* of Jansenism led not only to a general turnaround in the state's education and school policy, in which the Jesuits were stripped of their power, but also more generally to a looser, enlightened relationship of state and church, which prepared the ground for the subsequent Josephinian reforms.

The primary goal that Joseph II pursued with his reforms in the religio-ecclesiastical sphere after 1780 was to adjust the church to his enlightened ideas. It was chiefly the religious orders that were affected by this. In 1781,

Joseph issued an Edict of Toleration, which permitted the choice of confession under certain, of course still quite restrictive, conditions. At the same time, he decreed the radical dissolution of all monasteries that did not demonstrably fulfill charitable, scientific, or other public tasks. The dismissed monks and nuns were compensated, the monastic landholdings passed to a state-run fund for religion and university study.

The Josephinianism of the Habsburg lands was the "highpoint and culmination of the move by the absolutist state to take the church into its service";[97] of course, one must add that this move was thwarted in a variety of ways by resistance from the subjects. Against the backdrop of this resistance, which even took the form of an open rebellion in Brabant and Flanders, Joseph II was forced, shortly before his death in 1790, to rescind a number of his radical reforms.

Moravians (*Herrnhutter*) and Methodists

The so-called Moravian Brethren (*Brüdergemeine der Herrnhutter*) arose in the 1720s on the estate of Berthelsdorf in Lusatia. The dominant figure was from the beginning and until his death Count Nikolaus Ludwig von Zinzendorf (1700–60). In Berthelsdorf he gathered around himself a numerically small Brotherhood (*Brüderbund*), which, with the growing inclusion of Bohemian and Moravian brothers who had found refuge in and around Berthelsdorf, would develop into the Brethren (*Brüdergemeine*). In Berthelsdorf, the members jointly founded a colony they called Herrnhut (derived from *unter des Herrn Hut*, "under the lord's hat"). Within a very short time, the movement created in Herrnhut extended its reach far beyond Lusatia. The question of whether or not to separate from the established churches was decided at a celebration of the Lord's Supper on August 13, 1727, which proved enlightening to all participants: the group decided to remain within the Lutheran territorial church.[98] Still, like English Methodism, which arose only a short time later, the Moravian Brethren were, in the final analysis, a kind of free church, if one labels as free churches only those communities "who regulated their life in strict orders, and whose members gathered in separate houses of God and enjoyed the protection of magisterial toleration or privileges."[99] In spite of the fact that the Moravians renounced separatism, and in spite of the existence of many commonalities, there was a breach with Hallean Pietism, symbolized by the dismissal of the theologian August Gottlieb Spangenberg in Halle in 1730; Zinzendorf thereupon dispatched him to North America to scout the possibility of setting up Moravian colonies there.

The breach with Hallean Pietism signaled in general the beginning of a difficult phase for the Moravians, a phase marked by magisterial prohibitions and expulsions. The Brethren, like many radical Pietists, found temporary refuge and protection in the Wetterau. At the same time, though, in addition to their missionary activity in St. Thomas, Greenland, Lapland, Surinam, South Africa, and elsewhere, they extended their reach to England and North America, where, after some failed attempts in Savannah, Georgia, in the early 1740s, they began to establish their first settlements in Delaware and Pennsylvania.[100] Simultaneously, the Moravians began to find a style of piety that would characterize their subsequent history. This piety sought to symbolize distance to both Pietist legalism and to the Enlightenment; of course, given the natural or childlike approach to religious questions so vigorously promoted by Zinzendorf, for example, the doctrine of Christ that was so central to his thinking, it was impossible to prevent a relativization of Christ's suffering through the redemptive joy of the individual, as for example when Christ was referred to allegorically as "birdie of the cross" (*Kreuzluftvögelein*) or "Little worm of wounds" (*Wundenwürmlein*).[101] Incidentally, what one might call the everyday encounter with God was at the center of Moravian pedagogy, which was institutionalized in a school that evolved into a humanistic *Gymnasium* and in a seminary as a place to train the movement's clergy.[102]

After Zinzendorf's death in 1760, efforts were made to carefully correct "deviant developments" such as those just mentioned. At the same time, the initially hostile attitude of European government and authorities changed for the better in the face of the proverbial industriousness of the Moravians. Magistrates now authorized settlements in Prussia, Saxony, and Russia, later also in Denmark and Württemberg.

Alongside the German Society of Christendom (*Deutsche Christentumsgesellschaft*), the Moravian Brethren became, at the turn of the eighteenth century at the latest, the most important gathering place for the Awakened, who opposed both the rationalizing influence of the Enlightenment in theology and the church, and that of the French Revolution in culture and politics. For many pious believers, the French Revolution was an unmistakable omen of the imminent end of history.[103]

The Methodists

Scholars have noted this opposition to the French Revolution also with respect to British, and more specifically English, Methodism. Since Methodism, unlike the Moravians with their restrained missionary style, promised to become a real mass movement toward the end of the eighteenth century, some historians have argued that Methodism, because of its conservative mass suggestion, essentially prevented a radicalization of the English population in the 1790s. Writing from a neo-Marxist perspective, Edward P. Thompson, in his now classic study *The Making of the English Working Class* (first published in 1963), assigned Methodism the primary responsibility for influencing the ideology of the newly emerging English working class toward subordination to the existing sociopolitical conditions. As a result, no revolutionary consciousness was able to form among the English lower classes during the European wars at the turn of the eighteenth century, which meant that England remained the only country in Europe that saw no revolutionary upheaval in the late eighteenth and early nineteenth centuries.[104]

Since then, Jonathan Clark has offered a radically different perspective. Clark depicts English society before the reform of the electoral law in 1832 as an "ancien régime society" not unlike the estate-based society of pre-Revolutionary France. In this society, religion continued to play a central sociocultural role, and—to the extent that it was controlled by the state church—contributed to the stability of a "confessional state" that was, until 1832, dominated entirely by the high nobility and the gentry.[105] The destabilization of the conventional political system emanated—of course, without success in the age of the French Revolution—from the Dissenters, that is, from the Presbyterians, Independents, Baptists, and Quakers, who had left the state church in the 1660s, at the latest, and from the Methodists.[106] The Methodist preachers disseminated not only social conservatism, but in equal measure criticism of the sinfulness of the rich, the upper class, and many of the learned.

It cannot be said that Jonathan Clark exaggerated when he called attention to the criticism that Methodist preachers directed against the rich of the land. On November 17, 1759, John Wesley noted in his diary that it was indeed good if the number of the rich and noble who converted to a pious life increased. However, he would be pleased if this task were taken on by other preachers, as he preferred to continue preaching the Gospel to the poor.[107]

What Clark overlooks, however, is the consistent anti-Catholicism that pervades Wesley's sermons and diary entries, especially those dealing with Irish history.[108] In this way, Wesley contributed to strengthening the Protestant conformism of broad segments of the population, which also in the eighteenth century continued to measure itself against Catholicism as the un-British, negative yardstick par excellence.

For the most part, scholarship over the last twenty years has not followed Jonathan Clark's argument. Historians have pointed out, among other things, that while Protestantism at the time was a basic component of British national identity, "Great Britain was . . . not a confessional state in any narrower sense."[109]

At the same time, the one-sided interlocking of religious dissent and criticism of the political system has been refuted by a careful analysis of the various motives in those men who, in 1803, answered the government's call to form volunteer units for the defense of the country.[110] Moreover, others have repeatedly—and correctly—pointed to the "embourgeoisement," the gradual sociopolitical integration into the existing conditions, of Old Dissent, that is, the Presbyterians, Independents (or Congregationalists), Baptists, and Quakers of the eighteenth century.[111] At the beginning of the eighteenth century, Old Dissent comprised approximately 334,000 persons—with a strongly downward trend. The number of Methodists grew to about 77,000 by 1796. In view of these figures, it may seem dubious to attribute to Methodism larger political weight with respect to the tensions of the 1790s,[112] to which we must add that Methodism at the time was certainly not a monolithic movement with uniform political goals.

The religious horizon of the founder of the Methodist movement, John Wesley (1703–91), had been shaped during his student years in Oxford by a zeal for personal salvation through charity and the preaching of the Gospel, a zeal that surpassed the boundaries of conventional Anglican piety. Still, like the eighteenth-century Moravians, the main current of Methodism, founded by John and his brother Charles Wesley, remained loyal to the state church. Incidentally, Methodism, much more so than the Moravian church, addressed the questions raised by the Christian Enlightenment. What characterized John Wesley was a religiosity that thoroughly pervaded his life, combined with exceptional rhetorical gifts, which enabled him—sometimes in critical and dangerous situations—to reach and touch the hearts of even the most bitter opponents. Through his tireless travels in England and on the European continent, as well as in Ireland, Scotland, and North America, he was able to shape the entire, continually growing movement of Wesleyan Methodism through his personal authority. When John Wesley claimed, in a diary entry in 1770, that he had by then covered more than 100,000 miles on horseback, he was overestimating; still, historians today believe that he had traveled 25,000 miles by the time of his death in 1791 and had preached 40,000 sermons.[113]

In 1739, following a journey to America with German Moravians (1735–38), there began the Methodist campaign of Awakening, the same year in which Wesley met Ludwig von Zinzendorf for the first time in London; subsequently, Wesley visited Herrnhut and Halle on a trip to Germany.[114] In Bristol, where the pulpits of the churches remained closed to him, the preacher George Whitefield, who had been part of the closest circle around John and Charles Wesley, began to deliver his sermons in the open. His audience grew rapidly into the thousands. In March of 1739, John Wesley, who first had to overcome his reluctance to preach outside of a church, continued this campaign of Awakening. Scholars have spoken in this context of the "outbreak" of the Methodist movement of Awakening.[115]

The movement did not remain unified: it was not long before it split into a Calvinist line led by George Whitefield (also called Primitive Methodism) and a Wesleyan one, which had an Arminian imprint, though the contacts between the two currents remained very close. Although the two Wesley brothers can be described, with some justification, as "true-blue Anglicans," there were still conflicts with the state church, chiefly because the Methodist preachers violated the territorial principle of the parishes. The appearance of Methodist *lay* preachers further intensified the conflicts with the Anglican clergy.[116] Still, unlike Primitive Methodism, eighteenth-century Wesleyan Methodism remained loyal to the state church.

Like the Moravians, with whom the Wesley brothers and their circle felt a close bond, the Methodists also established communities in North America. In addition, they carried out missionary work in Scotland—though with only modest success—and in Ireland, where they addressed their sermons of awakening especially at the Anglicans who lived there.

With respect to the social composition of English Methodism, during the lifetime of John Wesley, the ratio of artisans and "skilled workers," which included the numerous miners especially in the north of England, played a very crucial role, similar to the Moravians. Scholars have calculated that this class made up 47.4% of the Methodists during the first five decades (1740–90), while small peasants, cottagers, rural laborers, fishermen, sailors, and soldiers made up 29.1%, with the remaining social groups participating only to a very minor extent (with the exception of farmers, who comprised 12.2%).[117] As we have seen, the total number of Methodists at the time of Wesley's death stood at 74,000, though the trend was strongly upward. Historians have often overestimated the share that the lower classes—at the time the largest segment of the British population numerically—had in the Methodist movement. The share was comparatively highest within the movement of the Primitive Methodists.[118] What made Methodism so attractive to the social groups that embraced it most fervently was—beyond the fascination of the religious message in the more orthodox sense[119]—undoubtedly the circumstance that the mental world of popular religiosity was more accessible to Methodist preachers than to the conventional clergy of the state church, given the movement's openness toward supernatural phenomena (for example, in the realm of magic) and towards religiously motivated emotionalism.[120]

PART II

The Integrated, Outcasts, and the Elect

3

Community

Reformation, Counter-Reformation, and Community

Reformation scholarship of the last few decades has been strongly
inspired by the path-breaking study *Reichsstadt und Reformation*
(Imperial Cities and the Reformation), by Bernd Moeller, a church
historian from Göttingen, published in 1962. Moeller tried to explain
the special appeal that the Reformation message had in the imperial
cities of the German southwest and Switzerland in the 1520s by
noting, among other things, the interaction of the urban-corporative
legal and constitutional tradition, which was so strongly developed in
this geographical region, and the Reformation theology of Zwingli
and Bucer, with its urban imprint. Through this theology, the urban-
corporative tradition of the southwest German and Swiss imperial
cities was, so to speak, sacrally transfigured.[1]

The 1970s saw some vehement debates about Moeller's interpretation. Social historians criticized it, with some justification, on
the grounds that it harmonized the social and political tensions
that existed within the cities in the fifteenth and sixteenth centuries;
since Moeller's approach always implied that the city community
was a unified entity, it prevented these tensions from being considered in the attempt to explain specific processes.[2]

In the 1980s, the communal aspects of the Reformation events
that Moeller and others had placed front and center were investigated
more intensively, especially in the circle around the Bern historian

Peter Blickle. In her 1984 dissertation on the reception of Reformation theology in the rural territory of the city of Strasbourg, Franziska Conrad concluded that the peasant communities of Strasbourg defined the role of the
Gospel "differently from how it was defined in the evangelical doctrine of
salvation." Villagers saw the Gospel "not as the good news of salvation, but as
instructions for behavior that was pleasing to God."[3] They did not understand
the Reformers' doctrine of justification: "The villagers grasped the affinity
between the demands explained by the preachers and presented as God's
command, and basic principle of their communal life.... The message of the
Reformation," Conrad concluded, "thus resonated in the countryside because
the communal ideal and social ethics corresponded to the village community's
perception of itself; its reception led [in the Peasants' War of 1525] to the
assertive defense of the principle of cooperative community [*Genossenschaft*]."[4]
In the countryside, the Reformation message was thus, in a way, filtered
through a prior communal understanding and therefore understood primarily
in the sense of the Ten Commandments.

The insights gained from concrete regional examples were summed up
and confirmed in 1985 by Peter Blickle in his more broadly conceived, programmatic study on the topic of the "communal reformation."[5] The general
thesis of Blickle's book, which he has since reinforced in a number of publications, emphasizes that "the original, undistorted character of the Reformation" as a social and religious movement was "its expression as communal
reformation." The general thesis applies to a geographical area that corresponds more or less (though not entirely) to the area affected by the Peasants'
War of 1525. It is bounded in the north by Erfurt and Fulda, in the west by
Mainz or Lorraine and Burgundy, in the east by Bavaria. The southern boundary for the geographical diffusion of the "communal reformation" ran "from
Solothurn across the Zurich countryside to St. Gall, and from there via Rhaetia
to the Trentino and finally into the Salzburg area."[6] Decades before the Reformation, this region already saw growing demands by the rural population
not only that the local priests reside in the community, but also that they
provide more intensive pastoral care. In tandem with these demands there
arose opposition to the ecclesiastical court, although this opposition showed
strong regional variations. These demands eventually culminated, at the beginning of the Reformation, in the claim that priests should be chosen by the
community, as was unmistakably articulated in the Peasants' War of 1525.

According to Blickle, the goal of the common man in the early years of
the Reformation was the "comprehensive and total communalization of the
church." This goal implicitly challenged the existence of the hierarchically
constituted Roman Church in a fundamental way. The linkage and mutual

interconnection between the calls for the pure Gospel, on the one hand, and the realization of divine law as laid out by the Gospels, on the other, gave rise to a theoretical conception of a political order that was built upon community. This conception was articulated with particular clarity in the Peasants' War in southern and southwestern Germany.[7]

In the Swiss Confederation, these demands by the rural population were for the most part cushioned, defused, and integrated into the subsequent unfolding of the Reformation emanating from the cities. North of the Rhine, in the old empire, by contrast, the crushing of the Peasants' War of 1525 was followed by the suppression of the communal reformation. After 1525, Blickle has argued, the Reformation in the empire gradually turned into a princes' Reformation. Luther's theology in the end promoted this development, while, according to Blickle, the theology of the southern German and Swiss reformers especially that of Zwingli, could be much more serviceable, in the understanding of the common people, to the demand for the communalization of the church. It is unmistakable that Bernd Moeller's old arguments are being revived here and incorporated into a new line of argumentation.

How, then, can we connect the course of the rural and the unfolding of the urban Reformation? What the reformationist efforts in the countryside prior to 1525 shared with those in the cities was especially the call for the "pure Gospel," even if in the urban setting, unlike in the countryside, it did not give rise to the demand that the community choose its own priest. Blickle firmly believes that the rural and urban Reformation movements of the early 1520s were closely related, indeed mutually interlocked. In one of the many essays he subsequently published on the same topic, he noted almost programmatically that "the comparison of urban and rural reformationist ideas confirms that they were highly compatible, indeed, largely identical."[8]

Still, the problem of the reciprocal relationship between the respective developments in city and country is the Achilles' heel, so to speak, of Blickle's suggestive communalization model. This becomes clear, for example, in his effort to subordinate the notion of communalism (*Gemeinschaft*) to that of community (*Gemeinde*). The result is that he is forced largely to ignore the social tensions that could exist not only in the city but most definitely also in the countryside, even though scholars today must start from the assumption that religio-ecclesiastical, social, and political demands were closely interconnected at the beginning of the Reformation. This latter reason is why I believe that the communalism model cannot grasp and explain the entire early Reformation in its full breadth. A critical reading of a short essay that Blickle wrote more than a decade ago on the question of why the towns and villages in the central Swiss Confederation did not become Protestant will illustrate my reservations.

The pre-Reformation communalization of the church holds a central place in Blickle's argumentation:

> On the eve of the Reformation, the parishes or political communities of Inner Switzerland . . . held nomination and presentation rights to about thirty parishes. In other words, to put what I have said more incisively: nearly all pastoral posts in the modern cantons of Uri, Schwyz, Nidwalden, and Obwalden, and many in the neighboring territories (in Glarus and Zug), were assigned . . . by either the parish community or the city or territory. Crucial changes took place in the organization of the Church in the pre-Reformation period.[9]

Blickle argues that these changes resulted primarily from a growing need on the part of the population for good pastoral care, with primary interest focused on the issue of where the clergy resided. The communalization of the church that was sought after in this way was supposedly much more advanced in Inner Switzerland than elsewhere on the eve of the Reformation: "From all this one can conclude that the conditions for the reception of the Reformation were substantially less favorable in Inner Switzerland than in other regions of central Europe. The community, by its own efforts, had organized the church in a way that met its ideas of piety and its religious needs.[10] In Lucerne, Zug, Schwyz, and the other communities of Inner Switzerland there was thus no urgent desire to introduce the Reformation; as a result, they adhered to the old faith.[11]

If we accept the line of argumentation offered by Blickle, it would follow that the absence of a need for reformation should have existed also in Bern, for example, where the city council, in the course of the fifteenth century, had been able to communalize the local church and subject it to its control to a degree that was quite comparable to what occurred in Inner Switzerland. Nevertheless, a religious break took place here in February 1528, which was, in the final analysis, forced through by the guilds against the Small Council.

To my mind, what makes the causal reduction of the events of the Reformation to the complex of factors labeled "communalization of the church" problematic is primarily the fact that it excludes almost entirely the sphere of the history of religious mentalities. In other words, the communalization approach is not able, in the end, to provide a comprehensive explanation of how pious followers of traditional forms of belief and religious practice could become, virtually overnight, supporters of, or even actors in, Reformation iconoclasm. That religiosity (as noted in my introduction) is not experienced independent of social and—as the case may be—political factors; that it was, already in the early sixteenth century, subject to complex mechanisms of mediation between the individual and the collective desire for salvation, and that the individual need for salvation was not necessarily fully satisfied within collective salvation—all of this falls outside of the interpretive scheme offered here.

Peter Blickle has argued that "the danger of the republicanization of the Empire" was averted with the quashing of the Peasants' War of 1525, the criminalization of leagues and associations as "forms of political social organization that competed with noble society," and the simultaneous control that the territorial princes began to assert over the evangelical churches.[12] In his eyes, what the princes and noble society made of the Reformation in the old empire after 1525 suppressed its communal foundations. In a comparable vein, the British historian John Bossy has noted the destruction of the traditional, medieval village community erected on family and clan by the Counter-Reformation, especially in France and Italy.[13] The result, according to Bossy, was a stronger isolation of individuals.

In light of the more recent scholarly debate and Bossy's one-sided focus on normative sources (for example, the decrees of the Council of Trent), his findings must be modified, at least as they pertain to Italy.[14] At the same time, the Counter-Reformation's reorganization of the system of confraternities, for example, to the extent that it was successful on a local level, undoubtedly entailed a clear turning-point in the communal tradition. In the region encompassed by the diocese of Lyon, the long-term—and paradoxical—result of the Tridentine-inspired reorganization of the confraternities was that the local community fell under state control and was, thus, secularized.[15]

While the local clergy of the ancien régime in this French diocese was largely able to gain control of the confraternities, some Italian confraternities tried to disconnect themselves from their local priest and to evade Episcopal control by financing their own clergy. Even though there was an impressively large number of confraternities newly established in Italy by the Counter-Reformation, Hersche, who knows the subject well, estimates that the extent of their Tridentine "churchification" was relatively low: in Venice and Genoa, because they were protected by the state; in the Alpine region, because the autonomy of the confraternities was equated with the autonomy of the communities and was, consequently, emphatically defended; and in southern Italy, because the Tridentine reforms had never really been able to gain traction there in the first place.[16]

The community was composed of the community of the house-fathers. But not all house-fathers were equal: important differences of social rank existed. Today this is most strikingly evident in the Protestant churches in which the old pews from the sixteenth and seventeenth centuries have survived. The different sociopolitical weight of the house-fathers and their families within the community is demonstrated not only by the way in which the seating was fashioned; the arrangement of the pews within the church space also symbolized the prevailing order of social rank—in the same way, incidentally, as did the arrangement of graves in the church cemeteries of all early modern confessions at this time. In fact, the early modern English chronicler Richard Gough took the arrangement of the pews as the starting point for a real social history of his parish of Myddle in Shropshire.[17] For women, who usually sat separate from men at services, the church was, especially since they were excluded from public functions, "a very central space in which to display and create their ranking order amongst themselves and to engage in conflicts with each other. Taking note of these aspects and regulating them through special rules allowed the ecclesiastical authorities time and again to highlight the dependence of the female gender on male dominance."[18] Of course, in some Reformed churches, benches replaced actual chairs. In the seventeenth and eighteenth centuries, however, this development symbolized the fracturing of the parishes into households and families, and thus the erosion of the communal-associational cohesion.

As this discussion has shown, "community" in the early modern period was in some respects understood in religious terms. The commune with its traditional legal and political structures provided the external framework for this. "Community," by contrast, was not a given, but had to be continuously renegotiated among those who were part of it. Historical-anthropological methods are best suited for studying the "community" from the inside, so to speak.

David Sabean, in his historical-anthropological studies of Württemberg society in the early modern period, has offered insights into the complex mediating mechanisms of neighborly community, mechanisms that are still far from having been researched in sufficient depth. He points to various processes that led individuals, because of tensions within the community by which they were personally affected, to absent themselves from the community of the Last Supper for some period of time.[19] In both Catholic and Protestant churches, the celebration of the Eucharist was above all a commemoration of Christ's redemptive sacrifice, but it also had the function of reinforcing the Christian community. Anyone who was not at peace with his neighbors or relatives and was not able to forgive should not participate in the Last Supper. In this early modern understanding of neighborliness, commune, community, and association (*Genossenschaft*) appear not merely as an almost automatic bundling, as it were, of individual interests. Instead, they strike us as a rather unstable construction, at least under conditions of discord, a construction that rested also (but by no means exclusively) in questions of faith on the accommodation of the interests of individual persons or groups.

Marriage and Family

The contrast between "public" and "private" spheres of life is a modern one, with a very limited applicability to the pre-Enlightenment society of Europe,[20] and the same can be said for marriage and family. More so than it does in modern society, marriage represented a rite of passage in the early modern world. It was connected with both the end of parental guardianship and the establishment of a household of one's own, which entailed political rights and responsibilities for the new house-father. For the woman, marriage meant in a sense the optimization of her social standing, but not the attainment of autonomy. In the estate-based, patriarchal society of early modern Europe, she remained subject to the guardianship of her husband in his capacity as house-father.[21] Marriage in the early modern era was always both an emotional and material community of interests. Although love between future spouses was not an indispensable requirement for marriage, the latter did presuppose at least some degree of what R. van Dülmen has called "emotional feeling of solidarity" between the prospective partners.

Reformation and Counter-Reformation brought fundamental changes in their wake with respect to the social and ecclesiastical function of marriage and family. However, these changes did not come about overnight. Instead, the rules and regulations that governed gender relationships on the eve of the Reformation on the basis of the three late-medieval guiding ideas of celibacy for the clergy, marriage for adult laypeople, and public prostitution for adult men not yet or no longer married, had ceased "to correspond to the new social realities. Shifting the church's power to establish norms and exert control to secular authorities was not enough to solve these problems. Guidance from new conceptions of marriage was also needed."[22]

The new ideas of marriage propagated by the Reformers contained the categorical rejection of celibacy and, conversely, not only an enhanced status for the institution of marriage, but also a new and positive assessment of marital sexuality. At the same time, however, sexuality was confined strictly to the sphere of marriage and thus reserved for married women and men. The public urban brothels were closed down and prostitution was henceforth vigorously fought against. Premarital sex was declared a sin worthy of punishment from the church's perspective—a sin against which the Protestant church campaigned with little success in many places, especially in the countryside, as late as the seventeenth and eighteenth centuries, as a study of the activities of the marriage court of Schaffhausen has shown, for example.[23] The customary norms governing the relationship between the sexes permitted premarital intercourse if both partners had promised marriage. Against this tradition, the Protestant churches—both Lutheran and Reformed—tried to assert and enforce the claim that only a church wedding established a legitimate marital bond. In practice, however, the "customary forms of marriage . . . proved exceedingly robust."[24]

Still, from the beginning of the seventeenth century the authorities sought to punish premarital sexuality more and more emphatically. Prior to 1600, for example, the morals court in the East Frisian town of Emden had not dealt with a single case of premarital sexuality. By the second half of the 1640s, 6.7% of all cases already involved sexual behavior, and in the 1740s that ratio had risen to no less than 70%.[25] The same is true for the Episcopal court in the northern French city of Cambrai, where 75% of the cases before the marriage court in the eighteenth century concerned premarital sexuality.[26]

In the late Middle Ages, and into the early sixteenth century, marriage was a purely secular matter. As we have seen, in the eyes of contemporaries, the promise of marriage between two partners, usually confirmed by a gift from the man to the woman, permitted premarital sexual intercourse. The only way the churches—Protestant as well as Catholic—would be able to achieve anything in this regard was by trying to subject marriage to ecclesiastical regulation. And in fact, the entire early modern period is characterized by a tendency toward the "churchification" of marriage.[27] This also meant that all three confessions sought to suppress the so-called clandestine marriages that took place not only outside the church, but in most cases also without the consent of the parents. The necessity of such consent acquired a much more prominent place, especially in Protestantism, and this, too, is an indirect sign that the Reformation strengthened the social position of the house-father and family father.

It has been emphasized that the new Protestant view of marriage was in complete agreement with the interests of the secular authorities or the state.[28] While this new conception of marriage and marital sexuality deprived women of self-realization in a monastic setting and consigned them to the house and marriage as the sphere of personal realization, at the same time it also provided a new accent to the socially accepted image of man: henceforth, "the real man was a household head, a little patriarch ruling over wife, children, servants, journeymen, and apprentices. Like the city father on the council, he was vested with the power to chastise; like them his good governance consisted in careful stewardship of the household's limited resources."[29]

The Reformation led to the dissolution of convents in Protestant territories. This deprived the burgher class, and especially the nobility, of the option of pursuing the placement of daughters as part of the family's deliberate strategy of caring for its members. For their part, women were now bound into family life more than ever, and were subjected to the authority of family fathers. The possibility of withdrawing into a convent or joining a tertiary, either to follow an inner calling or simply to avoid familial bonds, no longer existed. To this we must add that the Reformation, by abolishing the pre-Reformation confraternities, in which women often had been very active, curtailed the previous share that women had in the religious life of the community.[30] Henceforth, the emphasis was on domestic practices of piety.

For women, opportunities to break out of the prescribed social order of the genders came especially during the early years of the Reformation, in the Peasants' War (1525), and in the Anabaptism of the 1520s and 1530s.[31] It has been noted that the social status of women in Anabaptism was enhanced by the fact that these movements generally allowed women to leave their husbands if the latter were not willing to join the Anabaptists also.[32] Leaving aside the practice of outside spouse-selection among the Brethren of Moravia and the introduction of polygamy in Münster in 1534, a real break with the traditional forms of spouse-selection and marital sexuality within Anabaptism occurred only where the movement took on ecstatic forms in the 1520s and 1530s. Such ecstatic currents, in which free love, among other things. was practiced, appeared briefly in St. Gallen and in the Appenzell region, in Erlangen near Nuremberg, in Spahl, and in Mühlhausen in Thuringia. The practice of polygamy that was introduced in the short-lived Kingdom of Münster should be mentioned here. The background to this development was atypical, in that on average more than twice as many men than women joined the Anabaptist movement between 1528 and 1618.[33] In more recent times, similar transgressions against the universally valid social norms occurred in parts of radical Pietism, especially in the antinomian approach to sexuality in the circle around Eva Buttlar in the first two decades of the eighteenth century, but also in the ascetic rejection of any and all marital sexuality by other radical Pietists on religio-mystical grounds.[34]

In Catholicism, by contrast, the convent was already in the pre-Tridentine period the sphere in which women could seek a self-realization that was not subject to the conventional (secular) norms. It was very much in line with the decrees of the Council of Trent that the Catholic Church, in the wake of the Council, worked to isolate convents more strongly. Some of the sixteenth and seventeenth-century nuns who were later beatified or even canonized preserved their independence—even against the increasing post-Tridentine control by the male world—in their spiritual devotion to the mysticism of Christ. That is true for, among others, saints Theresa of Avila (1515–82), Maria Magdalena dei Pazzi (1566–1607) of Florence, Rosa of Lima (1586–1617), and Marie de l'Incarnation.[35] Yet these women were not always able to escape the controlling claims of the male-dominated world, even in mystical contemplation and (at times collective) meditation. I am thinking here, for example, of the various Spanish nuns during those two centuries—from Teresa of Avila to Madre Catalina de Jesus—who were investigated by the Inquisition.[36]

Different, but no less emphatic, was the claim of renewal and control put forth by state and church in Reformed territories. At this point we must remind ourselves once again that the institutionalization of ecclesiastical and moral discipline was from the outset a crucial characteristic of the Reformation in southern Germany and Switzerland. It began with the proclamation of the Zurich marriage code on May 10, 1525.[37] After prostitution was made part of the jurisdiction of the marital judges, the court transformed itself between March and June 1526 into a morals court with substantially expanded authority. In this form, as we have seen, it became the model for the institutionalization of other morals courts in Protestant cities—from Konstanz and Basel to Strasbourg and Geneva.

Since the Reformation reduced the sacraments from seven to two (baptism and Last Supper), marriage lost its previously sacramental character in Protestant territories and thus also ceased to be indissoluble. The new Protestant marriage law granted the judges of marriage and morals courts the power to dissolve marriages under certain conditions; for example, in cases of impotence or if a marriage was so damaged that there was no longer any hope of a sufficient reconciliation between the spouses. However, there were characteristic differences among the Reformers in this regard:

> Luther limited the grounds for divorce with a right of remarriage
> for the "innocent party" to impotence, adultery, . . . and refusal to
> perform the "conjugal work." "Irreconcilable differences" between
> spouses, however, permitted only a separation of table and bed.
> Zwingli expanded the grounds for divorce by adding "malicious
> abandonment" and infectious diseases, reasons that had led to separation already under canon law.[38]

As another reason for divorce, the authorities in Basel added the case where one spouse was found guilty of a capital crime. However, the new, Reformed morals courts by no means dealt primarily with divorces. In Basel, "only 244 of 1,344 cases heard between 1550 and 1592 were suits for divorce."[39] In the sizeable Huguenot community in the southern French city of Nîmes, the activities of the communal morals court are documented by two voluminous registers for the years between 1561 and 1563 and between 1578 and 1583. In addition to cases of prostitution and adultery, the morals court also dealt with blasphemy, magical practices, lax attendance at sermons or catechism lessons, and with verbal confrontations, brawls, gambling, drinking, dancing, indecent dress, and participation in a charivari put on by a neighborhood or young boys.[40]

The church's attempt to channel sexuality into marriage could have purely material limitations, as we can see for Italy in synodal decrees condemning the practice of two unmarried persons of the opposite sex sleeping in the same bed. In such cases, no rarity in the early modern period outside of Italy as well, the implementation of the new ecclesiastical prescriptions was not a question of morality, but first and foremost a question of the available rooms and the material means.[41]

The new discourse on marriage initiated by the Reformation in the sixteenth century lasted essentially into the period of the Enlightenment. Beginning in the seventeenth century, it was in (Reformed) Protestantism intimately linked with a discourse on purity, which sought to stigmatize premarital sexuality as a dishonoring stain not only on a person's individual body, but also on the social body, the community, and which tried increasingly to assign responsibility for proper sexual conduct outside of marriage unilaterally to women.[42] The Catholic counterpart of this Reformed discourse on purity was, in a certain sense, the intensified Marian piety of the Baroque period, which was actively promoted by the Jesuits and at times assumed wildly exuberant forms.

The Council of Trent, however, was chiefly concerned, in its decree *Tametsi*, to suppress clandestine marriages. Henceforth, marriages without witnesses would no longer be valid. In addition, a minimum age was prescribed (20 for men, 18 for women), and remarriage was prohibited even if it resulted from marital infidelity.[43] The rejection of any right to divorce clearly set this decree apart from the Reformed regulation of marriage.

Heide Wunder has emphasized that it was left to the new, Enlightened discourse about nature and culture to redefine

the "nature of woman" and gender relations. While the married couple as the central social institution dominated the social discourse during the sixteenth century, the family became the crux of all reflections in the eighteenth century. If the chief task of the public institution of marriage was to provide order, the family in the eighteenth century becomes a resource for the new generation of respectable burghers, hard-working taxpayers, and loyal soldiers.[44]

However, this re-orientation was presumably less profound than the trend— brought about by the Reformation as well as the Counter-Reformation— toward the "churchification" of marriage, because it overturned and rejected many customs that were deeply rooted in traditional popular culture and were also protected by canon law. The revaluation and upgrading of marriage in the sixteenth century, together with the consequences this entailed, takes us once again into the sphere of popular religiosity, and to its relationship with the established churches, a relationship that was not infrequently rife with tensions.

Popular Religiosity as a Collective Ritual

In the early modern period, popular religiosity was part of a cultural web of relationships that also encompassed the religiosity of the upper and educated classes and the (in the narrower sense) ecclesiastical forms of religiosity. Seen in this way, the ritual independence of early modern popular religiosity appears in a new light. The point here is not to deny the very close relationship that existed between church-approved religiosity and popular religiosity at certain times and in certain situations or regions. We should picture the relationship between "established" and less official forms of religiosity as a continuous spectrum reaching from mutual interconnectedness to relative independence.

I have already discussed both essential aspects of post-Reformation piety—that is, Baroque as well as "classicistic," French Catholicism—and the tense relationship that existed in many areas between ecclesiastical or official and "unofficial" piety.[45] Here I will examine various independent aspects of early modern popular religiosity or piety that strike me as important. At the same time, a look at the problem of independence also raises the question of the continuity of popular religious practice—for instance, about elements connecting the piety of the pre-Tridentine period and that of the post-Tridentine period. Can it be said, for example, that the sacramental institution of confession (which was so vigorously promoted by the Tridentine Church) led to a breach with the earlier forms of piety, because it was aimed at personal contrition and thus shifted the accent from collective sins to the hidden guilt of the individual, and from family and clan to the individual? The realization of the "new model of the individual Christian responsible before God for his own sins" was confined within Catholic society largely to the spiritual elite.[46]

Early modern society was—depending on the region—from 80 to 90% agrarian. Even in Protestantism, the practices of piety were strongly shaped by the rhythm of the agricultural year and by the corresponding calendar of saints' days—even though the traditional feast days were no longer observed. In the countryside, early modern piety thus had a material foundation largely unchanged since the Middle Ages and strongly interwoven with the productive cycle of the agricultural year. This also explains why the changes initiated by the Reformation, with its rejection of many traditional forms of piety, often made only slow progress in the countryside and had to overcome a good deal of resistance.[47]

His contextually rich studies of peasant piety in early modern Bavaria have led Hermann Hörger to the following observation:

> Where it was possible to integrate nature—in its temporal unfolding with all its irregular or unforeseen occurrences—seamlessly into a closed, if multi-layered system of pious practices ... the theological or official church statement contained in the respective pious exercise was also fully integrated into the sphere of peasant belief. But where this was not possible, it was rejected like an indigestible foreign body.[48]

This confirms once again the thesis I formulated in the introduction: religious experience in the early modern period was filtered in crucial ways through the priorities of daily life.

In the world as imagined by early modern people, there was no self-contained microcosm of daily life. Rather, dangers that threatened to upset the order of everyday life were constantly lurking, so to speak. These dangers included the nefarious machinations of the Devil (to be discussed in more detail in the following section), the behavior of the dead, to the extent that they interfered with the daily life of the living, and, finally, transgressive natural occurrences. Since an animistic picture of nature was dominant on the level of popular religiosity, these transgressive occurrences encompassed not only crop failures, hunger, and epidemics, but also the doings of demons and spirits. It becomes clear, once again, why religion and magic can be distinguished only along a sliding spectrum when it comes to the religiosity of the pre-Enlightenment age.

It is not sufficient or satisfactory, however, to describe religiosity as the mere function of fear-reducing reflexes. Hermann Hörger made his task too easy when he wrote that the utter dependence of early modern peasants on the whims of nature created fear, and that the "peasant religiosity" of that time had its "final roots" in this fear and dependence.[49] Still, there can be no doubt that its fear-assuaging function constitutes a crucial aspect of early modern religiosity, and the same can be said for magical practices that were used with the intent of manipulating nature.

Existential fears assume their most striking form in the fear of comets that was so widespread in the sixteenth and especially the seventeenth century. In Germany, the number of comet pamphlets rose from around 20 in response to the comet of 1572, to around 140 that dealt with the comet of 1680. Way stations along this upward trajectory were the comets of 1577, 1618, and 1664/65. The content of most of these pamphlets can be summed up under the headings of repentance and devotion: "A comet was seen as a 'Divine Awakener of Repentance' or 'Fiery Rod of Punishment' (1675), as 'God's Terrible Rod of Wrath and Wonder' (1682), as a 'Divine Work of Wonder and Warning' (1676), or a 'Divine Sign of Punishment and Affliction' (1680)."[50] Most comet pamphlets sought to channel people's anxieties by linking the fear of natural catastrophes with the fear of divine punishment announced by the comets. To avert God's impending punishment, they called for repentance and devotion. In many cases, crop failures, natural catastrophes, diseases, and epidemics were understood as God's punishment for individual or collective sins. Alternatively, it was of course also possible to lay the blame on a sorcerer or a witch.[51] Hartmut Lehman established a causal link between the great fear of comets and the crisis of the seventeenth century. As he describes it, this crisis was "a long phase—beginning in the late sixteenth and extending into the early eighteenth century—of economic depression and in part even contraction, of political repression, social upheavals, and demographic irritations, with all the attendant sociopsychological effects."[52]

How a comet could be seen concretely as an omen is illustrated by Johannes Stumpf in his *Swiss Chronicle* of 1548. There he refers to a comet that was observed in 1532, at a time when Emperor Charles V was preparing for another campaign against the Turks. The comet, according to Stumpf, "was followed by great bloodshed, great wind, unnatural weather, heat and cold at unseasonable times, cruel fevers, such as had never been seen, many dying of it, heart pains, headaches, frenzy, strange paralysis, sadness of the people. Many killed themselves by hanging and drowning. There was a great and protracted rise in prices, warlike shouting, disloyalty, treachery, practices that left no estate of humankind untroubled."[53]

Judging by the provenance of the pamphlets, the belief in comets was particularly widespread in Protestantism. On a general level it can be considered part of the contemporary belief in omens. Omens of special occurrences were, first of all, unusual meteorological events (ranging from unusual light or cloud phenomena in the sky to alleged blood rain). Next came other unusual natural occurrences, such as birth deformities and the monstrosities described by reports in corresponding broadsheets and pamphlets—repulsive, fantastic creatures, sometimes part animal, part human, such as the "papal donkey" popularized by the visual propaganda of the early Reformation, which had supposedly appeared in Rome, or the so-called "monk-calf of Wittenberg," one of the rare examples of early anti-Reformationist pictorial propaganda.[54] But these fabulous creatures were by no means simply the inventions of their authors. Bob Scribner, in his pioneering study of the pictorial propaganda in the German Reformation, has convincingly demonstrated that the visual propaganda of the 1520s and 1530s owed its evident success precisely to the fact that it deliberately appropriated the pictorial and imaginative worlds of popular culture.[55]

Just like the comet pamphlets, the numerous broadsheets and pamphlets of the sixteenth and seventeenth centuries that dealt with omens were also aimed at inspiring devotion, while at the same time calling upon their readers to repent: "The heathens have allowed themselves to be moved to religion and fear of God by dreams and useless manifestations: but we Christians do not allows ourselves to be moved by any favor / nor indeed by any kind of sign of punishment that God places before our eyes / such as death / disease / hunger / rising prices / war / earthquakes / comets / eclipses."[56] Incidentally, one can also read in such statements the great yearning for an ordered world and the reproach against the unpredictability of nature this entailed—although nature was of course by no means understood as autonomous, but as the instrument of reward *and* punishment in the hands of God.

God, contemporaries believed, permitted birth deformities and monstrous manifestations as a reminder of our sins and punishment for these sins (or an omen of such punishment). It was no accident that monstrosities often had something diabolical about them; after all, the Devil in the form of a human with a horse's foot represented something like the personification of human sinfulness.[57] Of course, this was only one of many forms in which the Devil manifested himself. Deformed births, monstrosities, and other omens were exemplars, as it were, of a nature gone haywire. As such they simultaneously alluded to the very widespread notions of a world turned upside down. Signs pointing to disorder in nature were also signs pointing to disorder in the moral conduct of humanity. In the Reformation era, such an understanding of omens was a widespread phenomenon among all strata of the population. In the late seventeenth century, by contrast, deformed births and monstrosities were treated as divine signs only in ballads, broadsheets, and occasionally in pious pamphlets directed mostly at the common people.[58] In the upper classes and among the educated, the time of belief in omens had largely passed by the turn of the seventeenth century. Belief in comets, however, and the popularity of comet pamphlets persisted unchanged. Pierre Bayle's early-Enlightenment critique of these things had little effect.

Like the miracles that were recorded in the miracle books at Catholic pilgrimage sites, omens, as long as they were seen as being based on divine intervention, were understood as so-called prodigies, that is, miraculous signs;

thus the phrase "belief in prodigies" is sometimes used instead of "belief in omens." Scholars have noted a secularization of the interpretive schema both in Protestant collections of prodigies and in Catholic miracle books of the seventeenth century. When it came to comets, monsters, and deformed births, the people of the seventeenth century asked themselves

> with increasing frequency whether these absurdities were really at-
> tributable to divine intervention, and they began to ponder whether
> "blood rain" and other catastrophes could possibly have other causes.
> Alongside religious explanatory patterns we increasingly find new
> patterns. Parallel to the fractures that open up in the rhetoric of the
> miracle books, growing doubts in sacral interpretations also appear
> in the collections of prodigies.[59]

The miracle books were the indirect product of the prayers of the faithful in pilgrimage churches or in front of the picture of the local saint or his relics. For if these prayers were answered, the faithful were obliged to report this as a miracle to the priest, who would then enter a report into the miracle book. Here, too, we can observe a fundamental change between the late sixteenth and the early eighteenth centuries: the texts become increasingly "profane, fictional, [and] literary." In the process, they ceased to represent popular narrative material. "The miracle book leaves oral culture" and becomes part of written culture, with its dominant urban imprinting.[60]

The Jesuits, and above all the Capuchins, put the popular belief in miracles to use for their missionary activities in the sixteenth and seventeenth centuries. In the process, the Jesuits especially sought to promote the belief in the miraculous efficacy of church sacraments and sacramentals. The annual reports of the Jesuit branches in Austria, Moravia, and Bohemia in the late sixteenth century often speak of the miraculous effect of confession and Communion; their wrong use or neglect could lead to illness.[61] From Prague comes a report in 1557 that no small number of the critically ill had recovered in miraculous fashion through confession and Communion; from Gross Meseritsch in Moravia comes word in 1599 that three seriously ill or crippled individuals had miraculously recovered their physical strength after taking Holy Communion.[62] From the perspective of these Jesuits reports, confession was undoubtedly the most effective antidote to the Devil and demons:

> For example, one possessed individual in Brünn in 1589 first had an
> Agnus Dei (a consecrated wax picture of the lamb of God) placed
> around her neck, whereupon the demon in her merely began to act
> up wildly; holy water was sprinkled and consecrated palm fronds

were held in front of her; she was instructed in the Catholic faith, from which she had lapsed, yet the Devil simply became more incensed by this and harassed her day and night, until she took Communion after having made a full confession.[63]

It is not difficult to detect the aspect of confessional propaganda in such reports. At the same time, however, it becomes clear that so-called sacramentals (objects consecrated by a priest, from holy water to amulets), which were already widespread in the late Middle Ages, continued to be widely used as protection against the Devil, demons, and witches after the Tridentine Council. In addition, the blessing of fields, orchards, animal flocks and herds, wells, houses, and marital beds by a priest, to mention only a few examples, persisted, even though Pope Paul V sought to curtail such practices severely in 1614.[64]

It is hardly possible to separate the belief in miracles from the belief in magic in the way the people dealt with sacramentals. This is also true of pilgrimages in the Baroque period. However, many well-known pilgrimage sites of the pre-Reformation period did not survive the Reformation. In Germany, in the wake of the Counter-Reformation, it was especially the pilgrimages to Weingarten in Upper Swabia and to Frankish Walldürn in the eastern Odenwald that experienced a revival. By the middle of the eighteenth century, Walldürn had evolved into a large enterprise with 50 priests, who heard confession daily and celebrated more than 7,000 Masses each year.[65] Clearly, the pilgrimage filled a broad and deeply rooted need for miracle cures. The fact that the Counter-Reformation pilgrimage in Germany and Austria reached its highpoint only in the eighteenth century, when the Enlightenment began to take hold also of the southern German-Catholic realm, has prompted Peter Hersche to ask whether we are perhaps looking at a (popular) protest against the Enlightenment.[66] Pilgrimage in the eighteenth century was a mass phenomenon. Year after year, millions of people in Catholic Europe were on the road for several days. When we read in critical reports of the late eighteenth century that pilgrims crowded into the churches in such numbers that the pews broke under their weight, this was no invention of critical enlighteners who were trying to discredit the pilgrims: the account books document repairs and replacement purchases.[67]

Alongside Weingarten and the pilgrimage to the Holy Blood of Walldürn, in southern Germany it was the Marian pilgrimage in particular that surged in the wake of the Thirty Years' War. Here we should mention Altötting and Mariahilf in Passau above all; as many as 130,000 pilgrims made their way to Mariahilf each year in the first half of the eighteenth century.[68]

Ronnie Hsia has emphasized that the cult of Mary at Mariahilf attracted members of all estates and social classes.[69] Peter Hersche, however, speaking in generalizing terms of the Baroque pilgrimage in southern Germany and Austria, has pointed out that the reports in miracle books and registers of confraternities have little to say about the social class or occupations of pilgrims, and that, in contrast, the extant ex voto images "document many typical farming accidents." He concludes that one should generally presume a ratio of the peasant population between 70% and 80%. The rest was distributed among "urban artisans and, at a ratio of a few percent, the upper class (officials, the nobility, the clergy)," whereby the nobility certainly still promoted pilgrimages in the seventeenth century, but increasingly withdrew in the eighteenth century.[70]

There were also "hired" pilgrims. While studying in Montpellier, the later Basel physician Felix Platter met Swiss Brothers of Saint Jacob who were passing through the city on their way to Santiago de Compostela on behalf of others. In the Upper Valais in 1605, Hans Jergien of Münster contracted a pilgrimage to Compostela from Peter Warin of Rottenburg, promising him "after successful completion 18 crowns, one pair of new shoes, '1 new linen cloth and 1 new shirt.'" In 1630, Margaretha Schmideyden of Münster promised Heinrich Brunner upon his return from a completed pilgrimage to Saint Jacob "16 pounds, 3 ells of cloth," one cheese and one pair of shoes.[71]

The basis of the practice of pilgrimages was the veneration of saints and relics. The Catholic Church of the later sixteenth and the seventeenth centuries sought to bring the veneration of saints increasingly under its control, and, above all, to prevent new, local, and thus relatively autonomous saints' cults from springing up, virtually over night. The corresponding post-Tridentine strategy of the papal curia resulted in demonstrative restraint on the level of beatifications and canonizations—a restraint that contrasts starkly with the belief in miracles among the laity.[72] In the post-Tridentine period it was especially the veneration of the Holy Family that became more prominent, and in connection with this the cult of Mary. The Reform orders of the Jesuits and Capuchins promoted the latter with everything at their disposal.

To the faithful, saints represented not least exemplars of how to behave. In contrast to the late medieval saints, among whom saints of noble or at least aristocratic backgrounds were numerically dominant, the veneration of Mary since the later sixteenth century overcame the hierarchical aspect implicit in the saints' cults of the late Middle Ages. Several functions that previously could be exercised only by different saints were "inseparably fused" in the mother figure of Mary, who was also a patron saint. Mary thus fulfilled her tasks in equal measure as ruler and subject:

The ideal she embodied was rule and power in serving obedience, in submission to the Lord, who granted to her participation in rule in accordance with the measure of her availability, until she would eventually—as Queen of heaven endowed with all rights of the King—unite the world, the Church, and heaven with all its powers under her benevolent rule. The synthesis that had thus been achieved surpasses by far all previous models of conduct.[73]

Alongside the cult of Mary, in the post-Tridentine period the Church upgraded, above all, those saints whose veneration it hoped would stabilize the Church's edifice of faith and doctrine shaken by the Reformation. Among them were the Church Fathers, especially Ambrose, and also Carlo Borromeo and Ignatius of Loyola, sixteenth-century Church reformers who were canonized in the seventeenth century, as well as Teresa of Avila, who quickly became a popular saint of the people.[74]

We know from countless examples, especially in the Mediterranean region, where already in the Middle Ages the veneration of saints had been more intense than north of the Alps, that the cult of the saints could certainly take on bilateral forms, since believers expected certain saints to deliver what was asked of them in prayer or by good works without any ifs or buts. There are documented cases of disappointed believers who took revenge on a saint's statue because the requested help was not forthcoming. This reciprocal thinking was also reflected in the fact that miracle stories occasionally contained the warning—even since the fifteenth century—that saints who were challenged or insulted by believers were perfectly capable of taking revenge.[75] The prevailing notions of the sacral were, in the early modern period, closely interlinked with conceptions of power and domination that could manifest themselves not only in the spiritual sphere, but also in concrete concerns of everyday life.

The veneration of saints responded to a deep desire on the part of believers not only for personal and collective protection against dangers, but also for the presence of the sacral in one's own daily life in a familiar, human form. That is why the Lutheran Reformation in Germany was not able to simply eradicate this desire. Bob Scribner, in an essay on popular forms of Luther veneration, noted cases in which portraits of Luther miraculously survived house fires in the seventeenth century that burned up everything else. The conceptual world articulated in Protestant reports about these events is, according to Scribner, entirely congruent with that of Catholic saint worship, for relics and the host were also seen as incombustible in contemporary Catholicism. Incidentally, the Luther iconography of the late sixteenth and the seventeenth centuries demonstrates that Luther was in fact venerated as a saint in a multitude of ways.[76]

Alongside the deep-seated desire for the miraculous working of God and the saints, the wish for personal knowledge about one's own fate was also an essential aspect of early modern religiosity, and this is where astrology came in. In the sixteenth and seventeenth centuries, many women and men of all social strata and every confession had recourse to what it had to offer. It was only in the later seventeenth century that the upper and educated classes gradually began to distance themselves from prognosticating astrology, leaving this field increasingly to the lower social strata in the cities and to the rural peasant population.

The association of religiosity and belief in astrology may seem surprising. Magical ideas, however, established a bridge, so to speak, between the more orthodox forms of religiosity and astrology. This bridge rested essentially on the magical notion of "sympathy," the idea—which goes back to antiquity—that an invisible exchange of forces takes place between the planetary macrocosm and the human microcosm. Analogously, people also imagined a magical–spiritual exchange of powers between objects or between persons. In early modern society, fortune-telling on an astrological basis was the province especially of wise women and sorcerers, who, incidentally, could also help with everyday problems, such as finding lost objects.[77]

Not all forms of early modern religiosity show collective aspects. Astrology, for example, could be put to use for highly personal and private purposes. The same is true of magical practices. Still, early modern popular religiosity as a whole is marked, not least, by its references to the collective. Here, too, the "community" proves to be a fundamental and important dimension of religiosity within the period under discussion. That applies especially to the practice of pilgrimages and saint worship. It is equally true, on the Protestant side, of the belief in omens, for the divine punishments announced by omens were usually directed at the community, even when it was the sins of individuals that led to the threat of divine sanction.

4

Outcasts

Marginalized: The Jews

When it comes to dividing Jewish history of the early modern era (1500–1800) into periods, the only thing scholars agree on is that there were two currents that developed in different ways: Sephardic Judaism (Spanish-Portuguese in origin), and Ashkenazi Judaism of the German-speaking lands and central Europe. While Friedrich Battenberg distinguishes between a medieval phase that lasted to the end of the Thirty Years' War and a subsequent early modern phase with its processes of change and assimilation,[1] Jonathan Israel locates a turning point in the history of European Jewry as early as between about 1570 and 1600, which signaled in western and central Europe a gradual end to the expulsion of the Jews.[2] This transition period led to a phase of consolidation between 1600 and 1620, which was followed in turn by a flowering of Jewish culture in the years from 1650 to 1713. Israel's scheme is undoubtedly oriented much more strongly than Battenberg's toward political history. Battenberg, in contrast, is guided primarily by the internal development of European Jewry.

Throughout nearly all of central and western Europe, the history of the Jews in the late Middle Ages and throughout most of the sixteenth century is marked by processes of marginalization and even outright expulsion—from England, the south of France, Spain, and Portugal, as well as from most of the larger cities in the Netherlands,

Germany, and Switzerland. Where Jews continued to be tolerated in urban areas, for example, in the imperial cities of Frankfurt and Worms and in some cities of northern Italy, their growing marginalization was manifested in the process of ghettoization that began in the sixteenth century.[3] At the same time, in Central Europe the fallback on money-lending as the primary source of income, a process that had been going on since the late Middle Ages, reinforced the supportive internal structure of Jewry and simultaneously, from the inside out, the isolation imposed by the outside world.

In England, following a series of harassments and accusations of the ritual murder of Christian children, King Edward I expelled the Jews from the realm in 1290. A gradual resettlement did not occur until the 1650s, initially under Oliver Cromwell, who was motivated chiefly by economic and political considerations.[4] While Cromwell had taken this step over the opposition of many critics, the almost sensationally early plan by the Pelham government in 1753 to emancipate the Jews legally was thwarted by the pressure of public opinion, which included anti-Jewish riots in the streets and public squares of English cities.[5]

France saw orders of expulsion by the crown at the beginning and the end of the fourteenth century; the first order of 1306 had been temporarily rescinded. Against the backdrop of the pressure of an anti-Jewish sentiment, a Jewish exodus from almost all of France took place in the course of the fifteenth century. Exceptions were the southwest, where many forcefully converted Portuguese Jews, known as *conversos*, settled in the sixteenth and seventeenth centuries, the Papal lordships of Comtat Venaissin and Avignon, as well as the Alsace (at that time not yet under French control) and scattered cities and towns in Lorraine (which did not come under French suzerainty until the eighteenth century). In Lorraine, an important Jewish community—endowed with a royal privilege—arose in the former imperial city of Metz, which had fallen to France in 1552.[6]

The development of Spanish and Portuguese Jewry had an incomparably greater impact in shaping the respective national histories of these countries. In the Middle Ages, the Iberian peninsula was home to members of three religions living together and side by side—although this *convivencia* was rarely a community free of conflict.[7] In the fifteenth century, the Jews felt a strong pressure toward integration especially from two sides: first, from the crown, which, in the wake of the *reconquista* (the conquest of territories previously controlled by the Moors), also pursued the stronger integration of the Jews into the new, strongly Catholic polity; and second, from preachers of the mendicant orders, like Vincente Ferrer, who from the late fourteenth century made increasingly vigorous efforts to convert the Jews. "In a holy war against Islam," as John H. Elliott has rightly noted, "the priests automatically acquired a privileged position."[8] Following on the heels of a large pogrom in Castile (1391), in which the clergy was by no means free of blame, most conversions took place under duress; we should not overlook, however, that on occasion there were relatively voluntary conversions, either out of inner conviction or because the individuals in question were also hoping to derive social advantages from this step.[9] This gave rise to the new class of conversos or New Christians. "Relapsed" conversos, who secretly remained faithful to the religion of their ancestors, were called *marranos*. The Moors, too, were subjected to a massive campaign of conversion, which culminated in 1502 in a decree by King Ferdinand and Queen Isabella ordering the expulsion of all non-converted Muslims.[10] Already ten years earlier, the history of the Sephardic (Iberian) Jewry had entered a new phase.

During the fifteenth century, no small number of conversos had risen into important positions as financiers, tax farmers, and ecclesiastical dignitaries, thereby contesting the existing elite's monopoly on power. One clear expression of the widespread resentment are the *limpieza de sangre* statutes of the sixteenth century, purity-of-blood decrees by which cathedral chapters, monasteries, and state institutions tried to protect themselves against the unregulated admission of so-called New Christians. After the middle of the sixteenth century, they were used throughout the country. The *limpieza de sangre* contained proof of untainted (which meant non-Jewish) descent. It was indeed "ominous" that Philip II, in 1556, authorized his royal privilege for such a statute by the cathedral chapter in Toledo with the comment that "all heresies in Germany, France, and Spain have been sown by the offspring of Jews."[11] Do the roots of modern, racial anti-Semitism reach back into the Spain of Philip II? Should we be speaking here of anti-Semitism rather than hostility toward the Jews or anti-Judaism? Scholars of Jewish history are divided on how to answer these questions. To be sure, to an expert like Hermann Greive, "the question of this use of different words does not hold the kind of importance that it is sometimes accorded."[12] As I see it, the overwhelming consensus of historical scholarship still holds that the term "anti-Semitism" should be used only for the situation of the nineteenth and twentieth centuries.

It was not only the rapid social rise of many conversos that aroused suspicion within the traditional upper class; the crown, too, under the influence of its clergy, was increasingly concerned about the lack of orthodox beliefs in many New Christians. The coercive character of baptisms by no means ensured that the New Christians were in fact committed Christians, even though the clergy and no doubt a considerable segment of the Old Christians expected just that of them. The widespread belief in the miraculous powers of Church sacraments reinforced this expectation. All the more reason why the fact that more than a few conversos secretly continued to practice the Jewish faith of their ancestors and its rituals met with growing consternation. It was primarily the related anxieties (alongside more political motives) that eventually gave rise to the Inquisition as a special ecclesiastical tribunal concerned with the orthodoxy of the subjects. The Inquisition began its activities in Castile in 1478, and nine years later in Aragon and Catalonia.[13]

Until the turn of the fifteenth century, the Inquisition was devoted almost exclusively to the problem of the heterodoxy of the conversos. It has been estimated that within this period, about 2,000 victims were burned during the well-known autos-da-fé for heresy and apostasy alone, and that an even greater number were "reconciled" with the Church as a result of an inquisitorial investigation against them. These reconciliados, as they were called, had to engage in acts of public humiliation and penance. In serious cases, the reconciliados— like those condemned to the stake—had to expect the confiscation of their property. One cannot dismiss the possibility that this also provided an incentive to prosecute the New Christians, many of whom were well-off.

The exodus of the Spanish conversos began after the royal conversion decree of March 30, 1492. In it, Isabel of Castile and Ferdinand of Aragon ordered all Jews not yet baptized to convert to Christianity; those who refused would be banished from Spain. Somewhere between half and two-thirds of Spanish Jews left the realm—followed by many conversos. A few emigrated to North Africa, others to Northern Italy and thence to the Ottoman Empire; the majority, however—Jonathan Israel estimates their number at 70,000, at the most[14]—migrated into neighboring Portugal.

At this time Portugal did not yet have an Inquisition. On the contrary, King Manuel (1495–1521) was initially willing to protect the Jews against the widespread anti-Judaism of the population. Eventually, however, he was forced to yield to Spanish pressure on this issue. In 1497 he decreed the compulsory baptism of all Jewish children, and later that year the baptism of all adult Jews.[15] Portuguese Jewry, among them the refugees from neighboring Spain, had to submit to a mass conversion on a vast scale.

Over the next decades, the Spanish development repeated itself in Portugal. The social rise of no small number of New Christians was followed by growing anxieties and resentment within the old Christian population regarding the orthodoxy and the social influence of the conversos. This increasingly explosive mood erupted in a larger massacre of conversos in 1506—here, too, preachers from the mendicant orders played an ignominious role as instigators. Then, under King John (1521–48), who was evidently impressed by the harsh religious policy of Charles V in Spain, the Portuguese Inquisition was established in 1531 along the lines of the Castilian model. At first, influential conversos were able to impede its functioning by intervening with the Roman curia, but it swung into full operation beginning in 1539–40. Here, too, the thrust of the penal actions was initially targeted at the Judaizing New Christians, whereby this suspicion was surely not justified in every case. At the first autos-da-fé in Lisbon (1540) and Evora (1542), a number of allegedly Judaizing conversos were executed for their apostasy.

Against this backdrop, a strong exodus of conversos from Portugal commenced in the 1530s, and, despite various measures by the crown, which sought to stop it, continued over several decades. As a result, already existing communities of Iberian conversos in the rest of Europe and the Levant saw a considerable influx of refugees.[16]

A hundred years before Castile, southern Italy witnessed the first pogrom-like excesses against Jews and forced baptisms against the background of accusations of ritual murder in Trani in 1290.[17] As a result the Jewry of northern Italy grew in numbers, with money-lending and pawnbroking, in particular, as possible ways of earning a living. The massive deterioration of living conditions for many Jews in western and central Europe in the fifteenth century is also evident in (northern) Italy. For one thing, the mendicant orders (especially the Franciscans) sought to incite the population against the Jews in Italy as well; for another, the Jews faced competition from the charitable institutions of the *Monti di pietà* Hostility toward the Jews reached a high point in 1475 in the accusations of ritual murder against the Jews of Trent.[18] Shortly after these events, the boy Simon, the alleged victim of the ritual murder, was beatified as a martyr.

Still, no real expulsion from Italy took place. Instead, in 1492 and thereafter, Iberian and Sicilian Jews found refuge in Italian cities, quite apart from the many conversos, whom I will discuss in more detail presently. Especially in the sphere of influence of the Papal States, living conditions for Jews were comparatively tolerable under the Renaissance popes in the first half of the sixteenth century.[19] That changed in the 1550s, when a new spirit began to pervade the Roman curia. Even before the religious zealot and Jew-hater Cardinal Caraffa assumed the papal throne as Pope Paul IV (1555–59), burnings of Jewish books took place in Rome, and they quickly spread to other cities in northern Italy.[20] With his discriminatory bull *Cum nimis absurdum* (1555), Paul IV promoted, among other things, the creation of Jewish ghettos in Italian cities. Meanwhile, the Roman Inquisition ensured orthodoxy among the Portuguese conversos of Ancona: 24 men and women were burned at the stake, others were condemned to the galleys.[21]

The new papal policy of repression continued under Pius V (1566–72) and had negative repercussions for the conditions of Jewish life nearly everywhere in Italy; expulsions took place not only in the Papal States. Still, a change of course began to take shape also in Italy in the last third of the sixteenth century, driven primarily by economic motives, especially because of the importance of trade with the Levant, which led to a more tolerant attitude among the princes of the land.[22]

The 1475 ritual murder trial in Trent created a stir not only in northern Italy, but also in the old empire. Despite the concerns of the papal commissioner about the trial proceedings, the accused were sentenced and executed. Indeed, the incident shows unmistakably "that the popularized articles of faith, because of the constant agitation especially by mendicant monks, had become so entrenched that even the authority of the Pope was now powerless against them."[23] At the same time, however, we should not overlook the fact that in the cities of the empire, as in Italy, money-lending constituted the chief source of income for Jews, and in the face of growing Christian competition, the economically less significant pawnbroking became increasingly important. The Jews were economically less interesting than they had been. And that is probably the chief motivation behind the early expulsions from Strasbourg 1389, Basel 1397, Vienna 1421, Cologne 1423/24, Freiburg im Breisgau 1424/25, and Augsburg 1440.[24] The second half of the fifteenth century saw successive expulsions from Breslau, Mainz, Bamberg, and Ulm. The last larger urban expulsion took place in Regensburg in 1519, where a Marian pilgrimage chapel was erected on the site of the demolished synagogue. In all of these cities, the incendiary preaching by the Franciscans and Dominicans was undoubtedly an additional motivation behind the expulsions.[25]

The Dominicans of Cologne also played a role in the quarrel between the baptized Jew Johannes Pfefferkorn and the humanist and Hebraist Johannes Reuchlin. It broke out in 1509 over Pfefferkorn's writings, in which he called for the destruction of Talmudic text, since the conversion of the Jews would be possible only if one took away their writings. For Reuchlin, however, the study of the Hebrew language on the basis of traditional Jewish texts was an indispensable prerequisite for a study of the Bible in the humanist sense. The affair grew into a major quarrel between Pfefferkorn, the Dominicans of Cologne, and the humanists and reformers who supported Reuchlin.[26] Now, it would be wrong to conclude from this incident that all humanists assumed an attitude of interest and tolerance toward the Jews. The example of Erasmus of Rotterdam, with his deep-seated hatred of the Jews, teaches us otherwise.[27]

Nor did the Reformation in Germany bring any relief for the Jews. Martin Luther, because of a faith in the approaching end times that formed a constant undercurrent in his thinking, expected the conversion of the Jews (or at least some of them) that was prophesied in the apocalyptic passages of the

Bible. Three years before his death he felt so deceived that he wished for terrible punishment upon the Jews in his—from a modern perspective highly disturbing—tractate *Of the Jews and Their Lies* (1543).[28]

In view of the expulsions and persecution in western and central Europe, the time between the late fifteenth and the late sixteenth century was marked by the eastern migration of the Jews, either (in the Mediterranean region) to the Levant, where the Ottoman Empire offered greater tolerance than the Christian lands, or into the Polish-Lithuanian region and the Ukraine. After around 1570, then, within a generation the tide turned in favor of a return to the toleration of Jews in Bohemia, Italy, Germany, France, and the Netherlands. This turnaround was, presumably, an indirect result chiefly of the crisis of the faith of the sixteenth century, which led to a more pragmatic attitude toward the Jews within the educated and leading social strata, and especially among the territorial princes of the Empire and Italy.[29]

Although the Jews of central Europe certainly did not escape the losses inflicted by the Thirty Years' War, we can observe that the Jewish population in cities like Prague, Vienna, Speyer, Hamburg, and the neighboring settlements of Altona and Wandsbek did not decline, and even increased in outright fortress towns like Breisach, Philippsburg, and others, even though the latter were not spared by the war.[30] In demographic terms, however, it was above all the strong growth of eastern European Jewry that was of the greatest consequence. In the second half of the seventeenth century, Jews made up about 7% of the total population of Poland and Lithuania, while in Bohemia and Moravia they accounted for only 1%, and even less in the rest of the Empire. And the 10,000 Hungarian, 8,000 Dutch, and 12,000 French Jews made up an even more modest share of the overall population in their respective countries, although these figures do not include the hard-to-gauge number of secretly Judaizing conversos in the Netherlands and in France.[31]

More drastic and far-reaching than the experiences of the Thirty Years' War were, without any doubt, the massacres that were committed in 1648 and the following years among the Jews of Poland and Ukraine by the rebellious Cossacks under the leadership of Bogdan Khmelnitski. Between 100,000 and 150,000 Jews fell victim to this unimaginable slaughter. Although the Jewish population recovered fairly rapidly demographically, the negative economic, social, and cultural consequences persisted and motivated many to seek greater existential security: "To some extent, the migration of Jews from West to East began to reverse itself."[32]

An anonymous letter from Frankfurt an der Oder, which dates presumably from the 1560s, relates that the Prince Elector of Brandenburg was holding captive a man from Augsburg who was claiming that both his parents and two spirits had prophesied to him that "he is to lead an expedition to the East," namely as the leader of a large Jewish army, "for the Jews throughout the world wish to come together so that they might recover their kingdom, and that this was true, and that the Jews were arming themselves."[33] Although we know nothing about the subsequent fate of the prisoner, this strange letter does reflect indirectly the great hope and longing for salvation that pervaded sixteenth-century Jewry. Against the backdrop of the experience of the Khmelnitski massacre and the rediscovery and new discovery of the ancient mystical teachings of the Kabala within Mediterranean and Polish Jewry, this attitude of messianic expectation crystallized once again in the 1650s and 1660s. It was inspired especially by the appearance of Sabbatai Zevi of Smyrna, who was proclaimed the messiah by his prophet Nathan of Gaza in 1664.[34] The memoirs of Glikl Bas Judah Leib (Glückel of Hameln) illustrate the widespread enthusiasm that seized European Jewry in 1665/66, and it would appear that this enthusiasm resonated especially—and not only in Hamburg, to which Glikl refers—among the Sephardic descendants (whom Glikl calls the "Portuguese") of the forcefully converted Jews:

> Our joy, when the letters arrived [from Smyrna] is not to be told.
> Most of them were addressed to the Sephardim who, as fast as they
> came, took them to their synagogue and read them aloud; young
> and old, the Germans too hastened to the Sephardic synagogue. The
> Sephardic youth came dressed in their best finery and decked in
> broad green silk ribbons, the gear of Sabbatai Zevi.[35]

But when Sabbatai Zevi a short while later converted to Islam in the prison of the Ottoman sultan, his credibility vanished.

Incidentally, the special significance of 1666 as the year of salvation in kabbalistic prophesies prompted Duke Christian August von Pfalz-Sulzbach to settle Jewish families in Frankish Sulzbach. Under the patronage of this prince, Christian Knorr von Rosenroth published his *Kabbala Denudata* between 1677 and 1684.[36] Other princes of the old empire also drew closer to Judaism in the second half of the seventeenth and the early part of the eighteenth centuries, though their motives, needless to say, were more economic than intellectual, spiritual or philosemitic. This was the time of the so-called court Jews, who, during the expensive wars of the age of Louis XIV of France and the heightened need for money this created among the princes, exerted considerable influence at the courts of Germany, Austria, and the Netherlands as financiers and general entrepreneurs. For the very same reason, however, their vulnerability equaled their power, as can be seen from the example of

Joseph Süss Oppenheimer, who was executed in 1738 for allegedly treasonous activities after the death of his princely patron.[37]

If some court Jews were already highly assimilated into their Christian courtly environment, the Christian–Jewish rapprochement intensified further during the Enlightenment of the second half of the eighteenth century. Of course, this was a phenomenon exclusively of the upper social strata. The previously mentioned example of the virulent opposition that forced the English government in 1753 to withdraw its proposal for the civic emancipation of the Jews is sufficient testimony to that fact. In Germany, the lead in the struggle for the emancipation of the Jews was taken especially by Gotthold Ephraim Lessing, with his drama *Nathan the Wise* (1779), and Christian Wilhelm von Dohm, with his programmatic tract *On the Civic Improvement of the Jews* (1781/1783).[38] Needless to say, we must not overlook the fact that these commendable pioneers of emancipation were essentially thinking chiefly of the relatively small Jewish upper class, and surely not of the impoverished Jews that were becoming a growing social problem in Germany in the eighteenth century.

The final legal equality for Jews did not occur in Germany until 1871, in Austria-Hungary in 1867, and in Switzerland as late as 1874. Following the failed attempt by the English government to emancipate the Jews in 1753, Revolutionary France became the first European country to decree the legal equality of the Jews in 1791. We should not forget, though, that the decrees and laws issued in the 1780s by Joseph II in Austria in the spirit of the Enlightenment, even if they contained only individual privileges and did not alter the fundamental status of the Jews, prompted people far beyond Austria to ponder the political-legal status of the Jews and their possible legal emancipation.

The Jewish Enlightenment made no small contribution to the secularization of Jewish identity, and in that sense it can also be seen—especially in regard to the German-speaking lands—as an important step along the path to growing assimilation. To the west, this intellectual and cultural movement radiated as far as Metz and Nancy, as well as to the Alsace. In 1781, the Alsatian military contractor Herz Cerff-Berr financed the publication of the tractate *On the Civic Improvement of the Jews*, which was the work of the Protestant historian Christian Wilhelm von Dohm.[39] The history of the Jewish Enlightenment is intimately linked with the name of Moses Mendelssohn (1729–86); from Mendelssohn and his Berlin circle there "emanated decisive impulses for Jewish Enlightenment as a whole," which over the long-term radiated especially into the Eastern European lands.[40] In Berlin, Aaron Salomon

Gumpertz, a descendant of a family of court Jews, introduced Mendelssohn to the educated and learned circles in which Lessing also moved. For all his "rational" understanding of his own religion, which this son of a Torah scribe from Dessau advocated in his widely read publications beginning in 1767, Mendelssohn himself remained faithful to his Jewish roots. The educated world of enlightened Berlin included, far into the Romantic period, the salons of Rahel Varnhagen von Ense, née Levin, who had converted to Christianity but whose sense of self-identity remained deeply rooted in Judaism, and of Henriette Herz, née Lemos.[41]

Tensions: The Witch Persecutions

Before the later seventeenth century slowly led educated circles to distance themselves from popular notions of an animate world, the worldview of both the common people and the educated was dominated by animistic ideas. To be sure, nature stood under God's command, but on a small scale it was ruled by good and evil spirits. The openings of the human body represented entry points, so to speak, through which demons, in the form of evil spirits, were able to take possession of human bodies.

Exorcism as a means of expelling evil spirits from the body gained in popularity in the wake of the Counter-Reformation, since it was used systematically, especially by the Jesuits and the Capuchins, as a tool of confessional propaganda. This propagandistic purpose was revealed, for example, by the Viennese Jesuit priest Georg Scherrer in a printed sermon, in which he recounted how he had freed sixteen year-old Anna Schlutterbauer from 12,652 devils. Scherer noted with concern "that if the clergy and Catholic priests had not driven out these spirits, no doubt our enemies would have cast it in the most disreputable light and our entire holy religion would have received abuse because of it, seeing that a number of them were already starting to rejoice merely because of the delay."[42]

It would be wrong, however, to presume that exorcism was in a sense foisted upon the members of the Church. Rather, this practice was in tune with a long and deeply-held world of the imagination, one that even the Reformation in Protestant areas was evidently not able to completely eradicate: numerous sources not only of the sixteenth, but as late as the eighteenth century, tell of Protestants who sought help from Catholic exorcists. The official *Rituale Romanum* of 1614 created the still valid *Ritus exorcisandi obsessos a daemonio*. The exorcism of demons was thus regulated through official Church channels. Three forms of exorcism were distinguished: exorcism at baptism;

the small exorcism for people who were being threatened by demons but were not possessed, and for foodstuffs like water, salt, and oil to ensure their purity; and the great exorcism, which could be applied only by a priest with permission from a bishop and on persons who were possessed.[43] Jean Delumeau has argued that the unmasking of the Devil was "one of the great enterprises of European educational culture at the beginning of modernity," but his observation is difficult to reconcile readily with the exorcisms that took place between the sixteenth and the eighteenth centuries.[44]

The animistic worldview, to which one can assign ideas about demoniacal possession, also provided the foundation for the contemporary belief in witches.[45] Accordingly, there were connections between possession and witchcraft; witches could incite the Devil to take complete possession of a person. The *Malleus Maleficarum* of 1486, a handbook of contemporary demonology that was widely read and consulted for many decades, devoted the entire tenth chapter to this aspect.[46]

With a view to the pre-Enlightenment worlds of imagination and experience, we must distinguish three forms of magic. The first was the art of so-called wise women and male sorcerers, who are found throughout Europe in the sixteenth and seventeenth centuries. Like the medicine man and shamans of premodern societies today, they were believed to possess special magical powers, particularly with respect to the cure of illnesses. The second form of magic was regarded as sorcery, for in the understanding of the time, witches and sorcerers were in contact exclusively with evil spirits (demons) and thus sought to practice their art with the help of the Devil. The product of their magical manipulations was *maleficium*, maleficent magic. The third type of magic and witchcraft involved the witches' Sabbath with all its attendant rituals. I will return to this in a moment.

We should linger for a moment on *maleficium*, for it represented by far the most common and widespread form of witchcraft in the world of imagination at the time, and thus also in the court proceedings. The *Traité des superstitions* (1679 and 1697) from the pen of the French *abbé* Jean-Baptiste Thiers, a comprehensive handbook of everything the author believed could be classified as popular superstition, contains a very extensive list of possible forms of maleficent magic.[47] Prominently featured is *le nouement de l'aiguillette*, the knotting of leather thongs which caused impotence or sterility. In his travel accounts, Thomas Platter the Younger describes how extraordinarily widespread the fear of this maleficium was in southern France in the 1590s.[48] The contemporary French scholar Jean Bodin, who made a name for himself not only as a legal and political philosopher, but also as the author of a well known work on witchcraft, knew of no fewer than 50 different types of this witchcraft.[49] Next on Thiers' list were plagues of animals and insects—from wolves that were set upon sheep to moles in the garden—that could be attributed to witchcraft, followed by illnesses in humans and animals induced by sorcery. There are also references to weather magic or to dolls, for example, that could represent real-life individuals; maltreating the dolls was supposed to harm the person in question through sympathetic or analogous magic.[50] This is just a small selection from Thiers' compendium. Some of the ideas classified by Thiers were limited to certain regions, as is evident from the example of impotence and infertility caused by witchcraft. In southern Germany, for instance, unlike in southern France, this notion appears to have played no role at all, even though the *Malleus Maleficarum* of 1486 devoted a good deal of attention to it.[51]

Considering their wide distribution, so-called wise women—and women were in the majority, although we occasionally find male magical healers— were rarely accused of witchcraft in the sixteenth and seventeenth centuries.[52] Still, the clergy of the established churches occasionally regarded them as undesirable competition. This was the case, for example, with the "soul mother" (*Seelenmutter*) of Küssnacht on the Rigi. The trial, which ended with her death at the stake on November 19, 1573, was instigated by the clergy of the deanery of Lucerne.[53] According to the contemporary observer Renward Cysat, she was "an old woman in Küsnacht . . . who was more skilled than all others in this witchcraft and sorcery, and experienced especially in the invocation of spirits and souls, which is also why she was simply called the soul mother." Her counsel, which, Cysat says, she dispensed with the help of the Devil, was much sought after. People came to her from near and far: "And the number of people who came from everywhere was so great that she had to spend several hours of the day listening and giving advice to the people who came to her for help and counsel."[54] These accounts by Lucerne's city clerk Renward Cysat reveal that he firmly believed in the pact between witches and the Devil. This is evident not only in his claim that this "soul mother" was in league with the devil; it also comes out in this report: "I saw a witch like this burned here in 1560. She used to lead good, pious, and simple-minded women to deserted locations outside the town, where they engaged in the damnable, wretched union and intercourse with the Devil."[55]

"Union and intercourse" refers to sexual intercourse with the Devil, which witches practiced as part of their pact with Satan. This fantastic notion was part of the theory of the witches' Sabbath, which can be classified here as the third from of magic and witchcraft that we encounter in the period between the late Middle Ages and the eighteenth century.

The learned theory of the witches' Sabbath arose in the fourteenth century. In the 1480s, it was fully incorporated into the first comprehensive handbook for the battle against witches, the *Malleus Maleficarum* (1486; the title means "Hammer of Witches"), written by two Dominicans, Jacob Sprenger and Heinrich Institoris. Thereafter, it engaged the energies of a host of demonologists in various European countries. In the sixteenth and even for most of the seventeenth century, the academic discussion of theological, philosophical, and legal aspects of witchcraft was a recognized branch of university studies.[56]

What was the concrete content of the theory of the witches' Sabbath? Four elements are most prominent. First on the list is the pact with the Devil: a person, in the majority of documented cases a woman, "concludes with the Devil, who appears to her as a man, a pact while renouncing God. Second, this pact is concluded in a very particular form, namely as a marriage consummated through sexual intercourse. This was followed, third, by cases of maleficent magic, of harm and destruction inflicted on persons and animals." Then came, fourth, participation in the witches' Sabbath, an orgiastic and ritualized gathering of witches under the leadership of the Devil, to which all witches rode on brooms or goats. This last aspect was undoubtedly of profound importance to the spread of the "witch mania," because the conventional idea of the witches' Sabbath implied "that every witch had to know other witches, because she had seen them at these assemblies."[57]

Whether or not something like a pagan cult of the witches' Sabbath—a kind of counter-cult—did in fact exist during the period under examination is not a question I will deal with at length here. Suffice it to say that I think it is exceedingly unlikely that it did. The idea goes back to the well known nineteenth-century French historian Jules Michelet, and was later revived by prominent historians like Pierre Chaunu and Emanuel Le Roy Ladurie. In England it was chiefly Margaret Murray who championed similar ideas in the period between the wars.[58]

The theory of the witches' Sabbath was a learned theory, which means that it did not spring from the imagination of popular culture. It therefore behooves us to see the persecution of witches in the early modern period as a process of negotiation by which, case by case, so to speak, judges, accusers, and witnesses had to arrive at a cultural understanding. As this understanding became more and more difficult, witch trials grew increasingly rare from about the last third of the seventeenth century—apart from some local divergences.

What made this question of a cultural understanding even more difficult was the fact that by no means all members of the educated class believed in witches, let alone their pact with the Devil. One early critic was Johann Weyer (ca. 1515–88). From 1550 to 1578 he was active in Düsseldorf as the personal physician to the dukes of Cleves-Jülich and Berg. During this time he also wrote *De praestigiis daemonum et incantatoribus ac veneficiis* (Of the deceptions of demons and of enchantments and poisonings), first published in Basel in 1563. The basic idea of the book is that witches were not heretics in the religious sense or evildoers in the legal sense, "but ignorant and melancholy women deceived by the Devil."[59] Weyer's book was widely read and stirred up an intense discussion, in which Thomas Erastus and Jean Bodin, among others, made a name for themselves as enemies of Weyer.[60] But nothing more happened, since critics like Weyer represented merely a small minority in the late sixteenth and early seventeenth centuries. Public criticism of the persecution of witches was not without danger, as we learn from the example of the Catholic theologian Cornelius Loos: persuaded by Weyer's arguments, he was subsequently forced to recant by the nuncio of Cologne and was banished from the city. Later, as a priest in Brussels, his implacable opposition to witch trials landed him in prison for a while.[61]

The particular danger that critics of witch trials faced was the charge of atheism, which all too readily could have legal consequences. Another early critic of witch persecutions who spoke out against trials in spite of this danger was the Englishman Reginald Scot, in his 1584 work *The Discoverie of Witchcraft*. This polemical tract prompted James VI of Scotland (the future James I of England), for example, to arrange for the publication in Edinburgh in 1597 of a treatise on demonology directed against Scot and others like him.[62]

The last phase of the battle over witch persecutions in the publishing arena was marked from the middle of the seventeenth century by, on the one hand, the reception of Descartes' philosophy, whose physics categorically ruled out the existence of spirits and demons, and, on the other hand, the early Enlightenment in general. In this context we should mention the Cartesian criticism of the belief in witches by Thomas Hobbes in his *Leviathan*, first published in 1653, and by the Dutch theologian Balthasar Bekker in *De betoverde Wereld* (1681), as well as the emphatic rejection of demonological theories by the German Christian Thomasius in his writings of 1701 and 1712.[63]

The dates of the published works I have mentioned also trace the chronological framework of the larger witch persecutions in the early modern period. It extends essentially from around 1560 to the last third of the seventeenth century. To be sure, witches had been persecuted before, in the late Middle Ages, but larger, panic-like persecutions did not occur until about 1560. Persecutions declined rapidly in the later seventeenth century, while the eighteenth century saw only a few scattered trials, until the whole process came to a halt for good, with the exception of a few ignominious, late trials.

What geographical area was covered by this chronology? The eastern European region was largely excluded. The real epicenter of the European witch persecutions lay in Germany and France. Persecutions began late—after the turn of the sixteenth century—in Scotland, Ireland, Scandinavia, and North America. In Italy, only the north was affected; the southern Italian *mezzogiorno* witnessed virtually no witch trials. The same is true for Spain—with the exception of the Basque region. England played a special role in this regard, since here—unlike in neighboring Scotland and continental Europe—Roman law with its inquisitorial procedures, which included the application of torture, did not become established, and, moreover, the theory of the witches' Sabbath was of hardly any consequence.[64]

The persecutions were not everywhere marked by the same fervor and intensity, nor did the chronology and geography of the European witch persecutions that I have briefly sketched out overlap. Let us look, for example, at the witch persecutions in the Basque lands, which the Danish folklorist Gustav Henningsen has studied in detail.[65] This region saw two larger waves of persecution in 1608–10 and 1610–11, which the inquisitorial court in Logroño had to deal with. The second wave of persecutions was painstakingly supervised by the chief official of the Inquisition in Logroño, Alonso de Salazar Frias, and the statements by the accused witches, with their numerous contradictions, prompted him to become increasingly skeptical. Although Salazar Frias did not question the existence of witches, because of his skepticism not one of the women arrested in 1610 was burned as a witch, a marked contrast to the first wave of persecutions. Moreover, as a result of his memoranda that were passed on to the highest officers of the Inquisition, no witch burnings took place in Spain at all after 1614—that is, much earlier than the rest of Europe. In Italy, too, where persecutions occurred only in the northern periphery and exclusively in the sixteenth century, the absence of further witch hunting can be explained chiefly by the extraordinarily cautious restraint on the part of the Inquisition.[66]

The opposite extreme can be found in the Salzburg *Zaubererjackl* trials between 1675 and 1690.[67] This was one of the last great witch trials in the old empire. Its victims numbered around 200, virtually without exception members of the lower class of beggars and vagrants. Moreover, what is surprising is the large number of children and adolescents among the accused, most of them boys and young men. Of the 133 delinquents who were executed between 1675 and 1681, "about two-thirds were younger than 21, and more than a third had not passed the age of 15."[68] These rather startling figures do not agree very well with the stereotyped image of the evil old witch, which was confirmed in every way, for example, by the case of the "soul mother" of

Küssnacht. The explanation lies "for one, in the peculiar nature of the investigative practices (the authorities were looking for the *Zaubererjackl,* the chief sorcerer of the inveterate vagrants, but found only his beggar accomplices), and, for another, in the worsening beggar problem in the seventeenth century."[69]

Trials like the Salzburg *Zaubererjackl* of the late seventeenth century were reactions by the state, of the kind we are familiar with from other ecclesiastical principalities of the old empire, for example in the Electorate of Trier. The attempt by the authorities to cast the suspicion of magic upon the begging culture as a whole was "a strategy for the social marginalization of begging, a political strategy that was pursued by the state authorities, and especially by the Counter-Reformation Church," to deepen "the chasm between the population and those undesirable marginal groups" that were beyond the reach of the Church.[70] While this explanation is persuasive for the case in question, it is little suited to a more general interpretation of witch persecutions in the early modern period. For example, in the Spanish Basque region, it was, on the contrary, the assertion of control over the legal proceedings by the centralized authority of state and church that defused the entire problem. Moreover, there were areas in Europe in which the participation of the authorities in the emergence of witch trials was marginal or virtually nonexistent. One example is the Saarland, where "community committees" that were established on a communal basis "had the village mandate to prepare, initiate, and supervise the witch trials that were wanted and approved of by the collective."[71]

Among French historians, Robert Muchembled some time ago advanced the thesis that the witch persecutions in France were primarily an expression of what he called the acculturation of traditional rural culture by the Counter-Reformation Church and the absolutist state, and the uncertainties this entailed on the level of the village. The Scottish persecutions, which occurred chiefly between the 1590s and the 1670s, have been interpreted in a similar vein as well.[72]

In a regional study of the witch persecutions in Cambrésis in northern France, however, Muchembled also pointed emphatically to the economic events that formed the backdrop: the first wave of witch persecutions, he notes, followed directly in the wake of a longer economic crisis in the last third of the sixteenth century.[73] In the light of newer research on the witch problem, the causal link between economic crises, the social destabilization they produced, and individual waves of persecutions strikes me as more plausible than the general causal connection between witch persecutions and the growing assertion of power by the early modern state, and the claims of confessionalization advanced by the post-Reformation and post-Tridentine churches.

The example of the witch persecutions in the Saar region, in particular, refutes such a statist interpretation in the most direct way.

Other scholars have pointed to the link between specific waves of persecution and crop failures in the late sixteenth and the seventeenth centuries. In the process, they have made it clear just how much these evident causal connections point to the need to study the phenomenon of witch persecutions primarily on the level of the village community:

> In the village, more so than anywhere else, one can see the elemental link between crop failures, food shortages, the increase in hunger and disease, and the death of both man and animal. The village was therefore the first and primary locus where all this misery had to be explained. And this was, accordingly, also the place where the desire to eliminate the causes was most pronounced. Characteristically enough, then, in rural witch trials specific individuals were generally accused of having threatened, harmed, or destroyed another person, animal, or object through a *maleficium*.[74]

A particular clear case for the causal link between local crises and panic-like forms of witch persecutions is offered by Geneva, where outbreaks of the plague in the city (1545, 1567/68, 1571, and 1615) were regularly attended by rumors that so-called *engraisseurs*, who were in league with the Devil, had exacerbated the impact of the epidemic. According to a contemporary chronicler, seven men and 24 women were executed in Geneva in 1545 for conspiring with the Devil to use lethal ointments (hence the term *engraisseurs*) "to poison those in the city whom the plague had spared."[75] However, it must be noted that this kind of causal link can evidently not be established in the other witch trials in Geneva in the sixteenth and seventeenth centuries, and that those trials were also characterized by a striking restraint when it came to sentencing of the accused. Only about 20% of the accused were executed during these later proceedings, while the corresponding ratio in Zurich was 33% in the sixteenth and seventeenth centuries, and in Lucerne no less than 51% between 1550 and 1675.[76] By contrast, in southern Germany, and not least along the upper Rhine, where a large, almost epidemic-like wave of persecution swept the land between 1627 and 1632 and seized, among other places, Mergentheim, the margraviate of Baden, the imperial cities of Offenburg and Gengenbach, and the Ortenau region, the percentage of accused who were found guilty was probably extremely high.[77]

All this still leaves the question to what extent local forms of conflict management through accusations of witchcraft were distorted, so to speak, through the intervention by the state. In England, direct state intervention in this area was not possible. In Scotland, on the other hand, every single accusation of witchcraft reached either the Royal Council or Parliament, where the witch persecutions of 1649 and around 1660 were employed as an instrument for creating national unity.[78] It would thus surely be false to regard the Salzburg *Zaubererjackl* trial as a unique or special case of the state instrumentalizing the events for its own purposes. Still, in my view the interpretative framework that focuses on the local community is, on the whole, a more promising approach, although one must bear in mind, of course, that the phenomenon of witch persecutions can be explained only if it is seen within the context of a permanent dialogue between popular and educated culture.

This observation applies especially to the historical explanation of the decline of witch persecutions from the last third of the seventeenth century, at the latest. Here we should note, first of all, the fact—well documented, particularly for France in the sixteenth and seventeenth centuries—that the spontaneous lynching of alleged witches and sorcerers occurred again and again on a local level. The 1580 tract *La démonomanie des sorciers*, in which Jean Bodin advocated the harsh legal persecution of witches and sorcerers, was, among other things, testimony to the worry that higher officials were paying too little attention to the concerns of the common people, thereby tolerating an utterly irregular popular justice aimed at those believed to be witches.[79] Of course, the measures taken by the Parlement of Paris between 1587 and the decree of 1624, which in witch trials conducted by lower courts allowed for an appeal to the Parlement, were not at all along the lines of Bodin's proposals. Rather, they reflected the conscious moderation on the part of the Parlement, and their result was that within its jurisdiction, by far the largest in France at the time, only sporadic witch trials took place after the 1640s.[80] Still, as late as 1785 the region of Béarn in southwestern France saw sporadic "witchcraft crises" with accusations of harmful magic, especially in cases of illness, but the courts no longer reacted to them.[81]

Incidentally, something similar can be reported about the development in Brandenburg-Prussia. There, Frederick Wilhelm I (1713–40), through an edict of 1714, reserved any further witchcraft trials for the royal government and the highest judicial panels: "The trials were thus removed from the often zealous irrationalism of local judges. The burning of witches came to an end in Prussia."[82]

In this context, it is interesting to note that a whole series of cases of village lynching-law against witches is documented for England as late as the eighteenth century, that is, at a time, when the courts finally and openly refused to be drawn any longer into witchcraft trials. In other words, witchcraft trials before a court presupposed a certain consensus regarding the belief in witches among officials (judges and jurors), who in England usually hailed from the educated classes, and the average village population. When the officials overturned this consensus once and for all at the beginning of the eighteenth century, the persecution of witches on the village level, where the belief in witches was alive and well, could continue only in the form of spontaneous popular justice. There is much to suggest, therefore, that in England the increasingly realistic worldview of the educated classes, and the resulting skepticism toward ideas about witchcraft, was crucial in putting an end to the legal persecution of witches. Conversely, however, this also means that it was only the broad criminalization of the witch by the judicial apparatus of the state since the 1560s that helped the witchcraft phenomenon, which had already existed for some time on a local level, to attain new prominence in the first place. This realization prompted Larner to draw the conclusion, not without good reason, that only the criminalization of witchcraft in Scotland in 1563 and around the same time in the rest of Europe, coupled with the growing interest of authorities and the state in persecuting witches, invested the local witch with its real potential of threat.[83]

This interpretation could be applied even to the Saar region, for while the initiative for the persecutions came primarily from the individual communities, it is also true that demonology's new image activated "ideas—anchored in the magical thinking of the rural population—about harmful magical possibilities, female unpredictability, and fantastic creatures that existed in oral popular culture."[84] On the other hand, the help of the Enlightenment was not required to bring the persecutions to an end in the Saar region, where their end resulted largely from the destruction of the existing village communities by the Thirty Years' War.[85]

Compared to the developments in the Saar region and in the north of the old empire, it took longer for the witch mania to be overcome in southern Germany and in Austria. Here the influence of the eighteenth-century Enlightenment was crucial. To be sure, leaving aside the hereditary Habsburg lands, the eighteenth century saw only scattered trials. Gerhard Schormann has emphasized that "for Germany as a whole, one can assume that the great persecutions came to an end in the last two decades of the seventeenth century."[86] The last isolated witch trial in southern Germany took place in 1775 in the *Reichsstift* of Kempten. In Switzerland, the last alleged witch, Anna Göldi, was executed in Glarus seven years later, after here, too, the trials had already dried up completely in various regions during the eighteenth century.

The delayed subsiding of the witch trials in southern Germany and in the Habsburg lands, where a few larger trials were held as late as the first half of the eighteenth century (especially in Hungary), might be seen, at first glance, as an indication that the response to witches was much harsher in Catholic territories than it was in the Protestant north. A closer look reveals, however, that in the old empire there is no clear confessional difference between the persecutions in Protestant and in Catholic territories. Incidentally, this is also true of the link between processes of confessionalization inside German territorial states and the witch persecutions, for such a link cannot be documented. In other words, it is not possible to show that in Catholic territories, for example, the followers of the new doctrines were especially hard hit by the persecutions.[87] That the events across Europe can hardly be subsumed under confessional stereotypes is already demonstrated by the difference between the Catholic Basque region, where, as we have seen, no witches were executed after 1612 (the same is also true for the rest of Spain), and the Archbishopric of Salzburg or the Habsburg lands, where larger persecutions still occurred toward the end of the seventeenth and into the first decades of the eighteenth century.

The last victim of a witch trial in Germany, held in Kempten in 1775, "was the daughter of a mercenary and day-laborer, left homeless at an early age and probably also ragged and unkempt." Anna Göldi, executed in Glarus in June of 1782, was a poor maidservant. This case confirms Norbert Schindler's previously mentioned thesis that the victims in the late witch trials of the Alpine region were predominantly women and men from the lower and underprivileged social classes. Of course, that points merely to a regional trend. What, more broadly, *was* the social background of the victims, here and outside of the Alpine region, from the beginning of the larger persecutions in the 1560s?

In the case of England, Keith Thomas has summarized the overall picture he found with regard to the social background of the victims in one sentence: "they were poor, and they were usually women."[88] Alan Macfarlane has further noted that in England the witches were generally poorer than the persons they were accused of having sought to harm with their magic. Thomas and Macfarlane thus place their explanatory approach within the context of the strong growth in the lower peasant classes in England in the late sixteenth and seventeenth centuries, and the dissolution of the traditional village community this entailed. I will return to the gender-specific aspect of the situation, but first let us linger for a moment over the question of the social status of the accused.

In the Westphalian principality of Büren, the accused were evidently "in the majority from the lower peasant classes," that is, the class of day-laborers, cottagers, and the like.[89] Research on the witch persecutions in Cambrésis in northern France has also essentially confirmed Macfarlane's thesis, while at the same time pointing out that witches should not be understood simply as the target of the campaign by the authorities—which was gaining momentum in the seventeenth century—against poverty, vagrancy, and begging.[90] This latter observation is surely correct, even though the Salzburg *Zaubererjackl* trial of the 1690s would suggest a different conclusion. Incidentally, this unusual Salzburg trial was not the only exception; the same holds true for the panic-like conflagrations in southwest Germany. Where the persecutions temporarily assumed epidemic forms, because the torture of the accused rapidly produced a growing list of those who allegedly participated in the witches' Sabbath, members of the well-situated urban bourgeoisie also fell victim to the witch hunts. That was the case especially in Mergentheim (1628–31) and Ellwangen (1611–15).[91] Incidentally, in southern Germany children were also involved in the trials with growing frequency in the course of the seventeenth century. Leaving aside the exceptions I have indicated, however, we can assume that a large percentage of the accused generally came from the lower bourgeois and lower peasant classes.

What was the gender distribution among the total number of victims? In Germany, there were regions

> with a relatively high ratio of male victims—for example, in the trials documented for the Duchy of Westphalia, nearly half of the accused were men—but that does not alter the overall picture in any way. A comparison between various regions in Europe for which we have the relevant information shows that, on average, 80% of victims were women, with a high of 95% in certain areas of the Jura region ... and a low of 58% in the Pays de Vaud and 64% in Freiburg in Switzerland.[92]

In southwestern Germany (Baden-Würtemberg),

> the ratio of women ranged from 72 to 95%, likewise in the Saar region and in the Walloon areas of Luxembourg; in the Bishop-ric of Basel, in Denmark, and in the Counties of Namur and Essex it was as high as 92–95%. The ratio of women stood at 80% in the canton of Solothurn, in the Department du Nord, in the canton of Neuchâtel ..., in Scotland and Norway, while women accounted for up to 70% in the German-speaking regions of Luxembourg, in Franche-Comté, Geneva, the Country of Burgundy, and in Toledo.[93]

Of course, these are averages and do not tell us anything about changes in the gender distribution over the decades. That such shifts did occur is revealed by the example of the lordship of Neuchâtel: whereas men hardly registered among the accused before 1600, after 1600 their number rose to about 20%.

How were the female accused in concrete cases? The persons accused of being *engraisseurs* in Geneva in 1571–72 included 90 women and 9 men. About half of these were day-laborers or the wives of day-laborers; the rest came from the class of small artisans or fishermen. What is surely more striking is the fact that only one in twelve accused was a man.[94] A study of the witch trials in Besançon in the years 1602, 1608, and 1609 has identified a high ratio of widows and of unmarried women from the lower classes among the victims. Since a comparably high ratio of unmarried and widowed women can also be found elsewhere, William Monter has concluded that "witchcraft accusations can best be understood as projections of patriarchal social fears onto atypical women, those who lived apart from the direct male control of husbands or fathers."[95]

The claim that the witch persecutions can be attributed chiefly to social fears and misogyny no longer holds up in this generalized form.[96] In the case of English witch trials, scholars have by now shown that in a whole series of trials it was almost exclusively women who figured among the accused as well as the accusers; in other words, it was not unusual that it was chiefly women who brought cases of witchcraft before the courts in the first place. Of course, there is no need to emphasize that the court was then composed exclusively of men. What is important, however, is the reference to the emergence of accusations within a local framework and to the possible motives that might have played a role in this process. That neighborly and social tensions had a motivating effect is evident; however, in trials that arose within an exclusively female sphere, we can simply rule out patriarchal fears and misogyny as a contributing factor.[97]

Lyndal Roper's research on Augsburg leads to similar conclusions. That city saw no panic-like persecutions and no witch trials of any kind prior to 1625. After this date there were some scattered trials of individuals. All together, 18 persons were executed in Augsburg in the seventeenth and the early eighteenth centuries. That is far fewer than the 101 individuals who lost their lives in Mergentheim in 1628/29, and a far cry from the more than 300 persons who fell victim to the witch persecutions in Ellwangen between 1611 and 1615.[98]

The typical accused in Augsburg in the seventeenth century was the *Kindsamme*, who assisted new mothers in childbed, and who were generally older women who could no longer bear children themselves. The accusations usually came from the women they had cared for and concerned either the premature death of the newborn or its physical deformities. Men were strictly excluded from the environment of women in childbed, until the latter, six weeks after giving birth, were ritually readmitted into the circle of parishioners, or at least that was the practice in Catholicism and Lutheranism. The primary context of witchcraft accusations in Augsburg that emanated from a purely female environment was motherhood. The conflicts that gave rise to these accusations "were not concerned with the social construction of gender but were related much more closely to the physical changes a woman's body undergoes when she bears children."[99] In other words, they had to do chiefly with the *physical* reality of gender identity. Roper seeks to explain the conflicts that led, in seventeenth-century Augsburg, chiefly to accusations of witchcraft psychohistorically as an expression of individual efforts to cope with problems of motherhood. And this does not stand in contradiction to the fact that after the turn of the seventeenth century, it was almost exclusively children and not older women who fell under suspicion of witchcraft in Augsburg, since "the dynamics of much witch-hunting have to be sought in the relationship between mother and child."[100]

Of course, this raises complex questions of historical methodology—especially about the legitimacy of psychohistorical approaches—which cannot be addressed here. It is clear, however, that the picture of the Augsburg trials has once and for all put a large question mark over older, feminist approaches that saw in the witch persecutions primarily a deliberate campaign to eliminate midwives, who were then replaced by the male physician as birth helper in the course of the seventeenth and eighteenth centuries. A direct cause for this explanation was the special suspicion that the two authors of the *Malleus Maleficarum* of 1486 had cast upon midwives.

To be sure, there is no dispute that this professional displacement—from female to male birth helpers—did in fact take place. And while it can also be shown that "midwives were clearly overrepresented among the victims of the witch trials," on the whole they were only "a small minority."[101] The midwife, like the *Kindsamme* of the lying-in period, cannot be presented as the chief victim of the persecutions, even though she, like the *Kindsamme*, played a difficult role in the problematic area of motherhood, and was all too readily singled out as the guilty party if the child was stillborn or there was some other mishap during birth.

In any case, the more recent works on the role of women in the witch trials in England and Augsburg that I have discussed here show that the theory of a deliberate extermination of midwives is in no way able to explain the European witch persecutions as an alternative to the conventional scholarly debate. At the same time, however, a look at the "midwife theory" also demonstrates the limitations of a psychohistorical explanation of the witch persecutions. The same is true for the generalized approach mentioned earlier, which argues that the persecutions were an expression of both patriarchal fears and tangible misogyny. The witch persecutions were too complex a phenomenon to fit neatly into this explanatory template, as the presence of men and children among the accused demonstrates.

The generalizing explanatory approaches include, fourth, those that seek to link the witch persecutions with disciplinary measures by the state and the church, as, for example, when the persecutions are seen as a battle by the Church to eradicate popular magic. But in the end this approach, too, falls short as a theory with a sole claim to validity, because it ignores the extent to which witch trials could originate entirely from the village level without having been in any way initiated "from above." The previous discussion has also made it clear that the witch persecutions cannot be explained by way of confessional conflicts, which is a fifth global explanation that turns out in the end to be inadequate.

The witch persecutions of the early modern period cannot be squeezed into any monocausal explanatory scheme. In the vast majority of cases—to return to the title of this section—the issues revolved around questions of community and neighborliness.[102] It would be wrong, however, to see early modern witch persecutions from a contemporary perspective as merely an aberration, a mishap, so to speak, in the wake of what has been called the "disenchantment" of the world that supposedly began with the Reformation. There were no unresolvable contradictions between the conventional Protestant ways of thought and a mentality that accepted the working of the Devil in this world.[103] At least in the sixteenth and seventeenth centuries, the belief in magic was an integral phenomenon of early modern history. Seeing it as merely an aberration on the road to the individualism of the Enlightenment and the rationalism of modernity would be a failure to fully appreciate this belief and all its ramifications.

5

Separatism

I will preface my discussion of some representative separatist church movements of the early modern period with two remarks about the concepts of "church" and "sect," taking guidance from the still-important ideas of the theologian Ernst Troeltsch.

First, the presence of the established churches in social life has gradually declined in the postwar societies of central and western Europe. Many people today declare themselves to be indifferent when it comes to religion or the church, or have joined non-church groups and organizations that are concerned with investing life with meaning—from Astro to Tao, so to speak. Still, in spite of this evident pluralism, the term "sect" carries something pejorative and derogatory with it to this day. Yet this implicit value-judgment, which is oriented toward the perspective of the official state churches, is not very helpful, for, as Troeltsch observed of early modern sects, "Very often in the so-called 'sects' it is precisely the essential elements of the Gospel which are fully expressed; they themselves always appeal to the Gospel and to Primitive Christianity, and accuse the Church of having fallen away from its ideal; these impulses are always those which have been either suppressed or undeveloped in the official churches...."[1] Here we should recall, for example, the emergence of the idea of religious tolerance in the early modern period:[2] it took place at best at the margins of the established churches, and in most cases outside of them.

Second, beyond implicit pejorative value judgments, there are, of course, also substantive reasons for a distinction between churches and sects, since an established church is an "institution" in the sense that one is born into it. It is an objective organism which, in the final analysis, exists independently of the quality and performance of its institutional bearers. By contrast, the sect is "a voluntary community whose members join it of their own free will. The very life of the sect, therefore, depends on actual personal service and co-operation.... An individual is not born into a sect; he enters it on the basis of conscious conversion; infant baptism, which, indeed, was only introduced at a later date [in the post-biblical period], is almost always a stumbling block."[3]

In fact, sects are pervaded by a general skepticism toward the sacramental ideas of the established churches. Sacraments are seen not so much as instruments of piety, but rather as *signs* of a piety already achieved through personal effort before the reception of the sacraments. In the Spiritualists of the sixteenth century, such as Sebastian Franck and Kaspar Schwenckfeld, this notion of sacrament is an expression of an unmistakable individualization of faith. The same is true of the Inspired and the Separatist Pietists. Among Anabaptists, Baptists, and Quakers, on the other hand, it meant, paradoxically, a solidification of the respective communities of faith. In the early modern period these were communities that were closed off against the outside world. As Troeltsch very rightly pointed out, the asceticism practiced by these latter communities in daily life was in no way in the tradition of mysticism. It was not "mortification of the senses in order to further the higher religious life; it is simply detachment from the world, the reduction of worldly pleasure to a minimum, and the highest possible development of fellowship in love."[4]

The Anabaptists

Baptism provides a look at what was numerically the most important movement within the radical Reformation.[5] Here I will limit myself primarily to the first half of the sixteenth century. The history of the Anabaptist movement in the late sixteenth and seventeenth centuries has been studied only in part. Summary statements about its insignificance in numerical terms have little credibility today; for example, the assertion, based on the extant court files, that the Anabaptists of southern and southwestern Germany were active only in the Palatinate, the Zurich *Oberland*, the Aargau, and—on a comparatively modest scale—Württemberg and Hesse.[6] It overlooks the fact that many Anabaptist families of the late sixteenth and seventeenth centuries in this geographical region were able to escape the long arm of the courts. Moreover, we must not forget the considerable spread of Mennonite Anabaptism in the middle of the sixteenth century in the northern Netherlands and in northern Germany. In Krefeld, for example, the Mennonites, who had been settled there beginning around 1583 at the initiative of Count von Moers, became the founders of that city's silk manufacturing.[7]

The Radical Reformation had other currents besides the Anabaptists, chief among them the Spiritualists and the Antitrinitarians, which I will not discuss in detail here. The Spiritualists included, for example, Hans Denk, the Silesian nobleman Kaspar Schwenckfeld, Sebastian Franck, and in a certain sense also Sebastian Castellio. What mattered to the Spiritualists was the illumination of the individual in the Spirit of God. That is why, for them, the sacraments of baptism and the Lord's Supper did not play a central role. The immediate goal was the establishment of the invisible church of the true believers. In this sense Sebastian Franck saw himself and others like him in 1530 as the representatives of a fourth current of reform:

> Three chief faiths have arisen in our time, that is, the Lutheran,
> Zwinglian, and Anabaptist. The fourth is already on the way, in that
> all external preaching, ceremonies, sacraments, ban, and calling
> are to be eliminated as unnecessary, and an invisible spiritual church
> is to be established among all nations, in the unity of spirit and faith,
> and governed solely by the eternally invisible word without any ex-
> ternal means, for the Apostolic Church fell into disrepair soon after
> the departure of the apostles on account of the atrocities, and be-
> cause these are dangerous times.[8]

When it comes to his religious-theological stance, Paracelsus, too, should be situated within sixteenth-century Spiritualism. He was later invoked by Valentin Weigel and Jacob Böhme.

The roots of antitrinitarianism—that is, the rejection of the Church's doctrine of the trinity combined with an emphatic and strongly rationally-tinged assertion of the sole majesty of God—lie in sixteenth-century Italy. From there, religious refugees carried antitrinitarianism north across the Alps. Best known among these sixteenth-century refugees are Lelio Sozzini and his nephew Fausto Sozzini, who for a time founded a community of Antitrinitarians in Cracow in Poland, which was then forced out by the Counter-Reformation. Many Polish Antitrinitarians emigrated to North America in the seventeenth century. Incidentally, the term "socinianism," used to describe the antitrinitarian movement, goes back to the Sozzinis. A whole series of well-known figures of English scientific and intellectual life in the late seventeenth and early eighteenth centuries harbored secret sympathies for socinianism. Here

I will mention only the philosopher John Locke, the mathematician William Whiston, and Isaac Newton.

As we understand it today, the label "Radical Reformation" expresses the notion that the Anabaptists, the Spiritualists, and the Antitrinitarians of the sixteenth century tried to preserve and carry forward the original, radical impulse of the Reformation, while the established Reformation of Luther and Zwingli largely sacrificed and lost its original radicalism in the wake of its institutionalization. Hans-Jürgen Goertz has argued that the proponents of the Radical Reformation sought above all to continue cultivating the lay element (the emphasis on the priesthood of all believers) and the anticlerical thrust, both of which had played an important role in the early Reformation.[9]

Among the various currents of early sixteenth-century Anabaptism, some of which arose independently of one another, Swiss Anabaptism is chronologically the earliest.[10] At the beginning of 1522, the Zurich Reformer Huldrych Zwingli was still joining forces with his radical brethren. Present at the deliberately staged violation of the Lenten rules in Zurich were, alongside Zwingli, the priest of St. Peter, Leo Jud, the radical priest of the neighboring parish of Höngg, Simon Stumpf, as well as Heini Aberli and Bartholome Pur. These last three would shortly be among the first Zurich Anabaptists. At around that same time, however, a rift occurred over the issue of the tithe, that is, over the question of whether laypeople were obligated to support the holders of ecclesiastical benefices by paying the tithe. In 1522, Simon Stumpf, as the priest of Höngg, was the first of Zwingli's original companions who began to challenge the tithing duty in a fundamental way. The abbot of Wettingen was the holder of the parish benefice of Höngg. Simon Stumpf declared in his sermons that "the monks of Wettingen are good-for-nothings who have been stealing the people's livelihood long enough."[11] The first refusals to pay the tithe began. When other rural parishes around Zurich, radicalized by their preachers, began to assault the tithe rights of the chapter of the Great Minster in Zurich, the Zurich Council, and then indirectly also Zwingli, Leo Jud, and other preachers in the city, became a target for the radicals. For the Council held fast to the tithing obligation of the rural population, and Zwingli subsequently felt obliged to support this policy.

The real rift between the Zurich reformer and his radical compatriots occurred during and after the Second Zurich Disputation in October of 1523. This religious disputation, called for by the Zurich Council in 1523, centered on two questions: the abolition of the Mass, and the abolition of images. While images were removed from Zurich's churches in the summer of 1524 under the supervision of the Council, Mass continued to be read until Easter of 1525. In the face of this tentative stance, the radicals in and outside of Zurich insisted on the right of each individual parish to reform its religious services. This created an alliance between the radicals in the city and those outside.

According to James Stayer, it was only now, in 1524, that the radicals "launched their first attack on infant baptism. Once again the initiative came from the rural parishes outside of Zurich, from [Wilhelm] Reublin in Witikon [another radical preacher] and from Zollikon, who was evidently sailing in his wake." Baptism was to become a baptism of faith and therefore an adult baptism. At this point, the adult baptism of faith practiced in and outside of Zurich beginning in January 1525 by the radicals was not a separatist act of splitting off from the established, official church. The definitive break did not occur until after the Peasants' War of 1525.

The claim that the leading Zurich Anabaptists of the early days, men like Conrad Grebel and Felix Manz, along with their ally Balthasar Hubmaier, the radical priest of Waldshut, were in close contact with Thomas Müntzer in the fall of 1524 is evidently a later invention by Zwingli's successor Heinrich Bullinger, who was trying to purge Zurich in retrospect of the stain of having been the first seedbed of an Anabaptist movement.[12] But in September of 1524, Conrad Grebel and six other Zurich Anabaptists did in fact attempt to establish contact with Thomas Müntzer. We do not know, however, whether Müntzer ever received their letter, which opened with these words:

> To the truthful and faithful proclaimer of the Gospel, Thomas Müntzer, in Altstett am Hartz, our faithful and beloved fellow brother in Christ, etc.

> May the peace, grace, and mercy of God our Father and Jesus Christ our Lord be with us all, Amen. Dear brother Thomas, for God's sake do not be surprised that we address you without title and like a brother.

The writers let it be known that the word of Christ had prompted them to this brotherhood.[13] This long letter addressed a whole series of questions on the reform of the Church and the world, whereby the Zurich Anabaptists also outlined clear differences vis-à-vis Müntzer, as for example with respect to singing during the service, which they—like Zwingli—rejected. And, unlike Müntzer, they chose the path of non-violence: "One should also not protect the Gospel and its adherents with the sword nor should they do so themselves, which we have heard from our brother is what you believe and do. True believing Christians are sheep among the wolves."[14] The Anabaptist who is referred to merely as "our brother" in this passage was the goldsmith Hans

Huiuf from Halle an der Saale. There was, however, widespread agreement with Müntzer's understanding of baptism. He too recommended adult baptism, but we do not know whether he ever submitted to it himself.

Unlike Heinrich Bullinger and the older scholarship on Anabaptism, today we see the beginnings of Zurich Anabaptism not in the first adult baptisms of 1525, but in the tithe boycotts of 1522. Early Zurich Anabaptism had its origins between 1522 and 1525 in non-separatist congregationalism.[15] The term "congregrationalism" comes from Anglo-American church history. In England, Congregationalists are often described also as Independents. Congregationalism developed in England in the course of the 1640s in the face of the inability of the Puritans in Parliament and the Church to bring about a country-wide reform of the Church. While not separatists, Congregationalists asserted the autonomy of individual parishes and the independence of the Church from secular authority. Moreover, they rejected the office of the bishop and—unlike the Presbyterians—the synod, as well. Doctrinally, the Congregationalists, whose movement was particularly successful in colonial North America, were strict (and at times utterly unthinking) Calvinists.

The pacifism of the early Anabaptists in the city of Zurich is not symptomatic of the other Anabaptist movements in the canton of Zurich and in eastern Switzerland. In St. Gallen and in Schaffhausen there emerged within Anabaptism—against the backdrop of the Peasants' War—a strong willingness to engage in active resistance to the authorities and the established churches. This link between Anabaptism and the Peasants' War, which is also evident elsewhere, was most striking in the territory of Schaffhausen. According to Hans-Jürgen Goertz, the relevant sources "can easily be read in the light of the communal-revolutionary beginnings of Anabaptism, and suggest an interpretation that would imply an identification of Anabaptist and rebel interests."[16] In any case, the link between Anabaptism and the Peasants' War was much closer than the older scholarship believed. It was most pronounced in Hallau, which did not come under the suzerainty of Schaffhausen until 1521. The Hallauers made themselves into leaders of the armed insurrection of Schaffhausen's rural subjects against the city's overlordship, while in Hallau itself, the Anabaptist preacher Johannes Brötli drove the priest from the village and baptized all adult villagers.[17] The events in and around Hallau were closely tied to the uprising of the vintners in Schaffhausen: "Together with the peasants of the territory, they planned to overthrow the council and to establish a new government, and it is possible that hopes for a communalization of property were also awakened."[18] But here, as elsewhere, the uprising was eventually put down by force of arms.

It is the Schleitheim Confession, drawn up in 1527 primarily at the initiative of the Anabaptist Michael Sattler, that marks the true beginning of the separatism and pacifism of Swiss Anabaptism. This current did not draw on the experiences of the Anabaptists of Höngg, Zollikon, or Hallau, however, but on the experiences of those Anabaptist leaders who had failed in their effort to create a community. These included, first and foremost, the leading Zurich Anabaptists Conrad Grebel and Felix Manz. Only now, in the Schleitheim Confession, was the Anabaptist understanding of baptism moved emphatically to the foreground. As we have seen, in Swiss proto- or early Anabaptism, it played an important role only beginning in 1525. Following articles on baptism, the ban, and the breaking of bread at the Lord's Supper, the Confession states the following as Article 4: "We are agreed upon the separation. It shall be made from the evil and from the wickedness which the Devil has planted in the world. It shall be thus: we shall not have community with them [i.e., the non-Anabaptists] and not run with them in the chaos of their abominations."[19] Article 6 then justifies the pacifism of the so-called Swiss Brethren: "The sword is ordained of God outside the perfection of Christ; it punishes and puts to death the wicked, and protects and guards the good.... In the perfection of Christ, however, the ban is used."[20] From the Anabaptist perspective, it followed from this that no true Christian should be part of any kind of secular authority. Finally, Article 7 also rejects the oath, for "Christ, who teaches the perfection of the Law, prohibits all swearing to his followers."[21]

Most likely it was the theological positions as well as the strict separation, coupled with the rejection of military service and secular authority, that exposed the Anabaptists, far into the seventeenth century, to repeated, sporadic waves of persecution initiated by the authorities. Not a few Anabaptists paid for their convictions with their lives. As the seventeenth century progressed, opinions increasingly diverged on the question of the legitimacy of persecuting Anabaptists. The last persecution of Anabaptists in the canton of Zurich led in 1640 to the confiscation of a good deal of property in the lordships of Grüningen, Knonau, and Wädenswil, and to the emigration of around 70 men, 100 women, and 300 children, who went to the Alsace, the Palatinate, and the Netherlands. Outside of Switzerland the Zurich authorities were heavily criticized for this action, especially the confiscation of property.[22]

For a long time, early Zurich Anabaptism or the movement of the Swiss Brethren established in Schleitheim in 1527 were regarded as the real matrix of Anabaptism as such. However, all in all one must distinguish six larger groups within sixteenth-century Anabaptism, and we now know that not all of these groups had a demonstrable link with Swiss Anabaptism. This is especially true of southern German Anabaptism, which began in Augsburg in 1526, and for northern German–Dutch Anabaptism, which was established by Melchior Hoffman in Emden in 1530. In both instances we are dealing with absolutely independent movements.[23]

Southern German Anabaptism goes back to the Frankish bookkeeper Hans Hut, who was very close to Thomas Müntzer. To Müntzer he owed especially the strong apocalyptic tenor of his Anabaptist theology. The imminence of the Last Judgment infused him with a sense of urgency and drove him to fiery sermons. Within no more than a year (1527), the movement that originated with Hans Hut spread to Franconia and Bavaria, Upper and Lower Austria, the Salzburg region, and the Tyrol.

A third group took its guidance from the teachings of the furrier and lay preacher Melchior Hoffman. This current gave rise, in 1534/35, to the short-lived Anabaptist Kingdom in the episcopal city of Münster in Westphalia; its deterrent example led to sustained persecutions of Anabaptists through the old empire and beyond.

After a longer period of wandering, Melchior Hoffman had arrived in Strasbourg in 1529. Because of the relatively tolerant religious climate in the late 1520s and early 1530s, the city was home to a host of well-known Anabaptist leaders and Spiritualists. It was here that Hoffman made the final break with the established Reformation in its Reformed incarnation—having previously already turned his back on the Lutheran Reformation—and joined the circle around the Strasbourg prophetess Ursula Jost. Now the prophecy of the imminence of the Final Judgment solidified in Hoffman's thinking. This conviction, incidentally, was an essential part of the fascination that "gave Hoffmann such a mass-appeal and won him such a following."[24]

The visions of Ursula Jost reveal

> a murderous hatred of existing society and a willingness to resort to violence. "The bright light of God" shines from the Turks because they are prepared to destroy a corrupt society of tyrants and parasites. The conflict between ascetic morality and suppressed sensuality increases the desire to use force against those who "eat and drink" in comfort. Hopes are pinned on a charismatic leader who will lead the people out of servitude into freedom—into a new and spiritual life.[25]

This anticipated essential aspects of the program of the Anabaptist Kingdom of Münster. It made its way to the Netherlands, the lower Rhine, and Westphalia through Melchior Hoffman's numerous emissaries. Klaus Depperman has shown that in the Netherlands, it was "mainly the hungry and unemployed artisans" who joined the Melchiorite movement, as the current of Anabaptism that traces itself back to Melchior Hoffman is called. In Strasbourg, too, refugees formed the nucleus of the movement, suggesting that the famine crisis of the years 1529 to 1535 can be identified as the primary cause behind the "astounding growth of the movement."[26]

Beginning in the summer of 1533, we find in Hoffman's own, apocalyptically tinged prophecies the essential revolutionary ideas that laid the intellectual and spiritual groundwork for the Anabaptist Kingdom of Münster, specifically the following:

1. The idea that the godless will be rooted out *before* the Last Judgment.
2. The idea of an earthly dominion of saints, taking the form of an alliance between prophets (Jonah, Samson) and secular kings (Joseph, Solomon).
3. The expectation that Christ would only return after the second Solomon had appeared, who would prefigure Christos Pantocrator and prepare the earth to receive the Son of God.[27]

In the year 1534, radical Anabaptists from the lower Rhine and the Netherlands succeeded in gaining control of the episcopal city of Münster in Westphalia, where they proceeded to establish a kingdom in what they believed to be the Old Testament style, though it quickly degenerated into despotism. Melchior Hoffman was not directly involved in the creation of the Anabaptist Kingdom of Münster, since he was in prison in Strasbourg. The Anabaptist kingdom came to a bloody end in 1535, crushed by an army hired by the bishop of Münster. In the years that followed, Anabaptists were hunted down throughout the Empire and in the Netherlands. To give just one example: in Ensisheim in the Upper Alsace, seat of the Sundgau regiment of the Habsburgs, King Ferdinand established a special court in May of 1535 "for the specific purpose of sentencing Anabaptists to death."[28]

Following the debacle in Münster, the scattered groups and fragments of lower Rhenish-Westphalian and Dutch Anabaptism were slowly reassembled by the Dutch Anabaptist preacher Menno Simons (d. 1561), in part against the vehement opposition from Melchiorites like David Joris. Even before Menno Simon's death, the reorganization of Dutch–lower German and northern German Anabaptism emanated from Anabaptist communities at the periphery of the Empire, in Danzig and in Oldesloe in Holstein; ever since, it has become, in the form of the Mennonite movement, the international catch-basin for Anabaptism as such. Menno Simons condemned not only the excesses of the Münster Anabaptists, such as polygamy and the bloody persecution of nonbelievers, but in general every form of war and violence, though without going so far as to reject every form of secular authority, as the Schleitheim Articles had done.[29]

Another offshoot of sixteenth-century Anabaptism—and the last that I will examine more closely—were the Hutterites, named after their founder, Jakob Hutter. Within the bosom of this movement as well, the critique of existing social conditions played a crucial role, except that it did not lead to attempted revolutions, but rather the establishment of communist communities, which continue to exist to this day in Pennsylvania in an astonishingly unchanged form.

Whereas the idea of a community of property made only an occasional appearance in early south German–Austrian and in Swiss Anabaptism, the Hutterites in Moravia implemented it consistently beginning in the early 1530s. They held the firm belief—one they shared, incidentally, with many authors of sixteenth and seventeenth century utopias—that the private ownership of goods was the cause of all wars and bloodshed. In contrast to late medieval mysticism, *Gelassenheit* to Hutterites meant not the spiritualization of the individual for the purpose of drawing closer to God, but rather the renunciation of all worldly goods. Anyone who was incapable of making this renunciation, they believed, would never find God.[30]

Although sporadic persecutions of Anabaptists occurred also in Moravia (e.g., after the crushing of the Anabaptist Kingdom of Münster and in the late 1540s following the end of the Schmalkaldic War), in part at the command of the Habsburg overlords, the noble landlords had considerable autonomy in this region. Quite a few of them protected the Anabaptists, probably out of largely economic motives. As a result, beginning as early as the 1520s, Moravia acted as a magnet for no small number of persecuted Anabaptists from Austria, southern Germany, and Switzerland. Every year, the Hutterites sent out missionaries to recruit more followers and persuade them to emigrate to Moravia. Their Moravian brotherhoods of the late sixteenth century numbered between 7,000 and 20,000 individuals.[31] Emigration to Moravia was not driven only by religious motivations; poverty and hunger also influenced the emigrants. For example, the height of the emigration from Württemberg in the 1570s coincided with a dramatic rise in prices and with subsistence problems for the population.[32] It was only in the course of the Thirty Years' War that the Habsburg overlords were able to quash the Moravian Anabaptist movement and suppress it once and for all. The Moravian Anabaptists were forced to abandon their last 24 settlements in October of 1622. Many, among them the Hutterites, fled to Hungary, where the Habsburg confessional policy had little to no effect, depending on the region. There the Anabaptists found refuge on the estates of Hungarian magnates, in some cases for several generations.[33]

The price for the realization of a community of property was a functional hierarchy that was much more pronounced than in other Anabaptist communities. At the head of the Hutterite communities stood bishops, and below them the servants of the Word. These were followed, in descending order, by the secular servants. The differences between the living standard of this functional elite and that of the common Hutterites occasionally led to tensions, as we learn from the chronological records that were regularly and reliably kept in the various colonies. At the head of these colonies stood a servant of the Word and a secular servant, the latter fulfilling something like the role of house-father.

As in the contemporaneous utopias of Thomas More, Johann Valentin Andreae, or Tommaso Campanella, the nature and extent of the daily labor of the individual Hutterite was largely determined externally and did not involve any kind of personal remuneration. Moreover, individuals—and this, too, is reminiscent of More's *Utopia*—did not have the freedom to choose their spouses and did not have the right to supervise the upbringing of their own children. Daily life was truly ascetic. Even the "most innocent enjoyments, such as talking with friends over a glass of wine, were forbidden."[34] Then as now, true asceticism had its price.

Baptists and Quakers

When the Baptists in the revolutionary England of the 1640s evolved into a broader separatist movement, their enemies liked to denounce them as "Anabaptists." Evidently, the memory of the Anabaptist Kingdom of Münster was still so vivid—at least among the educated—that it was advantageous to associate ecclesiastical and religious opponents with it. The collective memory branded the Anabaptists of Münster as the embodiment of anarchy and lawlessness. In spite of such strategies of denigration, English Baptists had little to do with the Anabaptist movement of continental Europe. The English free churches of the Baptists, which today have a broad numerical base especially in the United States, were originally created by Puritan Separatists who turned their backs on the state church, which they regarded as papist and too lax in matters of church discipline.

One group that stands out is the Separatists, who left England in 1608 for reasons of faith and settled in the Netherlands.[35] Soon after they split into two parties that were led by dismissed Puritan clerics. The first group, under the leadership of John Smyth, opened itself to the influence of the Dutch Mennonites. They adopted adult baptism and rejected especially the Calvinist doctrine of predestination. In its place they put the teaching of the universality of divine grace—the idea, that is, that all humans are capable of redeeming their souls by virtue of their faith. Integration of these groups into the Dutch Mennonite movement, which seemed inevitable given these borrowings, was thwarted by the fact the majority of their members did not wish to give up their Puritan ideas of church discipline. Specifically Puritan in nature was the demand that the secular authorities should guarantee church discipline. Because the majority of the groups originally influenced by John Smyth held this positive view of the moral role of secular authority, they were not willing to accept the Anabaptists' principled distancing from all secular government. John Smyth's opponent on this issue, Thomas Helwys, a member of the gentry from Nottinghamshire, returned to England in 1612 and founded the first free church of the General Baptists in London.

The other segment of the 1608 emigrants remained largely immune to Mennonite influence and therefore did not, at first, make a complete or final break with the English state church. This break emerged only after members of this group had returned to London and the semi-separatist communities they established came under pressure of the new church governance of the Arminians in the course of the 1630s. It would appear that in this situation, especially radical members of this proto-Baptist communities separated themselves entirely from the state church; they began to baptize each other. Here, as in and around Zurich in 1525, the primary function of baptism was to serve as a visible sign of membership in the party of the pious.

These latter groups were the first Particular Baptists. What distinguished them from the General Baptists was above all that they clung to the Calvinist legacy and thus also to the doctrine of predestination. As far as baptism was concerned, in the early 1640s both Baptist Free Churches, following the example of the baptism of Christ by John, adopted the spectacular ritual of baptism by complete immersion. Around the middle of the seventeenth century, these two currents took great pains to set themselves apart from each other, in spite of their commonalities with respect to the ritual of baptism. This split was brought on by differing views on the question of predestination. In the eyes of the Particular Baptists as adherents to predestinarian theology, the General Baptists were nothing more than despicable heretics. The sociopolitical conditions of the 1640s and 1650s then gave both Baptist Free Churches a relatively free hand to pursue domestic missionary work within England. The movement grew markedly in size, especially during the 1640s, that is to say, before the Quakers began to compete with them.

The General Baptists, completely separated from mainstream Puritanism and the state church not least in the matter of doctrine, were the more radical of the two movements. Both currents drew their recruits primarily from London's lower bourgeoisie and the sub-bourgeois social strata, who tended to stand back from Puritanism as a movement especially of the middle and upper social strata. It is conceivable that this also had doctrinal in addition to other causes, for it would seem that the doctrine of the universality of grace promised the potential followers from the strata below the bourgeoisie and the peasant class more personal dignity than did the theology of predestination.[36] The majority of preachers were laymen, unskilled tradesmen-preachers, so-called Mechanick Preachers, who were the target of ridicule and derision from socially higher-ranking contemporaries and especially from the educated theologians of the state church. In the course of the 1640s, the General Baptists expanded their mission from London to all of England. An important missionary instrument were their services in the revivalist style. The General Baptists of the 1640s had little time for the kind of pacifist ideas that were part of the Mennonite movement. Instead, they joined the parliamentary army in large numbers and had a special predilection for serving in the New Model Army under Oliver Cromwell, who, like other Independents of his time, by no means took a negative view of the religious convictions of the Baptists. The General Baptists actively pursued their missionary activities also within the parliamentary army.

At the end of the decades of upheaval in the 1640s and 1650s, a time when a whole series of new religious groups in England sprang up, the Baptists as a whole numbered perhaps around 25,000, with the two Baptist Free Churches about equal in strength, all in all. That figure is less than 1% of the population of England at the time. However, historians have rightly pointed out that a mere percentage does not adequately capture the real influence of the Baptist movement, because it does not include either the numerous sympathizers or those supporters who were expelled from the two Free Churches for their excessively radical views.[37]

Around the middle of the seventeenth century, the local Baptist churches joined into regional associations that were coordinated by a system of representative assemblies, a system that was based on what were, in England, completely new democratic principles. The new associations also reveal the geographic distribution of the Baptists. Their presence was especially strong in the south and west of England, as well as in the Midlands. Only a handful of Baptist Free Churches existed in the northern counties, where the Quakers would shortly have missionary successes.

The occupational and social profile of the Baptists was dominated by the more humble tradesmen, such as weavers, shoemakers, tailors, smiths, bakers, and glove-makers. Despite this urban-artisanal preponderance, one should not underestimate the number of those Baptists who made a living from agriculture, even if they are less present in our sources. Alongside this majority of members from rather modest occupational and social backgrounds, there were also some rich merchants among the Baptists of the period of the English Revolution, especially in London (the likes of Samuel Moyer or the autobiographer William Kiffin), as well as members from the lower gentry. As already mentioned, many soldiers were at that time also followers of the movement. Between 1642 and 1660, they represented the largest—and most unpredictable—occupational group within both Baptist Free Churches. Finally, there was also a much less numerous group of educated clergy who had converted to Baptism. The leadership of the movement was thus—unlike the majority of the other members—anything but homogeneous. The glue that kept it together was the deep conviction that the true church was a community of the saints and that the sign of their community was the baptism of faith.

Between 1660 and the 1680s, following the restoration of the Stuarts, the Baptists, like the heirs of prerevolutionary Puritanism (especially the Presbyterians and the Independents) and the Quakers, came under strong pressure of conformity by the state. Not infrequently that pressure entailed charges in court, jail sentences, and other forms of harassment, all of which made many of those affected much more willing to emigrate to the New World. John Bunyan, surely the best-known Baptist preacher of the seventeenth century, was part of this group. He wrote his well-known spiritual autobiography, *Grace Abounding to the Chief of Sinners*, during his imprisonment. Bunyan became world famous through his work *The Pilgrim's Progress*, the first edition of which was published in two parts in 1678 and 1684. In the form of an allegory, it describes the path of the believing Christian past many trails, sometimes severe, humiliations, and obstacles toward the personal salvation of his soul; its success has made it one of the most widely read works of world literature.

It was less the king and more the so-called Cavalier Parliament of the early 1660s that subjected many of the former Puritans and all church Separatists to a rule of hardships and regular harassment. The goal of the Parliament with respect to church policy was the restoration of the state Episcopal Church on the basis of the 39 Articles of 1563 and the *Book of Common Prayer*.[38] In case of conflict, Parliament sought to further this goal by force and coercion.

The result was a series of laws enacted between 1661 and 1665 that were later referred to as the Clarendon Code, which—much against the intention of the king—were aimed at punishing the various "sects" and even the Presbyterians.[39] The first of these laws was the Corporation Act of December 1661, which obliged all magistrates of the land, from the mayor down to the clerk, to swear an oath of loyalty on the king and to take Communion in the Church of England. This was the first step toward the political—and to some extent also social—exclusion of the Presbyterians, Quakers, Baptists, and other groups, who were henceforth referred to as Dissenters or Nonconformists.

It was above all the Quakers—who had grown enormously as a movement in the late 1650s, and who attracted both special attention and fear through their peculiar behaviors—who now came to feel the full weight of the established classes' sense of social order.[40] It made no difference that Charles II did not hold it against the Quakers that they did not doff their hats to him, and that he even intended to legally free them from the obligation to swear oaths. The lower house of Parliament reacted to this tolerant stance with a law that made the refusal to swear the oath of homage to the king punishable by high fines and, in repeat cases, by prison or even "transportation," that is, deportation to North America. As the Quaker Act it became, in 1662, the second discriminatory law targeting the Dissenters.[41]

The best-known law of the Clarendon Code is the Act of Uniformity of 1662.[42] Its chief goal was to purge the state church of non-conforming and unorthodox clergymen. Although this is often the only act referred to in discussions of the discriminatory laws of the 1660s, it was an integral part of a series of similar ordinances from the years 1661 and 1662.

The law that Parliament passed on May 19, 1662, known as the Act of Uniformity, stipulated that every clergyman active within the Church of England would lose his office unless by St. Bartholomew's Day (August 24) he had officially accepted the *Prayer Book* in its entirety, had rejected Presbyterianism, and had abjured the idea of the subjects' right of resistance vis-à-vis the crown. At least 961 clergymen were unwilling to subject themselves to the rigid requirements of this law and were expelled from the official Church.[43] They accounted for about one-tenth of the entire parish clergy of England and Wales. Some counties, however, were more heavily affected than others. The state church was now also forced to do without some of its most capable and eloquent representatives. The latter, in turn, faced some tough times, but in many cases they were rescued by voluntary measures on the part of the parishes that remained loyal to them, and which thus turned into free churches. At least 5% to 10% of the laity—the concentration varied from region to region—were alienated from the state church.[44] The intolerant policies of the Cavalier Parliament were utterly incomprehensible to the Presbyterians especially, for they had actively supported the return of the king at the end of the 1650s.

Among the free church movements that were already organized along separatist lines before 1660, it was especially the more prominent Baptists who suffered alongside the Quakers. The successful London merchant William Kiffin recounted in his autobiography how, during this phase of intense discrimination against Dissenters, he was charged with conspiracy against the life of the king, though the accusation was dropped thanks to royal intervention. Subsequently he became embroiled in a trial of high treason for his participation in conventicles, but in the end he was able to get off lightly once again. Yet the only effect of these experiences was one the accuser had surely not intended, for they powerfully reinforced Kiffin's religious convictions: "You may hereby see," he wrote in his autobiography, "that it is not in vain to follow God in the way of duty; and to enquire after the knowledge of Jesus Christ betimes."[45]

The Quakers

The most serious competition for English Baptists in the years of upheaval, from 1642 to 1660, came from the Quakers. The vanguard of the Quakers came from the northern counties of England, where the influence of the Baptists was slight. Still, it is quite clear that the founder of the Quaker movement, George Fox (1624–1691), fell under the influence of the Baptists in the late 1640s. A substantial part of the teachings of the Quakers "is a radical extension of general redemption: the expression of true Christianity as moral conduct; the potential of all humanity to know the Spirit of God."[46] In the 1650s, the Quakers competed successfully with the Baptists for no small number of followers.

It therefore comes as no surprise that the spiritual autobiography of the Baptist preacher John Bunyan contains a detailed list of a total of 125 errors of the Quakers.[47] Bunyan notes, first and foremost, that the Quakers claimed that the Holy Scripture was not the work of God. It is certainly true that the Quakers accorded more weight to the divine inspiration of the individual through the light within than they did to Biblical revelation. Secondly, Bunyan—who was a Particular Baptist—criticized the Quaker's belief in general redemption. His fourth objection was directed at the Quaker notion that Christ dwelt in the true believers in flesh and blood. In fact, one can find among the early Quakers the belief in the perfectibility of the believer, and—in connection with it—a good measure of antinomianism, which refers to the conviction that the true believer is fully justified and can therefore no longer sin, that is, transgress against the law (*nomos*). In the religious history of the sixteenth and seventeenth centuries, antinomians often attract attention through transgressive behavior—for example the free choice of one's partner or a streak of destructive iconoclasm— by which they sought to demonstrate their state of grace to themselves and to their social environment. Even at item 125, John Bunyan had not exhausted the register of sins, as he emphasized how many more "ugly and despicable things" had been disseminated by the Quakers.[48]

The founder of Quakerism was the itinerant preacher George Fox, who, beginning in 1652, was able to unite various groups of separatist-inclined men and women into a new movement in the north of England. Soon a whole series of other, equally tireless Quaker missionaries became active alongside Fox. Many of the early converts worked in agriculture; no small number of them had clashed as farmers with their noble landlords during the period of the civil war. Quakerism was thus from the outset not merely a religious movement of renewal, but simultaneously also a movement of social and political protest.[49] At least that is true of the 1650s. Following the restoration of the Stuarts in 1660, the Quakers, too, had to come to terms with the existing conditions far more than before.

Though the movement began in the north of England, as early as the middle of the 1650s it began to spread in the south. Within the first decade, it grew to between 35,000 and 40,000 followers, perhaps even more. At any rate, at the beginning of the 1660s there were more Quakers than Baptists and Catholics in England.[50] Similar to the Baptists, the Quaker movement appealed—in addition to the rural elements—above all to the class of small artisans. Few Quakers came from either the gentry or the true underclasses.

George Fox was an exceptional personality. During missionary work that extended for more than forty years, Fox—much like John Wesley a hundred years later—was almost continuously on the move. He crisscrossed England a total of five times. In addition, he undertook missionary journeys to Wales, Scotland, Ireland, the Netherlands, Germany, and the North American colonies. He was imprisoned nine times, more often still he was maltreated by hostile mobs with blows and stones and occasionally left for dead; and yet, thanks to his robust constitution, he recovered every time and continued his work. He traveled the land wearing equally sturdy leather breeches and a white hat, and he wore his hair long, to the disgust of the Puritans. According to Michael Watts, the historian of the English Dissenters, his less attractive traits were his proverbial lack of humor and "the violent and frequently vulgar language with which he lambasted his opponents."[51]

George Fox and the early Quaker movement have been described repeatedly as a kind of deus ex machina or as an unforeseeable tidal wave. That view is accurate for, at most, the spectacular growth of Quakerism within a few short years, but not for the influences and precursors that worked on George Fox and other initial leaders. The collapse of the structure of the state church, as well as the censorship at the beginning of the 1640s and the spectacular failure of the Puritans in their effort to institute a country-wide church reform, combined with a whole host of other phenomena of this time of upheaval, had given rise, here and there, to completely new ecclesiastical-religious groups: alongside the Baptists and the sociopolitical movement of the Levellers that sprang from them, there were scattered Spiritualists (who were called Seekers), the antinomian group of the Ranters, and, in the early 1650s, the so-called Fifth Monarchists and the Muggletonians.

During his years of wandering, George Fox absorbed various impulses from some of these groups: for example, the condemnation of the university education of the theologians as a sufficient preparation for a Christian life, or the rejection of conventional church buildings as meeting places for *true* Christians. In George Fox's diary, which would become a model for a long series of other Quaker autobiographical works, churches are consistently given the pejorative label "steeple houses." These kinds of ideas were common in the English religious radicalism of the 1640s. Incidentally, the same is true for the doctrine of the light within—that is, of the direct, inner inspiration of the faithful by the Holy Spirit. At that time this notion was in the air, so to speak. One should also mention in this context that George Fox owned works by the Spiritualist mystic Sebastian Franck (1499–1542/43), though we do not know whether he ever read them.[52]

Much the same applies also to the new forms of behavior that George Fox introduced among his followers, and which made Quakers externally identifiable to their contemporaries. When God sent him out into the world, he wrote, the Lord in Heaven forbade him to doff his hat to anyone, and he instructed him "to 'thee' and 'thou' all men and women, without any respect to rich or poor, great or small." Everywhere there was great anger and outrage about this conduct: "Oh, the blows, punchings, beating, and imprisonment that we underwent for not putting off our hats to men!"[53]

Since the Quakers rejected the conventional forms of social intercourse, they fell under suspicion, in the ritual- and symbol-conscious society of their day, of spurning the existing social conditions in their entirety. In their rejection of the usual names for weekdays and months as pagan, and in their refusal to swear oaths, also abjured by the Anabaptists at that time, the Quakers drew especially on the practices of the Baptists. The Quakers were pioneers only with respect to their pacifism—at least in England. This pacifism was not present from the outset, however, but evolved only during the Restoration period, after 1660. As late as 1659, when the time of the Interregnum was coming to a close, individual Quakers like Edward Burrough were willing, in an apocalyptic mood, to risk their lives to establish a better world, to set up a government of the righteous and pious: "Oh then we should rejoice, and our lives would not bee Deare to lay downe."[54] The first, quasi-official statement by the Quakers that amounted to a general condemnation of any use of armed force dates only from the year 1661. What eventually made this position unavoidable was not only inner conviction, but undoubtedly also the desire for self-preservation in the face of the harsh climate to which the Quakers were exposed in the restored monarchy, as well as the disillusionment caused by their own, political marginalization.[55]

The early missionary work of the Quakers resembled in some ways the revivalist campaigns of the nineteenth century. In fact, leading missionaries practiced miracle healing and exorcisms, whose propaganda effect they were well aware of. In an account of the successful exorcism of a possessed woman in 1649, George Fox noted emphatically that their enemies could now no longer denounce them as "false prophets, deceivers, or witches."[56]

The early Quakers were not unsympathetic to the antinomian idea that the believer justified through the grace of God was no longer able to sin, and that the true believers thus had the possibility of becoming Christ-like through inner, divine inspiration. Such views are documented by the Quakers' own writings. Of course, as the second half of the seventeenth century unfolds, these texts also reveal a certain change: in pertinent writings of the late seventeenth century one encounters the notion from time to time that it is still possible to sin even after the inner conversion.

The Quaker preacher James Nayler, who was highly popular thanks to his extraordinary eloquence, is the personification of the antinomian tendencies of early Quakerism. On Palm Sunday in 1656, he rode into Bristol on a donkey while his followers hailed him as the embodiment of Christ. Parliament in Westminster, challenged and rattled by the Quaker movement, decided to make an example of Nayler. He barely escaped the death penalty, and the Lower House made the essentially unconstitutional decision to put Nayler in the pillory, and afterward to whip him through the streets of London, pierce his tongue with a hot iron, and have the executioner brand the letter B—for "blasphemer"—on his forehead. Shortly after Nayler was released from prison in September of 1656, literally a marked man, he was captured by highwaymen on the road from London to Wakefield and died from the maltreatment he suffered at their hands.[57]

The Nayler episode reveals the widespread fears of the representatives of the leading classes in the face of the new movement of Quakerism, which was, after all, from the very outset not merely a movement of religious renewal in the narrower sense, but also a sociopolitical protest movement. It can be shown that the widespread fear of the Quakers, who at this time had not unanimously renounced the use of force to establish the rule of the pious, was a factor of some importance in bringing about the restoration of the monarchy by the leading classes in 1659/60.[58]

The everyday culture of the Quakers, which was focused chiefly on religious principles, was plain and unpretentious. Both the spoken and written language was marked by a lack of rhetorical flourishes and an abstention from any ornamentation. The same was also true of clothing and of Quaker-inspired house and garden architecture. However, it did not prove possible to establish a rigid everyday culture within the movement: Quakerism was too heterogeneous for that, and the individual groups remained strongly rooted in contemporary popular culture. For example, the followers of Rhys John in Nottingham—who called themselves "Proud Quakers"—were known as excellent football players and wrestlers. On Sundays they gathered "to play at shovell board."[59] Incidentally, it is undeniable that the behavior of some Quakers began to become secularized in the last decades of the seventeenth and at the dawn of the eighteenth centuries, and that commercial success also brought a certain "embourgeoisement" with it. These tendencies become apparent in contemporary warnings by concerned Quakers against pride and vanity in their own ranks, against "striped silks, of divers Couleurs," "Broidered hair or pearls or Gold or Costly Array," and against "vaine and superfluous furniture" in the dwellings and houses of Quakers.[60]

The Revolution of 1688/89 and the Toleration Act of 1689, which did not by any means bring full religious toleration, though it did largely put an end to the persecution of the Dissenters by the state and its representatives, initiated a phase of rapprochement and gradual reconciliation between no small number of Quakers—and Dissenters of every stripe—and the existing social and political order. And so it came about that many Quakers gave up their refusal to pay the tithe, and that in eighteen-century Ireland, for example, Quakers were in fact highly sought after as leaseholders of farms, because the reputation of being very reliable—not least when it came to paying the rent—preceded them. In social and political terms, the light within that illuminated these farmers and the successful Quaker merchants of London, Bristol, Dublin, and Philadelphia in the eighteenth century was no longer that of a George Fox, Edward Burrough, or James Nayler.

Radical Pietism

If, as previously discussed, we follow Johannes Wallmann in positing a dual beginning of German Lutheran Pietism, we can date the onset of Pietism as a religio-social movement to the year 1675. Since the majority of Protestant

Separatists emerged out of Pietism (with the exception of the Mennonites and the Inspired, to be discussed shortly), one might assume that the relevant separatist tendencies do not become apparent until after 1675. Such a view would, however, be mistaken.

Already in the early seventeenth century there were smaller communities of Separatists; like Pietism, the movement had grown out of a serious effort to renew and reform the ecclesiastical and religious life of their time. What all these smaller communities shared was a basic apocalyptic mood and expectation. Moreover, similar to the proponents of the Radical Reformation of the sixteenth century, they placed less weight on the sacraments. One example is the Gichtelians (who called themselves the Brethren of the Angels), named after their founder Johann Georg Gichtel. They practiced a strict, nearly monastic withdrawal from the world, held property in common, and even rejected marriage and procreation and thus any form of sexuality.[61] The Gichtelians were strongly influenced by the mystical-spiritualist writings of Valentin Weigel and Jacob Böhme.

Much the same applies to the Englishwoman Jane Leade (1624–1704) and her completely interiorized form of religiosity. As with the Quakers, the direct, inner inspiration by God played an important role in her conception of religion; moreover, she believed in the perfectibility of the pious. On these foundations she established, around 1670, the Philadelphians as a community of the perfected, or more precisely, as a community of love of the true children of God, within which she herself assumed the role of divinely inspired prophetess. Pietists in the Netherlands, Germany, and Switzerland read her works with deep interest, and some were encouraged by them to become separatists. As a result, scattered Philadelphian communities appeared also on the continent within a short period, though they had no staying power and were largely replaced by the Inspiration movement in the first decades of the eighteenth century. In addition to shared apocalyptic expectations—the beginning of Christ's kingdom on earth was widely expected to occur in 1700—what united all of these new groups was the fact that they drew on the spiritualist-theosophical tradition of the seventeenth century, especially as embodied in Jacob Böhme. Among other things, that tradition gave rise to the belief in the original androgynism of humanity, by which was understood the dual-gender creation of humans in male–female form, and in the possibility of a mystical union of humans with the Divine Wisdom (*sophia*) as well as the mystical notion of the divine humanity of Christ.[62]

Yet this current of wisdom-mysticism based on Jacob Böhme and Jane Leade was only one of various manifestations of Radical Pietism. More than a century ago, the church historian Wilhelm Hadorn sought to understand all of these communities as the prevailing current in the last decades of the seventeenth century:

> People were yearning for something new. The spirit of prophesy was poured out, and prophets called by God came forward everywhere. The journeyman spur-maker Johann Georg Rosenbach preached in Heilbronn, in Nuremberg it was the wigmaker Tennhardt, who called himself the clerk [*Kanzlist*] of God, in Frankfurt it was the journey-man shoemaker Dauth who prophesied the fall of the German Em-pire, in Stuttgart the keeper of the Inn zum Hirschen, a man by name of Trautwein, had revelations, and in Silesia it was even chil-dren who were seized by the spirit of prayer. They began to preach and to pray on country roads and in city squares.[63]

To be sure, from our perspective today the reference to a prevailing "yearning for something new" is no longer an adequate historical explanation. Rather, the intense apocalyptic beliefs and the measures that the authorities every-where took against the Pietist conventicles played a crucial role, as did, un-doubtedly, the never-ending wars that began in the 1670s and extended into the eighteenth century, along with the economic troubles in their wake.

It was not only artisans who were seized by these currents of radical separatism; individual clergyman who were sympathetic to Pietism were also drawn in. The best-known example is Johann Wilhelm Petersen. Beginning in 1673, he lectured on theology at the University of Giessen, and from there he came into contact with Philipp Jacob Spener in Frankfurt—a meeting that had a profound impact: Petersen became a Pietist. After advancing through various church positions, he was eventually appointed Superintendant in the northern Germany city of Lüneburg in 1688. By then he was married to a kindred spirit, the noblewoman Johanna Eleonore von Merlau. Even before their move to Lüneburg, Petersen and his wife had been moving decisively in the direction of mystical separation and an exaggerated apocalypticism. In Lüneburg, Petersen clashed openly with the Lutheran clergy, and the conflict cost him his position. This is how Petersen and von Merlau became Sepa-ratists, central figures of separatist Radical Pietism with an extensive network of correspondence that they cultivated attentively. The apocalyptic faith of the Petersens expressed itself in a deeply felt chiliasm, in the firm conviction that Christ's thousand-year kingdom was imminent.

Central to Radical Pietism and its precursor currents was the importance of direct divine inspiration and chosenness, which meant that the role of the Bible in attaining a certainty of personal salvation tended to recede into the background. That is why awakening and spiritual rebirth played a far more important role here than they did in moderate, non-separatist Pietism. Terms such as "awakening" and "rebirth" should therefore not be used synonymously when speaking of Radical Pietism, since the former was a process brought on by external forces (preachers, prophets, or God himself), while the latter was the goal of an inner process.[64] On various occasions, both awakening and rebirth found expression also in autobiographical texts. A text of this sort served—much as it did in Quakerism, for example—as a testimony to the rest of the world and simultaneously as an instrument of missionary work. As a result, among Pietists (and not least Radical Pietists) such personal writings were often printed, just as they were among Quakers. Johann Heinrich Reitz's *History of the Reborn*, the first part of which was published in 1698, is an important example of this new written tradition,[65] as is the significant *Impartial History of the Church and Heresy* from the pen of Gottfried Arnold (1666–1714), who was for some time a Separatist. Like the biography of the Pietist Samuel König from Bern, who spent many years in exile in Wetterau, the life of Gottfried Arnold shows that the road leading to separation from the established churches was not necessarily a path of no return.

The Pietist conventicles established by Philipp Jacob Spener, the *Collegia pietatis*, as special circles of the pious,

> developed in Radical Pietism further into communes or life
> communities.... The chiliasm of the religiosity of Radical Pietism,
> the certainty that Christ's return was imminent . . . led, in reference to
> the Revelation of John, to the ingathering of the "true children of
> God" into a community.... Radical Pietists denied that preachers
> who were not among the reborn had the competence to teach or offer
> salvation, and the sacraments of the Church were rejected as features
> of the external, the Babylonian church. Instead, men and women constantly
> recreated community through readings from the Bible and
> from Johann Arndt's *True Christianity*, as well as through common
> worship involving prayers and singing.[66]

That the writings of Radical Pietists of a mystical-apocalyptic bent were also read and resonated in some of the more remote areas is revealed by the autobiographical writings of Daniel Müslin, a pastor in Bern. Beginning in 1702, when he served for a few years as pastor in Boltigen in the Simmental, he found himself compelled to provide special instruction in the vicarage to various members of the congregation following the weekly Sunday service, in order to counteract "leanings toward the false opinions and books of Dennhardt, Daut, and Peterson" in his village.[67] Among these Separatist-minded authors, the Nuremberg wigmaker Jacob Tennhardt was especially influential in

Switzerland. His conception of an intensive, personal piety, for which he drew on Johann Arndt, was combined with a resolute rejection of the established churches and their clergy. However, Tennhardt's special influence in Geneva did not produce an all-out separatism on the part of the local Pietists; instead, it led initially above all to a heightened formation of conventicles. When the authorities launched an investigation in 1718, it was determined that about 30 or 40 individuals were participating in the meetings, and that the readings included, alongside Thomas a Kempis's *Imitatio Christi* and Johan Bunyan's *Pilgrim's Progress*, not only the works of Tennhardt, but also those of the mystical-quietist Enthusiasts Madame Guyon and Antoinette de Bourignon.[68]

Like Geneva and the Thurgau in eastern Switzerland, Germany saw in those years a close interweaving of Separatist Pietism and the Inspiration movement. That is especially true of the Reformed counties of Isenburg, Sayn-Wittgenstein, and Berleburg in Wetterau (Hesse), which became a refuge par excellence for Radical Pietists and Inspired in the eighteenth century, and—somewhat later—also for the Moravians who were temporarily driven out of Lusatia.

In the early eighteenth century, the outstanding figure of Separatism in Wetterau, which was shaped in part by a number of women from the high nobility,[69] was the lone Spiritualist Ernst Christoph Hochmann von Hochenau (1670–1721). Community formation was not universally a constitutive characteristic of Radical Pietism. The mystical-spiritualist view of the path to salvation impeded the formation of a group—such as occurred, for example, in Hochmann's immediate neighborhood among the New Baptists (*Neutäufer*) of Schwarzenau. Hochmann's version of Pietism led, almost invariably, to a strong revaluation of the spiritual self-perfection of the individual. For along with the categorical rejection of the "Babylonian Church," one finds in his thinking heavy borrowings from a mysticism that reached back into the late Middle Ages, and, among other things, a notion—born of this orientation— that the true church was a purely spiritual church, as well as a doctrine of marriage which, in the sense of a spiritualized partnership, recommended a transcending of "external copulation."[70]

In stark contrast to the conception of marriage of Hochmann von Hochenau, free love as a ritual of sanctification and purification was practiced in the circle that established itself around Eva von Buttlar in Allendorf in northern Hesse in January of 1700. This community, denounced by contemporaries as the "Buttlarian gang," arose from the union of Radical Pietists from the Wetterau and northern Hesse who connected their hopes for the second coming of Christ and the beginning of the Golden Age with the start of the new century. When these hopes were dashed, the members of this group in no way abandoned their fundamental, intensely eschatological sentiment. Instead, their own community was now seen as a kind of sanctuary, "in which the true community was to be constituted until the second coming of Christ."[71] The group's controversial sexual practices led not only to its members being dismissed by contemporaries—as well as later historiography—as the "Buttlarian gang," but also to repeated expulsions, until finally, after 1706, Altona in Schleswig-Holstein offered a refuge to the group, which had by then evolved into a secret society.

Among the external characteristics the society assumed until it went into hiding (1706) was a particular hairstyle. For a while the women wore their hair short, and the men had special beards and clothing. In addition, the so-called love kiss was a sign of membership in the group: members (including those of the opposite sex) embraced and kissed each other. With the death of Eva von Buttlar in 1721, at the latest, the existence of the society, originally founded as a philadelphian community of love, came to an end.[72] What the British historian Lyndal Roper called the "sexual utopianism" of radical Anabaptists groups of the sixteenth century found its continuation here, in Radical Pietism.

The Inspired

After Louis XIV of France revoked the Edict of Nantes in 1685, thousands of Huguenots left that country, and there was no open resistance to the king's measures. The one exception was in the Cévennes mountains in the south of France, where the peasant population adhered to Calvinism more so than anywhere else in the country. At the turn of the seventeenth century, the Cévennes region saw an open revolt of the Huguenot camisards[73] against Louis XIV's drastic confessional policy. Louis was forced to wage a difficult guerrilla war, and it was several months before the last fortress of the Reformed was taken and leveled. Exaggerated apocalyptic speculations were part of the self-image of the camisards threatened by military destruction, and they also played a crucial role in the outbreak of open rebellion.[74] In this extraordinarily tense situation, various young women and men emerged as prophets who, as the direct mouthpieces of the Holy Spirit, gave expression to this apocalyptic sentiment. Their public appearances involved bodily convulsions and contortions. They stood, from our perspective today, at the beginning of the Inspired movement of the first half of the eighteenth century.

When the resistance to the royal troops seemed increasingly hopeless, a number of these camisard preachers decamped to Geneva, where they gathered a new band of followers. More consequential still was the circumstance that another small group of camisard prophets made it to London, where they be-gan, in the opening years of the eighteenth century, to form a community of followers who were composed of those recruited from the class of urban artisans and individual representatives of the educated class.[75] In the follow-ing years, delegates of the London camisards—called the French Prophets in English historiography—engaged in successful missionary work in the Nether-lands and in Germany. As a result, direct links to like-minded individuals in Halle were established in 1714/15 and to religious Separatists in the Wetterau. In the Wetterau, especially in the county of Wittgenstein, "Eberhard Ludwig Gruber (1665–1728) and Johann Friedrich Rock (1667–1749) were drawn into this movement, assumed leading roles, and established a code of rules for their religious gatherings."[76] Rock and Gruber undertook repeated missionary expeditions to Saxony, Württemberg, Bohemia, and Switzerland, where they were involved in the establishment of new communities of Inspired.

The Inspired would find a lasting resonance especially within Separatism with a Pietist flavor. These were kindred movements, not only by virtue of the special importance they placed on the inner word, but also in a number of other areas in which there was wide agreement: "In both movements we find an indifference toward the sacraments, a detailed, enthusiastic doctrine of things to come, a disdain for the estate of marriage among some, and a rejec-tion of the state church and its institutions."[77]

One area in which the two movements differed markedly, however, was in the tendency to form communities. Prophets needed listeners. In the In-spired movement, community formation took place on a comparatively much greater scale, which also had something to do, of course, with the seemingly indefatigable traveling and missionary activities of the leaders of the move-ment, which substantially promoted group cohesion.

Between 1719 and 1741, Johann Friedrich Rock traveled through Swit-zerland four times as a missionary and was able, in spite of clashes with clergy and the authorities, to score no small number of successes. At the time of his death in March of 1749, the movement of the Inspired had lost nearly all of its original impulse both in Germany and in Switzerland. In this situation, not a few Swiss Inspired communities joined up with Pietists who were outwardly loyal to the Church but kept an inner distance from the state church.[78] Al-though some of it was absorbed into distanced yet church-loyal Pietism, the Inspired movement represents, along with the New Baptists, the only com-munity of faith arising from Radical Pietism which has survived to this day—in a vanishingly small form, to be sure—as the Amana Colonies in the United States (Iowa).[79]

It would be wrong to assume that the Radical Pietists and the Inspired were universally rejected within the educated culture of their time. On the contrary, upon closer inspection we find a number of individuals who played the role of a connecting link, so to speak. Among them is Isaac Newton's friend Nicolas Fatio d'Huillier of Geneva, who was an excellent mathematician and at the same time one of the followers of the French Prophets in London in the first decade of the eighteenth century. For a time that group also included, within the circle of the Philadelphians in Wetterau, Johann Christian Edelmann, who would become, in the 1740s, something that was rather unusual for the German Enlightenment: a radical critic of Christian-Biblical tradition.

PART III

Fragmentation of Religiosity

6

The Privatization of Piety

The eighteenth century, especially the second half, brought changes that can be summed up under the heading "privatization of piety." In the case of Protestantism, scholars have emphasized that "what began to take shape increasingly after Pietism and the early Enlightenment was a style of church practice that was oriented toward the rhythm of the life-cycle. Both in the bourgeois milieu and in workers' communities [of the nineteenth century], the ties to the church focused on a personal religiosity of life-cycle rites."[1] It has been argued that in eighteenth-century French Catholicism, the increase in an economy of external ecclesiastical-religious gestures that is evident in the changes occurring in wills led invariably to a privatization of religiosity.[2] An apt description of the situation in England was given by Béat-Ludwig von Muralt, a representative of the early Enlightenment: "When it comes to religion, one could almost say that every Englishman has decided to either have everything, at least in his own way, or nothing at all, and that their country, unlike all others, therefore has no hypocrites." In addition to "professional free-thinkers," England also had many "fanatics," among whom were some with "extraordinarily extravagant religions."[3] This quote makes clear that the privatization of religiosity and piety was by no means automatically a process of secularization—and what I mean by secularization in this context, without aiming at a comprehensive definition, is the growing distance of social groups from the churches and a progressive indifference about questions of religious meaning and references to the supernatural.[4]

The following sections focus on aspects of secularization and "de-Christianization." But my intent is in no way to create the impression that the development of religiosity in eighteenth-century Europe was above all a story of decline and decay. The discussion in the previous chapters of Jansenists, Moravians, and Methodists is enough to show that there were important "countervailing"[5] trends to secularization, some of which reverberated uninterrupted into the nineteenth century and were, among other things, absorbed into Revivalism, the "Second Awakening," or Ultramontanism. These tendencies can be circumscribed with the terms "re-Christianization" and "sacralization," though for the reasons explained below, I prefer the second of the two. At the same time, it would be wrong to play late Jansenism, Pietism, and Methodism off against the Enlightenment (and vice versa).[6] There were also many points at which the two currents intersected—especially between the Catholic Enlightenment and Jansenism.[7]

Hartmut Lehmann has emphasized that the term "de-Christianization," favored until now by French historians in particular, "is much more precise in grasping the waning of a specific Christian influence, be it in politics and the establishment of a political order, in the maintenance of public morality, in the educational system, or in the approach to sickness and death"; consequently, it allowed for "a more precise formulation of scholarly questions."[8] This recommendation is problematic for a history of religion that proceeds from a perspective of society as a whole, in other words, one that seeks to fully embrace also the sphere of popular religiosity with all its so-called "syncretisms" (for lack of a better word), because it implies, on a case by case basis, that one must define what should be regarded as Christian. But with respect to the level of popular religiosity, whose relationship to the Church's view of orthodox piety was often also filled with tension, such determinations are dubious. For that reason, I continue to prefer the broader concept of "secularization" to that of "de-Christianization," and implicitly also the concept of "sacralization" to that of "re-Christianization."[9]

What factors stand behind the secularization of the eighteenth (and to some extent even of the seventeenth) century? It has been rightly pointed out that confessional differences and divergences demonstrated that religion was unsuitable as an instrument for the "social integration of society as a whole," and that the result of this realization could be the gradual transformation of religion "into an aspect of how one lived life that could be functionally detached and separated out."[10] Applied to Europe as a whole, however, this represents only *one* specific, causal explanation for the fact that from the middle of the eighteenth century, at the latest, the tension in the relationship between traditional religiosity and the sociocultural demands of everyday life increased and could thus, over the long term, lead to a decline in the importance of religion, especially in the public realm. How that process unfolded was very different from region to region. In Catholic southern Europe, especially on the Iberian peninsula, it did not pick up steam until the nineteenth century. In England, by contrast, it began to some extent as early as the late seventeenth century. So far, modern historical scholarship on religion and mentalities has not fully examined secularization phenomena on a transnational and comparative basis.[11] That is why three of the four following sections are embedded within the context of national histories. Such an approach is also justified by the fact that the national traditions of research on secularization are still very different at this time.

Enlightenment and Religion

Roughly between 1680 and 1720 there took place, among the learned and within the educated strata in western and central Europe, a transformation which—by completing what had already begun in humanism and the Renaissance—helped a new view of the world to achieve a breakthrough: a view in which the individual human being was understood once and for all and in every respect as the shaper of social, political-institutional, and historical reality.[12] The Enlightenment was beginning to gain its footing. Its emphatic focus on humanity and human abilities found an early and highly popular expression in Alexander Pope's *Essay on Man*, published between 1732 and 1734. Similar to Pope, the German-Jewish Enlightenment philosopher and writer Moses Mendelssohn summarized his intellectual goals in the statement, "At all times, I set the purpose [*Bestimmung*] of man as the measure and goal of all our efforts and endeavors."[13]

The associations of the Enlightenment period as the expression of a new, strongly bourgeois-flavored culture of the discursive conversation—from the Freemasonry lodges to the provincial academies to the reading societies—led indirectly to a weakening of conventional, estate-based forms of life, and, in connection with this, also to an individualization or privatization of the realm of socioreligious experience. Enlightened reason became the noblest and nimblest instrument of anthropocentric criticism of the intellectual and cultural tradition. Theology, too, came to feel this new breeze, although Catholicism clearly posed a greater challenge to enlightened criticism than did Protestantism.[14] For example, the corresponding processes of intellectual transformation were far less dramatic in Brandenburg-Prussia than in France. The well-known materialists of the Enlightenment are not found in Germany, England, Scotland, or Italy, but in France: Helvétius, d'Holbach, LaMettrie.

But even from a decidedly non-materialistic side, the Enlightenment made crucial contributions to the process that stripped theology of its place at the very top of the hierarchy of the disciplines. In general, though, the German Enlightenment was far less severe in its criticism of the Church than its French counterpart. As van Dülmen has noted, "For the critical engagement with the Church, religion, and Christianity, the eighteenth century was certainly still a Christian—indeed an ecclesiastical-confessional—century."[15] Sheridan Gilley cast his conclusion in even more general terms: "So in England, Scotland, Germany, Holland, and English North America, 'enlightenment' found a home *within* the Christian churches."[16]

Since the Enlightenment critique of theology included a fundamentally optimistic view of humanity, it was primarily concerned—in addition to the question of theodicy, proof of the goodness of God—with the doctrine of original sin. If the evil of human beings today was—as in Rousseau—merely the result of a false development of history and society and correctable through the proper education, there was no need for a proof of God.[17] When it came to his perfectibility, man was, henceforth, sufficient unto himself. It goes without saying that this view also posed a strong challenge to the traditional notion of divine punishments for collective sins in the form of natural catastrophes, epidemics, and wars. However, the massive earthquake in Lisbon in 1755, with its enormous destruction and loss of life, put a noticeable damper on the Enlightenment's optimistic view of humankind.

Closely linked with the discussion of traditional notions of human sinfulness and the problems of theodicy was the question of the eternal punishment of the damned. An intensive debate over the existence of hell had arisen as early as the seventeenth century, though we must not overlook the fact that it was not always a critical early Enlightenment stance that led to the rejection of the idea of the eternal torment of hell, but often an apocalyptic or chiliastic view of the world.[18]

It is evident, of course, that as early as late eighteenth century the Enlightenment had enemies who rejected the enlightened critique of religion and the church. These enemies came together in a stance that united Catholics and Protestants "against the secularization of the state, meaning above all against the officially promoted liberal sentiment, to which they opposed the Christian Gospel."[19] Here lie the roots (disparate as they were) that gave rise in the nineteenth century—against the backdrop of Romanticism and political restoration—to Catholic ultramontanism as a reaction to the liberalism of the preceding decades.

The primary reason behind the disparate nature of the roots of religious conservatism in the nineteenth century is that the eighteenth was the century not only of the Enlightenment, but also of religious "enthusiasts" like the Pietists, the Moravians, the Camisards, the Inspired, the Methodists, the Theosophists, and the Rosicrucians. The intellectual historian trained to be forward-looking may well dismiss the Rosicrucians as an "aberration." And yet one is left with the fact that they had a hand in shaping the age of the Enlightenment in western, central, and southern Europe, in addition to possessing a high degree of their own reasoned purpose. For even if those on

> the dark side of the Enlightenment . . . shielded themselves from the light of reason, because they feared its corrosive effect on the normative and social order on principled grounds, they did so out of a self-awareness whose modernity was in no way inferior to that of the proponents of the Enlightenment. Hence it was not only the Enlightenment that was Janus-headed: its conservative, admittedly anti-rational counterpart, also looked back to the past to shape modernity. And like the former, the latter also acted on the conviction that a human being was in his core a God-like being, whose second, liberating act of creation nature had merely been awaiting.[20]

And yet there is no denying that the Enlightenment's critique of religion and the church did have a certain impact. For example, it can be demonstrated that in France after 1750—especially in the Paris book market—there was a noticeable quantitative decline in printed matter with religious content, while the production of books in the sciences and arts increased strongly.[21] The catalogues of the Leipzig fair attest to a marked decline in theological literature in the second half of the eighteenth century. More revealing still, however, is the enormous surge (a sixteen-fold growth between 1740 and 1800) in the belles-lettres offered in Leipzig, from poetry to popular literature, which now took over the function of the Christian literature of edification.[22]

Microhistorical findings do not always confirm the large trends: in Laichingen in Württemberg, for example, it was largely the "religious attitude to reading matter and reading"—influenced not least by Swabian Pietism—that "brought forth the extraordinary wealth of books in Laichingen's households in the eighteenth and early nineteenth centuries."[23] This contrary finding is merely another clear indication that the only historical perspective that is able to do justice to the Enlightenment period is one that pays substantive attention both to the conventional Enlightenment phenomena and to the simultaneous, seemingly "countervailing" tendencies.

In Germany, the secularization of the state under the Enlightenment banner was deliberately promoted, especially by the cameralists among high government officials: "All cameralists were deeply interested in orderliness, diligence, and hard work, and religious education—as soon as it was adapted to the norms of religious policy—was regarded as the ideal instrument for changing popular mentality in the desired direction."[24] Such motives prompted officials trained as cameralists to take measures against pilgrimages, because the masses that came together for the larger pilgrimages were not amenable to social and moral supervision and control and were therefore a thorn in their sides. In fact, the question of the socioeconomic costs of Catholic piety became a fashionable topic among cameralists. The exceedingly detailed list of shortcomings compiled by the anonymous author of the polemical tractate *Why is the prosperity of Protestant countries so much greater than that of Catholic countries?* (1772), noted on the Catholic side that "the loss of time from thirty additional feast days, attendance at Mass, pilgrimages, processions, and carnival indulgences...adds up, along with the 'dissoluteness' that is usually involved,...to enormous damage to the national economy, which Protestant countries avoid."[25]

One of the key words in this area was "education," and self-criticism was occasionally heard even at the highest levels of the Church. For example, in the 1770s the Enlightenment theologian Pietro Tamburini, who was close to Jansenism, vehemently opposed the curia's traditional view that the laity should not be exposed to the Bible in the vernacular by asking—rhetorically—whether most of the conventional, popular devotional texts had not helped to promote "a childish and superstitious devotion, instead of a lasting and truly Christian piety."[26] The high point of cameralistic reforms on the Catholic side was undoubtedly Josephinism—some of whose longer-term effects, however, were indirectly undone by the French Revolution, as were some of the achievements of previous cameralistic reforms in this area. For as early as the 1790s, the revival of the only recently "abolished" pious practices seemed like a promising instrument for strengthening the population's ideological resistance to the influences of the French Revolution.[27]

The aloofness of proponents of the Enlightenment not only from religious enthusiasm, but also from the religiosity of the common people, is also reflected unmistakably in the contemporary discussion of melancholy. Especially popular in this discussion were reflections on whether artisans and artists who sat quietly were susceptible to melancholy. The lives and teachings of the two shoemakers Jacob Böhme and George Fox attracted renewed attention—though they could not expect to be met with approval, as the Enlightenment critique of Enthusiasts was approaching a popular-philosophical high point in Johann Christoph Adelung's seven-volume *History of Human Folly* (1785–89).[28] Moreover, Adelung argued that the Quaker George Fox had in a sense been born into his role by noting that his father had been a weaver: "And since this craft... easily produces melancholy (*Schwermut*) and gloominess (*Trübsinn*), our George may well have been born with a good portion of this disposition."[29]

As one looks at Europe in the age of the Enlightenment, it is important to bear in mind not only the enormous regional and sociocultural differences, but also the fact that *enlightened* Europe existed only at the top of a hierarchy of quite diverse and varied cultural worlds.[30] Of course there were also fundamental *social* processes in the eighteenth century that, sooner or later, transformed the relationship of all social strata to the supernatural and the hereafter. This is especially true of the decline in mortality. Although death did not yet disappear from daily life, as it has for the most part in modern industrial societies, compared to the seventeenth century it did lose some of its public presence, its undeniable reality notwithstanding. Above all, it was privatized—and thereby to a certain extent also secularized—and lost an essential part of its previously public dimension.[31]

Let me return to the cameralists. They and their Enlightenment allies vigorously pushed for a reduction in the number of feast days not only in Germany, but in nearly all Catholic areas of Europe. The "wave of reduction" triggered by them did not wane until the 1790s, after the outbreak of the French Revolution.[32] Within Catholicism, however, the trend reaches back into the pre-Enlightenment seventeenth century: as early as 1642, Pope Urban VIII reduced the traditional canon of feasts down to only thirty-four feast days commanded by the Church, and he justified this step on economic grounds.[33] On the Protestant side the old hymnal was replaced by a new one, brought up to date under Enlightenment influences. In some areas of Germany, these two measures encountered in part open resistance by the faithful.

The reduction of feast days in the second half of the eighteenth century constituted a radical intervention in the feast-day customs of traditional popular culture. Popular resistance to the relevant decrees was accordingly vehement, and it manifested itself chiefly in stubborn rebelliousness—for example, protests during Mass, as in the territory of Lucerne, in Bavaria, in Westphalia, and in the Bamberg area.[34] In the jurisdiction of Freiburg in Switzerland, the discontent merged with the resistance to other, unpopular measures by the city authorities and led, in 1781, to an uprising of the peasants—especially

in the area around Greyerz (Gruyère)—against the rule of the urban patrici-
ate; the revolt was led by Nicolas Chenaux and was bloodily suppressed.[35]
The most serious charge laid against the authorities in nearly all of these
instances of unrest was that they were acting like heretics. As Hersche has
explained,

> In spite of contract theory and natural law, the old theological legit-
> imization of political power had not vanished entirely even in the
> Europe of the Enlightenment.... Though the princes were now
> wavering between the various levels on which power was legiti-
> mated, for the people, who knew nothing of natural law and contract
> theory, the traditional theological arguments were decisive even in
> the age of the Enlightenment. So if the people denounced the ruler
> and his deputies, down to the local officials and the priest, as un-
> Catholic, they were—in a sense—stripping him of political legiti-
> macy.... At the same time, they were legitimizing for themselves all
> means of resistance to the heretical authorities, including the use of
> force.[36]

Enlightened reforms of hymnals were carried out in the late eighteenth
century in most Lutheran and Reformed territories of Germany. Like the reduction in feast days, this measure also led to resistance and protests, which
accompanied the introduction of the new hymnals in the years between 1767
and 1811.[37] The new Catholic songbooks also stirred up emotions in, for example, the Archdiocese of Mainz, Bamberg-Würzburg, and the Archbishopric
of Salzburg.[38] Although the nearly decade-long resistance in Württemberg,
for example, became increasingly politicized against the backdrop of the
French Revolution, the clashes even in this case document above all the obvious chasms between various socioreligious and cultural worlds. This is equally
true of the resistance to the reduction of Catholic feast days. While the Enlightened reformers sought "to make 'true religion' more tangible, visible, and
palpable to both the common and the educated person,"[39] the "common man"
saw in the rhetoric of the enlighteners a "perversion of religion, which he
regarded as his own."[40]

To the extent that the resistance to the new hymnals was occasionally
justified with the concern that the reforms pushed by the authorities and the
Church could lead to a return to Catholicism, there are clear parallels to the
situation in late eighteenth-century England. There, the largest English rebellion of the eighteenth century, the Gordon Riots of 1780, arose from popular
opposition to the legal measures that the government took to improve the
political status of Catholics.[41]

We can draw the following conclusions from this necessarily brief over view:

1. The effects of the Enlightenment in the countries I have examined more closely—England, France, and Germany—differed consider-ably, not only regionally, but also within the various religio-cultural worlds of the population. On occasion, enlightened reform efforts gave rise, as early as the last decades of the eighteenth century, to sus-tained resistance, not only within the educated class, but also among the common people; one can regard this resistance as the precur-sors of the Restoration.

2. The critique of religion and the church articulated by proponents of the Enlightenment, and the reform efforts by the Church under the banner of the Enlightenment, were always accompanied by other, "countervailing" tendencies—with respect to both radical ecclesiastical Separatism and the religious Awakening, and the activities of Rosi-crucians, Theosophists, and prophets such as Alexander, Count Cagliostro, and Franz Anton Mesmer. That these other tendencies were not always and automatically "countervailing" in the usual sense, is revealed by manifold crossover links to the Enlightenment, em-bodied in men like Gottfried Arnold or Johann Christian Edelmann.

The Beginnings of Secularization in England

In examining the secularization processes in England—chiefly in the period from the late seventeenth to the first half of the eighteenth centuries—I will start with the Camisards, the apocalyptic prophets from the Cevènnes region in southern France who began to gather a group of followers in London in the early years of the eighteenth century.[42]

The spectacular activities of the so-called French Prophets and the fact that three of their members were put in the pillory in December 1707 were the chief motivations behind the "Letter Concerning Enthusiasm" (1708) by Anthony Cooper, Earl of Shaftesbury.[43] In it, the philosopher Shaftesbury ar-gued emphatically that it was no longer necessary to use the force of the state against religious enthusiasts like the Camisards and their followers, and that included the pillory. Ridicule alone was sufficient to dismiss such movements for good. In the eyes of critical observers, the French Prophets had already disqualified themselves by the role that women prophets played in their midst.[44]

Shaftesbury was by no means the only English man of letters and philosopher to denounce religious enthusiasm at the time. In fact, he was under the influence, not least among others, of John Locke, who, in his work "The Reasonableness of Christianity" (1695), had sought—in agreement with the natural theology of his day—to highlight the natural dimensions of a Christian way of life, that is to say, those elements not derived from revelation. Shaftesbury, who, like Locke, stands at the beginning of the intensive discourse on virtue within the English and Scottish Enlightenment, was also eager to root the origins of civic values in this world, in humanity's natural dispositions. Needless to say, his critique of religious notions that did not fit into this concept was far more vehement than Locke's.

Shaftesbury's attack on religious "enthusiasts" was part of a conscious attempt to promote a new, virtuous "culture of politeness," the culture of "polite society," those members of the middle and upper classes who—unlike the rude and ignorant masses—were willing and able to square the new worldview of the educated, which was guided in large part by the discourse on the natural sciences, with the traditional tenets of Christianity.[45] In Scotland in the late eighteenth century, these efforts found their specific expression in the "academization of virtue."[46] In this context, Keith Thomas and other English historians have rightly pointed to the gradual "separation of popular from learned views of the natural world" that began in the late seventeenth century.[47]

The growing social and cultural significance of this process of separation is evident, for example, in the way in which the question of witchcraft and its persecution was dealt with at various cultural levels at the turn of the seventeenth century. The last execution for witchcraft in England took place in 1685, the last condemnation of a witch in 1712. In 1736, the crime of witchcraft was finally removed from the statute books with majority backing in Parliament. Although the courts increasingly refused to even entertain accusations of witchcraft, this change in court practice had little immediate impact on popular beliefs: we know of a whole series of cases between 1665 and 1751 in which alleged witches fell victim to "community justice" carried out by enraged neighbors or communities in the face of uncooperative courts.[48]

While we know that the paths of educated culture and popular culture in England diverged markedly in the closing decades of the seventeenth century, we still have little coherent understanding of the popular forms of religiosity in eighteenth and nineteenth-century England. Statements by clergymen indicate that church attendance, especially by the "meaner sort" of people, declined in the decades after 1660, following the Stuart Restoration.[49] Yet one must not place too much credence in such testimony: early modern clergymen everywhere, not only in England, were only too willing to complain loudly about their parishioners' laxity and lack of discipline. At any rate, there are good indications that the traditional forms of religiosity were preserved much better among the lower classes of English society in the course of the eighteenth century than among the middle and upper classes, as is suggested especially by the great success of the early Methodist domestic missionary work in the second half of the eighteenth century. Thus "countervailing" tendencies are found also, and especially, in England: in May of 1768, John Wesley complained in his diary that "the English in general, and indeed most of the men of learning in Europe, have given up all accounts of witches and apparitions, as mere old wives' tales." They were well aware that giving up the belief in witches was essentially tantamount to losing the Bible.[50]

We can trace the roots of the criticism of religious Enthusiasm within the educated classes of England back to the middle of the seventeenth century, and here we must posit a bundle of causal aspects and triggering factors.[51] One clearly evident cause was the danger that contemporaries believed they could perceive in the movement of the early Quakers and in other chiliastic groups of the late 1650s. The perception of this threat, whether realistic or not, was an important factor contributing to the Restoration of the Stuarts in 1659/1660. It was reflected, post factum, not only in the religious policy of parliament in the 1660s, which was deeply biased and crude, but also, and in a more differentiated way, in the attitudes of members of the Royal Society. Thomas Sprat's *History of the Royal Society*, written only a few years after the founding of this English scientific society in 1660, already reveals the extent to which leading members of the Royal Society had taken up the battle against "fanaticism" and "enthusiasm."[52]

The critical attitude of which I have spoken was further promoted by the fact that from the middle of the seventeenth century, a growing number of members of the English educated classes began to label believers in witches and miracles as "melancholy" or simply as "insane" in the psychiatric sense, as a way of distancing themselves from them: "By the middle of the eighteenth century the prevailing view among the educated elite was that people who claimed to have divine inspirations or devilish afflictions were insane."[53]

These kinds of labels were based, in part, on the scientific discourse about melancholy in the preceding decades. In part, however, they also refer to the simultaneous attempt by theologians (the so-called Latitudinarians) to reconcile the doctrinal orientation of the official church with the new, mechanistic natural philosophy. Moreover, there was a parallel track of efforts by other educated contemporaries to "rationalize" and systematize the observation of signs of divine providence in everyday life.[54]

What these contemporaries, like the Puritan theologian Matthew Poole around the middle of the seventeenth century, had in mind was a grandly conceived, systematic registry of all signs of divine providence, from unusual celestial phenomena to floods and earthquakes to monstrous births; the underlying belief was that compiling such signs would allow them to identify certain laws and thus enable them to demystify, as it were, God's presence in nature and in human history. From the perspective of the educated classes, such efforts left little justification for religious enthusiasm.

This stance opposed to enthusiasm was further reinforced by the pressure toward secularization that was exerted by the effective destruction of the Church of England's spiritual monopoly during the upheavals of the 1640s and 1650s. All of these various factors combined to bring about a marked decline in contemporary providentialism.[55]

Of course, this was a class-specific phenomenon. For example, the great popularity of religious tracts within the popular literature of the late seventeenth century points to a genuine interest in religious questions extending far beyond the circles of Nonconformists and Dissenters. The tremendous success of John Bunyan's *The Pilgrim's Progress*, first published in 1672, suggests that the rather streamlined natural theology of the Latitudinarians did not appeal to everyone, and especially that it was not in accord with the religious thinking and feeling of the common people.[56] In *Pilgrim's Progress* this becomes clear in various passages, as a kind of perspective from below—as when, for example, an atheist, whose name is "Shame," identifies himself as a representative of the upper class who is making fun of the lower classes and the modest living conditions of the "true pilgrims," that is, the real believers. "Shame" also reproaches the same believers for their "ignorance of the times in which they lived, and want of understanding in all natural science."[57] On several occasions Bunyan also targets the stigmatization of believers as melancholics.

It has been rightly pointed out that the educated class's criticism of the religiosity of the common people does not, in and of itself, automatically constitute a process of secularization.[58] However, within the specific context of England's religio-cultural development in the decades after 1660, this criticism joins many other factors to form an overall picture of a trend that can be seen as the foundation of a process of secularization. That trend is clearly visible in Shaftesbury, and the so-called mechanization of the scientific worldview also played a causal role.[59] The notion of mechanization is best illustrated by the analogy of the cosmos as a clockwork, which was prevalent among seventeenth-century scientists, from Kepler to Boyle. The image of God as clockmaker implied that He intervened only very occasionally in His own creation. Yet it was precisely the idea of daily divine intervention in the world that formed the basis of the traditional belief in God's special providence. English scientists of the seventeenth century thus found themselves confronted with the task of reconciling the doctrine of special providence with their own view of the order of nature.

Against this background, the opposition of the vast majority of influential English scientists of the later seventeenth century to the natural philosophy of Descartes, in general, and to the Cartesian Thomas Hobbes, in particular, makes perfect sense. Descartes was suspected of materialism, because in the eyes of many contemporaries his equation of matter and space made the presence of God in this world impossible. Until well into the eighteenth century, nearly all noted proponents of the natural sciences defended the notion of an "interventionist" God.[60] In spite of the materialist implications that could also be derived from his theory of gravity, Isaac Newton clung to this same notion until his death in 1727. This stance by the leading scientists undoubtedly slowed the secularization of thinking within the educated class.

At the turn of the seventeenth century, the Boyle Lectures became an important instrument in the defense of the traditional image of God. At his death in 1691, Robert Boyle had endowed eight public lectures to be delivered annually in one of London's churches. Their purpose was to provide—from both a theological and scientific perspective—proof of the necessity of the Christian religion. In their published form they represented for several decades an important means not only of spreading Boyle's concerns, but also of defending Newton's natural philosophy.[61]

It can thus be said that the worldview—and thus also the religious interpretation of the world—of England's middle and upper classes was unmistakably secularized beginning with tentative steps around the middle of the seventeenth century, and then on a much broader basis since the beginning of the eighteenth century. After all, "secularization" is not tantamount to "de-Christianization": in contrast, for example, to the French Enlightenment, with its sharp criticism of the church and religion, the propagation of a natural theology by leading members of the scientific establishment prevented free-thinking from exerting a broad effect in England. This process of secularization was, to a substantial degree, accompanied by a gradual separation between the educated and the popular worlds of cultural experience. By contrast, there are—at least for the later seventeenth and the eighteenth centuries—no truly discernible indications of a secularization of the worldview and lifestyle of the common people. It was only in the course of the nineteenth century that more pronounced inner adjustments to the external demands and temptations of modernity took place within this segment of the population.[62]

Déchristianisation in France

While certain tendencies toward secularization within the middle and upper strata already become visible in England before the Enlightenment of the eighteenth century, in France Enlightenment and secularization move essentially along parallel chronological tracks. It would be wrong, however, to regard the Enlightenment in general as the cause of the secularization processes in France. It was, undoubtedly, the reason for the wide diffusion of Freemasonry, but its influence on the changes in mentality in the later eighteenth century—of which I will speak presently—was, at best, indirect: "One must not forget that the vast majority of the population remains nearly completely unreceptive to the message of the [Enlightenment] philosophers.... To the extent that one can note changes in the religious practices of the French between 1760 and 1790, there is no doubt that the blame rests only in exceptional instances with Voltaire or Rousseau."[63] On the other hand, when it comes to the remarkable spread of Freemasonry in the decades before the Revolution, there is no doubt that one can see it as one result of the Enlightenment's critique of the church and religion.

Michel Vovelle has spoken of a profound change in mentality in the decades between the middle of the eighteenth century and the outbreak of the Revolution.[64] He emphasizes that we are talking not only about the well-known transformation in intellectual history from 1750 to 1770; rather, it was a much profounder change, one that cannot be explained simply as a reflex triggered by the Enlightenment. At the same time, he also rejects interpretations that claim that this watershed in the history of mentality in the second half of the eighteenth century was merely the end result of long-term trends reaching back into the seventeenth century. Vovelle is right when he declares that such interpretations are much too mechanical and teleological. He contends that before 1789—but within a fairly *short* period of time—a change occurred in the basic religious, moral, and social attitudes of a substantial part of the French population; this change was profound in some of its particulars and should be seen as an important precondition for the Revolution.

Mortality, especially infant mortality, was very high in the ancien régime.[65] Between 1650 and 1750, the average rate of mortality in France was more than three times what it is today. However, a comparison with modern conditions is not entirely appropriate: before 1750, unlike today (and this is precisely the point), mortality did not manifest itself in its statistic predictability, but assumed, in the many crises, unpredictable and therefore often catastrophic form. Coping with the constant proximity of death was therefore an important part of religious and ecclesiastical life. To be sure, within Catholicism, the doctrine of purgatory that had arisen in the twelfth century took the sting out of the Biblical distinction between those chosen by God for eternal salvation and those who were damned. Still, given the constant nearness of death, it was important to prepare oneself adequately, so that one would not be forced to stand before *the* judge—a judge against whose verdict and decree there was no appeal—completely unprepared. The theme of the imminence of death and the need for spiritual preparation was picked up repeatedly by many preachers of the time, and it made its way into a whole series of tracts that should be seen as part of the *ars moriendi* tradition, which examined, in other words, the proper way to die from a religious point of view.[66] Until around the middle of the eighteenth century, the religiosity and church life of a majority of the French people continued to stand in the shadow of the presence of death—both real and rhetorical.

That began to change in the middle of the century. Most of the population growth in France in the eighteenth century—which was rather modest compared to that in Spain, England, and Germany—fell into the period after the crises of the 1740s. What was new was that for the first time in French demographic history, this was not followed by a crisis-like setback. In other words, while the growth was relatively small, it remained constant during this period and promoted, to a not inconsiderable degree, the expansion of the cities and the urbanization of the country. And it was in the cities, even in smaller provincial ones, that the change in mentalities manifested itself most clearly. It was accentuated in the face of the accelerating population growth since the 1740s and the decline in mortality that began around the same time. In spite of further shortages and famines—which were not comparable to the great, periodic famines of the past—mortality declined slowly, yet noticeably, in many parts of the country. Under these conditions, the days of the spiritual *ars moriendi* literature were numbered: it gave way to what was, on the whole, a more optimistic sense of life.

An important source in which we can see reflected the attitude toward death by population groups that are otherwise anonymous to us are wills. Even if by no means all individuals drafted a will—the percentage of those who did fluctuated between 15% and 50%—analyses of last wills that cover longer periods of time can document changes in the piety and mentality of certain population groups. In French testaments from the sixteenth century, saints and the Virgin Mary hold a place that is nearly equal to that of God and Christ. Then, in the seventeenth and early eighteenth centuries, Mary and the saints wane in importance, and alongside God it is especially Christ who is invoked as the savior of the soul. In the case of Paris and the Provence, serial studies of testaments have shown that this development changed against the backdrop of a declining mortality between 1750 and 1770. A marked secularization of testaments is evident in the Provence after the middle of the century. The percentage of annual Masses that were endowed for the salvation of the donor's soul fell nearly by half in the cities, and then slowly also in the countryside. Michel Vovelle has spoken of a "profound transformation" (*mutation profonde*) following the decade 1750 to 1760.[67] In Provence, that transformation was initially far more pronounced among men than among the apparently "more traditional" women, especially when it comes to the endowment of Masses. In testaments from Paris, a steady secularization of the conventional content is already discernible beginning around 1720.[68] Additional research has now confirmed the substance of these findings for Paris and the Provence.[69] However, in the eighteenth century a very explicit departure from the once customary religious formulas and endowments is still limited primarily to the urban milieu. By contrast, few changes are discernible in the countryside (Anjou, for example), where, incidentally the Tridentine reforms were able to gain a foothold only from the beginning of the eighteenth century.[70]

In various cities—such as Auxerre in Burgundy, Bordeaux, Clamecy, and Rouen—as well as in a number of dioceses that have been studied to date, the number of twelve- and thirteen-year-olds who took First Communion plunged in the last decades of the eighteenth century, as did the number of new admissions to seminaries. The ecclesiastical fraternities, as well, suffered from an acute decline in their membership.[71] Given these facts, it is problematic to interpret—as Vovelle's critics have tried to do—the change in the testamentary formulas not as the expression of a turning away from the sacral, but rather as evidence that piety became interiorized. Instead, there is a good deal of evidence to suggest that it does indeed make sense to speak of a phenomenon of *déchristianisation* in this context. Of course, there is still something unsatisfactory about the concept. For in the end it remains unclear whether it refers to a general turning away from matters religious, or a process of "de-churchification"—even though it would seem to me that Vovelle's research puts the latter front and center. The rise of birth control, for example, could also be understood as a mere distancing vis-à-vis the Church and its dictates, and the same holds true for the decline in the number of new clergy.[72] This confirms, once again, that there are certain methodological objections to "de-christianization" as an analytical category in the history of religion.[73] More recent research has pointed above all to pronounced regional contrasts—especially in Bretagne and the adjoining regions, no comparable phenomenon is discernible in the eighteenth century—and even local differences. There is, however, no need to address again the thesis that the Christianization of the

French people essentially began only in the sixteenth century, a thesis that implicitly rules out a *déchristianisation* in the late eighteenth century.[74]

As a qualification of the notion of *déchristianisation*, we must therefore consider that the process did not in all cases mean an automatic turning away from religious ideas as such. For in spite of its vagueness, the concept of *déchristianisation* describes, after all, primarily a turning away from the Catholic Church and its rituals, and not—in all instances—a simultaneous, general process of secularization. If *déchristianisation* could be equated with secularization, it would be impossible to explain, for example, how spontaneous cults venerating the martyrs of the Revolution could arise after 1789, or how individual—no doubt over-excited—believers could feel that the Revolution marked the beginning of a new, good time and the first step toward the imminent millennium of Biblical prophecy.[75] This is further evidence that an examination of individual aspects of secularization or de-Christianization should not exclude "countervailing" tendencies.

It should also be noted that among the common people in the countryside, who in any case had until this time evaded the disciplinary reach of church and state, forms of religiosity and magical belief were retained into the period of the Revolution and far beyond. And so it should occasion no surprise that the campaign of de-Christianization that was carried from Paris into the countryside by Jacobins and members of the National Convention during the period of Jacobine rule from the winter of 1793 to the summer of 1794 ran into vehement opposition in various parts of the country, especially in the southeast, from Vivarais all the way to Burgundy.[76]

What did the so-called de-Christianization of the Jacobins entail? We learn the following from an entry (November 20, 1793) in the diary of Célestin Guittard, a member of the lower middle-class in Paris:

> Today is 30 Brumaire, *décadi*. A great ceremony took place at the section [the assembly of the Luxembourg quarter], a great procession lasting from three o'clock to five thirty. The procession set out from the square, the canons leading the way, then drummers, then a first group of citizens walking arm in arm, then young men; this was followed by a great crowd of girls dressed in white and women with tri-color sashes, then more drummers and many citizens arm in arm ... and a living goddess who was carried in a chair by eight men.
>
> We marched down the Rue de Vaugirard and the Rue du Regard, then up the Rue des Vieilles Tuileries ... to the Rue de Sèvres, where the section Croix-Rouge was assembled, all with red caps; in the middle of the street they had set up a kind of stage, on which

the Goddess of Liberty was set down, together with a band. . . . From there we went to the Croix-Roge square, where a pyre had been prepared. On top of it on one side stood a large painting with the pope's tiara, a mitre, a stole, and a censer, on the other side the golden escutcheon of monsieur [i.e., the king's brother] and the carved statue of Peter that was above the door to the sacristy at Saint Sulpice. All this was burned on the pyre along with other objects. From there we went to the church of Saint Sulpice, where, in the place of the altar, a kind of theater with decorations from the Comédie Italienne had been erected. . . . Here a philosophe gave speech, to the effect that there was now no religion and no god any more; everything was the work of nature.[77]

The de-Christianization ceremonies out in the countryside took a similar course, presumably with an even more pronounced carnevalesque atmosphere, almost as though popular culture was taking a late revenge for post-Tridentine disciplining.[78]

We know today that the campaign of de-Christianization in the country-side encountered more than acts of resistance on the part of tradition-bound Catholics. This particular campaign originated not only with the Jacobins of the French capital, but simultaneously also in the heartland of rural, peasant France—in the Nièvre.[79] Thus it was not merely a movement imposed from the top down, but in various regions of the country evidently also the spon-taneous expression of an alienation between the people and the Church that predates the Revolution. To be sure, one must draw a clear distinction be-tween these areas and other provinces, for example the Vendée and Brittany, in which the lower strata of the population remained consistently loyal to the village clergy and the church also during the period of the Revolution. It has been variously noted that in Brittany one can posit a continuity in religious-ecclesiastical terms between the ancien régime and modernity in which even the Revolution with its upheavals in the end left no permanent traces.[80] This was not, however, the product of a specifically Tridentine confessionalization; on the contrary, the latter was characterized by typically Baroque, and in some instances far-reaching, compromises between the Church's reformist pre-tensions and local traditions of piety. In fact, one could argue, with some justification, that it was precisely the specifically Tridentine reforms—where successful in France—that, paradoxically, prepared the secularizing thrust of the later eighteenth century.[81]

On the other hand, however, we can note that the Revolutionary oppo-sition to traditional Catholic religiosity and church life, which played no small role in dividing the nation during the revolutionary years, had its roots, in some instances, in the pre-revolutionary decades and thus evidently in the change of mentality that took place in the second half of the eighteenth century.

The growing distance from the Church as an institution became especially obvious after around 1750 in the increasing disapproval that the regular clergy (i.e., monks and nuns) encountered throughout the land. The French monasteries and convents experienced a crisis in the second half of the eighteenth century, which manifested itself above all in the dwindling interest in monastic life on the part of young people.[82] The decline in the number of new recruits occasionally assumed drastic dimensions in the cities, while in other parts of the country, specifically in Normandy and in the alpine zone of the southeast, the number remained above average. It would be wrong, however, to place the responsibility for the waning interest in monastic life, and the distancing from the established Church it expressed, entirely on the so-called process of de-Christianization. In some regions, as for example around Autun in Burgundy or in the south of the country, the influence of Jansenism was also at work, which had nothing but harsh and withering criticism for the Baroque lifestyle of the majority of the monastic clergy at the time. The point is that one must not overlook the fact that the phenomenon of *déchristianisation*, which spread especially in the urban environment, had its counterpart, in the same social environment, in the intensification of piety among a minority of the citizens, and to some extent also among the lower nobility, for the most part under the banner of Jansenism.

Manifested in the waning interest in monastic life was also a growing interest in new, worldly forms of social interaction among the learned. Historians have shown that among the civil servants in Provence and Toulouse, social interactions among the learned shifted from religious-ecclesiastical confraternities to the Freemason lodges. Before 1770, 36% of provincial lawyers and jurists belonged to an ecclesiastical confraternity of the *pénitents,* and only 19% were Freemasons. Within a relatively short period of time, 29% of these men were Freemasons and only 7% were still members of confraternities.[83] Moreover, in this context we should recall the success of other forms of enlightened sociability in the late eighteenth century, such as the salons and reading clubs and the French provincial academies.

The secularization of the way of life on the eve of the Revolution was undoubtedly most readily apparent within the educated class: it was here that the change in mentality I have been discussing merged with the influence of the Enlightenment (which was not from the outset identical with it), each current reinforcing the other and reverberating all the way into the visual arts, which reflected above all the taste of the educated class. The visual arts once and for all cast aside their Baroque pomp and created for themselves a new expressive medium, for example in the civic cult of the hero modeled after antiquity. A classic example of this trend is Louis David's *Oath of the Horatii*, painted in 1784.

By contrast, when it comes to the production of illustrated broadsheets for mass consumption, it is only in the Paris of the eighteenth century that we can observe a decline of religious themes and a corresponding rise of historical and landscape pictures as well as portrait and genre images. In the pictorial production by provincial printers, however, the individual image of religious content was able to hold its preeminent position until the end of the eighteenth century, and in many cases accounted for more than 50% of the relevant output. Yet the traditional broadsheet, which in the countryside retained its predominantly religious content, was joined in the eighteenth century by a series of newer, more profane pictorial printed works, such as illustrated calendars, patterns for drawing and ornamentation, and the illustrated political-satirical print, which was produced in large print runs.[84]

The change in mentality in the second half of the eighteenth century, which occurred chiefly in the urban milieu and took hold of the rural population only in a spotty way, and was, moreover, represented more by men than women,[85] includes, at least indirectly, also the transformation in the population's procreative behavior that is discernible in the urban sphere.

Compared to England, France had a remarkably low average rate of illegitimacy in the eighteenth century. It generally stood at 3% of all births in a given year, at most, with averages in the cities always a little higher than in the countryside. The picture changed within a fairly short period of time after the middle of the eighteenth century: illegitimate births began to increase from decade to decade—less so in the countryside, but all the more strongly in the cities.[86] Prior to the Revolution, the average annual rate rose from 8% to 12% in the larger cities, in Paris even as high as 30%, if one includes all the infants abandoned on the steps of poorhouses or orphanages. Along with the illegitimacy rate, the number of premarital births also showed a pronounced rise in the second half of the eighteenth century, reaching in some cities 10% to 15%—even 20%—of all births before the Revolution, as revealed by a comparison of marriage data with the data on first births.

The rapidly rising rates of illegitimacy and premarital births reflect a clear decline of the Church's influence on sexual morality, especially among urban dwellers. A similar conclusion should be drawn from the first signs of systematically practiced birth control that emerge from the urban population curves after 1770. Scattered indications of earlier birth control, at least as far as broad segments of the population are concerned, are found only in the English village of Colyton in Devonshire in the seventeenth century and in the small town of Saint Lambrecht in Styria.[87] Otherwise, given the current state of research, the assumption is that birth control in the later seventeenth and the eighteenth centuries was practiced only within upper-class families, as for example the ruling councilor families of Geneva and Zurich and the French high nobility.[88]

The first, and initially still scattered, indications from French cities come from the period after about 1740. They mark the beginning of an entirely new era in Europe's population history.[89] In the French countryside, birth control was able to gain a foothold only during and after the Revolution.[90]

Incidentally, the transformation in morality and manners that underlies this phenomenon is also reflected in the content of officially proscribed books: after about 1750, they likewise undergo a marked change.[91] We can infer this from the more than 1,500 prohibited titles of secretly circulating books contained in a list from the official chancery covering the years 1696 to 1773, from relevant police controls and confiscation lists, and from the business records of the Société typographique de Neuchâtel, which Robert Darnton has studied in great detail.[92] Alongside works that were deistic or atheistic in tenor, the prohibited texts circulating in the underground also included the *mauvais livres* genre, which seems to have become increasingly popular after 1750, in which biting criticism of the absolutist state entered into a strange symbiosis with crude pornography. This kind of underground literature could find a broader readership only against the background of the change in manners and morals that I have talked about.

The growing anticlericalism and the increasing distance to the Church; the phenomena that can be associated with the process of the *déchristianisation* of society at the end of the ancien régime; and, finally, the turning away from the Church's moral dictates, evident in the sexual behavior of larger segments of the population: from the perspective of the old order, all of this contributed to the spirit of insubordination which made the Revolution of 1789 and after possible in the first place. As I see it, there is good evidence that the change in mentality identified by Michel Vovelle for the years after 1750 was an important precondition for the Revolution. However, the beginnings of that change cannot be attributed in their entirety to the Enlightenment. Moreover, in contrast to Vovelle, we must remind ourselves emphatically of the "countervailing" tendencies of which I spoke at the beginning of this chapter.

We can even ask ourselves whether demographic change [i.e., the early decline in fertility compared to the rest of Europe] and political revolution were merely two accompanying manifestations of even deeper transformations, namely a change in mentality and the value system. In the end, though, all reflections give rise to a single question: Why did this happen in France? No answer can be found on a global or European level.[93]

Around the middle of the nineteenth century, Alexis de Tocqueville argued that state and society in the French ancien régime had increasingly developed along divergent paths. His important work *The Ancien Régime and the French Revolution* (1856) quite rightly saw that the attempts at centralizing and rationalizing monarchic rule under the banner of Absolutism went hand in hand with a disintegration and individualization of French society. From de Tocqueville's perspective, the Revolution was therefore not least a great sociocultural effort at reintegration, an attempt to bring state and society together again and to reintegrate the diverging parts and groups within the population into a collective framework. From the perspective of the pre-Revolutionary change in mentality, the question of the function of the French Revolution as a sociocultural hinge between the ancien régime and modernity must be framed somewhat differently, for especially in the sphere of manners and morals, the Revolution did not stop or slow down the process—beginning in the course of the eighteenth century—by which morality began to break away from the grip of the Church, that is to say, the individualization and secularization of manners and morals. In fact, the Revolution strengthened this process. In that sense, the Revolution stood at the threshold of a new time, not only politically but also culturally.

Secularization in the German-Speaking Realm

Some scholars have used the idea that Protestantism—especially what is called ascetic Protestantism (above all Puritanism and Pietism)—gave rise to secularization out of its own inherent nature as an answer to the emergence of individual self-control in Pietism. In the process, they have pointed especially to the psychologization of faith in Philipp Jacob Spener (1635–1705) and its influence on the subsequent development of the movement he helped establish:

> In Spener, the certainty of faith is established psychologically, faith is made psychologically plausible, according to Spener it must be anchored in the existence of man himself.... Whereas the old Protestant goal of the certainty of salvation remained the same compared to

the medieval Catholic goal, among the Reformers the path to the goal soon became more important than the goal itself, and in Pietism the path becomes the goal itself. . . . The place of God is imperceptibly taken by the Self.[94]

Adam Bernd's autobiography, the first part of which was published in 1738, and Karl Philipp Moritz's *Magazin zur Erfahrungsseelenkunde* (Magazine of Empirical Psychology), which first appeared in 1783, have been cited as proof of this thesis.

What is implied in this argument is that the process of secularization resulted from the tendencies toward individualization that are generally inherent in ascetic Protestantism. If that is true, it would mean that there existed, in the eighteenth century, a process of secularization that was relatively independent of Enlightenment influences, or, at the very least, that in Pietism the *decisive* impulses toward the secularization of religious self-understanding did not emanate from the Enlightenment. There is reason why one should question this all-too-unilinear perspective.

In the process of the growing secularization of Pietistic autobiography, which finally led in the last decades of the eighteenth century to Karl Philipp Moritz's magazine, among other things, the ascetic Protestant self-understanding and the Enlightenment stood in a potent and creative relationship of tension. Hans-Jürgen Schings has demonstrated this relationship especially in the autobiography of the Pietist Adam Bernd (1676–1748). It first appeared in printed form in Leipzig in 1738; seven years later, the author added a concluding part, which made the entire work grow to more than 1,200 pages. Already in Adam Bernd, the ascetical form of self-understanding anchored in the autobiographical tradition of Pietism encountered "competition" from philosophical and anthropological self-perception, "which expanded the field of observation by a full dimension and qualitatively altered the object of observation."[95] What fell within the purview of the observing gaze was, so to speak, the entire human being within the world.

It seems to me that there is no doubt about the directional trend of this development, provided one does not regard it as a developmental phenomenon inherent only in Pietism, or in *all* of Pietism. Schings believes that Adam Bernd, Karl Philipp Moritz, and other exponents of Pietism in the eighteenth century generally absorbed and adopted the anthropology of the Enlightenment.[96] By contrast, no comparable phenomena of secularization can be identified among Swiss representatives of (late) Pietism of a "middling level." Rather, the framework and means of the perception of self and others remained grounded in the older (Pietistic) tradition.[97]

Similar to what we have seen for Pietism, when looking at secularization phenomena in Germany in the eighteenth and early nineteenth century in general, one can posit a more pronounced fusion of Enlightenment and secularization than was the case in France, although it should be noted that while germanophone scholarship—in contrast to the historiography on France—has posed questions about changes in reproductive behavior, for example, it has not systematically examined them.[98] With respect to the German-speaking realm, I mentioned earlier that the upper class of Zurich practiced birth control in the seventeenth and eighteenth centuries.[99] Likewise, the statistical data for the small town of St. Lambrecht in Styria makes it clear that birth control was practiced there within families in the eighteenth century. In the eyes of the Catholic Church that was a mortal sin. Peter Becker was also able to demonstrate a general incongruity between the seasonality of marriage prescribed by the Church and conceptions in St. Lambrecht in the period from 1600 to 1850. In other words, "As soon as the act took on a public character, people adhered to the religiously prescribed forms. But in the seclusion of marital and non-marital beds, behavior was guided by different calculations."[100] When it comes to this example from Styria, there is thus every reason to believe that before the process of secularization began, sexual behavior followed one kind of logic in the public sphere under the control of the church, and another kind concerning private purposes. By contrast, in the Pietistic, Swabian village of Laichingen, it is only in the course of the nineteenth century that we find "the first indications of birth control... beginning in the 1850s, and then more emphatically since the 1880s."[101] Were St. Lambrecht and the comparable situation in the English village of Colyton in fact simply anomalies within a demographic environment that was characterized, in the countryside and extending far into the nineteenth century, not by birth control, but by traditional, natural fertility?[102]

When it comes to the German-speaking regions, the same situation prevails that we saw in the discussion of secularization in England: for the moment, we must admit that we have no precise understanding of how secularization unfolded in the lower strata of society. Rudolf Schlögl, in his pathbreaking work on secularization in Cologne, Aachen, and Münster, was forced to acknowledge that, in spite of an optimal selection of sources, he was unable to gain access "to the lower levels of the social pyramid."[103]

Were there other secularization trends that manifested themselves in the eighteenth century and at the beginning of the nineteenth century—not so much in Enlightened criticism or in governmental measures, but on the level of the history of mentalities?

A look at the libraries left behind by Catholic laypeople in the cities of Münster, Cologne, and Aachen between 1700 and 1840 leads to the conclusion that the "participants in the literate culture" had clearly turned away "from the matter of the church": "One of every three books in the recorded libraries owned by laity between 1760 and 1779 dealt with faith and religion. By the period 1780–1800, the ratio had dropped to 21%. In the first three decades of the nineteenth century, only about one out of every ten books fell within this field of knowledge."[104]

These findings are in line with the fact that the proportion of edifying titles in German book production as a whole showed a strong decline after about 1740—somewhat earlier than in the specifically urban-Catholic area. While the share of edifying literature was still about 20% around 1740, it dropped to 10% by 1770, whereas "belles lettres" more than doubled in the same period (1740–70), increasing from 5% to 15%. Given the rapidly growing interest in reading in the second half of the eighteenth century and the likewise rising number of total books printed, one can assume that at the turn of the eighteenth century approximately one half of the edifying titles published sixty years earlier (1740) were coming off the presses.[105] One might be tempted to see in all of this an expression of an explicitly Enlightenment-inspired critique of the church and religion. In fact, older works of intellectual history occasionally did just that in a comparable framework. However, there is reason to believe that the change I have described occurred on the level of mentalities, rather than within the context of a *conscious* embrace of the Enlightenment. In the German-speaking realm, as well, secularization was more than merely the product of the Enlightenment, because it occurred not only on the cognitive, but also the pre-cognitive level, that is to say, for example, under the influence of the general cultural change within the middle and upper social strata, an influence that may have been completely unconscious in individual instances.

Of course, we can detect "countervailing" tendencies also with respect to book ownership, most clearly in the composition of the libraries owned by rural Catholic vicars. Their book collections, which were inventoried after 1790, already reveal the beginnings of deliberate opposition and resistance to the Enlightened, rationalistic tendencies of their time:

> Instead of immersing themselves in doctrinal works, the vicars took guidance from the devotional books and sermon collections of the seventeenth century, and unlike almost all other clergy, they reaffirmed the value of case-based penitentials. Judging from their book collections, the vicars stood for a pastoral model of religiosity, one that was oriented toward the Baroque and thus pointed the way to the scholastic orthodoxy of the nineteenth century.[106]

The studies of book ownership have demonstrated a strong trend toward secularization among the urban-dwelling Catholic laity, though it is only in the last two decades of the eighteenth century that this trend becomes more clearly discernible. What insight can we derive from the serial analysis of last wills?

The Catholic wills that have been examined became almost completely secular in their language by the time we get to the decade from 1810 to 1820. Above all, it becomes very clear—the whole spectrum of ways of expression notwithstanding—that the picture of God began to change, especially in the second half of the eighteenth century. This change was a gradual turning away from the Baroque, punishing God who exacts vengeance. The God of the laity turned increasingly into a distant creator-God who no longer intervened in nature or in the collective and individual history of humanity.[107] Parallel to this important change, which also meant a privatization of piety, there was a considerable drop in the number of Masses for the dead and endowments provided for in wills, with the latter trend showing—apart from class differences (the nobility, for example, continued to cling to traditional forms)— especially differences between the genders. Endowments of Masses for the dead declined much more slowly, in the second half of the eighteenth century, in the wills of women, and in the nineteenth century, as well, women "gave expression more frequently than men to their belief in the efficacy of the Mass for the dead. This was an indication that the future Catholic practice of piety would have a female imprint."[108] Something similar has been noted for England in the first half of the nineteenth century: in the wake of the gradual dissolution of many traditional households in the early 1800s as a result of industrialization, women acquired a new and much more prominent role in the Church of England.[109]

7

The Self-Questioning of Early Modern Religiosity?

To what extent did early modern religiosity contain a dynamic that brought about, over several generations, a gradual relativization of religion's central place in social life? This is how Max Weber and Ernst Troeltsch, especially, sought to depict the process that created the western culture of modernity or the western process of rationalization (Weber), namely by trying to locate within sixteenth and seventeenth-century Protestantism the seed of its own, inner relativization and secularization. In the discussion that follows I use the word "internality" to describe the notion of such a dynamic. This will allow me to set it apart much more clearly from processes that brought a quite comparable relativization in Iberian Catholicism of the fifteenth and sixteenth centuries, but which did not arise primarily from an inner dynamic of religious belief. These latter developments I call processes of "externality."

"Externality": Individualization Among the Iberian Conversos

Medieval Spain was—to use modern parlance—a multicultural country par excellence, comprising, as it did, three population groups with distinctly different religions and cultures: Christians, Muslims, and Jews. Attempts by the monarchs of Aragon and Castille to create a unified religion and culture—attempts that sought to

Christianize the subjects and the institutions of the state and thus rejected the pluralism of the past—began in the late fourteenth century and gradually intensified as the fifteenth century unfolded. Forced baptism was the instrument of coercive integration that zealous clergy employed against the Jews, often with broad popular support. The first forced baptisms of this kind—accompanied by unrest in the cities—took place in 1391, and they were sporadically repeated throughout the fifteenth century. This created the new population group of the *conversos* or the "New Christians."

There is no need to revisit the subsequent history of the conversos in Spain and Portugal in the fifteenth and early sixteenth centuries.[1] Instead, my attention here will be focused on the scattered diaspora of the Sephardim that was created by the expulsions and the activities of the Inquisition in Spain and Portugal.

Many Portuguese conversos emigrated to Italy and the Levant, that is, the eastern Mediterranean. A number of towns in northern Italy that welcomed conversos occasionally served for the latter as way stations to the Levant. In some places there arose new settlements of this kind, tied together by a network of familial and commercial contacts. This network was influential especially in the gem trade, and for a time also in the sugar and spice trade with the Portuguese and Spanish colonies.

Most of the conversos who emigrated directly to the Ottoman Empire, where they settled chiefly in Saloniki, Adrianople, and Constantinople, officially returned to Judaism, especially since they did not have to fear being persecuted for doing so by the Ottoman population or the court of the Sultan.[2] Other settlements within the Ottoman sphere of influence grew up in Palestine, Cyprus, Egypt, and on the Balkans. Leaving aside the settlements of "Portuguese" in St. Esprit (a suburb of Bayonne) and in Bordeaux, which flowered primarily in the seventeenth and eighteenth centuries,[3] Antwerp was the most important first destination for most emigrants, and in the sixteenth century the city was home to the largest colony of Portuguese emigrants. The city fathers protected these Portuguese for economic reasons, even though rumors about their lack of orthodoxy would not abate. There is little doubt that Judaizing conversos could be found within the Portuguese colony of Antwerp, but the mention of economic interests applies not only to the councilors of the city but also to many of the Portuguese New Christians, who were willing—chiefly out of economic motivations—to assimilate to their Christian surroundings. For that is the only way to explain the failure of the measures—inspired above all by religious policy—that Charles V directed in the 1540s and 1550s against the growth of the colony in Antwerp. Commissioners, specially appointed by the emperor to deal with the stream of emigrants into the Spanish

Netherlands, organized the first larger proceedings against conversos in Antwerp in the 1530s and 1540s, prosecuting them for their Judaizing. In the face of the wars against the Turks—the Ottomans appeared before the gates of Vienna for the first time in 1529—it was especially the good personal and commercial contacts that Antwerp's conversos maintained with New Christians in the eastern Mediterranean and with the court of the Sultan in Constantinople that were subjected to close scrutiny. In the meantime, rumors ran wild—for example, that Portuguese merchants were not only supplying munitions for the war against the European Christians, but were teaching the Turks how to manufacture them. In this atmosphere, a commission of inquiry was set up in 1540 in Spanish-controlled Milan, which sought to take steps against alleged Judaizers by prosecuting them and confiscating property.[4] And in 1549 and 1550, Charles V called upon the Council of Antwerp to expel all Portuguese New Christians who had settled there since 1543, though with little success.

What, then, can we say about the Christian orthodoxy of the conversos?[5] What options were available to them with respect to their religious confession and religious practice? In the relevant literature, the term "converso" is not infrequently used synonymously with "marrano." As we understand the latter term today, marranos were Jews forced to convert or their descendants who continued to practice their faith more or less secretly, as for example the family of the apothecary Catalan, with whom the later Basel physician Felix Platter lived in the 1550s while studying medicine in the southern French city of Montpellier.[6] Were all the Portuguese conversos in the European and Levantine diaspora marranos?

Let us listen first to the words of the Venetian patrician Antonio Tiepolo: "All those who descend from Jewish fathers are called New Christians... From them, for the most part, come the people that in Italy we call marranos; the towns in Italy are full of them, and that rascal João Miquez comes of this accursed and fickle people."[7] João Miquez was a special thorn in the side of the Venetians of the second half of the sixteenth century, for he was a converso who, having arrived in Istanbul, returned to Judaism and under the name Joseph Nasi (his new Jewish name) rose high within the court of the Sultan, attaining the title of Duke of Naxos.[8] For reasons of trade policy and from private motivations, João Miquez or Joseph Nasi supported the Sublime Porte in its war against Venice. For Antonio Tiepolo, there was no distinction between conversos and marranos. But that was not the view of the Imperial Commissioner Johann Vuystinck in Colmar, who, in the summer of 1547, detained a group of Portuguese conversos who were passing through the city and questioned them. Before the detainees were released and allowed to continue on their way to Basel and northern Italy, they had to swear that they were good Christians and not marranos.[9]

The question that arises, then, is whether essentially all conversos, as so-called marranos, adhered to the religion of their fathers and ancestors and thus secretly practiced the Jewish religion with all its many rituals. The scholarly community is almost hopelessly divided on this issue. Some see marranism as a kind of subculture to which, when all is said and done, all conversos adhered. Others emphasize the broad spectrum of religious options that the conversos of the sixteenth century sought to make use of. Cecil Roth and Israel S. Révah—both scholars of the period between the two world wars and of the immediate post–World War II years—saw in marranism a specific form of crypto-Judaism, a kind of secret religion that was passed down from generation to generation.[10]

Jonathan Israel has argued on the other hand that a mass-subculture of crypto-Judaism existed in Portugal in the 1570s, while the remaining conversos in Spain were by this time effectively Christianized and could no longer be identified as such.[11]

However, a statement made by the Jew Chaim Saruc in 1580 as a witness before the inquisition in Venice reveals that the socioreligious disintegration was in a sense forced upon the conversos not only from the Christian side, but also from the old-Jewish side: "[A] marrano, as I said, is one who steers by two rudders: that is, he is neither Christian nor Jew."[12]

The strongest argument for the subculture thesis is surely the existence of cases of conversos who returned to the Judaism of their ancestors only after several generations. However, J. C. Boyajian was able to show that among the banking families of Lisbon in the first half of the seventeenth century, the primary motivation behind the return to the ancestral religion was in many cases not religion, but pragmatic considerations as well as financial and family interests.[13] Similarly, detailed research into the Portuguese in Antwerp—especially on economic history—raise doubts about Révah's thesis that the majority of the city's Portuguese between 1571 and 1666 were secret Judaizers and maintained contact with the Jews of Antwerp and Hamburg.[14] Rather, the studies support the thesis that the decision of a converso about his or her religious orientation was, in the final analysis, primarily an individual one.[15] This is already revealed by the mere fact that there were, at times, heated conflicts within families of conversos in Antwerp and northern Italy about which religious option to choose.[16] And in individual cases, not only the constraints imposed by one's environment but also the local possibilities of economic and social integration played an important role in this decision.

The conversos—a significant portion of whom were already dispersed by the middle of the sixteenth century among settlements in northwestern and southern Europe, in the Levant, and not least in Spain and Portugal's overseas colonies—were thus the first socioreligious population group of Europe in which a religious individualism began to spread already in the course of the sixteenth century as a result of external circumstances, and not from an inherent impulse within the core of the religion itself. Against this backdrop, the following incident occasions little surprise: in 1540, a Portuguese converso by name of "Loys Fernandez, an old man of eighty," who was one of those forcibly converted in 1497, was passing through Antwerp when the Imperial Commissioner questioned him about his faith. Loys Fernandez responded that there was an external and an internal faith, and the commissioner had no right to ask about his inner faith, for that was his private matter.[17] The life and work of the Dutch philosopher Baruch Spinoza (1632–77) illustrates that in subsequent generations this arc of tension connecting external and internal faith sometimes broke down. Spinoza was a Sephardic Jew who left the synagogue. His image of God was rejected and opposed by both Jewish and Christian contemporaries.

"Internality": The Weber Thesis

I have already discussed in sufficient detail the attempt to explain the connections between ecclesiastical-religious disciplining and the development from the medieval state of personal bonds to the bureaucratic, institutional state of modernity within the context of the concept of confessionalization.[18] There is therefore no need to address it again here, especially since questions concerning the history of mentalities will be at the center of the reflections that follow. The confessionalization concept incorporates these questions at best indirectly.

It is especially in the work of Max Weber (1864–1920) that we encounter a serious attempt to fathom the connections between early modern church doctrine or religiosity and the genesis of modernity. Weber pursued this attempt with universal historical breadth in his sociology of religion, including— in the process—also Islam, Judaism, and the Asiatic religions (needless to say, against the backdrop of the German-Protestant culture of his time) in his effort to explain what he called the process of "western rationalization."[19] Weber established a close link between the creation of a modern sense of business, the capitalistic mentality that shaped the modern world, and the ascetic forms of early modern Protestantism, especially English Puritanism and, to a limited extent, Pietism. The most comprehensive presentation of his thesis came in his long essay "The Protestant Ethic and the Spirit of Capitalism," published in two parts in 1904 and 1905[20]—an essay that triggered a still ongoing debate in the humanities and in neighboring disciplines.[21]

Weber believed he could find the core of the link between Protestantism and the spirit of capitalism in the predestinarianism of the Puritans, for among them the quest for God was—in contrast to pre-Reformation Catholicism and also, to some extent, to Lutheranism—focused entirely on the conduct of the individual believer in the world. Since no one could know whether he was among the chosen, he was under the religious compulsion to prove himself in his occupation, in the world, for this would at least allow the believer anxious about salvation to infer his inner state of grace from his outer state.[22] But let us listen to Weber in his own words:

> The inscrutability of predestination to either salvation or damnation was naturally intolerable to the believer; he searched for the *certitudo salutis*, for an indication that he belonged to the elect. Since otherworldly asceticism had been rejected, he could find this certainty, on the one hand, in the conviction that he was acting according to the letter of the law and according to reason, repressing all animal drives; on the other, he could find it in visible proofs that God blessed his work.... A person was judged elect or condemned as an entity; no confession and absolution could relieve him and change his position before God and, in contrast to Catholicism, no individual "good deed" could compensate for his sins. Therefore the individual could only be sure of his state of grace if he felt reason to believe that, by adhering to a principle of methodical conduct, he pursued the sole correct path in all his action—that he worked for God's glory. Methodical conduct, the rational form of asceticism, is thus carried from the monastery into the world.[23]

The explanatory reach of what is referred to as the Weber thesis is more comprehensive than one would have had reason to believe initially. Weber's friend and colleague Ernst Troeltsch (1865–1923) already saw this very clearly when he wrote that

> Weber's treatise in reality does not aim merely at the derivation of the capitalist spirit from the Calvinistic idea of vocation, but at the explanation of the modern bourgeois way of life, within which the "capitalist spirit" is only one element. He is concerned in the main

with the modern characteristics of the bourgeoisie, and not with the elements which modern capitalism has inherited from the ancient world and from the later Middle Ages.[24]

To what extent is there a connection between the issues addressed in these passages and the problems of individualization and secularization, to which this chapter is devoted? Both Weber and Troeltsch saw in Protestantism a religion of sentiment and conviction grounded in the belief in the sole validity of the Bible, in contrast to hierarchical-sacramental Catholicism. Both men also pointed to the trends toward individualization connected with the transition to a religion of sentiment and conviction brought about by the Reformation. According to Troeltsch, the religious individualism that was inherent in Protestantism in general was most pronounced in Calvinism:

> This individualism differs not only from Catholic and Lutheran individualism, but also from the optimistic, rationalistic individualism of the Enlightenment. Founded upon a crushing sense of sin, and a pessimistic condemnation of the world, without colour or emotional satisfaction, it is an individualism based upon the certainty of election, the sense of responsibility and of the obligation to render personal service under the Lordship of Christ. It finds expression in the thoughtful and self-conscious type of Calvinistic piety, in the systematic spirit of self-control, and in its independence of all that is "creaturely."[25]

Weber and Troeltsch were also in agreement that in spite of Protestantism's inherent tendencies toward individualization, especially in the ascetic version of Protestantism, there was no direct line of connection and tradition leading from the Reformation to the Enlightenment.

This is a broad outline of the development in religious history that led, according to Weber and Troeltsch, from the individualizing tendencies inherent in older Protestantism, above all in its ascetic manifestations, to the phenomena of secularization in the transition from the early modern period to modernity. We must qualify this line of argumentation by noting not only that it applies primarily to the development within German-speaking lands, but also that it leaves out the development within Catholicism.[26]

What do other scholars in the ongoing debate think about the Weber thesis? Here I will refer only to a few voices from the large, still growing, and in part rather dissonant chorus. The historian Paul Münch, taking a stance of critical distance from Max Weber, has pointed to the "process of growing diligence" (*Prozess der Verfleißigung*) as a longer-term trend of European history in the early modern period. According to Münch, the beginnings of that process date back to the late Middle Ages:

> Already in the fourteenth and fifteenth centuries, we can note a positive assessment of worldly work by theology. The urban burgher class, tied to artisanal labor and commerce, began to devise business regulations and codes of conduct. In so doing, they initiated the process of disciplining and rationalizing human labor, a process that was continuously pushed ahead until the end of the eighteenth century, though it did not enter a qualitatively new and more intensive stage of labor organization until the first era of industrialization. This deprives the Weberian thesis, according to which the emergence of the "spirit of capitalism" should be seen as an indirect result of Protestant dogma, of a critical basis. The battle against sloth and begging began in the late Middle Ages.

The adherents of Protestant and Catholic confessions carried on this battle in a comparable and similar way, until "it experienced a noticeable intensification with the establishment of workhouses and prisons," above all in the seventeenth and eighteenth centuries.[27]

In the final analysis, Paul Münch thus rejects the Weberian linkage between ecclesiastical-religious dogma and the process of "western rationalization" and points emphatically to what he believes were aspects of the process of increasing diligence that lay outside the church and religion. By contrast, Herbert Lüthy accepted the basic contention of Weber's thesis, though he criticizes the fact that Weber never asks why the beginnings of trends within the environment of late medieval Catholicism that would have favored a development toward capitalism ceased to exist after the Counter-Reformation, "as though the sudden cessation of an ascending line does not pose a far more genuine problem than its continuation." The scholarly debate has been carried on, Lüthy has argued, "as though we are dealing with a succession of phenomena—Catholicism equals Middle Ages, Protestantism equals the modern age, and all the misunderstandings of the nineteenth century were then piled onto this first, enormous distortion of history."[28]

Much like Herbert Lüthy, Karl-Ludwig Ay maintained that the possibility of the creation of a capitalistic spirit was not the product only of the Reformation and its repercussions. According to Ay, that possibility existed "already in the literary culture and in the urban economy of the Middle Ages, in humanism, and in the Renaissance."[29] Crucial to the survival of this late medieval trend beyond the Reformation was the degree of repression imposed by the princely policy of confessionalization. This explains why even in places "where Calvinism did not prevail, above all, for example, in Lutheran Saxony . . . , under favorable circumstances, the same tendency was able to continue developing and then occasionally unfold strong cultural and economic forces." Elsewhere, however, the same tendencies were "struck at their very root, depending on the severity and duration of princely repression in the confessional struggle."[30] According to Ay, the consequences "were most severe in the later Catholic Germany: in wide regions, the confessionalization carried out by the Old Church princes cut deeply into the cultural and economic development. For the price for the suppression of the Reformation was that the older traditions and lines of development that were free to unfold their specific dynamism under the Lutheran princes of the same period were severed." It is not difficult to see a contradiction in the argumentation of Lüthy and Ay and the theses of Paul Münch.

It should be noted here, by way of a brief excursus, that Peter Hersche, unlike Karl-Ludwig Ay, has tried to depict the economic backwardness of the spiritual principalities under the Catholic territorial states of the old empire in the eighteenth century as an "intentional backwardness"—with some of the responses to this contribution to the scholarly debate ranging from critical to negative.[31] I am rather skeptical whether Hersche's thesis can deliver what it promises, namely, the demonstration that a kind of alternative economic mindset was at work in the spiritual principalities of the eighteenth century, one that put itself in conscious opposition to the Protestant progress-oriented thinking—more implicit than explicit—that was posited by Weber, Troeltsch, and many others in the nineteenth and early twentieth centuries. More persuasive is his more recent call for research into the history of *mentalités* to clarify the decline of trade, commerce, and the financial sector in seventeenth-century Italy—a decline that did not result from purely economic necessity. In the scholarly literature, this reversal, which then brought a broad reagrarianization in its wake, has been described as the "loss of the commercial spirit" and "land rent mentality." We still know very little about the causes. Could it be that in Italy, "in the age of the Counter-Reformation, there arose moral qualms about embarking on the road to unrestrained, modern capitalism?"[32] Or is this an excessive backward projection of modern capitalism, to a time when it was barely discernible as a future development?

However, Herbert Lüthy's comment about the historical failure of the nineteenth century, especially under the banner of what has been called "cultural Protestantism," confirms a demand that has been articulated from another camp and is closer to Weber in substance: namely, that the so-called Weber thesis must be discussed within the context of the dominant scholarly-intellectual discourse in Germany before World War I, and should not be completely isolated from its embededness within the intellectual schemata and biases of the cultural Protestantism of the time.[33] The biases in question included the fact that scholars assumed, as a matter of course and without any further verification, that the Protestant regions of Germany were economically superior to the Catholic regions.

While one current in the debate over the Weber thesis is focused on contextualizing Weber's ideas and notions within the culture and scholarship of his own time, another moves within the sphere of seventeenth-century history, which is the chronological starting point of Weber's argument. I myself have tried to show—following consciously in the footsteps of some other interpreters of Weber—that his close interlinking of the Puritan work ethic with the belief in predestination surely cannot be sustained in the form he intended.[34] First, in the seventeenth century there were pronounced differences between the belief in predestination held by theologians and that of the laity; second, in their predestinarian beliefs, English Puritans tended to significantly tone down the implications of the doctrine of predestination; and third, it has been shown that Weber's chief witness for the close connection between the belief in predestination and Puritanism, the theologian Richard Baxter, was not a proponent of conventional predestinarian theology.[35]

Similar in their thrust are arguments that the discussion of the Weber thesis must not be conducted in too narrow a confessional framework. It has been pointed out, in this context, that Catholic devotional tractates of the seventeenth century were no different from relevant Protestant works in the way they argued about questions of occupational ethics.[36] John Bossy has emphasized in this regard that for Catholics, and "perhaps for everybody," catechism instruction, because it represented an instrument of church discipline, entailed the renunciation of larger spheres of traditional, everyday practices of social life. This tendency toward the regulation of Christian patterns of behavior— which Bossy believes was clearly successful and supra-confessional—reached their highpoint in Jean-Baptiste de la Salle's *Règles de la bienséance et de la civilité chrétienne* (Rules of Propriety and Christian Civility), published in 1713. By this time, the "trinity of catechism, civility and literacy was universally acknowledged in the west as the constellation which should govern the education of children."[37] The substantive points of contact between the position of Bossy and that of Paul Münch are evident. Still, one must bear in mind that by invoking la Salle and France, Bossy is trying to make the exception into the rule, because in France—as I have discussed in detail earlier—the reform efforts emanating from the Council of Trent found a comparatively richer seedbed than they did in the rest of Catholic Europe.[38]

For Hartmut Lehmann, these sorts of considerations give rise to two fundamental conclusions:

> On the one hand, it must be noted that forces of work ethic were being mobilized across all theological-confessional boundaries in seventeenth-century Christendom; both Protestant and Catholic authors saw in the difficult era in which they were living, in the faithful fulfillment of tasks within the world, a meaningful path of preparation for eternal salvation and a suitable means of achieving reconciliation with God. On the other hand, there is no denying that this mobilization could only take place and exert its influence within the framework of the political, social, and economic conditions of the various countries. Where the background conditions were favorable, as in England or the Netherlands, the more intensive, Christian occupational labor led to visible economic success, while in places where external conditions had a negative effect, as in France, Spain, and in many territories of the Old Empire, it produced no economic results worth mentioning.... It was a fundamental mistake on Weber's part to deduce the theological-ethical motivation of Puritan business people from their external success, and then in turn to deduce the external success from this motivation.[39]

Beyond these two fundamental observations, there is also a third argument—repeatedly tossed into the debate by Lehmann, Lüthy, and many others—one should consider, namely that religious dissident minorities have always played a special role, and not only in European history. Alongside the Puritans, Pietists, and Methodists of the seventeenth to nineteenth centuries, one could mention the Quakers, for example, whose doctrine of the light within has nothing in common with the notion of predestination, and to some extent also the Jews, especially those in western Europe. Finally, in the words of an expert, "the religious minorities in the Near East and in India, whose success surely had nothing to do with the Protestant ethic and yet shows certain common traits: in every case it is the response to the challenge of legal or social discrimination that compels and spurs people to greater accomplishments and discipline, provided the internal prerequisites and a minimum of external toleration are in place."[40]

The still ongoing debate about the dynamism inherent in Weber's thesis makes it impossible to conclude this chapter with some summary remarks. At this time there is no state of knowledge that is accepted by a majority of scholars and could be offered here as a summation (even if perhaps a very temporary one) of the discussion. Instead, I will lend my voice to the demand that has been raised by others, namely that Catholicism—and especially Weber's image of Catholicism—needs to be incorporated into the debate much more intensively than it has been. And on the positive side, the open, unfinished state of the scholarly debate about the Weber thesis testifies not only to the desire of some historians mentioned in this chapter to make a name for themselves in the profession. Rather, it reflects first and foremost the vigor of the scholarly conversation about the religious history of the early modern period.

Conclusion and Outlook

At least within the middle and upper classes of European society at the time, the world of early modern religiosity that I have tried to describe here experienced a profound transformation, primarily in the second half of the eighteenth century though in part earlier as well (I am thinking here of England), a transformation that made it forever a part of history—though I must state again that we know very little about changes in the religiosity of the common people. Only the Mediterranean world represents to some extent an exception to this scenario, because some of these same changes did not occur there until the nineteenth century. In western and central Europe and in Italy, the repercussions of the French Revolution accelerated the transformation, but at the same time they called forth the powers that clung to the old and resisted these innovations. When, in the first decades of the nineteenth century, reactions to Enlightenment, Revolution, and secularization set in with ultramontanism and the movement of Awakening, the old forms of religiosity could be revived only in part outside of the Mediterranean world. To be sure, one must not overlook the aspects of continuity; for example, "between the older Pietism and the movement of Awakening that began with the Biblical and missionary societies," as represented by the international conference of preachers founded by the Moravians; or between the ancien régime and the conservative Catholicism of the early nineteenth century in western and central France, where, in the face of the strong position of individual parishes and their clergy, the

Revolution could do little to change traditional forms of piety.[1] All in all, however, and in spite of the continuity in smaller details, something new did arise in the nineteenth century.

When Josephinism in the Habsburg lands was finally undone by the advancing troops and ideas of the French Revolution in the 1790s, there was an abrupt change of course, and official state support for traditional forms of popular religiosity was employed as a weapon of defense against Revolutionary influences:

> Since Austria bore the brunt of the battle [against the Revolution], it is not surprising that the first examples of a "popular piety" once again guided and protected by state authorities are reported from there: on 1 June 1796, Lombardy having just fallen to Bonaparte, the *Landstände* [territorial estates] of Tyrol in Bozen agreed upon the official introduction of the feast of the Sacred Heart, and prevailed upon Emperor Franz to approve it as a church–state feast day shortly thereafter; at the same time, in response to the efforts of his sister, the Abbess Maria Anna, the pilgrimage to Mariazell—outlawed since 1783—was revived.[2]

This observation provides another piece of evidence for the thesis that popular religiosity in the nineteenth century, as compared to the previous centuries, was "increasingly organized 'from above.' " The notion of an "organized mass religiosity" in this context has by no means been refuted.[3]

The mass religiosity of the nineteenth century played its part, not least, in ensuring that confessional stereotypes of judgment and behavior persisted into the second half of the twentieth century, with all their—sometimes subtle—repercussions in cultural and social life. In the 1980s and 1990s, new religious movements, most of them outside the churches, have provided further proof that secularization in the modern world has by no means led to the final disappearance of religious meaning and religious constructs in individual and collective life. And yet, those who study history today, as well as a broader public interested in the past, usually find it very difficult to perceive and recognize religiosity as a central aspect of the history of our ancestors. The present survey will have achieved one of its main goals if it has not only made it easier for the reader to arrive at this understanding, but has also conveyed something of the fascinating story of religion and piety in the early modern period.

Notes

INTRODUCTION

1. T. Luckmann, "Einleitung," in B. Malinowski, *Magie, Wissenschaft und Religion und andere Schriften* (Frankfurt a.M., 1973), ix.

2. See esp. P. Munz, "From Max Weber to Joachim of Floris: The Philosophy of Religious History," *The Journal of Religious History* 18 (1980): 185.

3. R. W. Scribner, "The Reformation, Popular Magic and the 'Disenchantment of the World,'" *Journal of Interdisciplinary History* 23 (1993): 476f., quoting Valerie Flint.

4. E. P. Thompson, *The Making of the English Working Class* (Harmondsworth, 1986), 12: "I am seeking to rescue the poor stockinger, the Luddite cropper, the 'obsolete' hand-loom weaver, the 'utopian' artisan, and even the deluded follower of Joanna Southcott, from the enormous condescension of posterity."

5. On this see R. Firth, "God and Anthropology," *Times Literary Supplement*, May 23, 1986, 557.

6. On this see C. Geertz, "'From the Native's Point of View': On the Nature of Anthropological Understanding," in *Meaning in Anthropology*, ed. K. H. Basso and H. A. Selby (Albuquerque, N.M.: 1976), 221–31.

7. Karl Marx, *The German Ideology*, in *Karl Marx: Selected Writings*, ed. David McLellan (Oxford, 1977), 164.

8. Ibid., 157.

9. Émile Durkheim, *The Elementary Forms of The Religious Life: A Study in Religious Sociology*, trans. Joseph Ward Swain (Glencoe, Ill., 1947), 47.

10. Ibid. 179f., see also 45f.

11. See "'Internality': Weber's thesis" in chapter 7.

12. See among others G. Levi, "On Microhistory," in *New Perspectives on Historical Writing*, ed. Peter Burke (Oxford, 1991), 93–113; H. Medick, "Mikro-Historie," in *Sozialgeschichte, Alltagsgeschichte, Mikro-Historie*, ed. W. Schulze (Göttingen, 1994), 40–53; H. Medick, "Entlegene Geschichte? Sozialgeschichte und Mikro-Historie im Blickfeld der Kulturanthropologie," in *Alltagskultur, Subjektivität und Geschichte: Zur Theorie und Praxis von Alltagsgeschichte*, ed. Berliner Geschichtswerkstatt (Münster, 1994), 94–109.

13. T. Welskopp, "Der Mensch und die Verhältnisse: 'Handeln' und 'Struktur' bei Max Weber und Anthony Giddens," in *Geschichte zwischen Kultur und Gesellschaft: Beiträge zur Theoriedebatte*, ed. T. Mergel and T. Welskopp (Munich, 1997), 39–70.

14. Max Weber, " 'Objectivity in Social Science and Social Policy," in *The Methodology of the Social Sciences*, ed. and trans. Edward A. Shils and Henry A. Finch (New York, 1949).

15. T. Mergel and T. Welskopp, "Geschichtswissenschaft und Gesellschaftstheorie," in *Geschichte zwischen Kultur und Gesellschaft: Beiträge zur Theoriedebatte*, ed. T. Mergel and T. Welskopp (Munich, 1997), 9–35.

16. M. Dinges, " 'Historische Anthropologie' und 'Gesellschaftsgeschichte': Mit dem Lebensstilkonzept zu einer 'Alltagskulturgeschichte' der frühen Neuzeit?," *Zeitschrift für historische Forschung* 24 (1997): 179–214.

17. Ibid., 192.

18. L. Hunt, "The Challenge of Gender: Deconstruction of Categories and Reconstruction of Narratives in Gender History," in *Geschlechtergeschichte und Allgemeine Geschichte: Herausforderungen und Perspektiven*, ed. H. Medick and A.-C. Trepp (Göttingen, 1998), 82f.

19. R. Schlögl, " 'Aufgeklärter Unglaube' oder 'mentale Säkularisierung'? Die Frömmigkeit katholischer Stadtbürger in systemtheoretischer Hinsicht (ca. 1700–1840)," in *Geschichte zwischen Kultur und Gesellschaft: Beiträge zur Theoriedebatte*, ed. T. Mergel and T. Welskopp (Munich, 1997), 95–121.

20. P. Burke, *Popular Culture in Early Modern Europe* (New York, 1978), prologue.

21. N. Schindler, "Spuren in die Geschichte der 'anderen' Zivilisation: Probleme und Perspektiven einer historischen Volkskulturforschung," in *Volkskultur: Zur Wiederentdeckung des vergessenen Alltags (16.–20. Jahrhundert)*, ed. R. v. Dülmen and N. Schindler (Frankfurt a. M., 1984), 13–77.

22. I.-M. Greverus, *Kultur und Alltagswelt. Eine Einführung in Fragen der Kulturanthropologie* (Munich, 1978), 52f.

23. In agreement with Schindler, "Spuren in die Geschichte," 54.

24. B. Scribner, *For the Sake of Simple Folk: Popular Propaganda for the German Reformation* (Oxford, 1994), 59.

25. The following discussion incorporates some revised passages from my essay "Grenzen zwischen Religion, Magie und Konfession aus der Sicht der frühneuzeitlichen Mentalitätsgeschichte," in *Grenzen und Raumvorstellungen (11.–20. Jh.)— Frontières et conceptions de l'éspace (11ᵉ–20ᵉ siècles)*, ed. G. P. Marchal (Zurich, 1996), 329–43.

26. R. Kieckhefer, *Magic in the Middle Ages* (Cambridge, 1989), 14.

27. "The Autobiography of Goodwin Wharton (1653–1704)," British Library, London, vol. 1, Additional Manuscript 20006, fol. 6 verso.

28. K. von Greyerz, "Religion in the Life of German and Swiss Autobiographers." By "syncretism" I mean the amalgamation of what are, *from a modern perspective*, not infrequently irreconcilable forms and practices relating to the supernatural.

29. L. Daston and K. Park, "Unnatural Conceptions. The Study of Monsters in Sixteenth and Seventeenth-Century France and England," *Past and Present* 92 (1981): 20–54.

30. R. Habermas, "Wunder, Wunderliches, Wunderbares: Zur Profanisierung eines Deutungsmusters in der Frühen Neuzeit," in *Armut, Liebe, Ehre: Studien zur historischen Kulturforschung*, ed. R. v. Dülmen (Frankfurt a. M., 1988), 38–66.

31. Quoted by A. G. Debus, "Science and History," in *Science, Pseudo-Science and Utopianism in Early Modern Thought*, ed. S. A. McKnight (Columbia, Mo., 1992), 16.

32. M. Hesse, "Reasons and Evaluation in the History of Science," in *Changing Perspectives in the History of Science: Essays in Honour of Joseph Needham*, ed. M. Teich and R. Young (London, 1973), 129.

33. Ibid., 143.

34. H. J. Dahms and U. Majer, "Wissenschaftsgeschichte," in *Wissenschaftstheoretisches Lexikon*, ed. E. Braun and H. Radermacher (Graz, 1978), cols. 671–72.

35. Thomas Kuhn, "The History of Science," in *International Encyclopedia of the Social Sciences* (New York, 1968), 14:74–83.

36. S. Shapin and S. Schaffer, *Leviathan and the Air Pump: Hobbes, Boyle and the Experimental Life* (Princeton, 1987). See also S. Shapin, *The Scientific Revolution* (Chicago, 1996).

37. On this see B. Vickers, "Francis Bacon and the Progress of Knowledge," *Journal of the History of Ideas* 53 (1992): 511.

38. See I. Stengers, *L'invention des sciences modernes* (Paris, 1995).

39. On what follows see M. Kempe, *Wissenschaft, Theologie, Aufklärung: Johann Jakob Scheuchzer (1672–1733) und die Sintflutheorie* (Frühneuzeit-Forschungen 10) (Epfendorf, 2003); R. Wolf, *Biographien zur Kulturgeschichte der Schweiz*, vol. 1 (Zurich, 1858), 181–228.

40. *Naturhistorie des Schweizerlandes*, 1st ed. (Zurich, 1716–18).

41. For a detailed discussion see Kempe, *Wissenschaft, Theologie, Aufklärung*. See also H. Dirlinger, "Das Buch der Natur: Der Einfluss des Physikotheologie auf das neuzeitliche Naturverständnis und die ästhetische Wahrnehmung von Wildnis," in *Individualisierung, Rationalisierung, Säkularisierung: Neue Wege der Religionsgeschichte* (Wiener Beiträge zur Geschichte der Neuzeit 22), ed. M. Weinzierl (Vienna and Munich, 1977), 156–85.

42. Quoted in E. Fueter, *Geschichte der exakten Wissenschaften in der schweizerischen Aufklärung (1680–1780)* (Aarau, 1941), 234–35, note 29.

43. Wolf, *Biographien*, 1:208.

44. Ibid., 224. I am grateful to Martin Mattmüller for additional information on this topic.

45. Quoted in ibid., 225.

46. F. Bacon, *The Advancement of Learning*, ed. G. W. Kitchin (London, 1973), 7–8.

47. W. Kutschmann, "Isaac Newton (1643–1727)," in *Klassiker der Natur-philosophie: Von den Vorsokratikern bis zur Kopenhagener Schule*, ed. G. Böhme (Munich, 1989), 175.

48. D. Kubrin, "Newton and the Cyclical Cosmos: Providence and the Mechanical Philosophy," *Journal of the History of Ideas* 27 (1967): 325–46; A. R. Hall, *Isaac Newton. Adventurer in Thought* (Oxford, 1992), 353–54.

49. Isaac Newton, *Optice: Sive de Reflexionibus, Refractionibus, Inflexionibus & Coloribus Lucis, Libri Tres* (London, 1706), 346–47.

50. Arianism is a belief that questions the three natures of God, the divine Trinity.

51. B. Vickers, "Analogy versus Identity: The Rejection of Occult Symbolism, 1580–1680," in *Occult and Scientific Mentalities in the Renaissance*, ed. B. Vickers (Cambridge, 1984), 114–15.

52. R. Boyle, "The Sceptical Chymist" (excerpts), in *English Science: Bacon to Newton*, ed. B. Vickers (Cambridge, 1987), 67–87.

53. B. J. Teeter Dobbs, *The Foundations of Newton's Alchemy or 'The Hunting of the Green Lyon'* (Cambridge, 1975), 80. On this see W. Pagel, "The Spectre of van Helmont and the Idea of Continuity in the History of Chemistry," in *Changing Perspectives in the History of Science: Essays in Honour of Joseph Needham*, ed. M. Teich and R. Young (London, 1973), 140f.

54. L. M. Principe, "Boyle's Alchemistic Pursuits," in *Robert Boyle Reconsidered*, ed. M. Hunter (Cambridge, 1994), 91. See also M. Hunter, "Alchemy, Magic and Moralism in the Thought of Robert Boyle," *British Journal for the History of Science* 23 (1990): 387–410.

55. B. J. Teeter Dobbs, *The Janus Faces of Genius. The Role of Alchemy in Newton's Thought* (Cambridge, 1990).

56. K. von Greyerz, "Alchemie, Hermetismus und Magie: Zur Frage der Kontinuitäten in der wissenschaftlichen Revolution," in *Im Zeichen der Krise: Religiosität im Europa des 17. Jahrhunderts* (Veröffentlichungen des Max-Planck-Instituts für Geschichte 152), ed. H. Lehmann and A.-C. Trepp (Göttingen, 1999), 415–32.

57. See, for example, M. Hunter, *John Aubrey and the Realm of Learning* (London, 1975), 22–24; M. Hunter, *Elias Ashmole 1617–1692: The Founder of the Ashmolean Museum and His World* (Oxford, 1983), 5–10.

58. H. Geertz, "An Anthropology of Religion and Magic, I," *Journal of Interdisciplinary History* 6 (1975): 71–89.

59. S. Clark, "The Scientific Status of Demonology," in *Occult and Scientific Mentalities in the Renaissance*, ed. B. Vickers (Cambridge, 1984), 351–74. See also his more recent monograph, *Thinking with Demons: The Idea of Witchcraft in Early Modern Europe* (Oxford, 1997).

60. M. Foucault, *The Order of Things: An Archeology of the Human Sciences* (London, 1970), 58–71.

61. S. J. Tambiah, *Magic, Science, Religion, and the Scope of Rationality* (Cambridge, 1990), 92.

62. Ibid., 105 and 108. Tambiah's reflections here were guided by ideas put forth by Claude Lévy-Bruhl.

63. Ibid., 92.

64. H. Cleveland, "Trois siècles après Newton," in *La mort de Newton*, ed. A. Forti et al. (Paris, 1996), 21–33.

65. See the section "Confessionalization and modernization" in chapter 1.

CHAPTER I

1. A survey of the relevant scholarship can be found in H.-C. Rublack, "Forschungsbericht Stadt und Reformation," in *Stadt und Kirche im 16. Jahrhundert* (Schriften des Vereins für Reformationsgeschichte 190), ed. B. Moeller (Gütersloh, 1978), 9–26; K. von Greyerz, "Stadt und Reformation: Stand und Aufgaben der Forschung," *Archiv für Reformationsgeschichte* 76 (1985): 6–63; B. Rüth, "Reformation und Konfessionsbildung im städtischen Bereich: Perspektiven der Forschung," *Zeitschrift der Savigny-Stiftung für Rechtsgeschichte, Kanonische Abteilung* 77 (1991): 197–282.

2. The classic study on this is still T. A. Brady, Jr., *Ruling Class, Regime and Reformation in Strasbourg, 1520–1555* (Leiden, 1978). See also his more recent *The Politics of the Reformation in Germany: Jacob Sturm (1489–1553) of Strasbourg* (Atlantic Highlands, N.J., 1997).

3. On the Peasants' War see P. Blickle, *The Revolution of 1525: The German Peasants' War from a New Perspective*, trans. T. A. Brady, Jr., and H. C. E. Midelfort (Baltimore and London, 1982).

4. R. van Dülmen, *Kultur und Alltag in der Frühen Neuzeit*, vol. 3: *Religion, Magie, Aufklärung, 16–18. Jahrhundert* (Munich, 1994), 26.

5. O. Chadwick, *The Reformation* (Harmondsworth, 1973), 160–61.

6. For this and what follows see, among others, E. Kouri, "La réforme royale en Scandinavie," in *L'Europe protestante aux XVIe et XVIIe siècles*, ed. H. Miller (Paris, 1997), 131–57.

7. See, among others, J. Guy, *Tudor England* (Oxford, 1988), 116–53.

8. P. Williams, *The Later Tudors: England 1547–1603* (Oxford, 1995), esp. 487–96.

9. E. Troeltsch, *The Social Teaching of the Christian Churches*, trans. Olive Wyon (London, 1956), 469.

10. H.-C. Rublack, "New Patterns of Christian Life," in *Handbook of European History*, ed. T. A. Brady, Jr., et al. (Leiden, 1995) 2:589–90.

11. Ibid., 586–87.

12. On this see, among others, P. Veit, "Das Gesangbuch in der Praxis Pietatis der Lutheraner," in *Die lutherische Konfessionalisierung in Deutschland*, ed. H.-C. Rublack (Gütersloh, 1992), 435–54 and 455–59 (discussion); E. François, "Les protestants

allemands et la Bible:Diffusion et pratiques," in *Le siècle des Lumières et la Bible*, ed. Y. Belaval and D. Bourel (Paris, 1986), 47–58.

13. R. B. Barnes, *Prophecy and Gnosis: Apocalypticism in the Wake of the Lutheran Reformation* (Stanford, 1988), esp. 13–59.

14. See "Anabaptism" in chapter 5.

15. W. Köhler, *Zürcher Ehegericht und Genfer Konsistorium*, 2 vols. (Leipzig, 1932–42).

16. W. E. Monter, "De l'Evêché à la Rome Protestante," in *Histoire de Genève*, ed. P. Guichonnet (Toulouse, 1974), 138; Köhler, *Zürcher Ehegericht* 2:614f.

17. On the practice of the parish court (*Chorgericht*) of Bern see H. R. Schmidt, *Dorf und Religion: Reformierte Sittenzucht in Berner Landgemeinden der Frühen Neuzeit* (Quellen und Forschungen zur Agrargeschichte 41) (Stuttgart, 1995).

18. This provision refers to partisans of the French king who received annual payments (*Pensionen*) for organizing, encouraging, or condoning the French levying of mercenary troops from the Swiss Confederation.

19. Quoted in H. R. Schmidt, "Die Christianisierung des Sozialverhaltens als permanente Reformation:Aus der Praxis reformierter Sittengerichte in der Schweiz während der frühen Neuzeit," in *Kommunalisierung und Christianisierung: Voraussetzungen und Folgen der Reformation, 1400–1600* (Berlin, 1989), 144–45.

20. See L. P. Wandel, *Voracious Idols and Violent Hands: Iconoclasm in Reformation Zurich, Strasbourg and Basel* (Cambridge, 1999).

21. "Aufzeichnungen eines Basler Karthäusers aus der Reformationszeit 1522–1532," in *Basler Chroniken*, vol. 1 (Leipzig, 1872), 447.

22. Moeller, "Basler Reformation," 21.

23. On this see Jean Delumeau, *La peur en Occident (XIVe–XVIIIe siècles): Une cité assiégée* (Paris, 1978), 184–85 and 189.

24. One overview can be found in H. Feld, *Der Ikonoklasmus des Westens* (Studies in the History of Christian Thought 41) (Leiden, 1990).

25. H. R. Schmidt, "Über das Verhältnis von ländlicher Gemeinde und christlicher Ethik: Graubünden und die Innerschweiz," in *Landgemeinde und Stadtgemeinde in Mitteleuropa: Ein struktureller Vergleich*, ed. P. Blickle (Munich, 1991), 455–87.

26. Rublack, "New Patterns of Christian Life," 593; also S. C. Karant-Nunn, "Churching and Reformation of Ritual," in *Problems in the Historical Anthropology of Early Modern Europe* (Wolfenbütteler Forschungen 78), ed. R. P.-C. Hsia and R. W. Scribner (Wiesbaden, 1997), 111–38.

27. R. W. Scribner, "The Reformation, Popular Magic and the 'Disenchantment of the World,'" *Journal of Interdisciplinary History* 23 (1993): 475–94.

28. H. R. Guggisberg, "The Problem of 'Failure' in the Swiss Reformation: Some Preliminary Reflections," in *Zusammenhänge in historischer Vielfalt: Humanismus, Spanien, Nordamerika* (Basler Beiträge zur Geschichtswissenschaft 164), ed. H. R. Guggisberg (Basel, 1994), 115–33; A. Zünd, *Gescheiterte Stadt- und Landreformationen des 16. und 17. Jahrhunderts in der Schweiz* (Basler Beiträge zur Geschichtswissenschaft 170) (Basel, 1999).

29. For this thematic complex as a whole see H.-J. Goertz, *Antiklerikalismus und Reformation: Sozialgeschichtliche Untersuchungen* (Göttingen, 1995), as well as A. Dykema and H. A. Oberman, eds., *Anticlericalism in Late Medieval and Early Modern Europe* (Studies in Medieval and Reformation Thought 51) (Leiden, 1993).

30. P. Blickle, *Communal Reformation: The Quest for Salvation in Sixteenth-Century Germany*, trans. Thomas Dunlap (Atlantic Highlands, N.J., 1992), e.g., 40–46.

31. E. G. Gleason, "Catholic Reformation, Counterreformation and Papal Reform in the Sixteenth Century," in *Handbook of European History*, ed. T. A. Brady, Jr., H. A. Oberman, and J. J. Tracy (Leiden, 1995), 2:317–45.

32. J. Delumeau and M. Cottret, *Le catholicisme entre Luther et Voltaire* (Paris, 1996), 92.

33. That is, justification only through grace and faith.

34. Delumeau and Cottret, *Catholicism*, 74–77.

35. On Borromeo's visitations see Accademia di San Carlo, *Studia Borromaica 10: Saggi e documenti di stori religiosa e civile della prima età moderna* (Milan, 1996).

36. A. Bucher and W. Schmid, eds., *Reformation und katholische Reform, 1500–1712* (Quellenhefte zur Schweizergeschichte 5) (Aarau, 1958).

37. R. P.-C. Hsia, *Social Discipline in The Reformation: Central Europe, 1550–1750* (London, 1989), 43f.

38. R. J. W. Evans, *The Making of the Habsburg Monarchy, 1550–1700* (Oxford, 1979); H. Schilling, *Höfe und Allianzen: Deutschland 1648–1763* (Berlin, 1989).

39. On this see K. J. MacHardy, *War, Religion and Court Patronage in Habsburg Austria: The Social and Cultural Dimensions of Political Interaction, 1521–1622* (New York, 2003); R. J. Gordon, "Patronage and Parish: The Nobility and the Re-catholicization of Lower Austria," in *The Reformation in Eastern and Central Europe* (St. Andrews Studies in Reformation History), ed. K. Maag (Aldershot, 1997), 211–27.

40. Hsia, *Social Discipline*, 65.

41. See "The limits of ecclesiastical discipline" in this chapter.

42. Delumeau and Cottret, *Le catholicisme entre Luther et Voltaire*, 105.

43. S. T. Nalle, "Inquisitors, Priests and the People during the Catholic Reformation in Spain," *The Sixteenth Century Journal* 18 (1987): 557–87.

44. P. Hersche, *Italien im Barockzeitalter (1600–1750): Eine Sozial- und Kulturgeschichte* (Vienna, 1999), 199, thesis 4.

45. R. P.-C. Hsia, *The World of Catholic Renewal, 1540–1770* (Cambridge, 1998), 51.

46. Ibid., 64–66, and 87–89.

47. On these questions see the controversy between Heinz Schilling and Wolfgang Reinhard, on the one side, and Heinrich Richard Schmidt, on the other. See, e.g., H. Schilling, "Disziplinierung oder 'Selbstregulierung der Untertanen'? Ein Plädoyer für die Doppelperspektive von Makro- und Mikrohistorie bei der Erforschung der frühmodernen Kirchenzucht," *Historische Zeitschrift* 264 (1997): 675–91, and H. R. Schmidt, "Sozialdisziplinierung? Ein Plädoyer für das Ende des Etatismus in der Konfessionalisierungsforschung," *Historische Zeitschrift* 265 (1997): 639–82.

48. H. Schilling, "Die Konfessionalisierung im Reich: Religiöser und gesellschaftlicher Wandel in Deutschland zwischen 1555 und 1620," *Historische Zeitschrift* 246 (1988): 1–45.

49. H. Schilling, "Nationale Identität und Konfession in der europäischen Neuzeit," in *Nationale und kulturelle Identität: Studien zur Entwicklung des kollektiven Bewusstseins in der Neuzeit,* ed. B. Giesen (Frankfurt a. M., 1991), 199.

50. Ibid., 202f.

51. B. Roeck, *Eine Stadt in Krieg und Frieden: Studien zur Geschichte der Reichsstadt Augsburg zwischen Kalenderstreit und Parität* (Schriftenreihe der Historischen Kommission bei der Bayerischen Akademie der Wissenschaften, vol. 37), 2 vols. (Göttingen, 1980), 1:94.

52. L. A. Veit and L. Lenhart, *Kirche und Volksfrömmigkeit im Zeitalter des Barock* (Freiburg i. Br., 1956), 55.

53. Roeck, *Eine Stadt in Krieg und Frieden,* 1:108.

54. E. Bloesch, *Geschichte der schweizerisch-reformierten Kirchen,* 2 vols. (Bern, 1898–99), 1:452.

55. See Hsia, *Social Discipline,* 19–21.

56. R. Beck, "Der Pfarrer und das Dorf: Konformismus und Eigensinn im katholischen Bayern des 17./18. Jahrhunderts," in *Armut, Liebe, Ehre: Studien zur historischen Kulturforschung,* ed. R. v. Dülmen (Frankfurt a. M., 1988), 107–43.

57. On this see G. Chaix, "Die schwierige Schule der Sitten: Christliche Gemeinden, bürgerliche Obrigkeit und Sozialdisziplinierung im frühneuzeitlichen Köln, etwa 1450–1600," in *Zeitschrift für historische Forschung, Beiheft: Kirchenzucht und Sozialdisziplinierung im frühneuzeitlichen Europa,* ed. H. Schilling (Berlin, 1994), 200–210.

58. W. Reinhard, "Was ist katholische Konfessionalisierung?" in *Die katholische Konfessionalisierung* (Schriften des Vereins für Reformationsgeschichte 198), ed. W. Reinhard and H. Schilling (Gütersloh, 1995), 419–52, and, ibid., note 7 for references to the author's earlier relevant essays.

59. P. Hersche, " 'Klassizistischer' Katholizismus: Der konfessionsgeschichtliche Sonderfall Frankreich," *Historische Zeitschrift* 262 (1996): 357–89.

60. Ibid., 371. See also G. Audisio, *Les Français d'hier.* Vol. 2: *Des croyants, XVe–XIXe siècle* (Paris, 1996).

61. F. Lebrun, *Être Chrétien en France sous l'Ancien Régime, 1516–1790* (Paris, 1996), 42–47.

62. Hsia, *Catholic Renewal,* e.g., 71f., has advanced a very similar argument.

63. Audisio, *Les Français d'hier,* 2:84.

64. P. Hersche, "Devotion, Volksbrauch oder Massenprotest? Ein Literaturbericht aus sozialgeschichtlicher Sicht zum Thema Wallfahrt: Von der kirchlichen über die volkskundliche zur sozialgeschichtlichen Wallfahrtsforschung," *Jahrbuch der österreichischen Gesellschaft zur Erforschung des achtzehnten Jahrhunderts* 9 (1994): 7–34.

65. On this, with a European-comparative perspective, see L. Châtellier, *The Europe of the Devout: The Catholic Reformation and the Formation of a New Society,* trans. Jean Birrell (Cambridge, 1989).

66. Ibid., 4–5.

67. Ibid., 27.

68. Ibid., 51.

69. A. Conrad, " 'Katechismusjungfrauen' und 'Scholastikerinnen.' Katholische Mädchenbildung in der Frühen Neuzeit," in *Wandel der Geschlechterbeziehungen zu Beginn der Neuzeit,* ed. H. Wunder and C. Vanja (Frankfurt a. M., 1991), and "Weibliche Lehrorden und katholische höhere Mädchenschulen im 17. Jahrhundert," in *Geschichte der Mädchen- und Frauenbildung,* ed. C. Opitz and E. Kleinau (Frankfurt a. M., 1996), 1:252–62.

70. Châtellier, 119 and 172.

71. The following sections draw heavily on my essay "Religion und Gesellschaft am Ende des Dreissigjährigen Kriegs," in *1998: Das Ende von Religion, Politik und Gesellschaft?,* ed. U. Fink and H. Gernet (Solothurn, 1997), 23–44.

72. See, among others, A. Bischof, "Translationen des Klosters St. Gallen und seiner Landschaften," in *Barock in der Schweiz,* ed. O. Eberle (Einsiedeln, 1930), 85–95; R. Häne, "Die Engelweihfeier zu Einsiedeln im Jahre 1659: Ein Beitrag zur Geschichte des barocken Gottesdienstes," in *Barock in der Schweiz,* ed. O. Eberle (Einsiedeln, 1930), 95–107; F. Dommann, *Der Einfluß des Konzils von Trient auf die Reform der Seelsorge und des religiösen Lebens in Zug im 16. und 17. Jahrhundert* (Beiheft Nr. 9 zum *Geschichtsfreund*) (Stans, 1966), 402–03.

73. Häne, "Engelweihfeier."

74. Ibid., 100.

75. Bischof, "Translationen," 90.

76. Hsia, *Social Discipline,* 94f.

77. O. Eberle, "Das Theater: Sein Sinn und seine Bedeutung," in *Barock in der Schweiz,* ed. O. Eberle (Einsiedeln, 1930), 132.

78. On this and what follows see Hersche, *Italien im Barockzeitalter,* 183–96.

79. Ibid., 192.

80. Roeck, *Eine Stadt in Krieg und Frieden;* E. François, *Die unsichtbare Grenze: Protestanten und Katholiken in Augsburg 1648–1806* (Sigmaringen, 1991).

81. P. Zschunke, *Konfession und Alltag in Oppenheim: Beiträge zur Geschichte von Bevölkerung und Gesellschaft einer gemischtkonfessionellen Kleinstadt der frühen Neuzeit* (Veröffentlichungen des Instituts für Europäische Geschichte 115) (Wiesbaden, 1984).

82. F. Volkland, "Konfessionelle Grenzen zwischen Auflösung und Verhärtung: Bikonfessionelle Gemeinden in der Gemeinen Vogtei Thurgau (CH) des 17. Jahrhunderts," *Historische Anthropologie* 5 (1997): 370–87; now also her *Konfession und Selbstverständnis: Reformierte Rituale in der gemischtkonfessionellen Kleinstadt Bischofszell im 17. Jahrhundert* (Veröffentlichungen des Max-Planck-Instituts für Geschichte 210) (Göttingen, 2005).

83. Quoted in T. Brügisser, "Frömmigkeitspraktiken der einfachen Leute in Katholizismus und Reformiertentum: Beobachtungen des Luzerner Stadtschreibers Renward Cysat (1545–1614)," *Zeitschrift für historische Forschung* 17 (1990): 1–26.

84. Quoted in R. E. Hofer, " 'Nun leben wir in der gefahrlichsten Zyth': Prolegomena zu einer Geschichte Schaffhausens im konfessionellen Zeitalter," *Schaffhauser Beiträge zur Geschichte* 72 (1995): 63.

85. See "Enlightenment and religion" in chapter 6.

86. H.-U. Bächtold, *Heinrich Bullinger vor dem Rat: Zur Gestaltung und Verwaltung des Zürcher Staatswesens in den Jahren 1531 bis 1575* (Zürcher Beiträge zur Reformationsgeschichte 12) (Bern, 1982), 70. See also Delumeau and Cottret, *Le catholicisme*, 381.

87. On this see J. Bossy, "The Counter-Reformation and the People of Catholic Europe," *Past and Present* 47 (1970): 51–70.

88. Oberman, "Impact of the Reformation," 6f. See also Rublack, "New Patterns of Christian Life," 597.

89. W. E. Monter, *Ritual, Myth, and Magic in Early Modern Europe* (Brighton, 1983), 45f.

90. E. Kouri, "La réforme royale en Scandinavie," in *L'Europe protestante aux XVIe et XVII siècles*, ed. J. Miller (Paris, 1997), 171.

91. H. Krawarick, "Neue Methoden zur Erforschung konfessioneller Strukturen der frühen Neuzeit," *Archiv für Kulturgeschichte* 70 (1988) 403.

92. H. Hörger, "Dorfreligion und bäuerliche Mentalité im Wandel ihrer ideologischen Grundlagen," *Zeitschrift für bayerische Landesgeschichte* 38 (1975): 156f.

93. M. Walker, *The Salzburg Transaction: Expulsion and Redemption in Eighteenth-Century Germany* (Ithaca, N.Y., 1992).

94. Hsia, *Catholic Renewal*, 74.

95. T. P. Becker, *Konfessionalisierung in Kurköln: Untersuchungen zur Durchsetzung der katholischen Reform in den Dekanaten Ahrgau und Bonn anhand von Visitationsprotokollen 1583–1761* (Veröffentlichungen des Stadtarchivs Bonn 43) (Bonn, 1989), 169.

96. Hersche, *Italien im Barockzeitalter*, 197–212, quote p. 203.

97. H. Klueting, *Das Konfessionelle Zeitalter, 1525–1648* (Stuttgart, 1989), 150.

98. Ibid.

99. See "Marriage and the family" in chapter 3.

100. G. Oestreich, "Strukturprobleme des europäischen Absolutismus," in his *Geist und Gestalt des frühmodernen Staates: Ausgewählte Aufsätze* (Berlin, 1969), 179–97. See also W. Schulze, "Gerhard Oestreichs Begriff der 'Sozialdisziplinierung,'" *Zeitschrift für historische Forschung* 14 (1987): 265–302.

101. This thrust—on a largely social-anthropological basis—was already present at a comparatively early time in the work of Robert W. Scribner. See his *Popular Culture and Popular Movements in Reformation Europe* (London, 1987). On a different basis it has also represented an important aspect in the work of Peter Blickle over the last fifteen years; see especially his *Communal Reformation*. Most recently, once again coming at the question from a different direction, Heinz Schilling has pondered the continuities extending from the late Middle Ages into the early modern period: "Reformation—Umbruch oder Gipfelpunkt eines Temps des Réformes?" in *Die frühe Reformation in Deutschland als Umbruch*

(Schriften des Vereins für Reformationsgeschichte 119), ed. B. Moeller (Gütersloh, 1998), 13–34.

102. R. W. Scribner, "Incombustible Luther: The Image of the Reformer in Early Modern Germany," *Past and Present* 110 (1986): 38–68; now in his *Popular Culture*, 323–53. See also A. Messerli, "Die Errettung des Paradiesgärtleins aus Feuers- und Wassersnot," *Fabula: Zeitschrift für Erzählforschung* 38 (1997): 253–79.

103. On this see C. Opitz and E. Kleinau, ed., *Geschichte der Mädchen- und Frauenbildung*, vol. 1 (Frankfurt a. M., 1996).

104. See Bächtold, *Heinrich Bullinger*, 189–231.

105. Ibid., 231.

106. M.-L. v. Wartburg-Ambühl, *Alphabetisierung und Lektüre: Untersuchungen am Beispiel einer ländlichen Region im 17. und 18. Jahrhundert* (Bern, 1981).

107. Quoted in Bloesch, *Geschichte*, 1:387.

108. Quoted in van Dülmen, *Kultur und Alltag*, 3:176.

109. Audisio, *Les Français d'hier*, 2:64.

110. Becker, *Konfessionalisierung in Kurköln*, 228f.

111. Quoted in ibid., 251.

112. Conrad, "Katechismusjungfrauen," 157f.

113. A. Conrad, "Weibliche Lehrorden und katholische höhere Mädchenschule im 17. Jahrhundert," in *Geschichte der Mädchen- und Frauenbildung*, ed. C. Opitz and E. Kleinau, vol. 1 (Frankfurt a. M., 1996), 252–62; R. Dürr, "Von der Ausbildung zur Bildung: Erziehung zur Ehefrau und Hausmutter in der Frühen Neuzeit," *Geschichte der Mädchen- und Frauenbildung*, vol. 1, 189–206.

114. Ibid., 178.

115. Van Dülmen, *Kultur und Alltag*, 3:168.

116. Schilling, "Nationale Identität," 241; see also H. R. Schmidt, *Konfessionalisierung im 16. Jahrhundert* (Enzyklopädie deutscher Geschichte 12) (Munich, 1992).

117. Burke, *Popular Culture*, 213. For Germany see also P. Münch, ed., *Ordnung, Fleiß und Sparsamkeit: Texte und Dokumente zur Entstehung der 'bürgerlichen Tugenden'* (Munich, 1984).

118. Beck, *Pfarrer und Dorf*, 135.

119. Ibid., 136.

120. Quoted in L. Zehnder, *Volkskundliches in der älteren schweizerischen Chronistik* (Schriften der schweizerischen Gesellschaft für Volkskunde 60) (Basel, 1976), 77.

121. Ibid., 381.

122. E. Lebec, ed. *Miracles et sabbats: Journal du Père Maunoir: Missions en Betagne, 1631–1650*, trans. from the Latin by A.-S. Cras and J. Cras (Paris, 1997), 70.

123. Veit and Lenhart, *Kirche und Volksfrömmigkeit*, 172.

124. Dommann, *Trient*, 368f.

125. See "Enlightenment and religion" in chapter 6.

126. P. Münch, "Volkskultur und Calvinismus: Zur Theorie und Praxis der 'reformatio vitae' während der 'Zweiten Reformation,'" in *Die reformierte Konfessionalisierung in Deutschland – Das Problem der 'Zweiten Reformation'*, ed. H. Schilling (Gütersloh, 1986), 300f. See also Bächtold, *Heinrich Bullinger*, 74f.

127. Münch, "Volkskultur und Calvinismus," 303.

128. Quoted in Zehnder, *Volkskundliches*, 308.

129. Dommann, *Konzil von Trient*, 375f. See also Veit and Lenhart, *Kirche und Volksfrömmigkeit*, 145f.

130. Quoted in Zehnder, *Volkskundliches*, 301.

131. Chaix, "Schwierige Schule der Sitten," 215.

132. Scribner, *Simple Folk*, 71–73.

133. N. Schindler, " 'Heiratsmüdigkeit' und Ehezwang: Zur populären Rügesitte des Pflug- und Blochziehens," in his *Widerspenstige Leute: Studien zur Volkskultur in der frühen Neuzeit* (Frankfurt a. M., 1992), esp. 202–08.

134. J. C. V. Johansen, "Faith, Superstition and Witchcraft in Reformation Scandinavia," in *The Scandinavian Reformation*, ed. O. P. Grell (Cambridge, 1995), 179–211.

135. Delumeau and Cottret, *Le catholicisme*, 329.

136. Ibid., 332.

137. Ibid., 345.

138. On this and what follows see especially S. Clark, "French Historians and Early Modern Popular Culture," *Past and Present* 100 (1983): 62–99.

139. N. Z. Davis, "Some Tasks and Themes in the Study of Popular Religion," in *The Pursuit of Holiness in Late Medieval and Renaissance Religion*, ed. H. A. Oberman and C. Trinkaus (Leiden, 1974), 307–36.

140. In, for example Lebrun, *Être chrétien en France*; and Audisio, *Les Français d'hier*, vol. 2, esp. 223: "Ainsi du dogme défini à la doctrine vécue, par l'intermédiaire clérical, la vérité chrétienne subit bien des déformations: Les clercs en furent globalement responsables."

141. C. Langlois, "Déchristianisation, sécularisation et vitalité religieuse: Débats de sociologues et practiques d'historiens," in *Säkularisierung, Dechristianisierung und Rechristianisierung im neuzeitlichen Europa: Bilanz und Perspektiven der Forschung*, ed. H. Lehmann (Göttingen, 1997), 166.

142. J.-C. Schmitt, " 'Religion populaire' et culture folklorique," *Annales Economies, Sociétés, Civilisation* 31 (1976): 946: "Une expérience n'ayant de sense que dans la cohésion présente."

143. E. Troeltsch, *Protestantism and Progress: The Significance of Protestantism for the Rise of the Modern World* (Philadelphia, 1986), 27.

144. W. Schulze, "Ende der Moderne? Zur Korrektur unseres Begriffs der Moderne aus historischer Sicht," in *Zur Diagnose der Moderne* (Munich, 1990), 96.

145. W. Reinhard, "Gegenreformation als Modernisierung? Prolegomena zu einer Theorie des konfessionellen Zeitalters," *Archiv für Reformationsgeschichte* 68 (1977): 234.

146. Ibid., 236.

147. Quoted in J. Osterhammel, "Modernisierungstheorie und die Transformation Chinas, 1800 bis 194: Kritische Überlegungen zur historischen Soziologie," *Saeculum* 35 (1984): 34; see also H.-U. Wehler, *Modernisierungstheorie und Geschichte* (Göttingen, 1975), 11–17.

148. H. Schilling, "Confessional Europe," in *Handbook of European History, 1400–1600* (Leiden, 1995), 2:641–81.

149. Ibid., 655.

150. Hersche, *Italien im Barockzeitalter*, 197–212, here 197.

151. Q. Skinner, *The Foundations of Modern Political Thought*, vol. 2: *The Age of Reformation* (Cambridge, 1978), 320.

152. Among the relevant historians I will mention, in chronological order, Paul Warmbrunn, Peter Zschunke, Bernd Roeck, Etienne François, and Peter Wallace.

153. F. Conrad, *Die Reformation in der bäuerlichen Gesellschaft: Zur Rezeption reformatorischer Theologie im Elsaß* (Stuttgart, 1984).

154. M. Forster, "The Counter-Reformation and the Traditional Church in the Villages of the Bishopric of Speyer," *Fides et Historia* 21 (June, 1989): 30–37; see also his *The Counter-Reformation in the Villages: Religion and Reform in the Bishopric of Speyer, 1560–1720* (Ithaca, N.Y 1992); J. Meier, "Die katholische Erneuerung des Würzburger Landkapitels Karlstadt im Spiegel der Landkapitelsversammlung und Pfarreivisitationen, 1579 bis 1624," *Würzburger Diözesangeschichtsblätter* 33 (1971): 51–125.

155. On this see, among others, H. E. Bödeker and E. Hinrichs, "Alteuropa—Frühe Neuzeit—Moderne Welt? Perspektiven der Forschung," in Bödeker and Hinrichs, eds., *Alteuropa—Ancien Régime—Frühe Neuzeit: Probleme und Methoden der Forschung* (Stuttgart, 1991), 11–50.

156. Hersche, *Italien im Barockzeitalter*, 60.

157. W. Schieder, "Säkularisierung und Sakralisierung der religiösen Kultur in der europäischen Neuzeit: Versuch einer Bilanz," in H. Lehmann, ed., *Säkularisierung, Dechristianisierung und Rechristianisierung im neuzeitlichen Europa: Bilanz und Perspektiven der Forschung* (Göttingen, 1997), 311f.

158. Osterhammel, "Modernisierungstheorie," 65–68.

159. The term *Musterbuch* was used by Winfried Schulze in his introductory lecture at the first meeting of the Working Committee on Early Modern History of the German Association of Historians, 28 September 1995. See *Frankfurter Allgemeine Zeitung* 242 (18 October 1995), p. N5.

160. H. Schilling, *Die reformierte Konfessionalisierung in Deutschland*.

161. H. J. Cohn, "The Territorial Princes in Germany's Second Reformation, 1559–1622," in *International Calvinism, 1541–1715*, ed. M. Prestwich (Oxford, 1985), 135–65.

162. See, among others, J. Wormald, *Court, Kirk and Community: Scotland 1470–1625* (Edinburgh, 1981), 95–139; T. C. Smout, *A History of the Scottish People, 1560–1830* (London, 1969), chapter 2.

163. V. Press, *Calvinismus und Territorialstaat: Regierung und Zentralbehörden der Kurpfalz, 1559–1619* (Stuttgart, 1970); C. D. Gunnoe, *Thomas Erastus in Heidelberg: A Renaissance Physician during the Second Reformation, 1558–1580*, Ph.D. thesis, University of Virginia (Ann Arbor, 1998; UMI Microform 9840364).

164. E. Büssem and M. Neher, ed., *Arbeitsbuch Geschichte: Neuzeit 1. Quellen* (Munich, 1977), 197.

165. V. Press, "Die 'Zweite Reformation' in der Kurpfalz," in *Die reformierte Konfessionalisierung in Deutschland,*' ed. H. Schilling, 107f.

166. L. D. Peterson, "Philippists," *The Oxford Encyclopedia of the Reformation,* ed. H. J. Hillerbrand (New York, 1996), 3:255–62.

167. R. v. Thadden, *Die brandenburgisch-preussischen Hofprediger im 17. und 18. Jahrhundert: Ein Beitrag zur Geschichte der absolutistischen Staatsgesellschaft in Brandenburg-Preussen* (Berlin, 1959).

168. K. Deppermann, *Der hallesche Pietismus und der preussische Staat unter Friedrich II (I).* (Göttingen, 1961).

169. C. Hinrichs, "Die universalen Zielsetzungen des Halleschen Pietismus," in his *Preußentum und Pietismus: Der Pietismus in Brandenburg-Preußen als religiös-soziale Reformbewegung* (Göttingen, 1971), 100.

170. On this see especially L. Schorn-Schütte, *Evangelische Geistlichkeit in der Frühneuzeit: Deren Anteil an der Entfaltung frühmoderner Staatlichkeit und Gesellschaft, dargestellt am Beispiel des Fürstentums Braunschweig-Wolfenbüttel, der Landgrafschaft Hessen-Kassel und der Stadt Braunschweig* (Gütersloh, 1996).

171. K. von Greyerz, *The Late City-Reformation in Germany: The Case of Colmar, 1522–1628* (Wiesbaden, 1980).

172. Ibid., 124–54.

173. B. Heyne, "Zur Entstehung kirchlicher Eigenart in Bremen," in *Hospitium Ecclesiae-Forschungen zur Bremischen Kirchengeschichte,* ed. B. Heyne and K. Schulz (Bremen, 1954), 15.

174. R. P.-C. Hsia, *Social Discipline,* 31.

175. Ibid.

176. On this see especially R. J. W. Evans, *The Wechel Presses: Humanism and Calvinism in Central Europe, 1572–1627* (Oxford, 1975).

177. W. Eberhard, "Reformation and Counterreformation in East Central Europe," in *Handbook of European History, 1400–1600,* ed. T. A. Brady, Heiko A. Oberman, and James D. Tracy, 2 vols. (Leiden, 1995), 2:567f.

178. R. J. W. Evans, "Calvinism in East Central Europe," in *International Calvinism, 1541–1715,* ed. M. Prestwich (Oxford, 1985), 182.

179. Ibid., 189.

CHAPTER 2

1. H. Lehmann, " 'Absonderung' und 'Gemeinschaft' im frühen Pietismus: Allgemeinhistorische und sozialpsychologische Überlegungen zur Entstehung und Entwicklung des Pietismus," *Pietismus und Neuzeit* 4 (1979): 54–82. Now in his *Religion und Religiösität in der Neuzeit: Historische Beiträge,* ed. M. Jakubowski-Tiessen and O. Ulbricht (Göttingen, 1996), 114–43.

2. See, among others, A. Pettegree, "Coming to Terms with Victory: The Upbuilding of a Calvinist Church in Holland, 1572–1590," in *Calvinism in Europe, 1540–1620,* ed. A. Pettegree et al. (Cambridge, 1994), 160–80.

3. A. Duke, "The Ambivalent Face of Calvinism in the Netherlands, 1561–1618," in *International Calvinism, 1541–1715*, ed. M. Prestwich (Oxford, 1985), 118f.

4. Ibid., 112.

5. R. A. Muller, "God, Predestination and the Integrity of the Created Order: A Note on Patterns in Arminius' Theology," in *Later Calvinism: International Perspectives*, ed. W. F. Graham (Kirksville, Mo., 1994), 431–46.

6. On what follows see especially J. van den Berg, "Die Frömmigkeitsbestrebungen in den Niederlanden [I]," in *Der Pietismus im 17. bis frühen 18. Jahrhundert*, ed. M. Brecht (Göttingen, 1993), 57–112, and F. A. van Lieburg, "From Pure Church to Pious Culture: The Further Reformation in the Seventeenth-Century Dutch Republic," in *Later Calvinism: International Perspectives*, ed. W. F. Graham (Kirksville, Mo., 1994), 69.

7. Van den Berg, "Frömmigkeitsbestrebungen," 69.

8. Ibid., 82.

9. Ibid., 74f.

10. Ibid., 77f.

11. Van Lieburg, "Further Reformation," 421–23.

12. On this see J. F. G. Goeters, "Der reformierte Pietismus in Bremen und am Niederrhein im 18. Jahrhundert," in *Der Pietismus im 18. Jahrhundert*, ed. M. Brecht and K. Deppermann (*Geschichte des Pietismus*, vol. 2) (Göttingen, 1995), 372–27, and idem, "Der reformierte Pietismus in Deutschland 1650–690," in *Der Pietismus vom 17. bis zum frühen 18. Jahrhundert*, ed. M. Brecht (*Geschichte des Pietismus*, vol. 1) (Göttingen, 1993), 241–277, and R. Dellsperger, "Der Pietismus in der Schweiz," in *Der Pietismus im 18. Jahrhundert*, ed. M. Brecht and K. Deppermann (*Geschichte des Pietismus*, vol. 2) (Göttingen, 1995), 588–16.

13. H. Lehmann, *Das Zeitalter des Absolutismus* (Stuttgart, 1980), 124f.

14. Most recently M. Gierl, *Pietismus und Aufklärung: Theologische Polemik und Kommunikationsreform der Wissenschaft am Ende des 17. Jahrhunderts* (Göttingen, 1997).

15. J. Wallmann, "Anfänge des Pietismus," *Pietismus und Neuzeit* 4 (1979): 11–53.

16. Ibid., 53.

17. M. Jakubowski-Tiessen and H. Lehmann, "Der Pietismus," in *Schleswig-Holsteinische Kirchengeschichte*, vol. 4 (Neumünster, 1984), 271f.

18. Hinrichs, "Zielsetzung," 33.

19. M. Schmidt, *Pietismus*, 2nd ed. (Stuttgart, 1978), 10.

20. Hinrichs, "Zielsetzung," 10f.

21. Van Dülmen, *Kultur und Alltag*, 3:128.

22. Lehmann, *Absolutismus*, 131f.

23. R. Dellsperger, *Die Anfänge des Pietismus in Bern: Quellenstudien* (Göttingen, 1984), 111f.

24. Lehmann, " 'Absonderung' und 'Gemeinschaft,' " 66.

25. Van Dülmen, *Kultur und Alltag*, 3:132f.

26. Dellsperger, *Anfänge des Pietismus*, 37.

27. R. Pfister, *Kirchengeschichte der Schweiz. Band 3: Von 1720 bis 1950* (Zurich, 1984), 23.

28. Ibid., 38–40. There is, however, disagreement about whether this movement can be considered a part of Pietism.

29. Paul S. Seaver, *Wallington's World: A Puritan Artisan in Seventeenth-Century London* (Stanford, 1985), 143.

30. Quoted in J. T. Cliffe, *Puritan Gentry: The Great Puritan Families of Early Stuart England* (London, 1984), 62.

31. M. M. Knappen, *Tudor Puritanism: A Chapter in the History of Idealism*, 3rd ed. (Chicago, 1970), 488.

32. Quoted in P. Collinson, *The Elizabethan Puritan Movement* (1967; Oxford, 1990), 27.

33. See P. Collinson, *The Religion of Protestants: The Church in English Society, 1559–1625* (Oxford, 1982), viii–ix.

34. For this and the following see S. Brigden, *New Worlds, Lost Worlds: The Rule of the Tudors, 1485–1603* (Harmondsworth, 2000).

35. Cross, *Church and People*, 87f. See also G. R. Elton, ed., *The Tudor Constitution: Documents and Commentary*, 2nd ed. (Cambridge, 1982), 397 and 406–08.

36. On this see, among others, Elton, *Tudor Constitution*, 372–77 (Act of Supremacy, 1559); 410–13 (Act of Uniformity, 1559).

37. W. Allen, *The Execution of Justice in England and A True, Sincere and Modest Defense of English Catholics*, ed. R. M. Kingdon (Ithaca, N.Y., 1965), 67f. Quoted in J.-U. Davids and R. Stinshoff, eds., *Rise Like Lions: Sozialgeschichte Englands in Quellen und Dokumenten, 1547–1915* (Oldenburg, 1982), 80f.

38. P. Collinson, "John Knox, the Church of England and the Women of England," in *John Knox and the British Reformations* (Aldershot, 1998), 74–96.

39. Guy, *Tudor England*, 291.

40. P. Christianson, *Reformers and Babylon: English Apocalyptic Visions from the Reformation to the Eve of the Civil War* (Toronto, 1978), 37.

41. Ibid., 39–41. See especially K. Firth, *The Apocalyptic Tradition in Reformation Britain, 1530–1645* (Oxford, 1979).

42. Christianson, *Reformers and Babylon*, 73.

43. Collinson, *Elizabethan Puritan Movement*, 243–88.

44. Collinson, *Religion of Protestants*, 248.

45. Ibid.

46. H. C. Porter, ed., *Puritanism in Tudor England* (London, 1970), 211.

47. P. Collinson, "England and International Calvinism, 1558–1640," in *International Calvinism, 1541–1715*, ed. M. Prestwich (Oxford, 1985), 213.

48. Ibid., 214.

49. Cross, *Church and People*, 171; P. Lake, "Calvinism and the English Church, 1570–1635," *Past and Present* 115 (1987): 32–76.

50. P. Collinson, "The Jacobean Religious Settlement: The Hampton Court Conference," in *Before the English Civil War: Essays on Early Stuart Politics and Government*, ed. H. Tomlinson (London, 1983), 27–51. See also the official contemporary report in J. R. Tanner, ed. *Constitutional Documents of the Reign of James I* (Cambridge, 1925), 60–69.

51. Collinson, "Jacobean Settlement," 49f.

52. On this and the following discussion see N. Tyacke, *Anti-Calvinists: The Rise of English Arminianism, c. 1590–1640* (Oxford, 1987).

53. See, among others, A. Foster, "Church Policies of the 1630s," in *Conflict in Early Stuart England: Studies in Religion and Politics, 1603–1642* (London, 1989), 203.

54. See, for example, Christianson, *Reformers and Babylon*, 184: "The experience of puritans in the 1630s and the apocalyptic filter through which they perceived the lessons of Laudian uniformity, in large part generated the militance with which they pushed for reform in the 1640s." See also ibid., 247.

55. See D. Hirst, "The Failure of Godly Rule in the English Republic," *Past and Present* 132 (1991): 33–66.

56. M. Watts, *The Dissenters*, vol. 1: *From the Reformation to the French Revolution* (1978; Oxford, 1985), 116.

57. Ibid., 221–62. See also the section on Baptists and Quakers in chapter 5 below.

58. On what follows see also K. von Greyerz, "Der alltägliche Gott im 17. Jahrhundert: Zur religiös-konfessionellen Identität der englischen Puritaner," *Pietismus und Neuzeit* 16 (1990): 9–28.

59. Collinson, "Jacobean Religious Settlement," 29.

60. H. Reventlow, *Bibelautorität und Geist der Moderne: Die Bedeutung des Bibelverständnisses für die geistesgeschichtliche und politische Entwicklung in England von der Reformation bis zur Aufklärung* (Göttingen, 1980), 163.

61. Quoted in Collinson, *Elizabethan Puritan Movement*, 191.

62. See Cliffe, *Puritan Gentry*, 40.

63. Ibid., 26.

64. Collinson, *Religion of Protestants*, 266f.

65. On these contexts see K. von Greyerz, *England im Jahrhundert der Revolutionen, 1603–1714* (Stuttgart, 1994).

66. Collinson, *Religion of Protestants*, 94–96.

67. On Bucer's influence see Reventlow, *Bibelautorität und Geist der Moderne*, 134–50.

68. On Richard Baxter see C. Lloyd Cohen, *God's Caress: The Psychology of Puritan Religious Experience* (New York, 1986), 115. On the following see also K. von Greyerz, "Biographical Evidence on Predestination, Covenant, and Special Providence," in *Weber's Protestant Ethic: Origins, Evidence, Contexts*, ed. H. Lehmann and G. Roth (Washington, 1993), 273–84.

69. K. von Greyerz, *Vorsehungsglaube und Kosmologie: Studien zur englischen Selbstzeugnissen des 17. Jahrhunderts* (Göttingen, 1990), esp. chapter 4.

70. M. Walzer, *The Revolution of the Saints: A Study in the Origins of Radical Politics* (London, 1966). On this see, among others, Collinson, *Religion of Protestants*, 177–79. K. Sharpe, *The Personal Rule of Charles I* (New Haven, 1992), is trying to revive Walzer's theses.

71. Watts, *The Dissenters*, 129f. See also Cliffe, *Puritan Gentry*, 206–09, on the apocalyptic thinking within the Puritan gentry on the eve of the Civil War.

72. For a more detailed discussion see the section on Weber's "internality" in chapter 7 below.

73. See above, note 68.

74. G. Birkner, *Heilsgewissheit und Literatur: Metapher, Allegorie und Auto-biographie im Puritanismus* (Munich, 1972), 170.

75. Collinson, *Religion of Protestants*, 250–52. See also K. von Greyerz, "Spuren eines vormodernen Individualismus in englischen Selbstzeugnissen des 16. und 17. Jahrhunderts," in *Ego-Dokumente: Annäherungen an den Menschen in der Geschichte*, ed. W. Schulze (Berlin, 1996), 131–45.

76. A. Macfarlane, ed., *The Diary of Ralph Josselin, 1616–1683* (Oxford, 1976), 130.

77. See "Counter-Reformation" in chapter 1.

78. P. Hersche, *Der Spätjansenismus in Österreich* (Vienna, 1977), 23.

79. R. Briggs, "The Catholic Puritans, Jansenists and Rigorists in France," in *Puritans and Revolutionaries: Essays in Seventeenth-Century History presented to Christopher Hill* (1978; Oxford, 1982), 337f.

80. Delumeau and Cottret, *Le catholicisme*, 208–10.

81. E. Walder, ed., *Staat und Kirche in Frankreich I* (Bern, 1953), 78: "son jugement n'est pourtant pas irréformable, à moins que le consentement de l'église n'intervienne."

82. Briggs, *Catholic Puritans*, 347f.

83. Delumeau and Cottret, *Le Catholicisme*, 218.

84. Hersche, " 'Klassizistischer' Katholizismus," 376.

85. On this and the following see P. Loupès, "*La vie religieuse en France au XVIIIe siècle* (Paris, 1993). The relationship of the "Second Jansénisme" to the French Revolution is at the center of M. Cottret, *Jansénismes et Lumières: Pour un autre XVIIIe siècle* (Paris, 1998).

86. Lebrun, *Être Chrétien*, 64f.

87. Cottret, *Jansénismes et Lumières*, 117–42.

88. Hersche, *Spätjansenismus in Österreich*, 31f.

89. Delumeau and Cottret, *Le catholicisme*, 220.

90. Ibid., 30.

91. *Pensées de Pascal sur la religion et sur quelque autres sujets*, Nouvelle édition (Paris, n.d.), 441–46: "Comparaison des chrétiens des premiers temps avec ceux d'aujourd'hui," quote 441f.

92. Briggs, *Catholic Puritans*, 351.

93. Delumeau and Cottret, *Le catholicisme*, 237f.

94. On this see Rosa, *Settecento religioso*.

95. On this and the following see P. Hersche, *Der Spätjansenismus in Österreich*.

96. Ibid., 118–24.

97. H. Schilling, *Höfe und Allianzen: Deutschland 1648–1763*, 323.

98. D. Meyer, "Zinzendorf und Herrnhut," in *Der Pietismus im achtzehnten Jahrhundert*, ed. M. Brecht and K. Deppermann (Göttingen, 1995), 3–106.

99. H.-J. Goertz, *Religiöse Bewegungen in der Frühen Neuzeit* (Munich, 1993), 53. Needless to say, the use of the term "sect"—still current because of a lack of

alternatives and, in the final analysis, pejorative—for all other separatist religious movements is not very satisfying from the perspective of a modern religious history.

100. D. Meyer, "Zinzendorf und Herrnhut," in *Der Pietismus im achtzehnten Jahrhundert*, ed. M. Brecht and K. Deppermann (Göttingen, 1995), 42f.

101. Ibid., 49f., quote, p. 50.

102. Ibid., 75–77.

103. H. Weigelt, "Der Pietismus im Übergang vom 18. zum 19. Jahrhundert," *Der Pietismus im achtzehnten Jahrhundert*, ed. M. Brecht and K. Deppermann (Göttingen, 1995), 700 and 744.

104. See E. P. Thompson, *The Making of the English Working Class* (London, 1963), chapter 11: "The Transforming Power of the Cross." Thompson adopted this thesis from Elie Halévy.

105. J. C. D. Clark, *English Society, 1688–1832: Ideology, Social Structure and Political Practice during the Ancien Régime* (Cambridge, 1985); idem, *Revolution and Rebellion: State and Society in England in the Seventeenth and Eighteenth Centuries* (Cambridge, 1986). On the concept of the "confessional state" see also his "England's Ancien Regime as a Confessional State," *Albion* 21 (1989): 450–74.

106. Clark, *English Society*, 366–83.

107. *The Journal of John Wesley: A Selection*, ed. E. Jay (Oxford, 1987), 143.

108. Ibid., passim, and C. Haydon, *Anti-Catholicism in Eighteenth-Century England, c. 1714–80: A Political and Social Study* (Manchester, 1993), 63.

109. L. Colley, *Britons: Forging the Nation, 1707–1837* (London, 1996), 19.

110. Ibid., chap. 7 ("Manpower").

111. R. Porter, *English Society in the Eighteenth Century* (London, 1982), 195f.

112. Ibid., 192 and 195.

113. *Journal of John Wesley*, 172 (entry of March 21, 1770). The revised figures in Porter, *English Society*, 192.

114. P. Streiff, "Der Methodismus bis 1784/1791," in *Der Pietismus im achtzehnten Jahrhundert*, ed. M. Brecht and K. Deppermann (Göttingen, 1995), 625f.

115. Ibid., 627.

116. Streiff, *Methodismus*, 629.

117. C. D. Field, "The Social Structure of English Methodism: Eighteenth–Twentieth Centuries," *British Journal of Sociology* 28 (1977): 199–25.

118. W. Gibson, *Church, State and Society, 1760–1850* (London, 1994), 88 and 152f.

119. This message was aimed chiefly at personal sanctification through regular prayer and Bible reading, frequent partaking in the Lord's Supper, and active charity (poor relief).

120. H. D. Rack, "Doctors, Demons and Early Methodist Healing," in *The Church and Healing*, ed. W. J. Sheils (Oxford, 1982), 151.

CHAPTER 3

1. B. Moeller, *Imperial Cities and the Reformation: Three Essays*, ed. and trans. by H. C. Erik Midlefort and Mark U. Edwards, Jr. (Durham, N.C., 1982).

2. For an overview see K. von Greyerz, "Stadt und Reformation," esp. 8–16.

3. F. Conrad, *Reformation in der bäuerlichen Gesellschaft*, 97.

4. Ibid., 114.

5. Peter Blickle, *Gemeindereformation: Die Menschen des 16. Jahrhunderts auf dem Weg zum Heil* (Oldenbourg, 1985); English translation by Thomas Dunlap, *Communal Reformation: The Quest for Salvation in Sixteenth-Century Germany* (Atlantic Highlands, N.J., 1992).

6. Ibid., 30–32, quote p. 32.

7. See Blickle, *The Revolution of 1525: The German Peasants' War from a New Perspective*.

8. Peter Blickle, "Die soziale Dialektik der reformatorischen Bewegung," in *Zwingli und Europa: Referate und Protokolle des Internationalen Kongresses aus Anlass des 500. Geburtstags von Huldrych Zwingli vom 26. bis 30. März 1984 in Bern*, ed. P. Blickle et al. (Zurich, 1985), 77.

9. Peter Blickle, "Warum blieb die Innerschweiz katholisch?," *Mitteilungen des Historischen Vereins des Kantons Schwyz* 86 (1994): 34.

10. Ibid., 38.

11. Concerning the development in Lucerne and Zug, see now also Zünd, *Gescheiterte Stadt- und Landreformationen*, 37–60.

12. Blickle, *Bauernkrieg*, 117f.

13. Bossy, "Counter-Reformation." See also his *Christianity in the West, 1400–1700* (Oxford, 1985), passim.

14. See "Confessionalization and the assault on popular culture" in chapter 1.

15. J.-P. Gutton, "Confraternities, Curés and Communities in Rural Areas of the Diocese of Lyon under the Ancien Régime," in *Religion and Society in Early Modern Europe, 1500–1800*, ed. K. von Greyerz (London, 1984), 202–11.

16. Hersche, *Italien im Barockzeitalter*, 87–102.

17. R. Gough, *The History of the Myddle*, ed. D. Hey (Harmondsworth, 1981). On Germany see J. Peters, "Der Platz in der Kirche: Über soziales Rangdenken im Spätfeudalismus," *Jahrbuch für Volkskunde und Kulturgeschichte* 28 (1985): 77–106.

18. C. Ulbrich, "Zankapfel 'Weiber-Gestühl,'" in *Historie und Eigen-Sinn: Festschrift für Jan Peters zum 65. Geburtstag*, ed. A. Lubinski et al. (Weimar, 1997), 114.

19. D. W. Sabean, *Power in the Blood: Popular Culture and Village Discourse in Early Modern Germany* (Cambridge, 1984), 37–60. See also his "Production of the Self during the Age of Confessionalism," *Central European History* 29 (1996): 1–18.

20. See, among others, U. Frevert, "Bürgerliche Familien und Geschlechterrollen: Modell und Wirklichkeit," in *Bürgerliche Gesellschaft in Deutschland. Historische Einblicke, Fragen, Perspektiven*, ed. L. Niethammer et al. (Frankfurt a. M., 1990), 90–98.

21. See R. van Dülmen, "Fest der Liebe: Heirat und Ehe in der Frühen Neuzeit," in *Armut, Liebe, Ehre: Studien zur historischen Kulturforschung*, ed. R. van Dülmen (Frankfurt a. M., 1988), 67.

22. Wunder, *He Is the Sun*, 42.

23. R. E. Hofer, *"Üppiges, unzüchtiges Lebwesen": Schaffhauser Ehegerichtsbarkeit von der Reformation bis zum Ende des Ancien Régime (1529–1789)* (Bern, 1993).

24. S. Burghartz, "Jungfräulichkeit oder Reinheit? Zur Änderung von Argumentationsmustern vor dem Basler Ehegericht im 16. und 17. Jahrhundert," in *Dynamik der Tradition: Studien zur historischen Kulturforschung*, ed. Richard van Dülmen (Frankfurt a. M., 1992), 39.

25. Hsia, *Social Discipline*, 149.

26. Audisio, *Les Français d'hier*, 2:315.

27. Van Dülmen, *Fest der Liebe*, 85; Bossy, *Christianity in the West*, 25.

28. Hsia, *Social Discipline in the Reformation*, 146.

29. L. Roper, *Oedipus and the Devil: Witchcraft, Sexuality and Religion in Early Modern Europe* (London, 1994), 46.

30. See S. C. Karant-Nunn, "Continuity and Change: Some Effects of the Reformation on the Women of Zwickau," *The Sixteenth Century Journal* 12 (1982): 35f.

31. See, among others, M. Kobelt-Groch, *Aufsässige Töchter Gottes: Frauen im Bauernkrieg und in den Täuferbewegungen* (Frankfurt a. M., 1993).

32. Ibid., 207; Roper, *Oedipus and the Devil*, 79–103 ("Sexual Utopianism in the German Reformation"), esp. 79–87.

33. C.-P. Clasen, *Anabaptism: A Social History, 1525–1618* (Ithaca, N.Y., 1972), 334.

34. B. Hoffmann, *Radikalpietismus um 1700: Der Streit um das Recht auf eine neue Gesellschaft* (Frankfurt a. M., 1996). More generally on the role of women in Pietism: R. Dellsperger, "Frauenemanzipation im Pietismus," in *Zwischen Macht und Dienst: Beiträge zur Geschichte und Gegenwart von Frauen im kirchlichen Leben der Schweiz*, ed. S. Bietenhard et al. (Berlin, 1991), 131–52.

35. Hsia, *Catholic Renewal*, 139–42.

36. Ibid., 144–46.

37. Köhler, *Zürcher Ehegericht*, 1: 35–37.

38. Wunder, *He Is the Sun*, 47–48.

39. Ibid.

40. R. A. Mentzer, Jr., "Disciplina nervus Ecclesiae: The Calvinist Reform of Morals at Nîmes," *The Sixteenth Century Journal* 18 (1987): 89–115.

41. Hersche, *Italien im Barockzeitalter*, 74–86.

42. Burghartz, "Jungfräulichkeit oder Reinheit?" See also her *Zeiten der Reinheit—Orte der Unzucht: Ehe und Sexualität während der frühen Neuzeit* (Paderborn, 1999).

43. Hsia, *Catholic Renewal*, 22f.

44. Heide Wunder, "Von der *frumkeit* zur *Frömmigkeit*: Ein Beitrag zur Genese bürgerlicher Weiblichkeit (15.–17. Jahrhundert)," in *Weiblichkeit in geschichtlicher Perspektive: Fallstudien und Reflexionen zu Grundproblemen der historischen Frauenforschung* (Frankfurt a. M., 1988), 186.

45. See "Confessionalization and the assault on popular culture" in chapter 1.

46. Hsia, *Catholic Renewal*, 198. See also J. Bossy, "The Social History of Confession in the Age of the Reformation," *Transactions of the Royal Historical Society* 25, 5th series (1975): 21–38.

47. R. W. Scribner, "Elements of Popular Belief," in *Handbook of European History*, ed. T. A. Brady, Jr., et al., vol. 1 (Leiden, 1995), 253f.

48. H. Hörger, "Dorfreligion und bäuerliche Mentalité im Wandel ihrer ideologischen Grundlagen," *Zeitschrift für bayerische Landesgeschichte* 38 (1975): 244–316.

49. Ibid., 284f.

50. H. Lehmann, "Die Kometenflugschriften des 17. Jahrhunderts als historische Quelle," in *Literatur und Volk im 17. Jahrhundert. Probleme populärer Kultur in Deutschland*, 2 Teile, ed. W. Brückner et al. (Wiesbaden, 1985), 685.

51. See "Tensions: witch persecutions" in chapter 4.

52. Lehmann, "Kometenflugschriften," 691.

53. Quoted in L. Zehnder, *Volkskundliches in der älteren schweizerischen Chronistik* (Basel, 1976).

54. Martin Luther, *Werke. Weimarer Ausgabe* 11 (Weimar, 1900), 357–85.

55. Scribner, *For the Sake of Simple Folk*.

56. Johannes Stumpf, quoted in Zehnder, *Volkskundliches*, 498.

57. Scribner, *For the Sake of Simple Folk*, 133.

58. L. Daston and K. Park, "Unnatural Conceptions: The Study of Monsters in Sixteenth and Seventeenth-Century France and England," *Past and Present* 92 (1981): 24.

59. Habermas, "Wunder," 60.

60. Ibid., 55f.

61. G. Heiss, "Konfessionelle Propaganda und kirchliche Magie: Berichte der Jesuiten über den Teufel aus der Zeit der Gegenreformation in den mitteleuropäischen Ländern der Habsburger," *Römische Historische Mitteilungen* 32/33 (1990/91): 122f.

62. Ibid., note 96.

63. Ibid.

64. Delumeau and Cottret, *Le catholicisme*, 308.

65. Hsia, *Social Discipline*, 155.

66. Hersche, "Devotion," 20f.

67. Ibid., 19f.

68. Hsia, *Social Discipline*, 157.

69. Ibid.

70. Hersche, "Devotion," 20f.

71. K. Anderegg, *Durch der Heiligen Gnad und Hilf: Wallfahrt, Wallfahrtskapellen und Exvotos in den Oberwalliser Bezirken Goms und Östlich-Raron* (Basel, 1979).

72. See on this P. Burke, "How to Be a Counter-Reformation Saint," in *Religion and Society in Early Modern Europe, 1500–1800*, ed. K. von Greyerz (London, 1984), 45–55.

73. Hörger, "Dorfreligion," 298.

74. Ibid., 301.

75. See, among others, Delumeau, *Le peur en Occident*, 61.

76. Scribner, "Incombustible Luther."

77. On this see, among others, Roper, *Oedipus and the Devil*, Part 1, 79–81.

CHAPTER 4

1. Friedrich Battenberg, *Das Europäische Zeitalter der Juden: Zur Entwicklung einer Minderheit in der nichtjüdischen Umwelt Europas*, 2 vols. (Darmstadt, 1990), 1:6–8.

2. J. I. Israel, *European Jewry in the Age of Mercantilism, 1550–1750* (Oxford, 1985), 32–52.

3. Battenberg, *Europäische Zeitalter der Juden*, 1:13.

4. Israel, *European Jewry*, 158f.

5. Battenberg, *Europäische Zeitalter der Juden*, 2:51f.

6. E. Benbassa, *Histoire des Juifs de France* (Paris, 1997), 97–106.

7. E. Schulin, "Die spanischen und portugiesischen Juden im 15. und 16. Jahrhundert: Eine Minderheit zwischen Integrationszwang und Anpassung," in *Die Juden als Minderheit in der Geschichte*, ed. B. Martin and E. Schulin (Munich, 1981), 93–95.

8. J. H. Elliott, *Imperial Spain, 1469–1716* (Harmondsworth, 1978), 32.

9. Schulin, "Die spanischen und portugiesischen Juden," 93–95.

10. See, among others, Elliott, *Imperial Spain*, 52. The subsequent development of the community of *moriscos* (converted Moors) until their final expulsion in the years 1608–14 will not be discussed here.

11. Quoted in Elliott, *Imperial Spain*, 222.

12. H. Greive, *Grundzüge des modernen Antisemitismus in Deutschland* (Darmstadt, 1983), viif. Compare also J. Friedman, "Jewish Conversion, the Spanish Pure Blood Laws and Reformation: A Revisionist View of Racial and Religious Antisemitism," *The Sixteenth Century Journal* 18 (1987): 3–29, with Battenberg, *Europäische Zeitalter der Juden*, 2:31, who, in keeping with the conventional view, distinguishes the anti-Judaism of the Middle Ages and the early modern period from the anti-Semitism of modern bourgeois society.

13. See H. Kamen, *Inquisition and Society in Spain in the Sixteenth and Seventeenth Centuries* (London, 1985); F. Bethencourt, *L'Inquisition à l'époque moderne: Espagne, Portugal, Italie (XVe–XIXe siècle)* (Paris, 1995).

14. Israel, *European Jewry*, 7, note 1.

15. On this and the following see C. Roth, *A History of the Marranos*, 1st ed. (New York, 1959), 54–73.

16. For the subsequent development of these diaspora communities in western and southern Europe and in the Levante, see " 'Externality': individualization among the Iberian conversos" in chapter 7.

17. On this and the following see H. Greive, *Die Juden: Grundzüge ihrer Geschichte im mittelalterlichen und neuzeitlichen Europa*, 4th ed. (Darmstadt, 1992), 53–56.

18. R. P.-Ch. Hsia, *Trent 1475: Stories of a Ritual Murder Trial* (New Haven, 1992). See also his *The Myth of Ritual Murder: Jews and Magic in Reformation Germany* (New Haven, 1988).

19. C. Roth, *The History of the Jews of Italy* (Philadelphia, 1946), 177f.

20. Battenberg, *Zeitalter der Juden*, 1:201.

21. Roth, *History of the Marranos*, 206f.

22. Israel, *European Jewry*, 44f.

23. Battenberg, *Europäische Zeitalter der Juden*, 1:131.

24. Greive, *Die Juden*, 107.

25. Battenberg, *Europäische Zeitalter der Juden*, 1:163f.

26. See, among others, H. A. Oberman, *Wurzeln des Antisemitismus: Christenangst und Judenplage im Zeitalter von Humanismus und Reformation* (Berlin, 1981), 40–43.

27. Ibid., 48–51.

28. Deppermann, "Judenhass," 115–25.

29. K. Deppermann, "Judenhass und Judenfreundschaft im frühen Protestantismus," in *Die Juden als Minderheit in der Geschichte*, ed. B. Martin and E. Schulin (Munich, 1981), 115–25.

30. Israel, *European Jewry*, 35–38 and 67.

31. Battenberg, *Europäische Zeitalter der Juden*, 2:2. On the conversos see " 'Externality': individualization among the Iberian conversos" in chapter 7.

32. H. Haumann, *Geschichte der Ostjuden* (Munich, 1990). For a critical view regarding the extent of this westward migration see Israel, *European Jewry*, 165.

33. Archives Départementales du Haut-Rhin, Colmar, 25 J (Sainte Croix-en-Plaine), no. 79. Contemporary copy of a letter to Johannes Kotschareuter (d. ca. 1570), *Vogt* of the city of Colmar in Heiligkreuz (Sainte Croix-en-Plaine), no sender, dated "Tuesday following St. Martin's in Frankfurt an der Oder," no year.

34. See, among others, Greive, *Die Juden*, 132f.

35. *The Memoirs of Glückel of Hameln*, trans. with notes by Martin Lowenthal (New York, 1977), 46.

36. On this see, among others, R. Zeller, "Der Paratext der Kabbala Denudata: Die Vermittlung von jüdischer und christlicher Weisheit," *Morgen-Glantz: Zeitschrift der Christian Knorr von Rosenroth-Gesellschaft* 7 (1997): 143–69.

37. Israel, *European Jewry*, 245f. Israel emphasizes that the court Jews were not an exclusively central European phenomenon; see ibid., 141.

38. Greive, *Die Juden*, 152f.

39. Benbassa, *Histoire de Juifs*, 123f.

40. Greive, *Die Juden*, 141. A discussion of Hasidism, which arose in Poland and Russia as a reaction to the Haskalah (Jewish Enlightenment) and is present to this day within Ashkenazi Jewry, falls outside the boundaries of the present book.

41. Battenberg, *Europäische Zeitalter*, 2:82.

42. Quoted in Heiss, "Konfessionelle Propaganda," 140f.; see ibid., 133–41.

43. C. Ernst, *Teufelsaustreibungen: Die Praxis der katholischen Kirche im 16. und 17. Jahrhundert* (Bern, 1972), 19.

44. Delumeau, *Le peur en Occident*, 243.

45. The literature on the belief in and persecution of witches in the early modern period has grown so immensely that it is impossible to keep track of. One survey (though focused largely on German-speaking lands) is provided by W. Behringer, "Erträge und Perspektiven der Hexenforschung," *Historische Zeitschrift* 249 (1989): 619–40.

46. Ernst, *Teufelsaustreibungen*, 24f.

NOTES TO PAGES 143–149   251

47. On this see J.-M. Goulemot, "Démons, merveilles et philosophie à l'âge classique," *Annales Economies, Sociétés, Civilisation* 35 (1980): 1223–50.

48. Thomas Platter der Jüngere, *Beschreibung der Reisen durch Frankreich, Spanien, England und die Niederlande (1595–1600)*, ed. R. Keiser, 2 vols (Basel, 1968), 1:274f.

49. Delumeau, *La peur en Occident*, 56.

50. Ibid., 59f.

51. H. C. E. Midelfort, *Witch Hunting in Southwestern Germany, 1562–1684* (Stanford, 1972).

52. See, for example, Johansen, "Faith, Superstition, and Witchcraft," 199.

53. Zehnder, *Volkskundliches*, 526, note 3.

54. Quoted in ibid., 525.

55. Quoted in ibid., 520.

56. For a comprehensive discussion of this see S. Clark, *Thinking with Demons*.

57. G. Schormann, *Hexenprozesse in Deutschland* (Göttingen, 1981).

58. See on this the discussion in Delumeau, *La peur en Occident*, 364–76.

59. Schormann, *Hexenprozesse*, 34f.

60. See, among others, Midelfort, *Witch Hunting*, 56.

61. Schormann, *Hexenprozesse*, 36.

62. C. Larner, *Witchcraft and Religion: The Politics of Popular Belief*, ed. A. Mac-Farlane (Oxford, 1984), 16f.

63. Sources on the published debate in W. Behringer, ed., *Hexen und Hexenprozesse in Deutschland* (Munich, 1988).

64. See, among others, Larner, *Witcchraft and Religion*, 16f.

65. On this and what follows see G. Henningsen, *The Witches' Advocate: Basque Witchcraft and the Spanish Inquisition (1609–1614)* (Reno, Nev., 1980).

66. Hersche, *Italien in Barockzeitalter*, 221.

67. N. Schindler, "Die Entstehung der Unbarmherzigkeit: Zur Kultur und Lebensweise der Salzburger Bettler am Ende des 17. Jahrhunderts," *Bayerisches Jahrbuch für Volkskunde* (1988): 61–130.

68. Ibid., 61.

69. Ibid., 61.

70. Ibid., 83.

71. E. Labouvie, *Zauberei und Hexenwerk: Ländlicher Hexenglaube in der Frühen Neuzeit* (Frankfurt a. M., 1991).

72. Larner, *Witchcraft and Religion*, 139.

73. R. Muchembled, "The Witches of Cambrésis: The Acculturation of the Rural World in the Sixteenth and Seventeenth Centuries," in *Religion and the People, 800–1700*, ed. J. Obelkevich (Chapel Hill, N.C., 1979), 257f.

74. H. Lehmann, "Frömmigkeitsgeschichtliche Auswirkungen der 'Kleinen Eiszeit,'" in *Volksreligiosität in der modernen Sozialgeschichte*, ed. W. Schieder (Göttingen, 1986), 43. See also Labouvie, *Zauberei und Hexenwerk*, esp. 214. The latter study also supports the thesis of the origins of the persecutions on the village level.

75. Quoted in Zehnder, *Volkskundliches*, 529: "d'empoisonner ce que la peste avoit laissé de reste en la ville."

76. W. E. Monter, *Witchcraft in France and Switzerland: The Borderlands during the Reformation* (Ithaca, N.Y., 1976), 46–49.

77. Midelfort, *Witch Hunting*, 149.

78. Larner, *Witchcraft and Religion*, 78.

79. See A. Soman, "La décriminalization de la sorcellerie en France," *Historie, économie et société* 4 (1985): 180f.

80. Ibid., 192–97.

81. Audisio, *Les Français d'hier*, 2:328.

82. G. Schwaiger, "Das Ende der Hexenprozesse im Heiligen Römischen Reich," in *Teufelsglaube und Hexenprozesse*, ed. G. Schwaiger (Munich, 1987), 162–78.

83. Larner, *Witchcraft and Religion*, 139.

84. Labouvie, *Zauberei und Hexenwerk*, 65.

85. Ibid., 251–53.

86. Schormann, *Hexenprozesse*, 54.

87. Ibid., 111f.

88. K. Thomas, *Religion and the Decline of Magic* (New York, 1971), 520.

89. Schormann, *Hexenprozesse*, 77.

90. Muchembled, "Witches of Cambrésis," 278.

91. Midelfort, *Witch Hunting*, 169–76.

92. Schormann, *Hexenprozesse*, 118.

93. Labouvie, *Zauberei und Hexenwerk*, 33f.

94. Monter, *Witchcraft*, 116–18.

95. Ibid., 124.

96. On this see C. Opitz, "Hexenverfolgung als Frauenverfolgung?," in *Der Hexenstreit. Frauen in der frühneuzeitlichen Hexenverfolgung*, ed. C. Opitz (Freiburg i. Br., 1995), 246–70.

97. See J. Sharpe, *Instruments of Darkness: Witchcraft in England, 1550–1750,* (Harmondsworth, 1997), chapter 7: "Women and Witchcraft."

98. Numbers are taken from the list of southwest German witch trials in Midelfort, *Witch Hunting*, 199–230.

99. Roper, *Oedipus and the Devil*, 203.

100. Ibid., 217.

101. Schormann, *Hexenprozesse*, 108.

102. On this see the reflections by A. Gregory, "Politics and 'Good Neighbourhood' in Early Seventeenth-Century Rye," *Past and Present* 133 (1991): 31–66.

103. Scribner, "Reformation," 491f.

CHAPTER 5

1. Troeltsch, *Social Teaching*, 1:334.

2. See H.R. Guggisberg, *Sebastian Castellio, 1515–1563: Humanist and Defender of Religious Toleration in a Confessional Age*, translated by B. Gordon (St. Andrews Studies in Reformation History) (Burlington, Vt., 2003).

3. Troeltsch, *Social Teaching*, 1:340.

4. Ibid.

5. The term describes those religious movements in sixteenth-century Protestantism which split off from the established Lutheran and Reformed Churches.

6. See Clasen, *Anabaptism*.

7. Klueting, *Konfessionelle Zeitalter*, 193.

8. Quoted in van Dülmen, *Kultur und Alltag*, 3:98.

9. H.-J. Goertz, *Pfaffenhaß und groß Geschrei: Die reformatorischen Bewegungen in Deutschland, 1517–1529* (Munich, 1987), esp. 184–220.

10. On this and the following see J. M. Stayer, "Die Anfänge des schweizerischen Täufertums im reformierten Kongregationalismus," in *Umstrittenes Täufertum 1525–1975*, ed. H.-J. Goertz (Göttingen, 1977), 19–49.

11. Ibid., 29.

12. See Clasen, *Anabaptism*, 6f.

13. *Quellen zur Geschichte der Täufer in der Schweiz*, vol. 1: *Zurich*, ed. L. von Muralt and W. Schmid (Zurich, 1952), 13–21.

14. Ibid., 17.

15. J. Stayer, "Anfänge des schweizerischen Täufertums," 20f.

16. H.-J. Goertz, "Aufständische Bauern und Täufer in der Schweiz," *Mennonitische Geschichtsblätter* 46 (1989): 90–112.

17. Ibid., 101–4; Stayer, "Anfänge des schweizerischen Täufertums," 42.

18. Goertz, "Aufständische Bauern," 101.

19. *Quellen zur Geschichte der Täufer in der Schweiz*, vol. 2: *Ostschweiz*, ed. H. Fast (Zurich, 1974), 26–35, 29f. (English translation based on that of J. C. Wenger).

20. Ibid., 31f.

21. Ibid., 33.

22. O. Sigg, "Das 17. Jahrhundert," in *Geschichte des Kantons Zürich*, vol. 2 (Zurich, 1996), 300.

23. J. M. Stayer et al., "From Monogenesis to Polygenesis: The Historical Discussion of Anabaptist Origins," *The Mennonite Quarterly Review* 49 (1975): 84–86.

24. K. Deppermann, *Melchior Hoffman: Social Unrest and Apocalyptic Visions in the Age of Reformation*, trans. Malcom Wren, ed. Benjamin Drewery (Edinburgh, 1987), 75.

25. Ibid., 210.

26. Ibid., 382.

27. Ibid., 259–60.

28. Ibid., 310.

29. J. M. Stayer, "The Radical Reformation," in *Handbook of European History, 1400–1600*, ed. Thomas A. Brady, Jr., et al. (Leiden, 1995), 2:273.

30. Clasen, *Anabaptism*, 193.

31. Ibid., 232 and 243f.

32. Ibid., 238.

33. Ibid., 213.

34. Ibid., 293.

254   NOTES TO PAGES 167–179

35. For this and the following see J. F. McGregor and B. Reay, eds., *Radical Religion in the English Revolution* (Oxford, 1984), 26.

36. On this see ibid., 29.

37. Ibid., 33.

38. Cross, *Church and People*, 224.

39. For this and what follows see Watts, *Dissenters*, 221–62.

40. Cross, *Church and People*, 233.

41. Watts, *Dissenters*, 224f.

42. J. P. Kenyon, ed., *The Stuart Constitution, 1603–1688. Documents and Commentary*, 2nd ed. (Cambridge, 1982), 353–56.

43. On this and the following see ibid., 176f.

44. J. Morrill, "The Later Stuarts: A Glorious Restoration," *History Today* 38 (1988): 12; P. Seaward, *The Restoration, 1660–1688* (London, 1991), 59f.

45. *Remarkable Passages in the Life of William Kiffin: Written by Himself*, ed. W. Orme (London, 1832), 46.

46. McGregor, *Radical Religion*, 60f.

47. For this and the following see J. Bunyan, "Grace Abounding to the Chief of Sinners," in *Grace Abounding and The Life and Death of Mr. Badman* (London, 1928), 39f.

48. Ibid., 40.

49. B. Reay, "Quakerism and Society," in B. Reay and J. F. McGregor, eds., *Radical Religion in the English Revolution* (Oxford, 1984), 141. See also his *The Quakers and the English Revolution* (London, 1985).

50. Reay, "Quakerism," 141.

51. Watts, *Dissenters*, 194.

52. Ibid., 189.

53. *The Journal of George Fox*, ed. J. L. Nickalls (Cambridge, 1952), 36f.

54. Quoted in Reay, "Quakerism and Society," 152.

55. Ibid., 153.

56. *The Journal of George Fox*, 43.

57. Watts, *Dissenters*, 211f., and especially L. Damrosch, *The Sorrows of the Quaker Jesus: James Nayler and the Puritan Crackdown on the Free Spirit* (Cambridge, 1996).

58. Reay, "Quakerism and Society," 163.

59. Reay, *Quakers and the English Revolution*, 120.

60. Ibid.

61. W. Hadorn, *Geschichte des Pietismus in den schweizerischen Kirchen* (Constance, 1902), 139.

62. H. Schneider, "Der radikale Pietismus im achtzehnten Jahrhundert," in *Der Pietismus im achtzehnten Jahrhundert*, ed. M. Brecht and K. Deppermann (Göttingen, 1995), 112.

63. Hadorn, *Geschichte des Pietismus*, 146.

64. Hoffmann, *Radikalpietismus*, 10.

65. G. Niggl, *Geschichte der deutschen Autobiographie im 18. Jahrhundert: Theoretische Grundlegung und literarische Entfaltung* (Stuttgart, 1977), 7f.

66. Hoffmann, *Radikalpietismus*, 9f.

67. Quoted in Hadorn, *Geschichte des Pietismus*, 158f.

68. Ibid., 171f.

69. Irina Modrow, "Frauen im Pietismus," in *Individualisierung, Rationalisierung, Säkularisierung: Neue Wege der Religionsgeschichte*, ed. M. Weinzierl (Vienna, 1977), 186–99.

70. See, among others, Schneider, "Der radikale Pietismus," 124–27.

71. Hoffmann, *Radikalpietismus*, 40.

72. See, among others, Hoffmann, *Radikalpietismus*, and Schneider, "Der radikale Pietismus," 133–35.

73. The name is derived from *camise* (peasant shirt or blouse).

74. C. W. Garrett, *Spirit Possession and Popular Religion: From the Camisards to the Shakers* (Baltimore, 1987), 13–34.

75. H. Schwartz, *The French Prophets: The History of a Millenarian Group in Eighteenth-Century England* (Los Angeles, 1980).

76. W. Grossmann, "Städtisches Wachstum und religiöse Toleranzpolitik am Beispiel Neuwied," *Archiv für Kulturgeschichte* 62/63 (1980/81): 224f.

77. Hadorn, *Geschichte des Pietismus*, 155.

78. R. Pfister, *Kirchengeschichte*, 24.

79. Schneider, "Der radikale Pietismus," 152. On the New Baptists in the New World, see ibid., 139.

CHAPTER 6

1. F. W. Graf, " 'Dechristianisierung': Zur Problemgeschichte eines kulturpolitischen Topos," in *Säkularisierung, Dechristianisierung, Rechristianisierung im neuzeitlichen Europa: Bilanz und Perspektiven der Forschung*, ed. H. Lehmann (Göttingen, 1997), 32–66.

2. P. Goubert and D. Roche, *Les Français et l'Ancien Régime*, vol. 2: *Culture et Société* (Paris, 1984), 169f.

3. Béat-Louis de Muralt, *Lettres sur les Anglais et les Français*, ed. P. Chappuis (Lausanne, 1972), 20f.

4. On the problem of secularization as a whole see H.-H. Schrey, ed, *Säkularisierung* (Darmstadt, 1981).

5. Placing "countervailing" in quotation marks is an expression of an effort on my part not to introduce into the discussion a new, teleologically-charged concept that could suggest any kind of inevitability.

6. On this see U. Gäbler, *"Auferstehungszeit": Erweckungsprediger des 19. Jahrhunderts* (Munich, 1991).

7. On this see the collection of essays by M. Rosa, *Settecento religioso: Politica della ragione e religione del cuore* (Venice, 1999).

8. H. Lehmann, "Von der Erforschung der Säkularisierung zur Erforschung von Prozessen der Dechristianisierung und Rechristianisierung im neuzeitlichen Europa," in *Säkularisierung, Dechristianisierung, Rechristianisierung*, ed. H. Lehmann, 9–16.

9. See also Audisio, *Les Français d'hier*, 2:424: "L'évolution indiquait bien plus la sécularisation de la sociéte que sa déchristianisation."

10. A. Hahn, "Religion, Säkularisierung und Kultur," in *Säkularisierung, Dechristianisierung, Rechristianisierung*, ed. H. Lehmann, 21.

11. O. Chadwick, *The Secularization of the European Mind in the Nineteenth Century* (Cambridge, 1975), is limited almost entirely to questions of intellectual history.

12. The essay by P. Hazard, *Le crise de la conscience européenne, 1680–1715*, 2 vols. (Paris, 1935), is still useful in terms of the overall picture, although it overestimates—as the older scholarship frequently did—the importance of (early) Enlightenment critique of the church and religion.

13. Quoted in H. Möller, *Vernunft und Kritik: Deutsche Aufklärung im 17. und 18. Jahrhundert* (Frankfurt a. M., 1986), 12,

14. P. Chaunu, *La civilisation de l'Europe des Lumières* (1971; Paris, 1982), 238.

15. Van Dülmen, *Kultur und Alltag*, 3:147.

16. S. Gilley, "Christianity and Enlightenment: An Historical Survey," *History of European Ideas* 1 (1981): 103–21; quote p. 104.

17. Möller, *Vernunft und Kritik*, 74.

18. See D. P. Walker, *The Decline of Hell: Seventeenth-Century Discussion of Eternal Torment* (London, 1964), esp. chapter 6 ("English Arians"). See also P. C. Almond, *Heaven and Hell in Enlightenment England* (Cambridge, 1994).

19. Van Dülmen, *Kultur und Alltag*, 3:150.

20. R. Schlögl, "Die Moderne und die Nachtseite der Aufklärung: Zum Verhältnis von Freimaurerei und Naturphilosophie," *Das achtzehnte Jarhundert* 21 (1997): 33–60.

21. Chaunu, *L'Europe des Lumières*, 197.

22. W. Ruppert, *Bürgerlicher Wandel: Die Geburt der modernen deutschen Gesellschaft im 18. Jahrhundert* (Frankfurt a. M., 1983).

23. Hans Medick, *Weben und Überleben in Laichingen, 1650–1900* (Göttingen, 1996), 475.

24. C. Dipper, "Volksreligiosität und Obrigkeit im 18. Jahrhundert," in *Volksreligiosität in der modernen Sozialgeschichte*, ed. W. Schieder (Göttingen, 1986), 84.

25. P. Münch, "Die Kosten der Frömmigkeit: Katholizismus und Protestantismus im Visier von Kameralismus und Aufklärung," in *Volksfrömmigkeit in der Frühen Neuzeit*, ed. H. Molitor and H. Schmolinsky (Munich, 1994), 113.

26. Quoted in M. Rosa, "L'‘Aufklärung' cattolica," in his *Settecento religioso*, 173.

27. On this see the chapter "Conclusion and Outlook" below.

28. H.-J. Schings, *Melancholie und Aufklärung: Melancholiker und ihre Kritiker in Erfahrungsseelenkunde und Literatur des 18. Jahrhunderts* (Stuttgart, 1977).

29. Quoted ibid., 214.

30. Chaunu, *L'Europe des Lumières* 14: "L'Europe des Lumières n'existe qu'au sommet."

31. Ibid., 128.

32. P. Hersche, "Wider 'Müßiggang' und 'Ausschweifung': Feiertage und ihre Reduktion im katholischen Europa, namentlich im deutschsprachigen Raum zwischen 1750 und 1800," *Innsbrucker Historische Studien* 12/13 (1990): 97–122.

33. P. Münch, *Lebensformen in der Frühen Neuzeit, 1500 bis 1800*, rev. ed. (Frankfurt a. M., 1996), 423.

34. Ibid., 116f.

35. G. Andrey and M. Michaud, "Das Ancien Régime—Von Spannungen zum Zusammenbruch," in *Geschichte des Kantons Freiburg*, ed. R. Ruffieux (Freiburg, Switzerland, 1981), 2:753–83; *Histoire et Légende: Six exemples en Suisse romande: Baillod, Bonivard, Davel, Chenaux, Péquinat et Farinet* (Lausanne, 1987).

36. P. Hersche, " 'Lutherisch werden'—Rekonfessionalisierung als paradoxe Folge aufgeklärter Religionspolitik," in *Ambivalenzen der Aufklärung: Festschrift für E. Wangermann*, ed. G. Ammerer and H. Haas (Vienna, 1997), 164.

37. See, among others, C. Maurer, "Aufgeklärte Gesangbücher und 'gemeine Leute': Äußerungen und Inhalte der Gesangbuchstreite des ausgehenden 18. Jahrhunderts im protestantischen Deutschland," in *Le livre religieux et ses pratiques: Etudes sur l'histoire du livre religieux en Allemagne et en France à l'époque moderne. Der Umgang mit dem religiösen Buch: Studien zur Geschichte des religiösen Buches in Deutschland und Frankreich in der frühen Neuzeit*, ed. H.-E. Bödeker et al. (Göttingen, 1991), 269–88, and H. Lehmann, "Der politische Widerstand gegen die Einführung des neuen Gesangbuches von 1791 in Württemberg: Ein Beitrag zum Verhältnis von Kirchen- und Sozialgeschichte," *Blätter für württembergische Kirchengeschichte* 66/67 (1966/67): 247–63.

38. Hersche, "Lutherisch werden," 158f.

39. So the argument of K. Guth, "Volksfrömmigkeit und kirchliche Reform im Zeitalter der Aufklärung: Ein Beitrag zur kirchlichen Aufklärung in den alten Bistümern Bamberg und Würzburg," *Würzburger Diözesengeschichtsblätter* 41 (1979): 200.

40. Maurer, "Aufgeklärte Gesangbücher," 275.

41. See, among others, Haydon, *Anti-Catholicism*, esp. 238–41.

42. The following section is a much-abbreviated version of my essay "Secularization in Early Modern England (1660–c. 1750)," in *Säkularisierung, Dechristianisierung, Rechristianisierung*, ed. H. Lehmann, 86–100, which also contains additional references.

43. H. Schwartz, *Knaves, Fools, Madmen, and That Subtile Effluvium: A Study of the Opposition to the French Prophets in England, 1706–1710* (Gainsville, 1978), 53f.; L. E. Klein, *Shaftesbury and the Culture of Politeness: Moral Discourse and Cultural Politics in Early Eighteenth-Century England* (Cambridge, 1994), 18f. and 160–69.

44. Schwartz, *French Prophets*, 134–46.

45. Klein, *Shaftesbury and the Culture of Politeness*. See also his "The Third Earl of Shaftesbury and the Progress of Politeness." *Eighteenth-Century Studies* 18 (1984/85): 186–214.

46. S. Bott, *"Friends and lovers of virtue": Tugendethische Handlungsorientierungen im Kontext der Schottischen Aufklärung, 1750–1800* (Frankfurt a. M., 1999), e.g., 27.

47. K. Thomas, *Man and the Natural World: Changing Attitudes in England, 1500–1800* (Harmondsworth, 1984), 80.

48. Thomas, *Religion and the Decline of Magic*, 453; J. Stevenson, *Popular Disturbances in England, 1700–1870* (London, 1979), 49.

49. C. Hill, *Some Intellectual Consequences of the English Revolution* (London, 1980), 76f.

50. *The Journal of John Wesley*, 163f.

51. An overview is provided by M. Heyd, "The Reaction to Enthusiasm in the Seventeenth Century: Towards an Integrative Approach," *Journal of Modern History* 53 (1981): 258–80.

52. Excerpts in B. Vickers, ed., *English Science, Bacon to Newton* (Cambridge, 1987), 160–82.

53. MacDonald, *Mystical Bedlam*, 170.

54. For this and what follows see K. von Greyerz, "Gottesbild und 'Mechanisierung' des gelehrten Weltbildes im England des 17. Jahrhunderts," in *Querdenken: Dissens und Toleranz im Wandel der Geschichte: Festschrift zum 65. Geburtstag von H. R. Guggisberg*, ed. M. Erbe et al. (Mannheim, 1996), 377–92.

55. Greyerz, "Vorsehungsglaube und Kosmologie."

56. On Latitudinarianism see, for example, Reventlow, *Bibelautorität und Geist der Moderne*, 370–469.

57. Bunyan, *The Pilgrim's Progress*, 107.

58. See R. W. Scribner, "Hidden Transcripts in Discourses about Religion, Science, and Skepticism," in *Säkularisierung, Dechristianisierung, Rechristianisierung*, ed. H. Lehmann, 117.

59. Given the intense interest of recent research in the alchemistic influences on the thought and work of prominent English scientists of the later seventeenth century, the term "mechanization" is now seldom found in the most recent literature on the history of science in England in the seventeenth century. While I continue to use it here, I must emphasize that it is by no means a sufficient descriptive label for the development of science in England during the period in question.

60. M. Jacob, *The Newtonians and the English Revolution, 1689–1729* (Ithaca, N.Y., 1976), 201–50; L. Stewart, *The Rise of Public Science: Rhetoric, Technology, and Natural Philosophy in Newtonian Britain, 1660–1750* (Cambridge, 1992).

61. See, among other, Jacob, *Newtonians and the English Revolution*, 143–61.

62. The resistance of rural popular culture and religion to attempts to change them is the topic of a fascinating study by B. Bushway, " 'Tacit, Unsuspected, but Still Implicit Faith': Alternative Belief in Nineteenth-Century Rural England," in *Popular Culture in England, c. 1500–1850*, ed. T. Harris (London, 1995), 189–215.

63. Lebrun, *Être chrétien en France*, 177.

64. On this see also Langlois, "Déchristianisation."

65. On this and what follows see also Langlois, "Déchristianisation."

66. See M. Vovelle, *La mort et l'Occident de 1300 à nos jours* (Paris, 1983), for example 296–301.

67. M. Vovelle, *Piété baroque et déchristianisation en Provence au XVIIIe siècle* (Paris, 1973), 125.

68. P. Chaunu, *La mort à Paris (XVIe, XVIIe, XVIIIe siècles)* (Paris, 1978), 432–56.

69. Vovelle, *La mort et l'occident*, 420.

70. F. Lebrun, *Les hommes et la mort en Anjou aux XVIIe et XVIIIe siècles* (Paris, 1971), esp. 413–15, and 493–95.

71. Goubert and Roche, *Les Français*, 341f.

72. Lebrun, *Être chrétien en France*, 180.

73. On this see the introduction to this chapter.

74. See "Confessionalization and the assult on popular culture" in chapter 1.

75. C. W. Garrett, *Respectable Folly. Millenarians and the French Revolution in France and England* (Baltimore, 1975).

76. M. Vovelle, "Dechristianization in Year II: Expression or Extinction of a Popular Culture," in *Religion and Society in Early Modern Europe, 1500–1800*, ed. K. v. Greyerz (London, 1984), 81f. See also his *Religion et Révolution. La déchristianisation de l'an II* (Paris, 1973).

77. U. F. Müller, ed., *Lust an der Geschichte. Die Französische Revolution, 1789–1799* (Munich, 1988), 254f., quoting the *Journal de Célestin Guittard de Floriban, Bourgeois de Paris sous la Révolution, 1791–1796*, ed. R. Aubert (Paris, 1974).

78. M. Vovelle, *La mentalité révolutionnaire. Société et mentalité sous la Révolution française* (Paris, 1985), 184.

79. Ibid, 177.

80. A. Croix and F. Roudaut, *Les Bretons, la mort et Dieu de 1600 à nos jours* (Paris, 1984), 217f.; M. Lagrée, *Religion et cultures en Bretagne (1850–1950)* (Paris, 1992).

81. This has been argued, for example, by Audisio, *Les Français d'hier*, vol. 2, 410f.

82. Lebrun, *Être chrétien*, 178; Audisio, *Les Français d'hier*, vol. 2, 94.

83. M. Agulhon, *La sociabilité méridionale (Confréries et associations dans la vie collective en Provence orientale à la fin du XVIIIe siècle)* (Aix-en-Provence, 1966), 344–80.

84. Goubert and Roche, *Les Français et l'Ancien Régime*, 275–79.

85. Vovelle, *La mentalité révolutionnaire*, 46.

86. F. Lebrun and A. Fauve-Chamoux, "Le mariage et la famille," in *Histoire de la Population Française*, ed. J. Dupâquier, vol. 2 (Paris, 1988), 313f.

87. A. Wrigley, "Family Limitation in Pre-industrial England," *Economic History Review*, 2nd series, 19 (1966): 82–109; P. Becker, *Leben und Lieben in einem kalten Land: Sexualität im Spannungsfeld von Ökonomie und Demographie. Das Beispiel St. Lambrecht, 1600–1850* (Frankfurt a. M., 1990).

88. For a summary review see U. Pfister, "Die Anfänge der Geburtenbeschränkung in Europa: Wege zu einer umfassenderen Analyse." In *Ehe, Liebe, Tod: Zum Wandel der Familie, der Geschlechts- und Generationsbeziehungen in der Neuzeit*, ed. P. Borscheid and H. J. Teuteberg (Münster, 1983), 213–32.

89. On this see Chaunu, *L'Europe des Lumières*, 100f.

90. Ibid., 255.

91. Goubert and Roche, *Les Français et l'Ancien Régime*, 231f.

92. See, among others, R. Darnton, *The Literary Underground of the Old Regime* (Cambridge, Mass., 1982).

93. J. Dupâquier, "Die Trendwende in der Geschichte der französischen Bevölkerung, 1750–1850," in *Deutschland und Frankreich im Zeitalter der Französischen Revolution*, ed. H. Berding et al. (Frankfurt a. M., 1989), 53f.

94. F. Stemme, "Die Säkularisation des Pietismus zur Erfahrungsseelenkunde," *Zeitschrift für deutsche Philologie* 72 (1953): 144–58.

95. Schings, *Melancholie und Aufklärung*, 102.

96. Ibid., 30.

97. L. Kansy, " 'Zu Ende dieses Jahres erfüllet sich dieser Traum . . . schon allbereit an meinem eigenen Leib. . .': Träume als Instrument biographischer Sinngebung." Unpublished licentiate dissertation, University of Basel, 1998.

98. C. Pfister, *Bevölkerungsgeschichte und Historische Demographie, 1500–1800* (Munich, 1994), 93.

99. U. Pfister, *Die Anfänge von Geburtenbeschränkung" Eine Fallstudie—Ausgewählte Zürcher Familien im 17. und 18. Jahrhundert* (Bern, 1985); see also note 88 above.

100. P. Becker, *Leben und Lieben*, 79; see also pp. 138 and 146f.

101. Medick, *Weben und Überleben*, 345.

102. This is the argument (regarding Colyton) of J. E. Knodel, *Demographic Behaviour in the Past: A Study of Fourteen German Village Populations in the Eighteenth and Nineteenth Centuries* (Cambridge, 1988), 317.

103. R. Schlögl, *Glaube und Religion in der Säkularisierung: Die katholische Stadt— Köln, Aachen, Münster, 1700–1840* (Munich, 1995), 31.

104. Ibid., 84f.

105. Lehmann, *Absolutismus*, 118.

106. Schlögl, *Glaube und Religion*, 123.

107. Schlögl, " 'Aufgeklärter Unglaube' oder 'mentale Säkularisierung'?," 109.

108. Ibid., 111.

109. Gibson, *Church and Society*, 87.

CHAPTER 7

1. See "The marginalized: Jews" in chapter 4.

2. A. Shmuelevitz, *The Jews of the Ottoman Empire in the Late Fifteenth and Sixteenth Centuries: Administrative, Economic, Legal and Social Relations as Reflected in the Responsa* (Leiden, 1984), esp. 11–40; A. Levy, *The Sephardim in the Ottoman Empire* (Princeton, 1992).

3. Benbassa, *Histoire des Juifs*, 87–95.

4. Roth, *History of the Marranos*, 200.

5. The following reflections are based on my essay "Portuguese *Conversos* on the Upper Rhine and the Converso Community of Sixteenth-Century Europe," *Social History* 14 (1989): 59–82, esp. 76–79.

6. F. Platter, *Tagebuch (Lebensbeschreibung), 1536–1567*, ed. V. Lötscher (Basel, 1976), 144 (note 172), 156f., 159f., 173, and 221.

7. Quoted in B. Pullan, *The Jews of Europe and the Inquisition of Venice* (Oxford, 1983), 171.

8. See P. Grunebaum-Ballin, *Joseph Naci, duc de Naxos* (Paris, 1968); C. Roth, *The House of Nasi: The Duke of Naxos* (Philadelphia, 1948). See also R. Calimani, *Die Kaufleute von Venedig: Die Geschichte der Juden in der Löwenrepublik*, trans. S. Höfer (Munich, 1988), 140–50.

9. Greyerz, "Portuguese *Conversos*," 76.

10. Roth, *History of the Marranos*; *History of the Jews of Italy*; I. S. Révah, "Les Marranes," *Revue des Etudes Juives* 118 (1959/60): 29–77, and especially his "L'hérésie marrane dans l'Europe catholique du 15e et 16e siècle," in *Hérésies et sociétés dans l'Europe préindustrielle, 11e–18e siècles* (Paris, 1968), 327–39, a good summary of Révah's arguments on this point.

11. Israel, *European Jewry*, 25; see also 58 and 82.

12. Quoted in Pullan, *Jews of Europe*, 209.

13. J. C. Boyajian, "The New Christians Reconsidered: Evidence from Lisbon's Portuguese Bankers, 1497–1647," *Studia Rosenthaliana* 13 (1979): 134.

14. H. Pohl, *Die Portugiesen in Antwerpen (1567–1648): Zur Geschichte einer Minderheit* (Wiesbaden, 1977).

15. Pullan, *Jews of Europe*, 204 and 242.

16. Israel, *European Jewry*, 82: "Furious divisions arose among émigrés in France, Italy, and at Antwerp, sometimes even within one family."

17. J. A. Goris, *Etude sur les colonies marchandes méridionales (Portugais, Espagnols, Italiens) à Anvers de 1488 à 1567: Contribution à l'histoire des débuts du capitalisme moderne* (Louvain, 1925), 573.

18. See "Confessionalization and the assault on popular culture" in chapter 1.

19. M. Weber, *Gesammelte Aufsätze zur Religionssoziologie*, 3 vols. (Tübingen, 1922–23).

20. Reprinted in Weber, *Gesammelte Aufsätze zur Religionssoziologie*, 1:17–236; also available in various reprints.

21. In addition to the contributions to this debate mentioned in notes 27–29 below, I should mention also H. Lehmann, "Asketischer Protestantismus und ökonomischer Rationalismus: Die Weber-These nach zwei Generationen," in *Max Webers Sicht des okzidentalen Christentums*, ed. W. Schluchter (Frankfurt am Main, 1988), 529–53, and H. Tyrell, "Worum geht es in der 'Protestantischen Ethik'? Ein Versuch zum besseren Verständnis Max Webers," in *Saeculum* 41 (1990), 130–77.

22. In early modern society, it was chiefly men who could "prove themselves in the world." In keeping with the tenor of his times, Weber's argumentation is limited with respect to gender.

23. Max Weber, *Economy and Society: An Outline of Interpretive Sociology*, ed. G. Roth and C. Wittich, trans. Ephraim Fischoff et al. (Berkeley, 1978), 2:1199–1200.

24. Troeltsch, *Social Teaching*, 2:894.

25. Ibid., 589–90.

26. For a discussion of the issues raised here that is broader both geographically and substantively see above Chapter 1.

27. P. Münch, "Welcher Zusammenhang besteht zwischen Konfession und ökonomischem Verhalten? Max Webers These im Lichte der historischen Forschung," in *Konfession—eine Nebensache?*, ed. H.-G. Wehling (Stuttgart, 1984), 69; see also his *Lebensformen*, 355–413 ("Arbeit und Fleiss").

28. H. Lüthy, "Variationen über ein Thema von Max Weber," in his *In Gegenwart der Geschichte. Historische Essays* (Cologne, 1967), 66.

29. K.-L. Ay, "Nachwirkungen der Konfessionalisierung in Wortkultur und Wirtschaft deutscher Regionen: Landesgeschichtliche Beobachtungen über Max Webers Protestantismus-These," *Sociologia Internationalis* 33 (1995): 21–47.

30. Ibid.

31. P. Hersche, "Intendierte Rückständigkeit: Zur Charakteristik des geistlichen Staates im alten Reich," in *Stände und Gesellschaft im Alten Reich*, ed. G. Schmidt (Stuttgart, 1989), 133–49.

32. Hersche, *Italien im Barockzeitalter*, esp. 167–69, quote p. 169.

33. R. van Dülmen, "Protestantismus und Kapitalismus: Max Webers These im Licht der neueren Sozialgeschichte," in *Max Weber: Ein Symposion*, ed. C. Gneuss and J. Kocka (Munich, 1988), 100.

34. Greyerz, "Biographical Evidence"; see also H.-C. Schröder, "Max Weber und der Puritanismus," *Geschichte und Gesellschaft* 21 (1995): 459–78.

35. On this see also "Thematic aspects" in chapter 2 above.

36. Lehmann, *Zeitalter des Absolutismus*, 148.

37. Bossy, *Christianity in the West*, 120f.

38. See "Baroque Catholicism" in chapter 1.

39. Lehmann, *Zeitalter des Absolutismus*, 150.

40. Lüthy, "Variationen," 57.

CONCLUSION AND OUTLOOK

1. Meyer, "Zinzendorf und Herrnhut," 67f.; J. Solé, *La Révolution en question* (Paris, 1988), 294.

2. Dipper, "Volksreligiosität," 93.

3. W. Schieder, "Konfessionelle Erneuerung in den christlichen Parallelkirchen Deutschlands im 19. Jahrhundert: Ein Kommentar," in *Säkularisierung, Dechristianisierung, Rechristianisierung*, ed. H. Lehmann, 227.

Literature and Sources

SOURCES

Academia di San Carlo, ed. *Studia Borromaica 10: Saggi e documenti di storia religiosa e civile della prima età moderna*. Milan, 1996.

Allen, W. *The Execution of Justice in England* and *A True, Sincere and Modest Defense of English Catholics*. Edited by R. M. Kingdon. Ithaca, N.Y., 1965.

"Aufzeichnungen eines Basler Karthäusers aus der Reformationszeit 1522–1532." In *Basler Chroniken*, 1:429–48. Leipzig, 1872.

"The Autobiography of Goodwin Wharton (1653–1704)." British Library. London, vol. 1, Add. Ms. 20006.

Bacon, F. *The Advancement of Learning*. Edited by G. W. Kitchin. London, 1973.

Behringer, W., ed. *Hexen und Hexenprozesse in Deutschland*. Munich, 1988.

Boyle, R. "The Sceptical Chymist" (selections). In B. Vickers, ed., *English Science: Bacon to Newton*, 67–87. Cambridge, 1987.

Bucher, A., and W. Schmid, eds. *Reformation und katholische Reform, 1500–1712*. Quellenhefte zur Schweizergeschichte 5. Aarau, 1958.

Bunyan, J. "Grace Abounding to the Chief of Sinners." In J. Bunyan, *Grace Abounding* and *The Life and Death of Mr. Badman*, 1–102. London, 1928.

———. *The Pilgrim's Progress*. Edited by R. Sharrock. Harmondsworth, 1965.

Büssem, E., and M. Neher, eds. *Arbeitsbuch Geschichte: Neuzeit 1: Quellen*. Munich, 1977.

Davids, J.-U., and R. Stinshoff, eds. *Rise Like Lions: Sozialgeschichte Englands in Quellen und Dokumenten, 1547–1915*. Oldenburg, 1982.

Elton, G. R., ed. *The Tudor Constitution: Documents and Commentary*. 2nd ed. Cambridge, 1982.

Journal de Célestin Guittard de Floriban, Bourgeois de Paris sous la Révolution, 1791–1796. Edited by R. Aubert. Paris, 1974.

The Journal of George Fox. Edited by J. L. Nickalls. Cambridge, 1952.

The Journal of John Wesley: A Selection. Edited by E. Jay. Oxford, 1987.

Kenyon, J. P., ed. *The Stuart Constitution, 1603–1688: Documents and Commentary*. 2nd ed. Cambridge, 1986.

Lebec, E., ed. *Miracles et sabbats: Journal du Père Maunoir. Missions en Bretagne, 1631–1650*. Translated from the Latin by A.-S. Cras and J. Cras. Paris, 1997.

Luther, Martin. *Werke [Weimarer Ausgabe]*, WA 11. Weimar, 1900.

Macfarlane, A., ed. *The Diary of Ralph Josselin, 1616–1683*. Oxford, 1976.

Münch, P., ed. *Ordnung, Fleiss und Sparsamkeit: Texte und Dokumente zur Entstehung der 'bürgerlichen Tugenden.'* Munich, 1984.

Muralt, B.-L. *Lettres sur les Anglais et les Français*. Edited by P. Chappuis. Lausanne, 1972.

Newton, I. *Optice: Sive de Reflexionibus, Refractionibus, Inflexionibus & Coloribus Lucis, Libri Tres*. London, 1706.

Pascal, B. *Pensées de Pascal sur la religion et sur quelques autres sujets*. Nouvelle ed. Paris, n.d.

Platter, F. *Tagebuch (Lebensbeschreibung), 1536–1567*. Edited by V. Lötscher. Basler Chroniken 10. Basel, 1976.

Platter, T. d. J. *Beschreibung der Reisen durch Frankreich, Spanien, England und die Niederlande (1595–1600)*. Edited by R. Keiser. 2 vols. Basler Chroniken 9. Basel, 1968.

Quellen zur Geschichte der Täufer in der Schweiz. Vol. 1: *Zürich*. Edited by L. v. Muralt and W. Schmid. Zurich, 1952.

Quellen zur Geschichte der Täufer in der Schweiz. Vol. 2: *Ostschweiz*. Edited by H. Fast. Zurich, 1974.

Tanner, J. R., ed. *Constitutional Documents of the Reign of James I*. Cambridge, 1925.

Walder, E., ed. *Staat und Kirche in Frankreich I*. Quellen zur neueren Geschichte 20. Bern, 1953.

SECONDARY LITERATURE

Agulhon, M. *La sociabilité méridionale (Confréries et associations dans la vie collective en Provence orientale à la fin du XVIIIe siècle)*. Aix-en-Provence, 1966.

Almond, P. C. *Heaven and Hell in Enlightenment England*. Cambridge, 1994.

Anderegg, K. *Durch der Heiligen Gnad und Hilf: Wallfahrt, Wallfahrtskapellen und Exvotos in den Oberwalliser Bezirken Goms und Östlich-Raron*. Schriften der Schweizerischen Gesellschaft für Volkskunde 64. Basel, 1979.

Andrey, G., and M. Michaud. "Das Ancien Régime—Von Spannungen zum Zusammenbruch." In *Geschichte des Kantons Freiburg*, edited by R. Ruffieux, 2:753–83. Freiburg, Switzerland, 1981.

Audisio, G. *Les Français d'hier*. Vol. 2: *Des croyants, XVe-XIXe siècle*. Paris, 1996.

Ay, K.-L. "Nachwirkungen der Konfessionalisierung in Wortkultur und Wirtschaft deutscher Regionen: Landesgeschichtliche Beobachtungen über Max Webers Protestantismus-These." *Sociologia Internationalis* 33 (1995): 21–47.

Bächtold, H.-U. *Heinrich Bullinger vor dem Rat: Zur Gestaltung und Verwaltung des Zürcher Staatswesens in den Jahren 1531 bis 1575.* Zürcher Beiträge zur Reformationsgeschichte 12. Bern, 1982.

Barnes, R. B. *Prophecy and Gnosis: Apocalypticism in the Wake of the Lutheran Reformation.* Stanford, 1988.

Battenberg, F. *Das Europäische Zeitalter der Juden: Zur Entwicklung einer Minderheit in der nichtjüdischen Umwelt Europas.* 2 vols. Darmstadt, 1990.

Beck, R. "Der Pfarrer und das Dorf: Konformismus und Eigensinn im katholischen Bayern des 17./18. Jahrhunderts." In *Armut, Liebe, Ehre: Studien zur historischen Kulturforschung*, edited by R. van Dülmen, 107–43. Frankfurt a. M., 1988.

Becker, P. *Leben und Lieben in einem kalten Land: Sexualität im Spannungsfeld von Ökonomie und Demographie: Das Beispiel St. Lambrecht, 1600–1850.* Frankfurt, 1990.

Becker, T. P. *Konfessionalisierung in Kurköln: Untersuchungen zur Durchsetzung der katholischen Reform in den Dekanaten Ahrgau und Bonn anhand von Visitationsprotokollen 1583–1761.* Veröffentlichungen des Stadtarchivs Bonn 43. Bonn, 1989.

Behringer, W. *Witches and Their Persecution.* Cambridge, 2003.

Benbassa, E. *Histoire des Juifs de France.* Paris, 1997.

Berg, J. van den "Die Frömmigkeitsbestrebungen in den Niederlanden [I]." In *Der Pietismus im 17. bis frühen 18. Jahrhundert (Geschichte des Pietismus*, vol. 1), edited by M. Brecht, 57–112. Göttingen, 1993.

Bethencourt, F. *L'Inquisition à l'époque moderne: Espagne, Portugal, Italie (XVe–XIXe siècle).* Paris, 1995.

Bideau, A., et al. "La mortalité." In *Histoire de la Population Française*, edited by J. Dupâquier, 2:221–91. Paris, 1988.

Birkner, G. *Heilsgewissheit und Literatur: Metapher, Allegorie und Autobiographie im Puritanismus.* Theorie und Geschichte der Literatur und der schönen Künste, Texte und Abhandlungen 18. Munich, 1972.

Bischof, A. "Translationen des Klosters St. Gallen und seiner Landschaften." In *Barock in der Schweiz*, edited by O. Eberle, 84–95. Einsiedeln, 1930.

Blickle, P. *Communal Reformation: The Quest for Salvation in Sixteenth-Century Germany.* Translated by Thomas Dunlap. Atlantic Highlands, N.J., 1992.

———. "Die soziale Dialektik der reformatorischen Bewegung." In *Zwingli und Europa: Referate und Protokolle des Internationalen Kongresses aus Anlass des 500. Geburtstags von Huldrych Zwingli vom 26. bis 30. März 1984 in Bern*, edited by P. Blickle et al., 71–89. Zurich, 1985.

———. *The Revolution of 1525: The German Peasants' War from a New Perspective.* Translated by T. A. Brady, Jr., and H. C. Erik Midelfort. Baltimore, 1981.

———. "Warum blieb die Innerschweiz katholisch?" *Mitteilungen des Historischen Vereins des Kantons Schwyz* 86 (1994): 29–38.

Bloesch, E. *Geschichte der schweizerisch-reformierten Kirchen.* 2 vols. Bern, 1898–99.

Bödeker, H. E., and E. Hinrichs. "Alteuropa—Frühe Neuzeit—Moderne Welt? Perspektiven der Forschung." In *Alteuropa—Ancien Régime—Frühe Neuzeit:*

Probleme und Methoden der Forschung, edited by H. E. Bödeker and E. Hinrichs, 11–50. Stuttgart, 1991.

Bossy, J. *Christianity in the West, 1400–1700*. Oxford, 1985.

―――. "The Counter-Reformation and the People of Catholic Europe." *Past and Present* 47 (1970): 51–70.

―――. "The Social History of Confession in the Age of the Reformation." *Transactions of the Royal Historical Society*, 5th ser., 25 (1975): 21–38.

Bott, S. *"Friends and lovers of virtue": Tugendethische Handlungsorientierungen im Kontext der Schottischen Aufklärung, 1750–1800*. Scottish Studies International 27. Frankfurt a. M., 1999.

Boyajian, J. C. "The New Christians Reconsidered: Evidence from Lisbon's Portuguese Bankers, 1497–1647." *Studia Rosenthaliana* 13 (1979): 129–56.

Brady, T. A., Jr. *The Politics of the Reformation in Germany: Jacob Sturm (1489–1553) of Strasbourg*. Atlantic Highlands, N.J., 1997.

―――. *Ruling Class, Regime and the Reformation at Strasbourg, 1520–1555*. Studies in Medieval and Reformation Theology 22. Leiden, 1978.

Brigden, S. *New Worlds, Lost Worlds: The Rule of the Tudors, 1485–1603*. Harmondsworth, 2000.

Briggs, R. "The Catholic Puritans: Jansenists and Rigorists in France." In *Puritans and Revolutionaries: Essays in Seventeenth-Century History presented to Christopher Hill*, edited by D. Pennington and K. Thomas [1978]. Oxford, 1982.

Brügisser, T. "Frömmigkeitspraktiken der einfachen Leute in Katholizismus und Reformiertentum: Beobachtungen des Luzerner Stadtschreibers Renward Cysat (1545–1614)." *Zeitschrift für historische Forschung* 17 (1990): 1–26.

Burghartz, S. "Jungfräulichkeit oder Reinheit? Zur Änderung von Argumentationsmustern vor dem Basler Ehegericht im 16. und 17. Jahrhundert." In *Dynamik der Tradition: Studien zur historischen Kulturforschung*, edited by R. van Dülmen, 13–40. Frankfurt a. M., 1992.

Burke, P. "How to Be a Counter-Reformation Saint." In *Religion and Society in Early Modern Europe, 1500–1800*, edited by K. von Greyerz, 45–55. London, 1984.

―――. *Popular Culture in Early Modern Europe*. New York, 1978.

Bushaway, B. " 'Tacit, Unsuspected, but Still Implicit Faith': Alternative Belief in Nineteenth-Century Rural England." In *Popular Culture in England, c. 1500–1850*, edited by T. Harris, 189–215. London, 1995.

Calimani, R. *Die Kaufleute von Venedig: Die Geschichte der Juden in der Löwenrepublik*. Translated by S. Höfer. Munich, 1988.

Chadwick, O. *The Reformation*. Pelican History of the Church, vol 3. Harmondsworth, 1973.

―――. *The Secularization of the European Mind in the Nineteenth Century*. Cambridge, 1975.

Chaix, G. "Die schwierige Schule der Sitten: Christliche Gemeinden, bürgerliche Obrigkeit und Sozialdisziplinierung im frühneuzeitlichen Köln, etwa 1450–1600." In *Zeitschrift für historische Forschung, Beiheft: Kirchenzucht und*

Sozialdisziplinierung im frühneuzeitlichen Europa, edited by H. Schilling, 200–210. Berlin, 1994.

Châtellier, L. *The Europe of the Devout: The Catholic Reformation and the Formation of a New Society*. Translated by Jean Birrell. Cambridge, 1989.

Chaunu, P. *La civilisation de l'Europe des Lumières* [1971]. Paris, 1982.

———. *La mort à Paris, (XVIᵉ, XVIIᵉ, XVIIIᵉ siècles)*. Paris, 1978.

Christianson, P. *Reformers and Babylon: English Apocalyptic Visions from the Reformation to the Eve of the Civil War*. Toronto, 1978.

Clark, J. C. D. "England's Ancien Regime as a Confessional State." *Albion* 21 (1989): 450–74.

———. *English Society, 1688–1832: Ideology, Social Structure and Political Practice during the Ancien Régime*. Cambridge, 1985.

———. *Revolution and Rebellion: State and Society in England in the Seventeenth and Eighteenth centuries*. Cambridge, 1986.

Clark, S. "The Scientific Status of Demonology." In *Occult and Scientific Mentalities in the Renaissance*, edited by B. Vickers, 351–74. Cambridge, 1984.

———. *Thinking with Demons: The Idea of Witchcraft in Early Modern Europe*. Oxford, 1997.

Clasen, C.-P. *Anabaptism: A Social History, 1525–1618*. Ithaca, N.Y., 1972.

Cleveland, H. "Trois siècles après Newton." In *La mort de Newton*, edited by A. Forti et al., 21–33. Paris, 1996.

Cliffe, J. T. *The Puritan Gentry: The Great Puritan Families of Early Stuart England*. London, 1984.

Colley, L. *Britons: Forging the Nation, 1707–1837*. London, 1996.

Collinson, P. *The Elizabethan Puritan Movement* [1967]. Oxford, 1990.

———. "England and International Calvinism, 1558–1640." In *International Calvinism, 1541–1715*, edited by M. Prestwich, 197–223. Oxford, 1985.

———. "The Jacobean Religious Settlement: The Hampton Court Conference." In *Before the English Civil War: Essays on Early Stuart Politics and Government*, edited by H. Tomlinson, 27–51. London, 1983.

———. "John Knox, the Church of England and the Women of England." In *John Knox and the British Reformations*. St. Andrews Studies in Reformation History, edited by R. A. Mason, 74–96. Aldershot, 1998.

———. *The Religion of Protestants: The Church in English Society, 1559–1625*. Oxford, 1982.

Conrad, A. " 'Katechismusjungfrauen' und 'Scholastikerinnen': Katholische Mädchenbildung in der Frühen Neuzeit." In *Wandel der Geschlechterbeziehungen zu Beginn der Neuzeit*, edited by H. Wunder and C. Vanja, 154–79. Frankfurt a. M., 1991.

———. "Weibliche Lehrorden und katholische höhere Mädchenschulen im 17. Jahrhundert." In *Geschichte der Mädchen- und Frauenbildung*, vol. 1, edited by C. Opitz and E. Kleinau, 252–62. Frankfurt a. M., 1996.

Conrad, F. *Die Reformation in der bäuerlichen Gesellschaft: Zur Rezeption reformatorischer Theologie im Elsass*. Veröffentlichungen des Instituts für Europäische Geschichte Mainz 116. Stuttgart, 1984.

Cottret, M. *Jansénismes et Lumières: Pour un autre XVIIIe siècle.* Paris, 1998.

Croix, A., and F. Roudaut. *Les Bretons, la mort et Dieu de 1600 à nos jours.* Paris, 1984.

Cross, C. *Church and People, 1450–1660: The Triumph of the Laity in the English Church.* Glasgow, 1976.

Dahms, H. J., and U. Majer. "Wissenschaftsgeschichte." In *Wissenschaftstheoretisches Lexikon,* edited by E. Braun and H. Radermacher, cols. 670–75. Graz, 1978.

Darnton, R. *The Literary Underground of the Old Regime.* Cambridge, Mass., 1982.

Daston, L., and K. Park. "Unnatural Conceptions: The Study of Monsters in Sixteenth and Seventeenth-Century France and England." *Past and Present* 92 (1981): 20–54.

———. *Wonders and the Order of Nature, 1150–1750.* New York, 1998.

Davis, N. Z. "Some Tasks and Themes in the Study of Popular Religion." In *The Pursuit of Holiness in Late Medieval and Renaissance Religion.* Studies in Medieval and Reformation Thought 10), edited by H. A. Oberman and C. Trinkaus, 307–36. Leiden, 1974.

Debus, A. G. "Science and History." In *Science, Pseudo-Science and Utopianism in Early Modern Thought,* edited by S. A. McKnight, 1–36. Columbia, Mo., 1992.

Dellsperger, R. *Die Anfänge des Pietismus in Bern: Quellenstudien.* Arbeiten zur Geschichte des Pietismus 22. Göttingen, 1984.

———. "Der Pietismus in der Schweiz." In *Der Pietismus im achtzehnten Jahrhundert* (*Geschichte des Pietismus,* vol. 2), edited by M. Brecht and K. Deppermann, 588–616. Göttingen, 1995.

———. "Frauenemanzipation im Pietismus." In *Zwischen Macht und Dienst: Beiträge zur Geschichte und Gegenwart von Frauen im kirchlichen Leben der Schweiz,* edited by S. Bietenhard, 131–52. Bern, 1991.

Delumeau, J. *La peur en Occident (XIVe–XVIIIe siècles): Une cité assiégée.* Paris, 1978.

———, and M. Cottret. *Le catholicisme entre Luther et Voltaire.* 6th ed. Paris, 1996.

Deppermann, K. *Der hallesche Pietismus und der preussische Staat unter Friedrich II. (I.).* Göttingen, 1961.

———. "Judenhass und Judenfreundschaft im frühen Protestantismus." In *Die Juden als Minderheit in der Geschichte,* edited by B. Martin and E. Schulin, 110–30. Munich, 1981.

———. *Melchior Hoffman: Soziale Unruhen und apokalyptische Visionen im Zeitalter der Reformation.* Göttingen, 1979.

Dinges, M. "'Historische Anthropologie' und 'Gesellschaftsgeschichte': Mit dem Lebensstilkonzept zu einer 'Alltagskulturgeschichte' der frühen Neuzeit?" *Zeitschrift für historische Forschung* 24 (1997): 179–214.

Dipper, C. "Volksreligiosität und Obrigkeit im 18. Jahrhundert." In *Volksreligiosität in der modernen Sozialgeschichte* (Geschichte und Gesellschaft, Sonderheft 11), edited by W. Schieder, 73–96. Göttingen, 1986.

Dirlinger, H. "Das Buch der Natur: Der Einfluss der Physikotheologie auf das neuzeitliche Naturverständnis und die ästhetische Wahrnehmung von Wildnis." In *Individualisierung, Rationalisierung, Säkularisierung: Neue Wege der Religionsgeschichte* (Wiener Beiträge zur Geschichte der Neuzeit 22), edited by M. Weinzierl, 156–85. Vienna and Munich, 1977.

Dommann, F. *Der Einfluss des Konzils von Trient auf die Reform der Seelsorge und des religiösen Lebens in Zug im 16. und 17. Jahrhundert.* Beiheft Nr. 9 zum *Geschichtsfreund.* Stans, 1966.

Duke, A. "The Ambivalent Face of Calvinism in the Netherlands, 1561–1618." In *International Calvinism, 1541–1715,* edited by M. Prestwich, 109–34. Oxford, 1985.

Dülmen, R. van "Fest der Liebe: Heirat und Ehe in der Frühen Neuzeit." In *Armut, Liebe, Ehre: Studien zur historischen Kulturforschung,* edited by Richard van Dülmen, 67–106. Frankfurt a. M., 1988.

———. *Kultur und Alltag in der Frühen Neuzeit.* Vol. 3: *Religion, Magie, Aufklärung, 16–18. Jahrhundert.* Munich, 1994.

———. "Protestantismus und Kapitalismus: Max Webers These im Licht der neueren Sozialgeschichte." In *Max Weber: Ein Symposion,* edited by C. Gneuss and J. Kocka, 88–101. Munich, 1988.

Dupâquier, J. "Die Trendwende in der Geschichte der französischen Bevölkerung, 1750–1850." In *Deutschland und Frankreich im Zeitalter der Französischen Revolution,* edited by H. Berding et al., 42–58. Frankfurt a. M., 1989.

Durkheim, E. *The Elementary Forms of the Religious Life: A Study in Religious Sociology.* Translated by Joseph Ward Swain. Glencoe, Ill., 1947.

Dürr, R. "Von der Ausbildung zur Bildung: Erziehung zur Ehefrau und Hausmutter in der Frühen Neuzeit." In *Geschichte der Mädchen- und Frauenbildung,* vol. 1, edited by C. Opitz and E. Kleinau, 189–206. Frankfurt a. M., 1996.

Dykema, A., and H. A. Oberman, eds. *Anticlericalism in Late Medieval and Early Modern Europe.* Studies in Medieval and Reformation Thought 51. Leiden, 1993.

Eberhard, W. "Reformation and Counterreformation in East Central Europe." In *Handbook of European History, 1400–1600,* edited by T. A. Brady, Jr., et al., 2:551–84. Leiden, 1995.

Eberle, O. " Theater: Sein Sinn und seine Bedeutung." In *Barock in der Schweiz,* edited by O. Eberle, 128–48. Einsiedeln, 1930.

Eliott, J. H. *Imperial Spain, 1469–1716.* Harmondsworth, 1978.

Enzyklopädie der Philosophie und Wissenschaftstheorie, vol. 4. Stuttgart, 1996.

Ernst, C. *Teufelsaustreibungen: Die Praxis der katholischen Kirche im 16. und 17. Jahrhundert.* Bern, 1972.

Evans, R. J. W. "Calvinism in East Central Europe." In *International Calvinism, 1541–1715,* edited by M. Prestwich, 167–96. Oxford, 1985.

———. *The Making of the Habsburg Monarchy, 1550–1700.* Oxford, 1979.

———. *The Wechel Presses: Humanism and Calvinism in Central Europe, 1572–1627.* Oxford, 1975.

Feld, H. *Der Ikonoklasmus des Westens.* Studies in the History of Christian Thought 41. Leiden, 1990.

Field, C. D. "The Social structure of English Methodism: Eighteenth–Twentieth Centuries." *British Journal of Sociology* 28 (1977): 199–225.

Firth, K. *The Apocalyptic Tradition in Reformation Britain, 1530–1645.* Oxford, 1979.

Firth, R. "God and Anthropology." *Times Literary Supplement,* 23 May 1986, 557.

Forster, M. "The Counter-Reformation and the Traditional Church in the Villages of the Bishopric of Speyer." *Fides et Historia* 21 (June 1989): 30–37.

———. *The Counter-Reformation in the Villages: Religion and Reform in the Bishopric of Speyer, 1560–1720.* Ithaca, N.Y., 1992.

Foster, A. "Church Policies of the 1630's." In *Conflict in Early Stuart England: Studies in Religion and Politics, 1603–1642,* edited by R. Cust and A. Hughes, 193–223. London, 1989.

Foster, R. F. *Modern Ireland, 1600–1972.* Harmondsworth, 1989.

Foucault, M. *The Order of Things: An Archeology of the Human Sciences.* London, 1970.

François, E. *Die unsichtbare Grenze: Protestanten und Katholiken in Augsburg 1648–1806.* Sigmaringen, 1991.

———. "Les protestants allemands et la Bible: Diffusion et pratiques." In *Le siècle des Lumières et la Bible,* edited by Y. Belaval and D. Bourel, 47–58. Paris, 1986.

Frevert, U. "Bürgerliche Familien und Geschlechterrollen: Modell und Wirklichkeit." In *Bürgerliche Gesellschaft in Deutschland: Historische Einblicke, Fragen, Perspektiven,* edited by L. Niethammer et al., 90–98. Frankfurt a. M., 1990.

Friedman, J. "Jewish Conversion, the Spanish Pure Blood Laws and Reformation: A Revisionist View of Racial and Religious Antisemitism." *The Sixteenth Century Journal* 18 (1987): 3–29.

Fueter, E. *Geschichte der exakten Wissenschaften in der schweizerischen Aufklärung (1680–1780).* Aarau, 1941.

Garrett, C. W. *Respectable Folly: Millenarians and the French Revolution in France and England.* Baltimore, 1975.

———. *Spirit Possession and Popular Religion: From the Camisards to the Shakers.* Baltimore, 1987.

Geertz, C. " 'From the Native's Point of View': On the Nature of Anthropological Understanding." In *Meaning in Anthropology,* edited by K. H. Basso and H. A. Selby, 221–31. Albuquerque, N.M., 1976.

Geertz, H. "An Anthropology of Religion and Magic, I." *Journal of Interdisciplinary History* 6 (1975): 71–89.

Gibson, W. *Church, State and Society, 1760–1850.* London, 1994.

Gierl, M. *Pietismus und Aufklärung: Theologische Polemik und Kommunikationsreform der Wissenschaft am Ende des 17. Jahrhunderts.* Veröffentlichungen des Max-Planck-Instituts für Geschichte 129. Göttingen, 1997.

Gilley, S. "Christianity and Enlightenment: An Historical Survey." *History of European Ideas* 1 (1981): 103–21.

Gleason, E. G. "Catholic Reformation, Counterreformation and Papal Reform in the Sixteenth Century." In *Handbook of European History, 1400–1600,* edited by T. A. Brady, Jr., et al., 2:317–45. Leiden, 1995.

Goertz, H.-J. *Antiklerikalismus und Reformation: Sozialgeschichtliche Untersuchungen.* Göttingen, 1995.

———. "Aufständische Bauern und Täufer in der Schweiz." *Mennonitische Geschichtsblätter* 46 (1989): 90–112.

————. *Pfaffenhass und gross Geschrei: Die reformatorischen Bewegungen in Deutschland,*
1517–1529. Munich, 1987.

————. *Religiöse Bewegungen in der frühen Neuzeit* (Enzyklopädie deutscher Geschichte
20). Munich, 1993.

Goeters, J. F. G. "Der reformierte Pietismus in Bremen und am Niederrhein im 18.
Jahrhundert." In *Der Pietismus im achtzehnten Jahrhundert (Geschichte des*
Pietismus, vol. 2), edited by M. Brecht and K. Deppermann, 372–427. Göttingen,
1995.

————. "Der reformierte Pietismus in Deutschland 1650–1690." In *Der Pietismus vom*
17. bis zum frühen 18. Jahrhundert (Geschichte des Pietismus, vol. 1), edited by
M. Brecht and K. Deppermann, 241–77. Göttingen, 1993.

Gordon, J. R. "Patronage and Parish: The Nobility and the Recatholicization of Lower
Austria." In *The Reformation in Eastern and Central Europe.* St. Andrews
Studies in Reformation History, edited by K. Maag, 211–27. Aldershot, 1997.

Goris, J. A. "Étude sur les colonies marchandes méridionales (Portugais, Espagnols,
Italiens) à Anvers de 1488 à 1567: Contribution à l'histoire des débuts du
capitalisme moderne." (Université de Louvain, Receuil des travaux publiés par
les membres des Conférences d'Histoire et de Philologie, 2e série, 4e fascicule.)
Louvain, 1925.

Goubert, P., and D. Roche. *Les Français et l'Ancien Régime.* Vol. 2: *Culture et Société.*
Paris, 1984.

Gough, R. *The History of Myddle.* Edited by D. Hey. Harmondsworth, 1981.

Goulemot, J.-M. "Démons, merveilles et philosophie à l'âge classique." *Annales*
Economies, Sociétés, Civilisation 35 (1980): 1223–50.

Graf, F. W. " 'Dechristianisierung': Zur Problemgeschichte eines kulturpolitischen
Topos." In *Säkularisierung, Dechristianisierung, Rechristianisierung im neuzeitlichen*
Europa: Bilanz und Perspektiven der Forschung. Veröffentlichungen des Max-
Planck-Instituts für Geschichte 130), edited by H. Lehmann, 32–66. Göttingen,
1997.

Greive, H. *Die Juden: Grundzüge ihrer Geschichte im mittelalterlichen und neuzeitlichen*
Europa. 4th ed. Darmstadt, 1992.

————. *Grundzüge des modernen Antisemitismus in Deutschland.* Darmstadt, 1983.

Greverus, I.-M. *Kultur und Alltagswelt: Eine Einführung in Fragen der Kulturanthropo-*
logie. Munich, 1978.

Greyerz, K. von "Alchemie, Hermetismus und Magie: Zur Frage der Kontinuitäten in
der wissenschaftlichen Revolution." In *Im Zeichen der Krise: Religiosität im Europa*
des 17. Jahrhunderts (Veröffentlichungen des Max-Planck-Instituts für Geschichte
152), edited by H. Lehmann and A.-C. Trepp. Göttingen, 1999.

————. "Biographical Evidence on Predestination, Covenant, and Special Providence."
In *Weber's Protestant Ethic: Origins, Evidence, Contexts,* edited by H. Lehmann
and G. Roth, 273–84. Washington, D.C., 1993.

————. "Der alltägliche Gott im 17. Jahrhundert: Zur religiös-konfessionellen
Identität der englischen Puritaner." *Pietismus und Neuzeit* 16 (1990): 9–28.

————. *England im Jahrhundert der Revolutionen, 1603–1714.* Stuttgart, 1994.

272   LITERATURE AND SOURCES

———. "Gottesbild und 'Mechanisierung' des gelehrten Weltbildes im England des 17. Jahrhunderts." In *Querdenken: Dissens und Toleranz im Wandel der Geschichte. Festschrift zum 65. Geburtstag von H. R. Guggisberg*, edited by H. Erbe et al., 377–92. Mannheim, 1996.

———. "Grenzen zwischen Religion, Magie und Konfession aus der Sicht der frühneuzeitlichen Mentalitätsgeschichte." In *Grenzen und Raumvorstellungen (11.–20. Jh.)—Frontières et conceptions de l'éspace (11ᵉ–20ᵉ siècles)*, edited by G. P. Marchal, 329–43. Zurich, 1996.

———. *The Late City-Reformation in Germany: The Case of Colmar, 1522–1628.* Veröffentlichungen des Instituts für Europäische Geschichte Mainz 98. Wiesbaden, 1980.

———. "Portuguese *Conversos* on the Upper Rhine and the Converso Community of Sixteenth-Century Europe." *Social History* 14 (1989): 59–82.

———. "Religion in the Life of German and Swiss Autobiographers (Sixteenth and Early Seventeenth Centuries)." In *Religion and Society in Early Modern Europe, 1500–1800*, edited by K. von Greyerz, 223–41. London, 1984.

———. "Religion und Gesellschaft am Ende des Dreissigjährigen Kriegs." In *Das Ende von Religion, Politik und Gesellschaft?*, edited by U. Fink and H. Gernet, 23–44. Solothurn, 1997.

———. "Secularization in Early Modern England (1660–c. 1750)." In *Säkularisierung, Dechristianisierung, Rechristianisierung im neuzeitlichen Europa: Bilanz und Perspektiven der Forschung.* Veröffentlichungen des Max-Planck-Instituts für Geschichte 130, edited by H. Lehmann, 86–100. Göttingen, 1997.

———. "Spuren eines vormodernen Individualismus in englischen Selbstzeugnissen des 16. und 17. Jahrhunderts." In *Ego-Dokumente: Annäherungen an den Menschen in der Geschichte. (Selbstzeugnisse der Neuzeit: Quellen und Darstellungen zur Sozial- und Erfahrungsgeschichte*, vol. 2), edited by W. Schulze, 131–45. Berlin, 1996.

———. "Stadt und Reformation: Stand und Aufgaben der Forschung." *Archiv für Reformationsgeschichte* 76 (1985): 6–63.

———. *Vorsehungsglaube und Kosmologie: Studien zu englischen Selbstzeugnissen des 17. Jahrhunderts.* Veröffentlichungen des Deutschen Historischen Instituts London 25. Göttingen, 1990.

Grossmann, W. "Städtisches Wachstum und religiöse Toleranzpolitik am Beispiel Neuwied." *Archiv für Kulturgeschichte* 62/63 (1980/81): 207–32.

Grunebaum-Ballin, P. *Joseph Naci, duc de Naxos.* Ecole pratique des Hautes Etudes, 6ᵉ section, Etudes Juives 13. Paris, 1968.

Guggisberg, H. R. "The Problem of "Failure" in the Swiss Reformation: Some Preliminary Reflections." In *Zusammenhänge in historischer Vielfalt: Humanismus, Spanien Nordamerika* Basler Beiträge zur Geschichtswissenschaft 164, 115–33. Basel, 1994.

———. *Sebastian Castellio, 1515–1563: Humanist and Defender of Religious Toleration in a Confessional Age*, translated by B. Gordon. St. Andrews Studies in Reformation History, Burlington, Vt., 2003.

Gunnoe, C. D. *Thomas Erastus in Heidelberg: A Renaissance Physician during the Second Reformation, 1558–1580.* Ph.D. thesis, University of Virgina (UMI Microform 9840364), Ann Arbor, Mich., 1998.

Guth, K. "Liturgie, Volksfrömmigkeit und kirchliche Reform im Zeitalter der Aufklärung: Ein Beitrag zur kirchlichen Aufklärung in den alten Bistümern Bamberg und Würzburg." *Würzburger Diözesangeschichtsblätter* 41 (1979): 183–201.

Gutton, J.-P. "Confraternities, Curés and Communities in Rural Areas of the Diocese of Lyons under the Ancien Régime." In *Religion and Society in Early Modern Europe, 1500–1800,* edited by K. von Greyerz, 202–11. London, 1984.

Guy, J. *Tudor England.* Oxford, 1988.

Habermas, R. "Wunder, Wunderliches, Wunderbares: Zur Profanisierung eines Deutungsmusters in der Frühen Neuzeit." In *Armut, Liebe, Ehre: Studien zur historischen Kulturforschung,* edited by R. van Dülmen, 38–66. Frankfurt a. M., 1988.

Hadorn, W. *Geschichte des Pietismus in den schweizerischen Kirchen.* Constance, 1902.

Hahn, A. "Religion, Säkularisierung und Kultur." In *Säkularisierung, Dechristianisierung, Rechristianisierung im neuzeitlichen Europa: Bilanz und Perspektiven der Forschung* (Veröffentlichungen des Max-Planck-Instituts für Geschichte 130), edited by H. Lehmann, 17–31. Göttingen, 1997.

Hall, A. R. *Isaac Newton: Adventurer in Thought.* Oxford, 1992.

Häne, R. "Die Engelweihfeier zu Einsiedeln im Jahre 1659. Ein Beitrag zur Geschichte des barocken Gottesdienstes." In *Barock in der Schweiz,* edited by O. Eberle, 95–107. Einsiedeln, 1930.

Haumann, H. *Geschichte der Ostjuden.* Munich, 1990.

Haydon, C. *Anti-Catholicism in Eighteenth-Century England, c. 1714–80: A Political and Social Study.* Manchester, 1993.

Hazard, P. *La crise de la conscience européenne, 1680–1715.* 2 vols. Paris, 1935.

Heiss, G. "Konfessionelle Propaganda und kirchliche Magie: Berichte der Jesuiten über den Teufel aus der Zeit der Gegenreformation in den mitteleuropäischen Ländern der Habsburger." *Römische Historische Mitteilungen* 32/33 (1990/91): 103–52.

Henningsen, G. *The Witches' Advocate: Basque Witchcraft and the Spanish Inquisition (1609–1614).* Reno, Nev., 1980.

Hersche, P. *Der Spätjansenismus in Österreich.* Veröffentlichungen der Kommission für Geschichte Österreichs 7. Vienna, 1977.

———. "Devotion, Volksbrauch oder Massenprotest? Ein Literaturbericht aus sozialgeschichtlicher Sicht zum Thema Wallfahrt: Von der kirchlichen über die volkskundliche zur sozialgeschichtlichen Wallfahrsforschung." *Jahrbuch der österreichischen Gesellschaft zur Erforschung des achtzehnten Jahrhunderts* 9 (1994): 7–34.

———. "Intendierte Rückständigkeit: Zur Charakteristik des geistlichen Staates im alten Reich." In *Stände und Gesellschaft im Alten Reich,* edited by G. Schmidt, 133–49. Stuttgart, 1989.

———. *Italien im Barockzeitalter (1600–1750): Eine Sozial- und Kulturgeschichte.* Vienna, 1999.

———. "'Klassizistischer' Katholizismus: Der konfessionsgeschichtliche Sonderfall Frankreich." *Historische Zeitschrift* 262 (1996): 357–89.

———. "'Lutherisch werden'—Rekonfessionalisierung als paradoxe Folge aufgeklärter Religionspolitik." In *Ambivalenzen der Aufklärung: Festschrift für E. Wangermann,* edited by G. Ammerer and H. Haas, 155–68. Vienna and Munich, 1997.

———. "Wider 'Müssiggang' und 'Ausschweifung': Feiertage und ihre Reduktion im katholischen Europa, namentlich im deutschsprachigen Raum zwischen 1750 und 1800." *Innsbrucker Historische Studien* 12/13 (1990): 97–122.

Hesse, M. "Reasons and Evaluation in the History of Science." In *Changing Perspectives in the History of Science: Essays in Honour of Joseph Needham,* edited by M. Teich and R. Young, 127–47. London, 1973.

Heyd, M. "The Reaction to Enthusiasm in the Seventeenth Century: Towards an Integrative Approach." *Journal of Modern History* 53 (1981): 258–80.

Heyne, B. "Zur Entstehung kirchlicher Eigenart in Bremen." In *Hospitium Ecclesiae—Forschungen zur Bremischen Kirchengeschichte,* edited by B. Heyne and K. Schulze, 7–21. Bremen, 1954.

Hill, C. *Some Intellectual Consequences of the English Revolution.* London, 1980.

Hinrichs, C. "Die universalen Zielsetzungen des Halleschen Pietismus." In C. Hinrichs, *Preußentum und Pietismus: Der Pietismus in Brandenburg-Preußen als religiös-soziale Reformbewegung,* 1–125. Göttingen, 1971.

Hirst, D. "The Failure of Godly Rule in the English Republic." *Past and Present* 132 (1991): 33–66.

Histoire et Légende: Six exemples en Suisse romande: Baillod, Bonivard, Davel, Chenaux, Péquignat et Farinet. Mémoires et documents publiés par la Société d'Histoire de la Suisse Romande, 3ème série, tome 16. Lausanne, 1987.

Hofer, R. E. *'Üppiges, unzüchtiges Lebwesen': Schaffhauser Ehegerichtsbarkeit von der Reformation bis zum Ende des Ancien Régime (1529–1798).* Bern, 1993.

———. "'Nun leben wir in der gefahrlichsten Zyth': Prolegomena zu einer Geschichte Schaffhausens im konfessionellen Zeitalter." *Schaffhauser Beiträge zur Geschichte* 72 (1995): 23–70.

Hoffmann, B. *Radikalpietismus um 1700: Der Streit um das Recht auf eine neue Gesellschaft.* Frankfurt a. M., 1996.

Hörger, H. "Dorfreligion und bäuerliche Mentalité im Wandel ihrer ideologischen Grundlagen." *Zeitschrift für bayerische Landesgeschichte* 38 (1975): 244–316.

———. *Kirche, Dorfreligion und bäuerliche Gesellschaft: Strukturanalysen zur gesellschaftsgebundenen Religiosität ländlicher Unterschichten des 17. bis 19. Jahrhunderts, aufgezeigt an bayerischen Beispielen,* Part I. Studien zur altbayerischen Kirchengeschichte 5. Munich, 1978.

Hsia, R. P.-C. *The Myth of Ritual Murder: Jews and Magic in Reformation Germany.* New Haven, 1988.

———. *Social Discipline in the Reformation: Central Europe, 1550–1750.* London, 1989.

———. *Trent 1475: Stories of a Ritual Murder Trial*. New Haven, 1992.

———. *The World of Catholic Renewal, 1540–1770*. Cambridge, 1998.

Hunt, L. "The Challenge of Gender." In *Geschlechtergeschichte und Allgemeine Geschichte: Herausforderungen und Perspektiven*, edited by H. Medick and A.-C. Trepp, 57–97. Göttingen, 1998.

Hunter, M. "Alchemy, Magic and Moralism in the Thought of Robert Boyle." *British Journal for the History of Science* 23 (1990): 387–410.

———. *Elias Ashmole 1617–1692: The Founder of the Ashmolean Museum and his World*. Oxford, 1983.

———. *John Aubrey and the Realm of Learning*. London, 1975.

Israel, J. I. *European Jewry in the Age of Mercantilism, 1550–1750*. Oxford, 1985.

Jacob, M. *The Newtonians and the English Revolution, 1689–1720*. Ithaca, N.Y., 1976.

Jakubowski-Tiessen, M., and H. Lehmann. "Der Pietismus." *Schleswig-Holsteinische Kirchengeschichte* 4 (Neumünster, 1984): 269–334.

Kamen, H. *Inquisition and Society in Spain in the Sixteenth and Seventeenth Centuries*. London, 1985.

Kansy, L. " 'Zu Ende dieses Jahres erfüllete sich dieser Traum ... schon allbereit an meinem eigenen Leib': Träume als Instrument biographischer Sinngebung." Unpublished licentiate dissertation, University of Basel, 1998.

Karant-Nunn, S. C. "Continuity and Change: Some Effects of the Reformation on the Women of Zwickau." *The Sixteenth Century Journal* 12 (1982): 17–42.

———. "A Women's Rite: Churching and Reformation of Ritual." In *Problems in the Historical Anthropology of Early Modern Europe* (Wolfenbütteler Forschungen, vol. 78), edited by R. P.-C. Hsia and R. W. Scribner, 111–38. Wiesbaden, 1997.

Kempe, M. *Wissenschaft, Theologie, Aufklärung: Johann Jakob Scheuchzer (1672–1733) und die Sintfluttheorie*. Frühneuzeit-Forschungen 10. Epfendorf, 2003.

Kieckhefer, R. *Magic in the Middle Ages*. Cambridge, 1989.

Klein, L. E. *Shaftesbury and the Culture of Politeness: Moral Discourse and Cultural Politics in Early Eighteenth-Century England*. Cambridge, 1994.

———. "The Third Earl of Shaftesbury and the Progress of Politeness." *Eighteenth-Century Studies* 18 (1984/85): 186–214.

Klueting, H. *Das Konfessionelle Zeitalter, 1525–1648*. Stuttgart, 1989.

Knappen, M. M. *Tudor Puritanism: A Chapter in the History of Idealism*. 3rd ed. Chicago, 1970.

Knodel, J. E. *Demographic Behaviour in the Past: A Study of Fourteen German village Populations in the Eighteenth and Nineteenth Centuries*. Cambridge, 1988.

Kobelt Groch, M. *Aufsässige Töchter Gottes: Frauen im Bauernkrieg und in den Täuferbewegungen*. Frankfurt a. M., 1993.

Köhler, W. *Zürcher Ehegericht und Genfer Konsistorium*, 2 vols. Quellen u. Abhandlungen zur schweizerischen Reformationsgeschichte 7 und 10. Leipzig, 1932–42.

Kouri, E. "La consolidation du Luthéranisme en Scandinavie." In *L'Europe protestante aux XVIe et XVIIe siècles*, edited by J. Miller, 159–92. Paris, 1997.

————. "La réforme royale en Scandinavie." In *L'Europe protestante aux XVIe et XVIIe siècles*, edited by J. Miller, 131–57. Paris, 1997.

Krawarick, H. "Neue Methoden zur Erforschung konfessioneller Strukturen der frühen Neuzeit." *Archiv für Kulturgeschichte* 70 (1988): 375–410.

Kubrin, D. "Newton and the Cyclical Cosmos: Providence and the Mechanical Philosophy." *Journal of the History of Ideas* 27 (1967): 325–46.

Kuhn, T. S. "Die Entstehung des Neuen: Studien zur Struktur der Wissenschaftsgeschichte." Edited by L. Krüger, translated by H. Vetter, 4th ed., 169–93. Frankfurt a. M., 1992.

Kutschmann, W. "Isaac Newton (1643–1727)." In *Klassiker der Naturphilosophie: Von den Vorsokratikern bis zur Kopenhagener Schule*, edited by G. Böhme, 171–86. Munich, 1989.

Labouvie, E. *Zauberei und Hexenwerk: Ländlicher Hexenglaube in der frühen Neuzeit.* Frankfurt a. M., 1991.

Lagrée, Michel. *Religion et cultures en Bretagne (1850–1950)*. Paris, 1992.

Lake, P. "Calvinism and the English Church, 1570–1635." *Past and Present* 115 (1987): 32–76.

Langlois, C. "Déchristianisation, sécularisation et vitalité religieuse: Débats de sociologues et pratiques d'historiens." In *Säkularisierung, Dechristianisierung und Rechristianisierung im neuzeitlichen Europa: Bilanz und Perspektiven der Forschung* (Veröffentlichungen des Max-Planck-Instituts für Geschichte 130), edited by H. Lehmann, 154–73. Göttingen, 1997.

Larner, C. *Witchcraft and Religion: The Politics of Popular Belief.* Edited by A. Macfarlane. Oxford, 1984.

Lebrun, F. *Être chrétien en France sous l'Ancien Régime, 1516–1790*. Paris, 1996.

————. *Les hommes et la mort en Anjou aux XVIIe et XVIIIe siècles.* Paris and The Hague, 1971.

Lebrun, F., and A. Fauve-Chamoux. "Le mariage et la famille." In *Histoire de la Population Française*, edited by J. Dupâquier, 2:293–347. Paris, 1988.

Lehmann, H. " 'Absonderung' und 'Gemeinschaft' im frühen Pietismus: Allgemeinhistorische und sozialpsychologische Überlegungen zur Entstehung und Entwicklung des Pietismus." *Pietismus und Neuzeit* 4 (1979): 54–82.

————. "Asketischer Protestantismus und ökonomischer Rationalismus: Die Weber-These nach zwei Generationen." In *Max Webers Sicht des okzidentalen Christentums*, edited by W. Schluchter, 529–53. Frankfurt a. M., 1988.

————. *Das Zeitalter des Absolutismus.* Christentum und Gesellschaft 9. Stuttgart, 1980.

————. "Der politische Widerstand gegen die Einführung des neuen Gesangbuches von 1791 in Württemberg: Ein Beitrag zum Verhältnis von Kirchen- und Sozialgeschichte." *Blätter für württembergische Kirchengeschichte* 66/67 (1966/67): 247–63.

————. "Die Kometenflugschriften des 17. Jahrhunderts als historische Quelle." In *Literatur und Volk im 17. Jahrhundert: Probleme populärer Kultur in Deutschland*, 2 parts (Wolfenbütteler Arbeiten zur Barockforschung 13), edited by W. Brückner et al., 683–700. Wiesbaden, 1985.

————. "Frömmigkeitsgeschichtliche Auswirkungen der 'Kleinen Eiszeit.'" In *Volksreligiosität in der modernen Sozialgeschichte (Geschichte und Gesellschaft, Sonderheft 2)*, edited by W. Schieder, 31–50. Göttingen, 1986.

————. "Von der Erforschung der Säkularisierung zur Erforschung von Prozessen der Dechristianisierung und Rechristianisierung im neuzeitlichen Europa." In *Säkularisierung, Dechristianisierung, Rechristianisierung im neuzeitlichen Europa: Bilanz und Perspektiven der Forschung* (Veröffentlichungen des Max-Planck-Instituts für Geschichte 130), edited by H. Lehmann, 9–16. Göttingen, 1997.

Leonhard, S. "Wege zum Selbst: Rituale der pietistischen Selbstvergewisserung dargestellt anhand von Selbstzeugnissen Sophie von Wurstembergers (1809–1878)." Unpublished licentiate dissertation, University of Basel, 1998.

Levi, G. "On Microhistory," In *New Perspectives on Historical Writing*, edited by P. Burke, 93–113. Oxford, 1991.

Levy, A. *The Sephardim in the Ottoman Empire.* Princeton, N.J., 1992.

Lieburg, F. A. v. "From Pure Church to Pious Culture: The Further Reformation in the Seventeenth-Century Dutch Republic." In *Later Calvinism: International Perspectives* (Sixteenth Century Essays and Studies 22), edited by W. F. Graham, 409–29. Kirksville, Mo., 1994.

Lloyd Cohen, C. *God's Caress: The Psychology of Puritan Religious Experience.* New York, 1986.

Loupès, P. *La vie religieuse en France au XVIIIe siècle.* Paris, 1993.

Luckmann, T. "Introduction." In B. Malinowski, *Magie, Wissenschaft und Religion und andere Schriften.* Frankfurt a. M., 1973.

Lüthy, H. "Variationen über ein Thema von Max Weber." In H. Lüthy, *In Gegenwart der Geschichte: Historische Essays*, edited by H. Lüthy, 39–100. Cologne, 1967.

MacDonald, M. *Mystical Bedlam: Madness, Anxiety, and Healing in Seventeenth-Century England.* Cambridge, 1981.

Macfarlane, A. *Witchcraft in Tudor and Stuart England.* London, 1970.

MacHardy, K. *War, Religion and Court Patronage in Habsburg Austria: The Social and Cultural Dimensions of Political Interaction, 1521–1622*, New York, 2003.

Marx, K. *Die Frühschriften.* Edited by S. Landshut. Stuttgart, 1968.

Maurer, C. "Aufgeklärte Gesangbücher und 'gemeine Leute': Äusserungen und Inhalte der Gesangbuchstreite des ausgehenden 18. Jahrhunderts im protestantischen Deutschland." In *Le livre religieux et ses pratiques: Etudes sur l'histoire du livre religieux en Allemagne et en France à l'époque moderne. Der Umgang mit dem religiösen Buch: Studien zur Geschichte des religiösen Buches in Deutschland und Frankreich in der frühen Neuzeit* (Veröffentlichungen des Max-Planck-Instituts für Geschichte 101), edited by H.-E. Bödeker et al., 269–88. Göttingen, 1991.

McGregor, J. F. "The Baptists: Fount of all Heresy." In *Radical Religion in the English Revolution*, edited by J. F. McGregor and B. Reay, 23–63. Oxford, 1984.

Medick, H. "Entlegene Geschichte? Sozialgeschichte und Mikro-Historie im Blickfeld der Kulturanthropologie." In *Alltagskultur, Subjektivität und Geschichte: Zur Theorie und Praxis von Alltagsgeschichte*, published by the Berliner Geschichtswerkstatt, 94–109. Münster, 1994.

———. "Mikro-Historie." In *Sozialgeschichte, Alltagsgeschichte, Mikro-Historie*, edited by W. Schulze, 40–53. Göttingen, 1994.

———. *Weben und Überleben in Laichingen, 1650–1900*. Veröffentlichungen des MPI für Geschichte 126. Göttingen, 1996.

Meier, J. "Die katholische Erneuerung des Würzburger Landkapitels Karlstadt im Spiegel der Landkapitelsversammlungen und Pfarreivisitationen, 1579 bis 1624." *Würzburger Diözesangeschichtsblätter* 33 (1971): 51–125.

Mentzer, R. A., Jr. "Disciplina nervus Ecclesiae: The Calvinist Reform of Morals at Nîmes." *The Sixteenth Century Journal* 18 (1987): 89–115.

Mergel, T., and T. Welskopp. "Geschichtswissenschaft und Gesellschaftstheorie." In *Geschichte zwischen Kultur und Gesellschaft: Beiträge zur Theoriedebatte*, edited by T. Mergel and T. Welskopp, 9–35. Munich, 1997.

Meyer, D. "Zinzendorf und Herrenhut." In *Der Pietismus im achtzehnten Jahrhundert* (*Geschichte des Pietismus*, vol. 2), edited by M. Brecht and K. Deppermann, 3–106. Göttingen, 1995.

Midelfort, H. C. *Witch Hunting in Southwestern Germany, 1562–1684*. Stanford, 1972.

Modrow, Irina. "Frauen im Pietismus." In *Individualisierung, Rationalisierung, Säkularisierung: Neue Wege der Religionsgeschichte* (Wiener Beiträge zur Geschichte der Neuzeit 22), edited by M. Weinzierl, 186–99. Vienna and Munich, 1977.

Moeller, B. "Die Basler Reformation in ihrem stadtgeschichtlichen Zusammenhang." In *Ecclesia semper reformanda: Vorträge zum Basler Reformationsjubiläum, 1529–1979*, edited by H. R. Guggisberg and P. Rotach, 11–27. Basel, 1980.

———. *Reichsstadt und Reformation*. Schriften des Vereins für Reformations-geschichte 180. Gütersloh, 1962; revised ed. Berlin, 1987.

Möller, H. *Vernunft und Kritik: Deutsche Aufklärung im 17. und 18. Jahrhundert*. Frankfurt a. M., 1986.

Monter, W. E. "De l'Evêché à la Rome Protestante." In *Histoire de Genève*, edited by P. Guichonnet, 129–83. Toulouse, 1974.

———. *Ritual, Myth and Magic in Early Modern Europe*. Brighton, 1983.

———. *Witchcraft in France and Switzerland: The Borderlands during the Reformation*. Ithaca, N.Y., 1976.

Morrill, J. "The Later Stuarts: A Glorious Restoration." *History Today* 38 (1988): 8–16.

Muchembled, R. "The Witches of Cambrésis: The Acculturation of the Rural World in the Sixteenth and Seventeenth Centuries." In *Religion and the People, 800–1700*, edited by J. Obelkevich, 221–76. Chapel Hill, N.C., 1979.

Muller, R. A. "God, Predestination and the Integrity of the Created Order: A Note on Patterns in Arminius' Theology." In *Later Calvinism: International Perspectives* (Sixteenth Century Essays and Studies 22), edited by W. F. Graham, 431–46. Kirksville, Mo., 1994.

Müller, U. F., ed. *Lust an der Geschichte: Die Französische Revolution, 1789–1799*. Munich, 1988.

Münch, P. "Die Kosten der Frömmigkeit: Katholizismus und Protestantismus im Visier von Kameralismus und Aufklärung." In *Volksfrömmigkeit in der*

Frühen Neuzeit, edited by H. Molitor and H. Schmolinsky, 107–19. Münster, 1994.

———. *Lebensformen in der Frühen Neuzeit, 1500 bis 1800*. Revised ed. Frankfurt a. M. and Berlin, 1996.

———. "Volkskultur und Calvinismus: Zur Theorie und Praxis der 'reformatio vitae' während der 'Zweiten Reformation.'" In *Die reformierte Konfessionalisierung in Deutschland—Das Problem der "Zweiten Reformation"* (Schriften des Vereins für Reformationsgeschichte 195), edited by H. Schilling, 291–307. Gütersloh, 1986.

———. "Welcher Zusammenhang besteht zwischen Konfession und ökonomischem Verhalten? Max Webers These im Lichte der historischen Forschung." In *Konfession—eine Nebensache?*, edited by H.-G. Wehling, 54–74. Stuttgart, 1984.

Munz, P. "From Max Weber to Joachim of Floris: The Philosophy of Religious History." *The Journal of Religious History* 11 (1980): 167–200.

Nalle, S. T. "Inquisitors, Priests and the People during the Catholic Reformation in Spain." *The Sixteenth Century Journal* 18 (1987): 557–87.

Niggl, G. *Geschichte der deutschen Autobiographie im 18. Jahrhundert: Theoretische Grundlegung und literarische Entfaltung*. Stuttgart, 1977.

Oberman, H. A. "The Impact of the Reformation: Problems and Perspectives." In *Politics and Society in Reformation Europe: Essays for Sir Geoffrey Elton on his Sixty-Fifth Birthday*, edited by E. I. Kouri and R. Scott, 3–31. London, 1987.

———. *Wurzeln des Antisemitismus: Christenangst und Judenplage im Zeitalter von Humanismus und Reformation*. Berlin, 1981.

Oestreich, G. "Strukturprobleme des europäischen Absolutismus." In G. Oestreich, *Geist und Gestalt des frühmodernen Staates: Ausgewählte Aufsätze*, 179–97. Berlin, 1969.

Opitz, C. "Hexenverfolgung als Frauenverfolgung?" In C. Opitz, *Der Hexenstreit: Frauen in der frühneuzeitlichen Hexenverfolgung*, 246–70. Freiburg i. Br., 1995.

Opitz, C., and E. Kleinau, eds. *Geschichte der Mädchen- und Frauenbildung*, vol. 1. Frankfurt a. M., 1996.

Osterhammel, J. "Modernisierungstheorie und die Transformation Chinas, 1800 bis 1949: Kritische Überlegungen zur historischen Soziologie." *Saeculum* 35 (1984): 31–72.

Pagel, W. "The Spectre of van Helmont and the Idea of Continuity in the History of Chemistry." In *Changing Perspectives in the History of Science: Essays in Honour of Joseph Needham*, edited by M. Teich and R. Young, 100–109. London, 1973.

Peters, J. "Der Platz in der Kirche: Über soziales Rangdenken im Spätfeudalismus." *Jahrbuch für Volkskunde und Kulturgeschichte* 28 (1985): 77–106.

Peterson, L. D. "Philippists." In *The Oxford Encyclopedia of the Reformation*, edited by H. J. Hillerbrand, 3:255–62. New York, 1996.

Pettegree, A. "Coming to Terms with Victory: The Upbuilding of a Calvinist Church in Holland, 1572–1590." In *Calvinism in Europe, 1540–1620*, edited by A. Pettegree et al., 160–80. Cambridge, 1994.

Pfister, C. *Bevölkerungsgeschichte und Historische Demographie, 1500–1800* (Enzyklopädie deutscher Geschichte 28). Munich, 1994.

Pfister, R. *Kirchengeschichte der Schweiz.* Vol. 3: *Von 1720 bis 1950.* Zurich, 1984.

Pfister, U. *Die Anfänge von Geburtenbeschränkung: Eine Fallstudie—Ausgewählte Zürcher Familien im 17. und 18. Jahrhundert.* Bern, 1985.

———. "Die Anfänge von Geburtenbeschränkung in Europa: Wege zu einer umfassenderen Analyse." In *Ehe, Liebe, Tod: Zum Wandel der Familie, der Geschlechts- und Generationsbeziehungen in der Neuzeit* (Studien zur Geschichte des Alltags 1), edited by P. Borscheid and H. J. Teuteberg, 213–32. Münster, 1983.

Pohl, H. *Die Portugiesen in Antwerpen (1567–1648): Zur Geschichte einer Minderheit.* Beiheft 63, *Vierteljahrsschrift für Sozial- und Wirtschaftsgeschichte.* Wiesbaden, 1977.

Pomata, G. "Partikulargeschichte und Universalgeschichte—Bemerkungen zu einigen Handbüchern der Frauengeschichte." *L'Homme: Zeitschrift für feministische Geschichtswissenschaft* 2 (1991): 5–44.

Porter, H. C., ed. *Puritanism in Tudor England.* London, 1970.

Porter, R. *English Society in the Eighteenth Century.* Harmondsworth, 1982.

Press, V. *Calvinismus und Territorialstaat: Regierung und Zentralbehörden der Kurpfalz, 1559–1619.* Kieler Historische Studien 7. Stuttgart, 1970.

———. "Die 'Zweite Reformation' in der Kurpfalz." In *Die reformierte Konfessionalisierung in Deutschland,* edited by H. Schilling, 104–29. Gütersloh, 1986.

Principe, L. M. "Boyle's Alchemical Pursuits." In *Robert Boyle Reconsidered,* edited by M. Hunter, 91–105. Cambridge, 1994.

Pullan, B. *The Jews of Europe and the Inquisition of Venice.* Oxford, 1983.

Rack, H. D. "Doctors, Demons and Early Methodist Healing." In *The Church and Healing* (Studies in Church History 19), edited by W. J. Sheils, 137–82. Oxford, 1982.

Reay, B. "Quakerism and Society." In *Radical Religion in the English Revolution,* edited by B. Reay and J. F. McGregor, 141–64. Oxford, 1984.

———. *The Quakers and the English Revolution.* London, 1985.

Reinhard, W. "Gegenreformation als Modernisierung? Prolegomena zu einer Theorie des konfessionellen Zeitalters." *Archiv für Reformationsgeschichte* 68 (1977): 226–51.

———. "Was ist katholische Konfessionalisierung?" In *Die katholische Konfessionalisierung* (Schriften des Vereins für Reformationsgeschichte 198), edited by W. Reinhard and H. Schilling, 419–52. Gütersloh, 1995.

Remarkable Passages in the Life of William Kiffin: Written by Himself. Edited by W. Orme. London, 1823.

Révah, I. S. "Les Marranes." *Revue des Etudes Juives* 118 (1959/60): 29–77.

———. "L'hérésie marrane dans l'Europe catholique du 15ᵉ et 16ᵉ siècle." In *Hérésies et sociétés dans l'Europe préindustrielle, 11ᵉ–18ᵉ siècles* (Civilisations et Sociétés 10), 327–39. Paris, 1968.

Reventlow, H. *Bibelautorität und Geist der Moderne: Die Bedeutung des Bibelverständnisses für die geistesgeschichtliche und politische Entwicklung in England von der*

Reformation bis zur Aufklärung. Forschungen zur Kirchen- und Dogmen-geschichte 30. Göttingen, 1980.

Roeck, B. *Eine Stadt in Krieg und Frieden: Studien zur Geschichte der Reichsstadt Augsburg zwischen Kalenderstreit und Parität*. Schriftenreihe der Historischen Kommission bei der Bayerischen Akademie der Wissenschaften, Bd. 37. Göttingen, 1989.

Roper, L. *Oedipus and the Devil: Witchcraft, Sexuality and Religion in Early Modern Europe*. London, 1994.

Rosa, M. "L 'Aufklärung'cattolica." In M. Rosa, *Settecento religioso*, S. 149–84. Venice, 1999.

———. *Settecento religioso: Politica della ragione e religione del cuore*. Venice, 1999.

Roth, C. *The History of the Jews of Italy*. Philadelphia, 1946.

———. *A History of the Marranos*. 3rd ed. New York, 1959.

———. *The House of Nasi: The Duke of Naxos*. Philadelphia, 1948.

Rublack, H.-C. "Forschungsbericht Stadt und Reformation." In *Stadt und Kirche im 16. Jahrhundert* (Schriften des Vereins für Reformationsgeschichte 190), edited by B. Möller, 9–26. Gütersloh, 1978.

———. "New Patterns of Christian Life." In *Handbook of European History*, edited by T. A. Brady, Jr., et al., 2:585–605. Leiden, 1995.

Ruffieux, R., ed. *Geschichte des Kantons Freiburg*, vol. 1. Freiburg i. Ue., 1981.

Ruppert, W. *Bürgerlicher Wandel: Die Geburt der modernen deutschen Gesellschaft im 18. Jahrhundert*. Frankfurt a. M., 1983.

Rüth, B. "Reformation und Konfessionsbildung im städtischen Bereich: Perspektiven der Forschung." *Zeitschrift der Savigny-Stiftung für Rechtsgeschichte, Kanonistische Abteilung* 77 (1991): 197–282.

Sabean, D. W. *Power in the Blood: Popular Culture and Village Discourse in Early Modern Germany*. Cambridge, 1984.

———. "Production of the Self during the Age of Confessionalism." *Central European History* 29 (1996): 1–18.

Schieder, W. "Konfessionelle Erneuerung in den christlichen Parallelkirchen Deutschlands im 19. Jahrhundert: Ein Kommentar." In *Säkularisierung, Dechristianisierung, Rechristianisierung im neuzeitlichen Europa: Bilanz und Perspektiven der Forschung* (Veröffentlichungen des MPI für Geschichte 130), edited by H. Lehmann, 223–28. Göttingen, 1997.

———. "Säkularisierung und Sakralisierung der religiösen Kultur in der europäischen Neuzeit: Versuch einer Bilanz." In *Säkularisierung, Dechristianisierung und Rechristianisierung im neuzeitlichen Europa: Bilanz und Perspektiven der Forschung* (Veröffentlichungen des Max-Planck-Instituts für Geschichte 130), edited by H. Lehmann, 308–13. Göttingen, 1997.

Schilling, H. "Confessional Europe." In *Handbook of European History, 1400–1600*, edited by T. A. Brady, Jr., et al., 2:641–81. Leiden, 1995.

———. "Die Konfessionalisierung im Reich: Religiöser und gesellschaftlicher Wandel in Deutschland zwischen 1555 und 1620." *Historische Zeitschrift* 246 (1988): 1–45.

————, ed. *Die reformierte Konfessionalisierung in Deutschland. Das Problem der "Zweiten Reformation."* Schriften des Vereins für Reformationsgeschichte 195. Gütersloh, 1986.

————. "Disziplinierung oder "Selbstregulierung der Untertanen"? Ein Plädoyer für die Doppelperspektive von Makro- und Mikrohistorie bei der Erforschung der frühmodernen Kirchenzucht." *Historische Zeitschrift* 264 (1997): 675–91.

————. *Höfe und Allianzen: Deutschland 1648–1763.* Berlin, 1989.

————. "Nationale Identität und Konfession in der europäischen Neuzeit." In *Nationale und kulturelle Identität: Studien zur Entwicklung des kollektiven Bewusstseins in der Neuzeit,* edited by B. Giesen, 192–252. Frankfurt a. M., 1991.

————. Reformation–Umbruch oder Gipfelpunkt eines Temps des Réformes? In *Die frühe Reformation in Deutschland als Umbruch* (Schriften des Vereins für Reformationsgeschichte 119), edited by B. Moeller, 13–34. Gütersloh, 1998.

Schindler, N. "Die Entstehung der Unbarmherzigkeit: Zur Kultur und Lebensweise der Salzburger Bettler am Ende des 17. Jahrhunderts." *Bayerisches Jahrbuch für Volkskunde* (1988): 61–130.

————. " 'Heiratsmüdigkeit' und Ehezwang: Zur populären Rügesitte des Pflug- und Blochziehens,." In N. Schindler, *Widerspenstige Leute: Studien zur Volkskultur in der frühen Neuzeit,* 175–214. Frankfurt a. M., 1992.

————. "Spuren in der Geschichte der 'anderen' Zivilisation: Probleme und Perspektiven einer historischen Volkskulturforschung." In *Volkskultur: Zur Wiederentdeckung des vergessenen Alltags (16–20. Jahrhundert),* edited by R. van Dülmen and N. Schindler, 13–77. Frankfurt a. M., 1984.

Schings, H. -J. *Melancholie und Aufklärung: Melancholiker und ihre Kritiker in Erfahrungsseelenkunde und Literatur des 18. Jahrhunderts.* Stuttgart, 1977.

Schlögl, R. " 'Aufgeklärter Unglaube' oder 'mentale Säkularisierung'? Die Frömmigkeit katholischer Stadtbürger in systemtheoretischer Hinsicht (ca. 1700–1840)." In *Geschichte zwischen Kultur und Gesellschaft: Beiträge zur Theoriedebatte,* edited by T. Mergel and T. Welskop, 95–121. Munich, 1997.

————. "Die Moderne auf der Nachtseite der Aufklärung: Zum Verhältnis von Freimaurerei und Naturphilosophie." *Das achtzehnte Jahrhundert* 21 (1997): 33–60.

————. *Glaube und Religion in der Säkularisierung: Die katholische Stadt—Köln, Aachen, Münster, 1700–1840.* Ancien Régime, Aufklärung und Revolution 28. Munich, 1995.

Schmidt, H. R. "Die Christianisierung des Sozialverhaltens als permanente Reformation: Aus der Praxis reformierter Sittengerichte in der Schweiz während der frühen Neuzeit." In *Kommunalisierung und Christianisierung: Voraussetzungen und Folgen der Reformation, 1400–1600,* edited by P. Blickle, 113–63. Berlin, 1989.

————. *Dorf und Religion: Reformierte Sittenzucht in Berner Landgemeinden der Frühen Neuzeit.* Quellen und Forschungen zur Agrargeschichte 41. Stuttgart, 1995.

————. *Konfessionalisierung im 16. Jahrhundert.* Enzyklopädie deutscher Geschichte 12. Munich, 1992.

———. "Sozialdisziplinierung? Ein Plädoyer für das Ende des Etatismus in der Konfessionalisierungsforschung." *Historische Zeitschrift* 265 (1997): 639–82.

———. "Über das Verhältnis von ländlicher Gemeinde und christlicher Ethik: Graubünden und die Innerschweiz." In *Landgemeinde und Stadtgemeinde in Mitteleuropa: Ein struktureller Vergleich*, edited by P. Blickle, 455–87. Munich, 1991.

Schmidt, M. *Pietismus.* 2nd ed. Stuttgart, 1978.

Schmitt, J.-C. " 'Religion populaire' et culture folklorique." *Annales Economies, Sociétés, Civilisation* 31 (1976): 941–53.

Schneider, H. "Der radikale Pietismus im 18. Jahrhundert." In *Der Pietismus im achtzehnten Jahrhundert (Geschichte des Pietismus*, vol. 2), edited by M. Brecht and K. Deppermann, 107–97. Göttingen, 1995.

Scholem, G. *Sabbatai Sevi: The Mystical Messiah, 1626–1676*, Princeton, N.J., 1973.

Schormann, G. *Hexenprozesse in Deutschland.* Göttingen, 1981.

Schorn-Schütte, L. *Evangelische Geistlichkeit in der Frühneuzeit: Deren Anteil an der Entfaltung frühmoderner Staatlichkeit und Gesellschaft, dargestellt am Beispiel des Fürstentums Braunschweig-Wolfenbüttel, der Landgrafschaft Hessen-Kassel und der Stadt Braunschweig.* Quellen u. Forschungen z. Reformationsgeschichte 62. Gütersloh, 1996.

Schrey, H.-H., ed. *Säkularisierung.* Darmstadt, 1981.

Schulin, E. "Die spanischen und portugiesischen Juden im 15. und 16. Jahrhundert: Eine Minderheit zwischen Integrationszwang und Anpassung." In *Die Juden als Minderheit in der Geschichte*, edited by B. Martin and E. Schulin, 85–109. Munich, 1981.

Schulze, W. "Ende der Moderne? Zur Korrektur unseres Begriffs der Moderne aus historischer Sicht." In *Zur Diagnose der Moderne*, edited by H. Meier, 69–97. Munich, 1990.

———. "Gerhard Oestreichs Begriff der 'Sozialdisziplinierung.' " *Zeitschrift für historische Forschung* 14 (1987): 265–302.

Schwaiger, G. "Das Ende der Hexenprozesse im Heiligen Römischen Reich." In G. Schwaiger, *Teufelsglaube und Hexenprozesse*, 162–78. Munich, 1987.

Schwartz, H. *The French Prophets: The History of a Millenarian Group in Eighteenth-Century England.* Los Angeles, 1980.

———. *Knaves, Fools, Madmen, and That Subtile Effluvium: A Study of the Opposition to the French Prophets in England, 1706–1710.* Gainsville, Fla., 1978.

Schwerhoff, G. "Vom Alltagsverdacht zur Massenverfolgung: Neuere deutsche Forschungen zum frühneuzeitlichen Hexenwesen." *Geschichte in Wissenschaft und Unterricht* 46 (1995): 359–80.

Scribner, R. W. "Elements of Popular Belief." In *Handbook of European History*, edited by T. A. Brady, Jr., et al., 1:231–62. Leiden, 1995.

———. *For the Sake of Simple Folk: Popular Propaganda for the German Reformation.* Cambridge, 1981.

———. "Hidden Transcripts in Discourses about Religion, Science, and Skepticism." In *Säkularisierung, Dechristianisierung, Rechristianisierung im neuzeitlichen Europa:*

Bilanz und Perspektiven der Forschung (Veröffentlichungen des Max-Planck-
Instituts für Geschichte 130), edited by H. Lehmann, 114–17. Göttingen, 1997.

———. "'Incombustible Luther': The Image of the Reformer in Early Modern
Germany." *Past and Present* 110 (1986): 38–68.

———. *Popular Culture and Popular Movements in Reformation Germany*. London,
1987.

———. "The Reformation, Popular Magic and the 'Disenchantment of the World.'"
Journal of Interdisciplinary History 23 (1993): 475–94.

Seaver, P. S. *Wallington's World: A Puritan Artisan in Seventeenth-Century England*.
London, 1985.

Seaward, P. *The Restoration, 1660–1688*. London, 1991.

Shapin, S. *The Scientific Revolution*. Chicago, 1996.

———, and S. Schaffer. *Leviathan and the Air Pump: Hobbes, Boyle and the
Experimental Life*. Princeton, N.J., 1987.

Sharpe, J. *Instruments of Darkness: Witchcraft in England, 1550–1750*. Harmondsworth,
1997.

Sharpe, K. *The Personal Rule of Charles I*. New Haven, 1992.

Shmuelevitz, A. *The Jews of the Ottoman Empire in the Late Fifteenth and the Sixteenth
Centuries: Administrative, Economic, Legal and Social Relations as Reflected in the
Responsa*. Leiden, 1984.

Sigg, O. "17. Jahrhundert." In *Geschichte des Kantons Zürich*, 2:282–363. Zurich, 1996.

Skinner, Q. *The Foundations of Modern Political Thought*. Vol. 2: *The Age of the
Reformation*. Cambridge, 1978.

Smout, T. C. *A History of the Scottish People, 1560–1830*. London, 1969.

Solé, J. *La Révolution en question*. Paris, 1988.

Soman, A. "La décriminalization de la sorcellerie en France." *Histoire, économie et
société* 4 (1985): 179–203.

Stayer, J. M. "Die Anfänge des schweizerischen Täufertums im reformierten
Kongregationalismus." In *Umstrittenes Täufertum 1525–1975*, edited by
H.-J. Goertz, 19–49. Göttingen, 1977.

———, et al. "From Monogenesis to Polygenesis: The Historical Discussion of
Anabaptist Origins." *The Mennonite Quarterly Review* 49 (1975): 83–121.

———. "The Radical Reformation." In *Handbook of European History, 1400–1600*,
edited by T. A. Brady, Jr., et al., 2:249–82. Leiden, 1995.

Stemme, F. "Die Säkularisation des Pietismus zur Erfahrungsseelenkunde."
Zeitschrift für deutsche Philologie 72 (1953): 144–58.

Stengers, I. *L'invention des sciences modernes*. Paris, 1995.

Stevenson, J. *Popular Disturbances in England, 1700–1870*. London, 1979.

Stewart, L. *The Rise of Public Science: Rhetoric, Technology, and Natural Philosophy in
Newtonian Britain, 1660–1750*. Cambridge, 1992.

Streiff, P. "Der Methodismus bis 1784/1791." In *Der Pietismus im achtzehnten
Jahrhundert (Geschichte des Pietismus*, vol. 2), edited by M. Brecht and
K. Deppermann, 617–65. Göttingen, 1995.

Tambiah, S. J. *Magic, Science, Religion and the Scope of Rationality*. Cambridge, 1990.

Teeter Dobbs, B. J. *The Foundations of Newton's Alchemy or "The Hunting of the Greene Lyon."* Cambridge, 1975.

———. *The Janus Faces of Genius: The Role of Alchemy in Newton's Thought.* Cambridge, 1991.

Thadden, R. von *Die brandenburgisch-preussischen Hofprediger im 17. und 18. Jahrhundert: Ein Beitrag zur Geschichte der absolutistischen Staatsgesellschaft in Brandenburg-Preussen.* Berlin, 1959.

Thomas, K. *Man and the Natural World: Changing Attitudes in England, 1500–1800.* Harmondsworth, 1984.

———. *Religion and the Decline of Magic.* New York, 1971.

Thompson, E. P. *The Making of the English Working Class.* [London, 1963] Harmondsworth, 1986.

Troeltsch, E. *Protestantism and Progress: The Significance of Protestantism for the Rise of the Modern* World. Philadelphia, 1986.

———. *The Social Teaching of the Christian Churches.* Translated by Olive Wyon. London, 1956.

Tyacke, N. *Anti-Calvinists: The Rise of English Arminianism, c. 1590–1640.* Oxford, 1987.

Tyrell, H. "Worum geht es in der 'Protestantischen Ethik'? Ein Versuch zum besseren Verständnis Max Webers." *Saeculum* 41 (1990): 130–77.

Ulbrich, Claudia. "Zankapfel 'Weiber-Gestühl.'" In *Historie und Eigen-Sinn: Festschrift für Jan Peters zum 65. Geburtstag,* edited by A. Lubinski et al., 107–14. Weimar, 1997.

Ulbricht, O. "Mikrogeschichte: Versuch einer Vorstellung." *Geschichte in Wissenschaft und Unterricht* 6 (1994): 347–67.

Veit, L. A., and L. Lenhart. *Kirche und Volksfrömmigkeit im Zeitalter des Barock.* Freiburg i. Br., 1956.

Veit, P. "Das Gesangbuch in der Praxis Pietatis der Lutheraner." In *Die lutherische Konfessionalisierung in Deutschland* (Schriften des Vereins für Reformationsgeschichte 197), edited by H.-C. Rublack, 435–59. Gütersloh, 1992.

Vickers, B. "Analogy versus Identity: The Rejection of Occult Symbolism, 1580–1680." In *Occult and Scientific Mentalities in the Renaissance,* edited by B. Vickers, 95–163. Cambridge, 1984.

———, ed. *English Science, Bacon to Newton.* Cambridge, 1987.

———. "Francis Bacon and the Progress of Knowledge." *Journal of the History of Ideas* 53 (1992): 495–518.

Volkland, F. "Konfessionelle Grenzen zwischen Auflösung und Verhärtung: Bikonfessionelle Gemeinden in der Vogtei Thurgau (CH) des 17. Jahrhunderts. In Historische Anthropologie 5 (1997): 370–87.

———. *Konfession und Selbstverständnis: Reformierte Rituale in der gemischtkonfessionellen Kleinstadt Bischofszell im 17. Jahrhundert.* (Veröffentlichungen des Max-Plack-Instituts für Geschichte 210), Göttingen, 2005.

Vovelle, M. "Dechristianization in Year II: Expression or Extinction of a Popular Culture." In *Religion and Society in Early Modern Europe, 1500–1800,* edited by K. von Greyerz, 79–94. London, 1984.

———. *La mentalité révolutionnaire: Société et mentalité sous la Révolution française.* Paris, 1985.

———. *La mort et l'Occident de 1300 à nos jours.* Paris, 1983.

———. *Piété baroque et déchristianisation en Provence au XVIIIe siècle.* Paris, 1973.

———. *Religion et Révolution: La déchristianisation de l'an II.* Paris, 1976.

Walker, D. P. *The Decline of Hell: Seventeenth-Century Discussion of Eternal Torment.* London, 1964.

Walker, M. *The Salzburg Transaction: Expulsion and Redemption in Eighteenth-Century Germany.* Ithaca, N.Y., 1992.

Wallace, P. G. *Communities and Conflict in Early Modern Colmar, 1575–1730.* Atlantic Highlands, N.J., 1995.

Wallmann, J. "Anfänge des Pietismus." *Pietismus und Neuzeit* 4 (1979): 11–53.

Walzer, M. *The Revolution of the Saints: A Study in the Origins of Radical Politics.* London, 1966.

Wandel, L. P. *Voracious Idols and Violent Hands: Iconoclasm in Reformation Zurich, Strasbourg and Basel.* Cambridge, 1999.

Warmbrunn, P. *Zwei Konfessionen in einer Stadt: Das Zusammenleben von Katholiken und Protestanten in den paritätischen Reichsstädten Augsburg, Biberach, Ravensburg und Dinkelsbühl von 1548 bis 1648.* Veröffentlichungen des Instituts für Europäische Geschichte Mainz III. Wiesbaden, 1983.

Wartburg-Ambühl, M.-L., von. *Alphabetisierung und Lektüre: Untersuchungen am Beispiel einer ländlichen Region im 17. und 18. Jahrhundert.* Bern, 1981.

Watts, M. *The Dissenters.* Vol. 1: *From the Reformation to the French Revolution.* Oxford, 1985 [1978].

Weber, M. *Gesammelte Aufsätze zur Religionssoziologie.* 3 vols. 2nd ed. Tübingen, 1922–23.

———. *Economy and Society: An Outline of Interpretive Sociology.* Edited by G. Roth and C. Wittich. Translated by Ephraim Fischoff et al. Berkeley, 1978.

———. "Objectivity in Social Science and Social Policy." In *The Methodology of the Social Sciences,* edited and translated by Edward A. Shils and Henry A. Finch. New York, 1949.

Wehler, H.-U. *Modernisierungstheorie und Geschichte.* Göttingen, 1975.

Weigelt, H. "Der Pietismus im Übergang vom 18. zum 19. Jahrhundert." In *Der Pietismus im 18. Jahrhundert (Geschichte des Pietismus,* vol. 2), edited by M. Brecht and K. Deppermann, 700–54. Göttingen, 1995.

Welskopp, T. "Der Mensch und die Verhältnisse: 'Handeln' und 'Struktur' bei Max Weber und Anthony Giddens." In *Geschichte zwischen Kultur und Gesellschaft: Beiträge zur Theoriedebatte,* edited by T. Mergel and T. Welskopp, 39–70. Munich, 1997.

Williams, P. *The Later Tudors: England 1547–1603. (The New Oxford History of England.)* Oxford, 1995.

Wolf, R. *Biographien zur Kulturgeschichte der Schweiz,* vol. 1. Zurich, 1858.

Wormald, J. *Court, Kirk and Community: Scotland, 1470–1625.* Edinburgh, 1981.

Wrigley, A. "Family Limitation in Pre-industrial England." *Economic History Review*, 2nd ser., 19 (1966): 82–109.

Wunder, H. *He Is the Sun, She Is the Moon: Women in Early Modern Germany.* Translated by Thomas Dunlap. Cambridge, Mass., 1998.

———. "Von der *frumkeit* zur *Frömmigkeit*: Ein Beitrag zur Genese bürgerlicher Weiblichkeit (15.–17. Jahrhundert)." In *Weiblichkeit in geschichtlicher Perspektive: Fallstudien und Reflexionen zu Grundproblemen der historischen Frauenforschung,* edited by U. A. J. Becher and J. Rüsen, 174–88. Frankfurt a. M., 1988.

Zehnder, L. *Volkskundliches in der älteren schweizerischen Chronistik.* Schriften der schweizerischen Gesellschaft für Volkskunde 60. Basel, 1976.

Zeller, R. "Der Paratext der Kabbala Denudata: Die Vermittlung von jüdischer und christlicher Weisheit." *Morgen-Glantz: Zeitschrift der Christian Knorr von Rosenroth-Gesellschaft* 7 (1997): 143–69.

Zschunke, P. *Konfession und Alltag in Oppenheim: Beiträge zur Geschichte von Bevölkerung und Gesellschaft einer gemischtkonfessionellen Kleinstadt der frühen Neuzeit.* Veröffentlichungen des Instituts für Europäische Geschichte 115. Wiesbaden, 1984.

Zünd, A. *Gescheiterte Stadt- und Landreformationen des 16. und 17. Jahrhunderts in der Schweiz.* Basler Beiträge zur Geschichtswissenschaft 170. Basel, 1999.

Index

spiritualism, 84, 159
Sprat, Thomas, 197
Sprenger, Jacob, 145
state, 148–51, 156, 166, 170, 176, 190, 192
    church, 70–71, 89–91, 93–96, 108–10,
        157, 167–71, 173, 182
    formation, 41–42, 66, 68–69
    medieval personal, 42
    territorial, 28, 42, 50–51, 59, 68–70,
        73–74, 76, 152, 221
Stayer, James, 161
Steinfurt, 72
Stock, Ambros Simon von, 105
Strasbourg, 30, 96, 114, 122, 138,
    164, 165
Stuart period, 90–93
Stumpf, Johannes, 126
Stumpf, Simon, 160
Stuttgart, 178
Styria, 207, 210
Sulzbach (Franconia), 140
Sulzer, Simon, 75
Sundgau, 165
supernatural, 15, 23, 63, 110, 188, 193
Supremacy
    Act of (1534), 29, 89
    oath, 89
Surinam, 107
surplice fees, 44, 89, 92
Süss Oppenheimer, Joseph, 141
Swabia, 129, 191, 210
Swammerdam, Jan, 19
Sweden, 29, 56
Swieten, Gerard van, 105
Swiss Brethren, 163
Swiss Confederation. See Switzerland
Swiss peasants' war (1653), 43
Switzerland, 3, 5, 18–19, 28, 30–31, 33,
    34–35, 37, 43, 45, 47–48, 53, 55, 61,
    62, 77, 81, 83, 86–87, 90, 92, 113,
    115–16, 122, 126, 130, 134, 141, 151,
    153, 160, 162–163, 166, 177, 180,
    182, 193, 209
synagogue, 138, 140, 217

syncretism, 14, 188
synod, 81, 91, 94, 162
    Synod of Dordrecht, Reformed (1618/
        19), 81, 92

Taffin, Jean, 81
Talmud, 138
Tambiah, Stanley J., 23
Tamburini, Pietro, 192
Tecklenburg, 72
Tennhardt, Jacob, 178, 179, 180
Teresa of Avila, 99, 121, 122, 131
tertiaries, 121
Thayngen, 51, 52
theater, 46, 48, 104, 204
    heroic play, 48
    spiritual, 48
Theatines, 35
theocracy, 31
theodicy, 190
theology
    natural, 196, 198–99
    critique of, 190
theosophy, 177, 191, 195
Thiers, Jean-Baptiste, 143, 144
Thirty Years' War, 31, 38, 42–43, 51, 54,
    69, 72–73, 75–76, 83, 97, 129, 133,
    139, 151, 166
Thomas, Keith, 22, 152, 196
Thomasius, Christian, 146
Thompson, Edward P., 6, 17, 108
Thurgau, 51, 180
Thuringia, 30, 121
Tiepolo, Antonio, 215
Tithe, 44, 160, 162, 176
Tocqueville, Alexis de, 208
Toledo, 39, 135, 153
tolerance, 73, 138–39, 157
Toleration Act (1689), 176
totemism, 7
Toulouse, 47, 205
trade, 138, 169, 214–15, 221
    merchants, 49, 93, 170, 176, 215

CPSIA information can be obtained at www.ICGtesting.com
Printed in the USA
LVOW03s1409050614

388774LV00003B/20/P